Communications
in Computer and Information Science 2088

Rationale

The CCIS series is devoted to the publication of proceedings of computer science conferences. Its aim is to efficiently disseminate original research results in informatics in printed and electronic form. While the focus is on publication of peer-reviewed full papers presenting mature work, inclusion of reviewed short papers reporting on work in progress is welcome, too. Besides globally relevant meetings with internationally representative program committees guaranteeing a strict peer-reviewing and paper selection process, conferences run by societies or of high regional or national relevance are also considered for publication.

Topics

The topical scope of CCIS spans the entire spectrum of informatics ranging from foundational topics in the theory of computing to information and communications science and technology and a broad variety of interdisciplinary application fields.

Information for Volume Editors and Authors

Publication in CCIS is free of charge. No royalties are paid, however, we offer registered conference participants temporary free access to the online version of the conference proceedings on SpringerLink (http://link.springer.com) by means of an http referrer from the conference website and/or a number of complimentary printed copies, as specified in the official acceptance email of the event.

CCIS proceedings can be published in time for distribution at conferences or as post-proceedings, and delivered in the form of printed books and/or electronically as USBs and/or e-content licenses for accessing proceedings at SpringerLink. Furthermore, CCIS proceedings are included in the CCIS electronic book series hosted in the SpringerLink digital library at http://link.springer.com/bookseries/7899. Conferences publishing in CCIS are allowed to use Online Conference Service (OCS) for managing the whole proceedings lifecycle (from submission and reviewing to preparing for publication) free of charge.

Publication process

The language of publication is exclusively English. Authors publishing in CCIS have to sign the Springer CCIS copyright transfer form, however, they are free to use their material published in CCIS for substantially changed, more elaborate subsequent publications elsewhere. For the preparation of the camera-ready papers/files, authors have to strictly adhere to the Springer CCIS Authors' Instructions and are strongly encouraged to use the CCIS LaTeX style files or templates.

Abstracting/Indexing

CCIS is abstracted/indexed in DBLP, Google Scholar, EI-Compendex, Mathematical Reviews, SCImago, Scopus. CCIS volumes are also submitted for the inclusion in ISI Proceedings.

How to start

To start the evaluation of your proposal for inclusion in the CCIS series, please send an e-mail to ccis@springer.com.

Enrico Borgogno Mondino · Paola Zamperlin
Editors

Geomatics for Environmental Monitoring: From Data to Services

26th Italian Conference, ASITA 2023
Virtual Event, December 18–20, 2023
Revised Selected Papers

Springer

Editors
Enrico Borgogno Mondino (iD)
University of Torino
Grugliasco, Italy

Paola Zamperlin (iD)
University of Firenze
Firenze, Italy

ISSN 1865-0929   ISSN 1865-0937 (electronic)
Communications in Computer and Information Science
ISBN 978-3-031-59924-8   ISBN 978-3-031-59925-5 (eBook)
https://doi.org/10.1007/978-3-031-59925-5

This Springer imprint is published by the registered company Springer Nature Switzerland AG
The registered company address is: Gewerbestrasse 11, 6330 Cham, Switzerland

If disposing of this product, please recycle the paper.

Preface

ASITAcademy2023 – the Italian Conference on Geomatics and Geospatial Technologies – held virtually on the 18th and 20th of December 2023, provided an opportunity to assess the latest developments of Geomatics specifically, but not only, in the Italian context: in particular, theoretical, technical and institutional issues related to instruments and applications were widely debated with reference to (i) the role of Geomatics in the Next Generation EU framework (Piano Nazionale di Ripresa e Resilienza - PNRR in Italy) through the presentation of first results from the ongoing related National projects; (ii) the state of the art and case studies involving geomatically based Official Products and Services from institutional subjects (e.g. Copernicus); (iii) instances related to the growing need for standardization and validation procedures of geographical and Earth Observation data/product/services with special concerns about the expected roles they can have within monitoring/control actions from institutional subjects (e.g. CAP controls, natural hazards, etc.).

This volume collects 19 selected articles showing a comprehensive exploration of the use of innovative geospatial analysis and technology in addressing critical environmental challenges, spanning climate change impacts, emergency response efficacy, and technological advancements in environmental monitoring. These papers were selected from 42 submissions after a single-blind review process in which each submission received at least two reviews.

Through diverse methodologies and interdisciplinary approaches, these studies offer significant contributions to the fields of environmental science, disaster management, and technological innovation. Each paper, through its unique lens, contributes to the overarching goal of leveraging technology and innovative methodologies to better understand and respond to environmental challenges, climate change impacts, and emergency situations. The studies collectively advocate for the integration of advanced remote sensing technologies, GIS, and photogrammetry in environmental monitoring, disaster management, and climate change mitigation efforts. They underscore the importance of data accuracy, standardization, and accessibility in enhancing the effectiveness of environmental surveillance and emergency response strategies.

Taking into consideration the different themes presented, the different methodologies, the objectives, and the results of the studies, the articles have been organized into three chapters.

The first chapter, titled *Natural Hazards Monitoring and Modelling*, groups papers that detail the use of cutting-edge technologies for monitoring environmental changes, assessing geohazards, and analyzing the impacts of events like forest fires and land deformations. It highlights advancements in remote sensing, photogrammetry, and Persistent Scatterer Interferometry (PSI) techniques.

Papers in the second chapter, *Technological Services for Territory Planning and Management*, emphasize the development of services and monitoring systems for environmental management and urban planning using remote sensing and geospatial technologies.

In the last chapter, *Methodological Advancements in Data Analysis and Processing*, have been grouped papers that propose new methodologies or significant advancements in existing techniques for data analysis and processing, particularly in the context of environmental monitoring, disaster management, and emergency response strategies. The studies presented in this category focus on the development of integrated systems, the application of machine learning, and other innovative approaches to data analysis.

Significant findings across the papers highlight the potential of satellite imagery and digital photogrammetry in accurately assessing changes in glacier volumes and land deformations, demonstrating the efficacy of aerial and drone surveillance in emergency response, and revealing insights into the complex dynamics of forest fires and their impact on ecosystems. These contributions are pivotal for advancing current knowledge and practices in environmental monitoring, offering new avenues for research, and informing policy and operational strategies to mitigate the adverse effects of climate change and natural disasters.

Moreover, we consider it important that the collaborative approaches demonstrated in several studies underscore the value of interdisciplinary research and multi-agency cooperation in tackling complex environmental issues. Future research should continue to explore innovative applications of technology in environmental monitoring, expand the use of geospatial analysis in disaster management, and further integrate scientific insights into policy and operational strategies to mitigate the adverse effects of climate change and natural disasters. The successful application of geospatial analysis and remote sensing technologies in these studies highlights the potential for further advancements in data collection, analysis, and application in addressing global environmental challenges. Policymakers and practitioners are encouraged to consider these insights in developing strategies for climate resilience, disaster risk reduction, and sustainable environmental management.

February 2024

Enrico Borgogno Mondino
Paola Zamperlin

Organization

Program Committee Chairs

Enrico Borgogno Mondino   Università di Torino, Italy
Paola Zamperlin   Università di Firenze, Italy

Program Committee

Stefania Bertazzon	University of Calgary, Canada
Angelo Besana	Università di Trento, Italy
Sandro Bimonte	INRAE, France
Filiberto Chiabrando	Politecnico di Torino, Italy
Elena Dai Prà	Università di Trento, Italy
Maria Antonietta Dessena	ENAS, Italy
Andrea Fiduccia	AMFM GIS Italia, Italy
Antonio Ganga	AMFM GIS Italia, Italy
Fabio Giulio Tonolo	Politecnico di Torino, Italy
Michele Grimaldi	Università di Salerno, Italy
Francesco Guerra	Università Iuav di Venezia, Italy
Maria Teresa Melis	Università di Cagliari, Italy
Stefano Nicolodi	SIFET, Italy
Francesco Pirotti	Università di Padova, Italy
Cinzia Podda	Università di Sassari, Italy
Monica Sebillo	Università di Salerno, Italy
Domenico Visintini	Università degli Studi di Udine, Italy

Additional Reviewers

Caterina Balletti	Alberto Cina
Massimo Blandino	Branka Cuca
Mirco Boschetti	Paolo Dabove
Giuseppe Borruso	Samuele De Petris
Mariano Bresciani	Marco Devecchi
Samuele Bumbaca	Alessandro Farbo
Alessandra Capolupo	Vanina Fissore
Enrica Caporali	Federica Ghilardi

Claudia Giardino
Tommaso Orusa
Gianni Pantaleo
Francesco Parizia
Luigi Perotti
Giovanni Pugliano
Antonello Romano

Filippo Sarvia
Marco Scaioni
Domenico Sguerso
Fabio Giulio Tonolo
Annalisa Viani
Andrea Virano
Domenico Visintini

Contents

Natural Hazards Monitoring and Modelling

Technological Services for Territory Planning and Management

Methodological Advancements in Data Analysis and Processing

Natural Hazards Monitoring
and Modelling

Assessment of the Vertical Accuracy of Satellite-Based Glacier Monitoring. The Rutor Glacier in Italy

Myrta Maria Macelloni[1](✉) (iD), Alberto Cina[1] (iD), Fabio Giulio Tonolo[2] (iD),
and Umberto Morra di Cella[3] (iD)

[1] DIATI, Department of Environment, Land and Infrastructure Engineering, Politecnico di Torino, Corso Duca degli Abruzzi 24, 10129 Turin, Italy
myrta.macelloni@polito.it

[2] DAD – Department of Architecture and Design, Politecnico di Torino, Viale Pier Andrea Mattioli 39, 10125 Turin, Italy

[3] Environmental Protection Agency of Valle d'Aosta, Climate Change Unit, Loc. Grande Charrière, 48, 11020 Saint-Christophe (AO), Italy

Abstract. Periodical monitoring of glacier extent and volume changes is a fundamental tool, considering the relevant changes and volume losses glaciers have been undergoing in recent years. The climatological changes leading to increasing hazards and related risks in alpine areas require complex and updated 3D models. Specifically, mountain environments are characterised by complex orography and limited accessibility and often require risky and expensive in situ campaigns. The presented case stay is the Rutor Glacier (Aosta Valley, Italy), monitored and studied in a multidisciplinary framework by the Glacier Lab of the Politecnico di Torino and the Aosta Valley Environmental Agency (ARPA VDA). Different remote sensing platforms are being used to carry out an annual survey to generate detailed 3D models enabling the estimation of the mass balance, focusing on the 3D positional accuracy of the metric products.

A very high-resolution Pleiades satellite image stereo pair acquired in September 2022 and a photogrammetric airborne survey carried out in the same month enable the comparison of 3D models based on different techniques and therefore characterised by different accuracies. In-depth analyses have been carried out to verify the suitability of satellite remote sensing for glacier monitoring, considering that a satellite-based approach would enable continuous monitoring over wide areas, including Alpine regions with limited access. The analyses are aimed at validating the 3D products by means of comparison with more accurate reference data as well as at evaluating the possibility of adopting synergistic multi-scale approaches, exploiting satellite and aerial platforms.

Keywords: Satellite · Glaciers · Aerial · Photogrammetry · Vertical accuracy · 3D models

E. Borgogno Mondino and P. Zamperlin (Eds.): ASITA 2023, CCIS 2088, pp. 3–15, 2024.
https://doi.org/10.1007/978-3-031-59925-5_1

1 Introduction

The Department of Environment, Land and Infrastructure Engineering (DIATI) at Politecnico di Torino thanks to the Italian Ministry for Education and Research (MIUR), Dipartimento di Eccellenza funded the CC-LAB, a multidisciplinary laboratory for the climate changes. The activities of the Glacier Lab are mainly focus on the evolution of the glacier and periglacial areas under the effects of climate change with a multidisciplinary approach. Under this project, several glaciers were monitored during the last years in collaboration with geomatic, hydraulic and geophysics research groups of Politecnico di Torino to understands the dynamics and vulnerabilities of these complex systems.

Since 2020, in collaboration with the Environmental Protection Agency of Aosta Valley (ARPA VdA) the Rutor glacier was monitored by yearly monitoring campaigns, aerial photogrammetric surveys and very high resolution satellite images.

In this framework, remote sensing techniques are valid tools to monitor the cryosphere often used in the last 20 years (Paul et al, 2007) both to monitor water kinematics and dynamics (Fieber et al., 2008) and glacier retreat (Prinz et al., 2018, Giulio Tonolo, F. et al., 2020).

Satellite glacier images are usually used to study and monitor ice masses, especially those difficult to reach that necessitate recurring analysis (Otosaka et al., 2023), but their use in these areas is often challenging and could lead to inaccurate estimates in glacial mass balances (Zhang et al., 2023).

Starting from a set of high-resolution aerial and Satellite photogrammetric images acquired a few days apart, the main goal of the research is to evaluate the positional accuracies of the related added-value cartographic products (orthoimagery and Digital Surface Models- DSMs). In particular, the accuracy of the 3D satellite models is estimated exploiting both independent Check Points (CP) and DSMs of known accuracy and precision as reference dataset. Following this approach, it is possible to compare two DSMs of the same area generated in different periods and from different remote sensing techniques to appreciate the statistical significance of the altimetric and volumetric variations.

2 Materials and Methods

2.1 Case Study

The Rutor Glacier is located in the north-western part of Italy, above La Thuile, at the border between Italy and France. It extends from 2540 m asl to 3486 m asl, and with its area of 7.9 km^2, is the third largest Aosta Valley glacier. The glacier has a gentle slope and is almost divided into two parts by the "Vedette du Rutor", ending with three different tongues into a periglacial area of around 4 km^2 characterised by lakes and moraines.

The Rutor glacier is retreating since Holocene maximum in 1820 when the extension was 12 km^2 (Villa et al., 2007) and has already lost 34% of its extent (Corte et al, 2023). The projections (Intergovernmental Panel on Climate Change, Representation Concentration Pathway 8.5 °C, IPCC RPC 8.5) of the climate scenarios estimate that the glacier will retreat up to 1.5 km in 2100 (Strigaro et al., 2016).

The continuous retreat strongly modifies the environment and the morphology and the hydrological system of the area and reduces the total water volume stored in the glacier. More specifically, the dynamics of the proglacial environment of the Rutor glacier created different moraines and lakes and sediment transport (Vergnano et al., 2023).

2.2 Reference Data

Aerial orthoimagery (Ground Sample Distance – GSD of 0.10 m, resampled to 0.5 m for these analyses) and DSMs (GSD of 0.5 m) based of the aerial photogrammetric flight carried out on 13th September 2022 were extracted from the 3D point cloud and used as reference dataset to validate the satellites products. These products are based on visible imagery acquired with a Phase One camera onboard an ultralight aircraft and were processed in Agisoft Metashape v. 1.8.3 (Metashape, 2023). The flight altitude was about 974 m and the ground resolution of 7,45 cm/pix and scale of 1:20 000.

The 628 images of the 2022 model were elaborated with 9 Ground Control Points (GCPs) and 6 Check Points (CPs), i.e. artificial plastered markers positioned and mea-sured with Global Navigation Satellite System (GNSS) receivers (Real time Kinematic - RTK mode) during ad-hoc field campaign. The reference system used is the RDN 2008 - EPSGS 6707.

A summary of the different data considered in this work is reported in Table 1.

Table 1. Reference data

Product	Data	GSD
Aerial flight	13th September 2022	0.1 m (resampled to 0.5 m)
Satellite acquisition	11th September 2022	0.72 m (resampled to 0.5 m by the data provider)

A very high resolution (VHR) satellite stereo pair acquired from the Pleiades 1-A platform on 11th September 2022 at 10:23 was also processed (mean off-nadir angle of 23° over an area of 211.873 km2 between Italy and France. The imagery includes visible (VIS) and near-infrared (NIR) information and is characterized by an actual GSD of 0.72 m for the panchromatic band and a 2.8 m for the multispectral ones.

The coverage of both aerial and Satellite acquisitions is shown in Fig. 1.

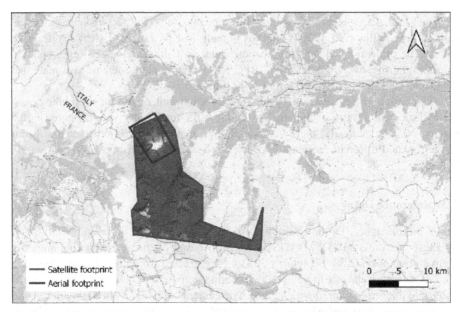

Fig. 1. Aerial (red) and Satellite (blu) coverage. Pléiades © CNES 2022 and AIRBUS DS. (Color figure online)

2.3 Data Processing

The satellite stereo pair was processed with CATALYST Professional Version 2223.0.1 (Catalyst, 2023) using the Rational Function Model (RFM or RPC, Rational Polynomial Coefficients) non parametric approach. The panchromatic and multispectral images were preliminarily pansharpened to obtain high resolution multispectral images characterized by the spatial resolution of the panchromatic band.

Thanks to the fact that the reference aerial products (orthophoto and DSM) were acquired only two days after the satellite acquisition, an automatic identification of stereo GCPs, CPs and Tie Points (TPs) was possible (due to the limited changes among the acquisitions). All the points automatically identified were manually checked and refined. After the image orientation phase and the generation of the epipolar pair, the DSM was extracted and two orthophotos were generated.

The knowledge of the accuracy and precision of a DSM is critical information when comparing two DSMs of the same area related to different time periods. More specifically, the metadata are mandatory to appreciate the statistical significance of elevation changes within a given probability threshold. The threshold value above which elevation differences are statistically meaningful is referred to as the Limit of Detection (LoD). Once the LoD is known, it is possible to apply the error propagation theory to determine the confidence intervals of the height variations of the glacial mass (mainly due to ice melting) (or the corresponding volume variations) between two different periods. We can determine the LoD of a DSM by comparison with independent reference products, generally following two alternative approaches:

- calculation of 3D residuals on a few CPs measured with GNSS RTK.
- comparison (pixel by pixel) against a reference DSM in areas considered stable, i.e. Difference of DSMs (DoD) approach, focusing on stable areas in the periglacial zone and exploiting aerial surveys carried out in previous years (which are not the focus of this manuscript) (Azmoon et al, 2022). In our case, given the almost simultaneous aerial and satellite acquisitions, the entire area covered by the photogrammetric flight can be considered unchanged.

Both paths have advantages and limitations that are summarised in the following.

CPs can be measured with topographic techniques with an horizontal precision of 1.5–2 cm and a vertical precision of 2–3 cm. As far as the aerial survey is concerned, CPs can be considered an independent references since they are unrelated to the photogrammetric process (the CP 3D accuracy is about 1/3 of the average aerial image GSD). However, CP numerosity is generally limited (6 in the specific case) since they need to be measured in the field and considering the accessibility constraints of a glacier environment.

The identification of control points on the imagery is often carried out manually with single pixel accuracy. Automatic sub-pixel accuracy is theoretically feasible using coded markers, but the operational constraints in the field make this approach mostly unusable in a glacier environment.

The second approach to determine the LoD is based on a statistical comparison with a DSM of known accuracy taken as reference. Being a pixel-by-pixel approach, the main advantage is that statistics are based on a very large number of points, but stable areas (without changes between the two datasets) must be defined to ensure that elevation differences are only due to measurement errors. It has to be highlighted that, even outside the glacier area subject to movements and melting, several phenomena may lead to variations, like instability processes, snow coverage, fluvial dynamics phenomena, water bodies, etc. Such areas induce errors in the image correlation phase leading to outliers in the DoD values that, if not properly filtered, severely impact on the statistics metrics.

In accordance to established testing practices in photogrammetry and topography, a maximum of 5% of the extreme values representing the tails of the DoD distribution have been excluded. Statistical analyses are carried out on this 95% sample, evaluating:

- Median over the entire sample, "robust" operator not influenced by the presence of gross errors;
- Mean and standard deviation of the DoD on the entire sample;
- Mean and standard deviation of the DoD on the 95% sample;
- Pearson indices based on skewness and kurtosis on the 95% sample (their value are close to zero if the distribution is normal).

Being one of the goals to assess the possibility of using only satellite imagery for glacier monitoring (especially when no aerial reference data is available), a detailed sensitive analysis on GCP spatial configuration and numerosity has also been carried out. A variable set of GCPs was evaluated, ranging from no GCPs (i.e. direct georeferencing approach) to 10 GCPs, with at least 5 CPs to evaluate the impact of the GCP configurations on the 3D positional accuracy.

Both approaches were followed to determine the LoD of DSMs generated from:

- Aerial photogrammetry - flights in 13 September 2022 (not the focus of this manuscript): 6 CP and DoD with respect to the 2021 aerial dataset
- Satellite photogrammetry - Pleiades images 11 September 2022: at least 5 CP and DoD with respect to the 2022 aerial dataset

For the assessment of the LoD of the satellite-based DSM, considering the two day difference between aerial and satellite acquisition dates, the DoD was carried out over the entire area (as shown in Fig. 2).

Fig. 2. Area considered for DoD on aerial orthophoto

3   Results

Concerning the evaluation of horizontal and vertical accuracy (i.e. DoD) of the satellite based products using CP residuals, different configurations of GCPs (Table 2 and Fig. 3) were tested when processing the satellite stereo-image.

The RMSEs on different configurations of CPs are reported in Table 2.

Table 2. Satellite RMSEs of different GCPs configurations

N GCPs	N CPs	GCPs ID	RMSE CP XY [m]	RMSE CP Z [m]
0	22	/	9.105	1.239
1	21	35	0.253	1.171
2	20	35,60	0.340	0.796
3	19	35,40,60	0.284	0.3650
5	13	35,39,40,60,61	0.140	0.651
10	8	all	0.147	0.760

It is clear from the results of Table 3 how the use of even just one GCP can eliminate horizontal and vertical systematic errors. Excellent results on the residuals calculated on the CPs are already obtained with only 3 GCPs. (see Table 4).

Fig. 3. Complete GCPs dataset spatial distribution and related ID

As already detailed, the satellite DSM is compared to the 2022 aerial DSM. Once the tails of the DoD distribution with significance level 5% are removed, the standard deviation of the altimetric differences is 56.8 cm (Fig. 4).

The trend of the deviations is shown in Fig. 4, the cumulative frequency diagrams present the values of the height deviations in the abscissa and the frequencies between 0 and 1 in the ordinate.

To assume the accuracy of the satellite DSM (10 GCPs configurations), we can consider:

$$\sigma^2_{DSMaerial} + \sigma^2_{DSMsatellite} = (56.8)^2 cm^2 \tag{1}$$

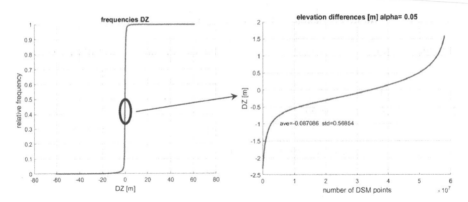

Fig. 4. Aerial 2022- satellite2022 - Alpha 5% - 10GCPs

In the case of DSM by area photogrammetry, the accuracy was estimated from vertical residuals on 7 CPs with an RMS of 7.3 cm (Table 3). Independent analyses, not covered in this work, were made by comparing the DSMs of the stable areas of the 2022 photogrammetric model with that of the previous year. The results substantially confirm the accuracy obtained from the CP analysis. From the error propagation law, it is then possible to obtain the standard deviation of the Satellite DSM, knowing the standard deviation of the reference aerial DSM (2).

$$\sigma_{DSMsatellite} = \sqrt{56.8^2 - 7.3^2} = \pm 56.3 \, cm \tag{2}$$

As far as the analysis on the CPs is concerned, the root mean square errors (RMSE) of the different models on the CPs is reported in Table 3.

Table 3. CP RMSE

Product	RMSE CP XY [m]	RMSE CP Z [m]
Aerial 2022 (9 GCPs, 6 CPs)	0.115	0. 073
Satellite 2022 (10 GCPs, 5 CPs)	0.147	0.760

The value obtained is slightly higher than the one obtained from the DoD analysis. We can therefore cautiously assume as LoD the value obtained in (2).

Based on the CPs, we then calculate the LoD of the differences between the DSMs (Fig. 5) to assess the significance threshold:

$$\sigma_{DSMaerial-satellite} = \sqrt{7.3^2 + 76.0^2} = \pm 76.3 \, cm \tag{3}$$

The two approaches lead to comparable LoD, which was used to classify the DoD, with the advantages and disadvantages highlighted in the previous section.

Fig. 5. DoD: Aerial 2022 – Satellite 2022

Additionally, to assess the accuracy of the different GCP configurations, using the procedure described above on the DoD area the statistics values are computed (Table 4 and Fig. 6).

Table 4. Statistical analysis of differences between DSMs according to different configurations

	NO GCP	1 GCPs	2 GCPs	3 GCPs	5 GCPs	10 GCPs
% outlier > 10 m	6.930	0.351	0.450	1.681	0.405	0.410
Median [m]	2.581	1.147	0.595	0.626	0.137	-0.118
Mean [m]	1.997	1.071	0.591	0.792	0.095	-0.156
Average without tails (5%) [m]	2.230	1.142	0.644	0.817	0.168	-0.087
Standard deviation without tails (5%) [m]	3.777	0.543	0.807	1.414	0.575	0.568
Skewness- Fisher range (without tails 5%)	-0.957	-0.223	0.142	0.661	-0.095	-0.068
Kurtosis- Fisher gamma 2 (no tails 5%)	1.798	0.921	0.413	3.035	1.115	1.022

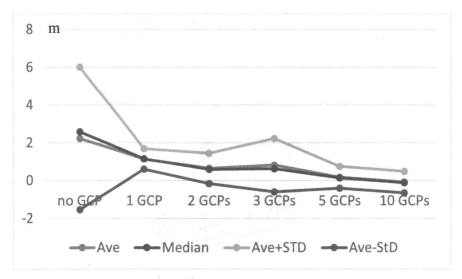

Fig. 6. DoD statistic metrics vs GCPs configurations

4 Discussion

As detailed in the Methods and Results sections, the assessment of the vertical precision of a DSM can be based on two approaches, exploiting as references:

- a (generally) limited number of CPs;
- a DSM of higher accuracy and with a dataset population of (generally) dozens of millions.

In the latter case, it is crucial to exclude outliers that may originate where correlation fails. Generally, this happens on water bodies areas due to homogeneous patterns (e.g. lakes) or to variability among different frames in case of runoff. Analyzing the percentages of outliers above a threshold of 10 m for this case study, it can be noted that outliers are less than 2% on a correctly georeferenced DSM. We then cautiously exclude 5% of the tails of the DoD distribution, according to usual cartographic validation approaches.

It should be noted that statistics calculated on very large samples or samples of only a few units do not have the same reliability. The preliminary conditions for the application of a parametric statistic are that observations and errors are independent of each other and normally distributed.

Small samples may not meet the assumptions of normal distribution. An alternative approach is to still use parametric tests relying on their robustness. However, the procedure applies to large samples and is generally not recommended (Krebs, 1999).

The hypothesis of Normal distribution can be verified by checking the skewness and kurtosis indices. The values of skewness and kurtosis of an experimental distribution, shown in Table 4 are given by Fisher's γ and γ_2 indices, respectively:

$$\gamma = \frac{m_3}{m_2^{\frac{3}{2}}}, \gamma_2 = \frac{m_4}{m_2^2} \tag{4}$$

with m_2, m_3 and m_4 moments of the second, third and fourth order, respectively. It is shown by the Central Limit Theorem that in a distribution of sample averages the measures of skewness and kurtosis tend to zero as sample size increases. In a normal distribution the Fisher indices have zero value. We can check with a two-sided test whether:

– the skewness index is non-zero - null hypothesis H_0: $\gamma_1 = 0$ and alternative hypothesis H_0: $\gamma_1 \neq 0$
– the kurtosis index is different from zero-null hypothesis H_0: $\gamma_2 = 0$ and alternative hypothesis H_0: $\gamma_2 \neq 0$ using the standardized variables for skewness Z_{Skw} and kurtosis indices Z_{Kurt}:

$$Z_{Skw} = \frac{\gamma - 0}{\sigma_1}, \sigma_1 = \sqrt{\frac{6}{n}}, Z_{Kurt} = \frac{\gamma_2 - 0}{\sigma_2}, \sigma_2 = \sqrt{\frac{24}{n}} \tag{5}$$

on n sample size

Table 4 shows that, normalizing the Fisher indices, the probability on both null hypotheses of skewness and kurtosis is practically equal to 1 on the 95% sample. This implies that the mean and standard deviation parameters of the DoD between the satellite and aerial DSM are well representative of a normal distribution. With this assumption we can say that the most representative value of LoD of the satellite DSM is 56 cm (68% probability interval: the value is double at 95% probability interval). This value is coherent with the nominal spatial resolution of the satellite images.

Concerning the use of GCPs for the orientation of the satellite stereo pair, it has to be remarked that – despite GCPs are crucial for the datum definition and for the final positional accuracy - there are several operational constraints related to GCP materialisation and measurement in glacial or periglacial areas. This operation should therefore be limited as much as possible. The statistical analysis of the result of different configurations of GCPs is aimed at identifying the minimum and optimal number of GCPs to be used.

Table 4 and Fig. 6 show the DoD statistic metrics with different configurations of GCPs. A direct georeferencing approach (i.e. no GCP) is possible (with a vertical accuracy of few meters), it is recommended to use at least 1 GCP to correct systematic effects. Increasing the number of GCPs leads to a significant improvement up to 5 GCPs.

5 Conclusions

In glaciological activities, the measurement of ground variations is used for the analysis of melting phenomena and related consequences. Such analyses are increasingly approached with photogrammetric surveys for the generation of 3D models: therefore, it is crucial to know their horizontal and vertical precision to statistically assess whether multitemporal elevation differences can be considered statistically meaningful.

Among the different platforms that can be used for photogrammetric surveys, satellites enable the acquisition of large areas (covering several glaciers) also if hardly accessible on the ground.

The analyses carried out for this research focused on very high resolution satellite stereo pairs. The results show that 5 GCPs, homogeneously distributed over the stereo pair footprint, enable to achieve sub-meter vertical accuracy (i.e. same order of magnitude of the image GSD) and imply a conservative but sustainable number of ground measurement operations. However, GCPs can be derived from photogrammetric products at larger nominal map scale (and therefore accuracy) when available.

The satellite DSM validation was carried out by evaluating elevation differences with respect to CPs and a reference aerial DSM. A LoD (at 68%, 1 standard deviation) of 73 cm and 56 cm respectively was estimated. According to the discussion section, the value of 56 cm seems a reasonable LoD since it is based on a sample of 60 M points.

The robustness of future multi-temporal analyses can be measured using parametric statistics, after verifying the hypothesis of DoD normal distribution based on skewness and kurtosis indices. This hypothesis is met by conservatively considering 95 percent of the DoD population, excluding the maximum and minimum values of the tails of the DoD distribution.

Funding. The Italian Ministry for Education and Research (MIUR), Dipartimento di Eccellenza, sui cambiamenti climatici, funded this research. (https://www.diati.polito.it/focus/dipartimento_di_eccellenza_sui_cambiamenti_climatici_2018_2022/laboratorio_multisito/cc_glacier_lab) and ARPA Valle d'Aosta.

The Pléiades satellite images were provided by AIRBUS Defense & Space in the framework ISIS License EU V4 -DIN-PGO-2022-HN-GRAN PARADIS.

References

1. Paul, F., Kääb, A., Haeberli, W.: Recent glacier changes in the Alps observed by satellite: consequences for future monitoring strategies. Glob. Planet. Change **56**(1–2), 111–122 (2007). https://doi.org/10.1016/j.gloplacha.2006.07.007
2. Fieber, K.D., Mills, J.P., Miller, P.E., Clarke, L., Ireland, L., Fox, A.J.: Rigorous 3D change determination in Antarctic Peninsula glaciers from stereo WorldView-2 and archival aerial imagery. Remote Sens. Environ. **205**, 18–31 (2018). https://doi.org/10.1016/j.rse.2017.10.042
3. Prinz, R., Heller, A., Ladner, M., Nicholson, L.I., Kaser, G.: Mapping the loss of Mt. Kenya's glaciers: an example of the challenges of satellite monitoring of very small glaciers. Geosciences (Switzerland) **8**(5) (2018). https://doi.org/10.3390/geosciences8050174
4. Giulio Tonolo, F., Cina, A., Manzino, A., Fronteddu, M.: 3D glacier mapping by means of satellite stereo images: the belvedere glacier case study in the Italian Alps. Int. Archiv. Photogrammetry Remote Sens. Spat. Inf. Sci. ISPRS Archiv. **43**(B2), 1073–1079 (2020). https://doi.org/10.5194/isprs-archives-XLIII-B2-2020-1073-2020
5. Otosaka, I.N., Horwath, M., Mottram, R., Nowicki, S.: Mass balances of the Antarctic and Greenland ice sheets monitored from space. Surv. Geophys. Springer Science and Business Media B.V. (2023). https://doi.org/10.1007/s10712-023-09795-8
6. Zhang, G., et al.: Underestimated mass loss from lake-terminating glaciers in the greater Himalaya. Nat. Geosci. **16**(4), 333–338 (2023). https://doi.org/10.1038/s41561-023-01150-1
7. Villa, F., De Amicis, M., Maggi, V.: GIS analysis of Rutor Glacier (Aosta Valley, Italy) volume and terminus variations. Geogr. Fis. Din. Quat. **30**, 87–95 (2007)
8. Corte, E., et al.: Multitemporal characterisation of a proglacial system: a multidisciplinary approach (2023). https://doi.org/10.5194/essd-2023-94

9. Strigaro, D., Moretti, M., Mattavelli, M., Frigerio, I., Amicis, M.D., Maggi, V.: A GRASS GIS module to obtain an estimation of glacier behavior under climate change: a pilot study on Italian glacier. Comput. Geosci. **94**, 68–76 (2016). https://doi.org/10.1016/j.cageo.2016.06.009

10. A Vergnano, A., Oggeri, C., Godio, A.: Geophysical–geotechnical methodology for assessing the spatial distribution of glacio-lacustrine sediments: the case history of Lake Seracchi. Earth Surf. Proc. Land. **48**(7), 1374–1397 (2023)https://doi.org/10.1002/esp.5555

11. Agisoft Metashape: Agisoft Metashape. (n.d.). https://www.agisoft.com/. Accessed 21 July 2023

12. Azmoon, B., Biniyaz, A., Liu, Z.: Use of high-resolution multi-temporal DEM data for landslide detection. Geosciences (Switzerland), **12**(10) (2022). https://doi.org/10.3390/geoscienc es12100378

13. CATALYST. Earth - Home. (n.d.). https://catalyst.earth/. Accessed 21 July 2023

14. Krebs, C.J.: Ecological Methodology, 2nd ed. Addison-Wesley Educational Publishers (1999)

A Multi-scale Approach to Detect Geomorphological Hazard in a Post-fire Scenario: A Case Study in Sardinia (Central Mediterranean)

Ilenia Murgia[1] ⓘ, Francesca Putzolu[2], Raffaella Lovreglio[2] ⓘ, and Antonio Ganga[3](✉) ⓘ

[1] Department of Agricultural, Food, and Environmental Sciences - Marche Polytechnic University, Via Brecce Bianche 10, 60131 Ancona, Italy
[2] Department of Agriculture, University of Sassari, Viale Italia, 07100 Sassari, Italy
[3] Department of Architecture, Design and Urbanism, University of Sassari, Via Pandanna, 07100 Sassari, Italy
aganga@uniss.it

Abstract. Several studies have documented a close relationship between forest fires and the instability of the soil-vegetation system. Furthermore, repeated wildfires, especially characterized by extreme severity and intensity, can induce hydrological and geomorphological effects that persist over several years, e.g., the temporary erosion rate intensification and the susceptibility increase of most significant downslope soil movement.

This study analyzes the close relationship between wildfires and soil instability by examining the mega-fire in July 2021 in the Montiferru – Planargia region (Sardinia, Central Mediterranean). The proposed multiscalar methodology provides management and plan indications to mitigate potential damages caused by extreme wildfire, especially in areas with high susceptibility from a hydrogeological perspective, using physical models supported by open geodata in a GIS-based workflow.

Keywords: Forest fire · Burn severity · Sentinel - 2 · NBR · Landslide · SlideforMAP · SOSlope · RUSLE

1 Introduction

Several studies worldwide [1–5] highlight a strong relationship between wildfires and increasing susceptibility to critical instabilities like surface erosion and shallow landslides. Fire influences soil hydro-mechanical behavior [2] due to removing vegetation cover, ash deposition, altering the structure of aggregates, and increasing the soil water repellency effect [6].

Fire severity determines the intensity of vegetation cover loss, dramatically exposing the soil to raindrop impact and to surface erosion by overland flow [3]. Although surface

E. Borgogno Mondino and P. Zamperlin (Eds.): ASITA 2023, CCIS 2088, pp. 16–29, 2024.
https://doi.org/10.1007/978-3-031-59925-5_2

damages are directly evident, the burning process alters soil hydro-mechanical properties improving its instability.

The burning of organic matter, damage to root systems [7], and death of pedo-fauna highly reduce soil cohesion [8] with different intensities depending on soil types and temperatures reached during the burning [9]. The organic content reduction affects particle size distribution, aggregate stability, bulk density, plasticity, and elasticity [2]. The production of ash and mineral particles from vegetation burning promotes the pH increase of solutions, leading to soil aggregate dispersion [10], also altering the soil water storage capacity, and reducing the storage capacity due to pore clogging [11]. Damage to root systems reduces their mechanical stabilizing effect, leading to strength loss and reduction of soil apparent cohesion [7, 12], and this effect can last for long periods. Gehring et al. (2019) observed that forests affected by moderate fires continue to provide adequate protection only to shallow (<0.5 m) and cohesive soils, while after high-severity fires, the protective ability is nullified for 15 years, and a significant slope failure probability remains for at least 40 years. This mainly depends on the condition and resilience ability of forests. Furthermore, root reinforcement decay is also promoted by crown fires [13].

Among hydrologic consequences, soil water repellency increases runoff and erosion [14]. The intensity and persistence of soil water repellency vary with fire severity and duration, vegetation type, moisture, soil texture, and time since burning [15, 16].

Surface erosion and precipitation-induced triggering of surface landslides result from the combination of the hydromechanical dynamics described above, with extended effects from the first rainy season immediately following the fire [17, 18], up to 1–2 years after the fire [1, 17], and even 10 to 30 years after fire [19].

Therefore, knowing the vulnerability degree of an area to hydrogeological instabilities, even independently of its fire history, is necessary to design and plan post-fire interventions. For this reason, slope stability models allow for assessing potential scenarios, e.g., land cover change after disturbances, and changes induced in the soil stability.

This study aims to analyze the relationship between forest fires and soil-vegetation system instability, considering the mega-fire that occurred in Sardinia in July 2021. The proposed multi-scalar methodology provides management and design guidance to mitigate the potential damage caused by forest fires, especially in areas of high vulnerability from a hydrogeological point of view, using physical models with geodata. Furthermore, this process and its results could be integrated into innovative civil protection systems and procedures [20].

2 Materials and Methods

The methodology implemented in this study aims to assess and quantify an area's vulnerability to rainfall-induced shallow landslides and surface erosion. The multiscalar approach (Fig. 1) includes a preliminary analysis concerning fire severity evaluation (Fig. 1a), a middle-scale slope stability analysis inside the burned area (Fig. 1b), and a large scale in a plot area identified considering high fire severity, high slope, shallow landslide susceptibility, and proximity to the urban center.

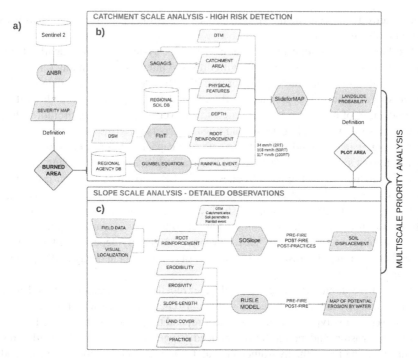

Fig. 1. Workflow diagram describing the multiscalar process to intervention priority analysis. In white shapes, data sources; in purple shapes, equations (oval) and software (hexagon) used; in gray shapes, field, lab, and visual process for obtaining input data; in yellow shapes input data used for soil stability assessment; in orange shapes output data. a) shows the fire severity detection to identify the burned area; b) shows middle-scale stability analysis to localize the plot area; c) shows the slope scale stability analysis for detailed observation of the plot area.

2.1 Study Area

The study area is located in the central-western part of Sardinia (Italy, Fig. 2), where a mega-fire spread over 13,000 hectares occurred in the summer of 2021. Following the concept of extreme wildfire event by [21], we can classify this event as an extreme one due to the extent of burnt surfaces and the unpredictable fire behavior and spread observed by the fire crews of the Sardinia Forest Service.

The site is characterized by variable morphology, with altitudes ranging from 0 to 1050 m asl. The main lithotypes are generated by Plio-Pleistocene volcanic activity, promoting a high soil variability strictly correlated to vegetation and topography. Deep and evolved soils dominate in the forested plain, while in slope and bare areas, soils are thin and affected by erosion, with scattered rock outcrop. According to the 1988 USDA Soil Taxonomy classification, the most represented soils at the subgroup level are *Lithic Xerorthents* and subordinately "*Xerochrepts*" [22]. The sea influences the climate; suddenly, condensation and precipitation are frequent. In the summit, the annual precipitation reaches 1000 mm/year. The pre-fire vegetational cover was composed of plants derived from recent tree plantations, mainly *Pinus nigra* (J.F.Arnold),

Pinus pinaster (Aiton), and *Pinus halepensis* (Mill.), associated with native species, in which *Quercus ilex* (L.) is the predominant specie.

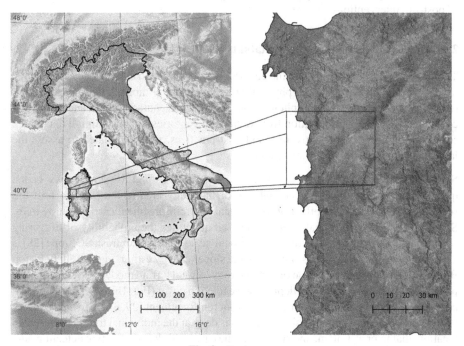

Fig. 2. Study area

2.2 Severity Detection

The severity measures the magnitude of the fire's impact on the ecosystem, indicating the degree of physical and ecological changes [23]. In recent decades, improving the remote sensing approach permits efficiently determining wildfire severity using satellite data [24]. This study used Sentinel-2 satellite images of the European Space Agency (ESA) collected in the Copernicus space project. Two multispectral images were acquired from the Sentinel-2A satellite, pre- and post-fire (24/07/2021), to detect the burnt area and create a severity map using a specific vegetation index. The Normalized Burn Ratio (NBR) [25] was calculated according to Eq. 1 (in brackets the bands relating to Sentinel images - 2):

$$NBR = (NIR(B8A) - SWIR(B12))/(NIR(B8A) + SWIR(B12)) \qquad (1)$$

The NBR assumes high values in correspondence with vigorous vegetation, and low values indicate a land cover change due to a fire. The difference between the pre-fire and post-fire NBR is used to calculate the delta NBR (dNBR), which helps estimate the damage severity. A higher dNBR value indicates severe damage, while negative dNBR values indicate vegetation regrowth [26]. According to the literature, these values are classified into 5 classes [25]. The ΔNBR allows for identifying wildfire boundaries and areas with the greatest damage, implementing all information to create a priority map of post-fire interventions.

2.3 Models for Estimating Slope Stability and Soil Loss

The slope stability evaluation and the general loss of soil due to erosion caused by heavy rainfalls were carried out using physical and mathematical models. Considering environmental factors related to morphology, water flows, soil characteristics, and vegetation cover, and processing information from regional inventories, such as rainfall data, three scenarios, namely pre-fire, post-fire, and post-practices, were simulated to assess the landslide susceptibility of the study area.

SlideforMAP and SOSlope. Two models, SlideforMAP and SOSlope (www.ecorsi q.org), were used to quantify the stability of the study area in the pre and post-fire scenarios and to verify the effect of mechanical soil reinforcement carried out by trees. SlideforMAP [27] is a probabilistic model that quantifies the probability of triggering rainfall-induced surface landslides over regional-scale areas. In contrast, SOSlope [28] is a deterministic model that tests stability at the slope scale by estimating the safety factor. Both models require information on morphology (digital terrain model), catchment area, physical soil characteristics and depth, and vegetation cover (Fig. 1b and c). Both models consider the forest effect by estimating the root reinforcement [29, 31] activated by trees to counteract soil movement. This estimation is done at the individual tree scale based on location, diameter at 1.30 m, and species. In the case of SlideforMAP, tree detection, and diameter dimensioning were done with the FInT model [32, 33]. Instead, for processing with SOSlope, cover reconstruction was done by considering measured field data and visually interpreting pre-fire orthophotos. Since this is an artificial planting, similar dimensions were considered for pinus trees.

To observe the effect of the forest, the potential instability scenario is simulated by completely neglecting the forest cover over the area of interest and comparing it with forested scenarios.

RUSLE. In order to estimate the risk of potential erosion on the plot area, the RUSLE Model [34] was utilized. This is the revision of the Universal Equation of Soil Loss elaborated by Wischmeier and Smith (1978). It is an empirical model that makes it possible to evaluate soil loss by estimating the factors that influence the erosion phenomenon, according to the following Eq. 2:

$$A = R * K * LS * C * P \qquad (2)$$

where A estimate of the average annual soil loss expressed in t ha^{-1} year^{-1}; R is the rainfall erosivity factor (MJ mm ha^{-1} h$-^{1}$year^{-1}); K is the soil erodibility factor (t ha h ha^{-1} MJ^{-1} mm^{-1}); LS is the topographic factor or slope length factor (dimensionless); C is the land use and land cover factor (dimensionless, range from 0 to 1) and P is the erosion control practices factor (dimensionless, range from 0 to 1).

For each factor, the data used are reported in Table 1.

Table 1. RUSLE data sources

Factor	Source	technical notes and literature
K	ESDAC data[1] integrated with field observations	[36]
R	ESDAC data[2]	[36]
LS	Digital Terrain model 1 m resolution	[37], elaborated with the SAGAGIS module
C	Remote sensing and field observation	C - classes values: [38]
P	Field Observation	P - classes values: [39]

[1] Available on: https://esdac.jrc.ec.europa.eu/themes/soil-erodibility-europe
[2] Available on: https://esdac.jrc.ec.europa.eu/content/rainfall-erosivity-european-union-and-switzerland

2.4 Experimental Plot Definition and Data Collection

According to a multiscalar approach, the experimental plot is detected using Slide-forMAP (Fig. 1b). The plot was identified within the burned area according to specific aspects: high fire severity, high slope, shallow landslide susceptibility, and proximity to the urban center. Within the plot area, field surveys were conducted to characterize the soil by collecting 15 samples according to a random pattern (with a spatial predicate that imposed a minimum distance of 20 m between points) and verify the soil depth. The laboratory analysis estimated some physical properties required from stability models (Fig. 1c), e.g., bulk density and texture. The classification of soils proposed in the literature and the soil map was validated directly by a field survey. Relative to the vegetation survey, data regarding the location, species, height, and diameter of trees after the fire were recorded to generate the dataset needed for pre- and post-fire simulations. Finally, rainfall data from the regional inventory were processed using the Gumbel equation to obtain rainfall intensities at different return times, 2, 50, 100, and 200 years (Fig. 1b).

3 Results and Discussion

3.1 Severity Map

Starting from ΔNBR, a severity map (Fig. 3) is redacted. The total area burned is 13.193 hectares, in which the high severity class is mainly located in the southern part, dominated by the broadleaf forest. The severity classes with the greatest extent are *low to moderate* (30% of the total) and *high* (26%), while the *moderate to high* and *low* classes are equally spread (23% and 21%, respectively).

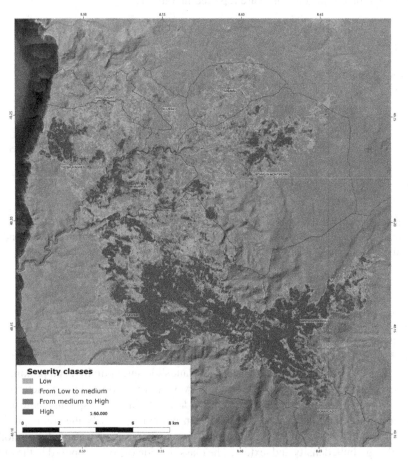

Fig. 3. Severity map.

3.2 Medium Scale Analysis - High-Risk Detection

Slideformap Analysis. Scenarios simulated with SlideforMAP show a strong correlation between failure probability with morphology and soil characteristics, with significant probability values in steeper areas and tributaries (Fig. 6A). Figure 4 shows the area extent referred to each failure probability class in the scenario of no forested cover and the one with forest. It is possible to observe a very minimal difference between the two scenarios, with higher values in the case of no cover (Figura 4a). Furthermore, considering different return times, an increase in the failure probability is observed between 2 and 50 years, which decreases sharply between 50 and 100 years. The presence of forest at this site shows little influence on the area.

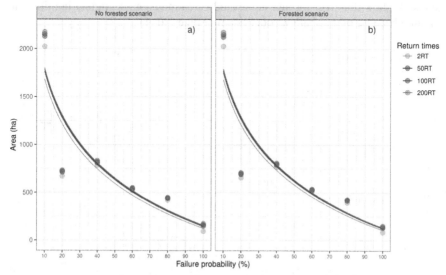

Fig. 4. The figure shows the extent expressed in hectares of areas belonging to a failure probability class (10 percentage classes). The curves refer to the return times considered in the analysis. a) is the scenario without forest, representing the potential instability; b) is the scenario with forest, representing the condition pre-fire.

Experimental Plot Definition. The experimental plot is defined through overlay GIS operation, using the risk map generated with SlideforMAP, Severity map, and land-use data. It is located at 8,48076° Longitude and 40,23953° of Latitude. The total area is 2.77 ha, the morphology is hilly with a north-east aspect, and the average slope is 26°. The soil taxonomy is congruent with the information in the soil map [22], with a maximum depth of 50 cm only in the downslope area. The mean bulk density registered is 0.871 g/cm^3, the minimum is 0.4826 g/cm^3, and the maximum is 1.1066 g/cm^3. The dominant texture is silt loam, with high coarse gravel content and rock outcrops.

3.3 Slope Scale Analysis - Detailed Observations

SOSlope Analysis. The simulations performed with SOSlope show the soil movement in an area of about 20% of the plot extent. In addition, a comparison among the surface subjected to soil movement for the three scenarios considered shows minimal differences or equal trends: in the Pre-Fire scenario the 16% of the area is subjected to soil movement (Fig. 6b), while in Post-Fire (Fig. 6c) and Post-Practices (Fig. 6c) scenarios the 18%, confirming morphology and pedology as the main predisposing factors. Also, Fig. 5a compares the Pre-Fire and Post-Fire scenarios, highlighting similar soil movements. The partial loss of vegetation cover resulted in a negligible increase, demonstrating its small influence on the plot stability. Figure 5b, however, shows an almost identical trend of the two curves, highlighting that the total removal of the vegetation component simulated in the Post-Practices scenario leads to no significant changes compared to the Post-Fire one. The results show that trees located in the study area intervene negligibly in mitigating instability because of the shallow root system of pine [40, 41].

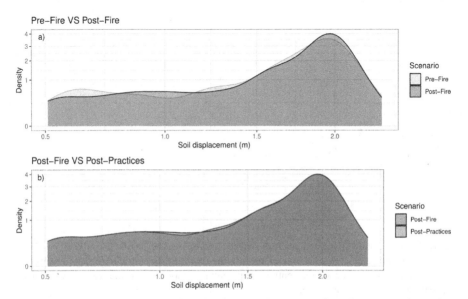

Fig. 5. The figure shows the density of cells reporting a specific soil displacement value, comparing the different scenarios of interest.

RUSLE Slope Scale Map. Two RUSLE simulations were produced and rendered in raster format with 5 m resolution (Fig. 6). The first simulation reports a pre-fire scenario in which the pre-existing vegetation has been reconstructed based on data collected in the field and goes through photo-interpretation. A second post-fire scenario is based on data collected in the field, mainly related to the presence of anti-erosion measures implemented by the Forest Service using standing dead trees to create wattle fences (Fig. 7). The values analysis demonstrates (Fig. 8) how the class of erosion values bigger than 300 $tha^{-1}y^{-1}$ has increased considerably. This is because the forest cover almost disappears, which exerts a high level of protection from water erosion. In the RUSLE model, factor C is relevant in burnt areas, especially forest areas [42]. Furthermore, it has been demonstrated that as the slope increases, the erosion rate increases more than proportionally [15, 43], especially if estimated using the RUSLE, which is particularly sensitive to topography [42]. The post-fire scenario shows a relevant increase in soil loss rate. This substantial increase aligns with the Mediterranean [44] and Sardinian frameworks [45]. However, the soil loss rates decrease rapidly due to the presence of post-fire mitigation interventions (Fig. 6) [45].

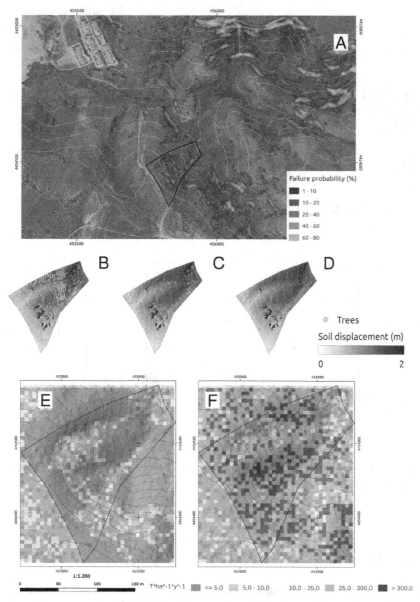

Fig. 6. A) Failure probability map using SlideforMAP referred to the rainfall scenario of 100 return time. B-C-D) Soil movement analysis using SOSlope considering respectively pre-fire, post-fire, and post-practice scenarios. E-F) Soil erosion maps using the RUSLE model in pre- and post-fire scenarios.

Fig. 7. The anti-erosive practice carried out by Sardinian Forestry Agency (FO.RE.S.T.A.S) with wattle fences produced in situ.

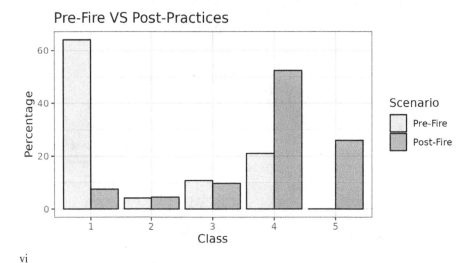

vi

Fig. 8. Distribution of the erosion percentage class: Class 1, ≤5; Class 2, 5–10; Class 3, 10–25; Class 4, 25–300; Class 5, ≥ 300 $tha^{-1}y^{-1}$.

4   Conclusions

The multi-level approach presented in this study enables the detection and quantification of the shallow landslide probability and potential soil erosion in a pre and post-fire scenario. The results showed that the soil erosion risk is preeminent over the loss of slope stability due to the specific characteristics of the soil and geological substrate. Stability analysis through SlideforMAP and SOSlope did not show a significant increase in the probability of initiation in the post-fire scenario compared to the pre-fire scenario, much less are effects due to silvicultural practices evident in the post-practices scenario.

In contrast, applying the RUSLE model to quantify soil erosion showed a significant percentage increase in the highest erosion classes (4 and 5).

The proposed multiscalar geo-hazard approach can be included for decision support in the planning and designing of post-fire interventions in urban-forest interface areas. Its application allows for identifying, prioritizing, and designing detailed and effective interventions. However, the role of data integration and processing (i.e., GIS, remote sensing, and physical model processing) is critical, both for human and financial resource management in this kind of scenario. In this sense, the study highlights the need for further research to integrate landslide and erosion model detection with another hazard model, especially for rockfall risk assessment and carbon loss stock estimation.

References

1. Meyer, G.A., Pierce, J.L., Wood, S.H., Jull, A.J.T.: Fire, storms, and erosional events in the Idaho batholith. Hydrol. Process. **15**, 3025–3038 (2001). https://doi.org/10.1002/hyp.389
2. Parise, M., Cannon, S.H.: Wildfire impacts on the processes that generate debris flows in burned watersheds. Nat. Hazards **61**, 217–227 (2012). https://doi.org/10.1007/s11069-011-9769-9
3. Shakesby, R., Doerr, S.: Wildfire as a hydrological and geomorphological agent. Earth-Sci. Rev. **74**, 269–307 (2006). https://doi.org/10.1016/j.earscirev.2005.10.006
4. Stoof, C.R., Vervoort, R.W., Iwema, J., van den Elsen, E., Ferreira, A.J.D., Ritsema, C.J.: Shakesby e doerr. Hydrol. Earth Syst. Sci. **16**, 267–285 (2012). https://doi.org/10.5194/hess-16-267-2012
5. Wagenbrenner, J.W., Ebel, B.A., Bladon, K.D., Kinoshita, A.M.: Post-wildfire hydrologic recovery in mediterranean climates: a systematic review and case study to identify current knowledge and opportunities. J. Hydrol. **602**, 126772 (2021). https://doi.org/10.1016/j.jhydrol.2021.126772
6. Certini, G.: Effects of fire on properties of forest soils: a review. Oecologia **143**, 1–10 (2005). https://doi.org/10.1007/s00442-004-1788-8
7. Gehring, E., Conedera, M., Maringer, J., Giadrossich, F., Guastini, E., Schwarz, M.: Sci. Rep. **9**, 8638https://doi.org/10.1038/s41598-019-45073-7
8. Mataix-Solera, J., Cerdà, A., Arcenegui, V., Jordán, A., Zavala, L.M.: Fire Effects on soil aggregation: a review. Earth-Sci. Rev. **109**, 44–60 (2011). https://doi.org/10.1016/j.earscirev.2011.08.002
9. Guerrero, C., Mataix-Solera, J., Garciâa-Orenes, F., Mez, I.G.: Different patterns of aggregate stability in burned and restored soils (2001)
10. Durgin, P.B.: Burning changes the erodibility of forest soils. J. Soil Water Conserv. **40**, 299–301 (1985)
11. Woods, S., Balfour, V.: The effect of ash on runoff and erosion after a severe forest wildfire, Montana, USA. Int. J. Wildland Fire **17** (2008). https://doi.org/10.1071/WF07040
12. DeGraff, J.V., Cannon, S.H., Parise, M.: Limiting the immediate and subsequent hazards associated with wildfires. In: Margottini, C., Canuti, P., Sassa, K. (eds.) Landslide Science and Practice, pp. 199–209. Springer, Berlin, Heidelberg (2013). ISBN 978-3-642-31336-3. https://doi.org/10.1007/978-3-642-31337-0_26
13. Swanson, F.: Fire and Geomorphic Process (1981)

14. Doerr, S.H., Shakesby, R.A., MacDonald, L.H.: Soil water repellency: a key factor in post-fire erosion. In: Fire Effects on Soils and Restoration Strategies, pp. 213–240. CRC Press (2009)
15. Huffman, E.L., MacDonald, L.H., Stednick, J.D.: Strength and persistence of fire-induced soil hydrophobicity under ponderosa and lodgepole pine. Colorado Front Range. Hydrol. Process. **15**, 2877–2892 (2001). https://doi.org/10.1002/hyp.379
16. Popović, Z., Cerdà, A.: Soil water repellency and plant cover: a state-of-knowledge review. CATENA **229**, 107213 (2023). https://doi.org/10.1016/j.catena.2023.107213
17. Cannon, S.H., Gartner, J.E.: Wildfire-related debris flow from a hazards perspective. Debris-Flow Hazards Relat. Phenom, 363 (2005)
18. Morton, D.: Distribution and frequency of storm-generated soil slips on burned and unburned slopes, San Timoteo Badlands, Southern California. Landslides Semi-Arid Environ. Emphas. Inland Val. South. Calif. **2**, 279–284 (1989)
19. May, C.L., Gresswell, R.E.: Processes and rates of sediment and wood accumulation in headwater streams of the Oregon coast range, USA. Earth Surf. Process. Landf. **28**, 409–424 (2003). https://doi.org/10.1002/esp.450
20. Sebillo, M., Vitiello, G., Grimaldi, M., Buono, D.D.: SAFE (Safety for Families in Emergency). In: Misra, S., Gervasi, O., Murgante, B., Stankova, E., Korkhov, V., Torre, C., Rocha, A.M.A.C., Taniar, D., Apduhan, B.O., Tarantino, E. (eds.) ICCSA 2019. LNCS, vol. 11620, pp. 424–437. Springer, Cham (2019). https://doi.org/10.1007/978-3-030-24296-1_34
21. Tedim, F., et al.: Defining extreme wildfire events: difficulties, challenges, and impacts. Fire **1**, 9 (2018). https://doi.org/10.3390/fire1010009
22. Aru, A., Baldaccini, P., Vacca, A.: Carta dei suoli della Sardegna in scala 1:250.000 (1991)
23. Guo, Q., Su, Y., Hu, T.: Chapter 12 - forest dynamics monitoring. In: Guo, Q., Su, Y., Hu, T., (eds.) LiDAR Principles, Processing and Applications in Forest Ecology, Academic Press, pp. 379–406 (2023). ISBN 978-0-12-823894-3
24. Szpakowski, D.M., Jensen, J.L.R.: A review of the applications of remote sensing in fire ecology. Remote Sens. **11**, 2638 (2019). https://doi.org/10.3390/rs11222638
25. Key, C.H., Benson, N.C.: Landscape Assessment (LA) **55** (2006)
26. Kelly, M., Meentemeyer, R.K.: Landscape dynamics of the spread of sudden oak death. Photogramm. Eng. **9** (2002)
27. van Zadelhoff, F.B., et al.: Introducing SlideforMap; a probabilistic finite slope approach for modelling shallow landslide probability in forested situations. Landslides and Debris Flows Hazards (2021)
28. Cohen, D., Schwarz, M.: Tree-root control of shallow landslides. Earth Surf. Dyn. **5**, 451–477 (2017). https://doi.org/10.5194/esurf-5-451-2017
29. Giadrossich, F., et al.: Methods to measure the mechanical behaviour of tree roots: a review. Ecol. Eng. **109**, 256–271 (2017). https://doi.org/10.1016/j.ecoleng.2017.08.032
30. Schwarz, M., Giadrossich, F., Cohen, D.: Modeling root reinforcement using a root-failure Weibull survival function. Hydrol. Earth Syst. Sci. **17**, 4367–4377 (2013). https://doi.org/10.5194/hess-17-4367-2013
31. Schwarz, M., Cohen, D., Or, D.: Spatial characterization of root reinforcement at stand scale: theory and case study. Geomorphology **171–172**, 190–200 (2012). https://doi.org/10.1016/j.geomorph.2012.05.020
32. Dorren, L.: FINT – Find Individual Trees. User Manual (2017)
33. Menk, J., Dorren, L., Heinzel, J., Marty, M., Huber, M.: Evaluation automatischer einzelbaumerkennung aus luftgestützten laserscanning-daten. Schweiz. Z. Forstwes. **168**, 151–159 (2017). https://doi.org/10.3188/szf.2017.0151
34. Renard, K.G.: Predicting Soil Erosion by Water: A Guide to Conservation Planning with the Revised Universal Soil Loss Equation (RUSLE). U.S. Department of Agriculture, Agricultural Research Service (1997). ISBN 978-0-16-048938-9

35. Wischmeier, W.H., Smith, D.D.: Predicting Rainfall Erosion Losses: A Guide to Conservation Planning. Department of Agriculture, Science and Education Administration (1978)
36. Panagos, P., et al.: The new assessment of soil loss by water erosion in Europe. Environ. Sci. Policy **54**, 438–447 (2015). https://doi.org/10.1016/j.envsci.2015.08.012
37. Panagos, P., Borrelli, P., Meusburger, K.: A new European slope length and steepness factor (LS-Factor) for modeling soil erosion by water. Geosciences **5**, 117–126 (2015). https://doi.org/10.3390/geosciences5020117
38. Rozos, D., Skilodimou, H.D., Loupasakis, C., Bathrellos, G.D.: Application of the revised universal soil loss equation model on landslide prevention. An example from N. Euboea (Evia) Island, Greece. Environ. Earth Sci. **70**, 3255–3266 (2013). https://doi.org/10.1007/s12665-013-2390-3
39. Panagos, P., Borrelli, P., Meusburger, K., van der Zanden, E.H., Poesen, J., Alewell, C.: Modelling the effect of support practices (P-Factor) on the reduction of soil erosion by water at European scale. Environ. Sci. Policy **51**, 23–34 (2015). https://doi.org/10.1016/j.envsci.2015.03.012
40. Danjon, F., Barker, D.H., Drexhage, M., Stokes, A.: Using three-dimensional plant root architecture in models of shallow-slope stability. Ann. Bot. **101**, 1281–1293 (2007). https://doi.org/10.1093/aob/mcm199
41. Genet, M., et al.: The influence of cellulose content on tensile strength in tree roots. Plant Soil **278**, 1–9 (2005). https://doi.org/10.1007/s11104-005-8768-6
42. Karamesouti, M., Petropoulos, G.P., Papanikolaou, I.D., Kairis, O., Kosmas, K.: Erosion rate predictions from PESERA and RUSLE at a mediterranean site before and after a wildfire: comparison & implications. Geoderma **261**, 44–58 (2016). https://doi.org/10.1016/j.geoderma.2015.06.025
43. Johansen, M.P., Hakonson, T.E., Breshears, D.D.: Post-fire runoff and erosion from rainfall simulation: contrasting forests with shrublands and grasslands. Hydrol. Process. **15**, 2953–2965 (2001). https://doi.org/10.1002/hyp.384
44. Valkanou, K., et al.: Soil loss potential assessment for natural and post-fire conditions in evia Island. Greece. Geosci. **12**, 367 (2022). https://doi.org/10.3390/geosciences12100367
45. Rulli, M.C., Offeddu, L., Santini, M.: Modeling post-fire water erosion mitigation strategies. Hydrol. Earth Syst. Sci. **17**, 2323–2337 (2013). https://doi.org/10.5194/hess-17-2323-2013
46. Vieira, D.C.S., Borrelli, P., Jahanianfard, D., Benali, A., Scarpa, S., Panagos, P.: Wildfires in Europe: burned soils require attention. Environ. Res. **217**, 114936 (2023). https://doi.org/10.1016/j.envres.2022.114936
47. Lovreglio, R., et al.: Observations on different post-fire bio-engineering interventions and vegetation response in a pinus canariensis C. Sm. Forest. Ann. Sylvic. Res. **45**, 83–91 (2020). https://doi.org/10.12899/asr-2034

Measuring Land Deformation Through PSI Technique in NE Sardinia (Italy): Roads to Einstein Telescope

Francesco Gabriele Dessì(✉) ⓘ and Maria Teresa Melis ⓘ

Department of Chemical and Geological Sciences, University of Cagliari, Cittadella
Universitaria-S.S. 554 Bivio per Sestu I, 09042 Monserrato, Italy
fdessi@unica.it

Abstract. The Einstein Telescope (ET) is a proposed underground infrastructure
to host a third-generation, gravitational-wave observatory. Currently, two European candidate-sites are competing to host it: one is located in the area of Sos
Enattos in Northern Sardinia (Italy), probably in the most favourable geological context, the second is in the Meuse-Rhine Euregion. The choice of the most
suitable site to host this new unique research infrastructure will be decided by
an international commission, considering the feasibility of the construction and
predicting the impact of the local environment on the detector sensitivity and operation. This site-characterization analyses are under way and the final decision is
expected by the end of 2024. The present study is part of the geological characterization of the site of Sos Enattos, and is focused on the evaluation of the surface
deformations of its area by means of Synthetic Aperture Radar (SAR) data. In this
framework, the PSI (Persistent Scattered Interferometry) technique with SAR data
provided by Sentinel-1 mission is the proposed approach for the analysis of a long
time-series imagery. Time-series of data were processed, exploiting the complete
Sentinel revisiting time, starting from 2014 to October 2022. The first results of
this analysis have been processed using the existing GNSS measures provided by
EUREF network as reference and the ground vertical displacement has been calculated after decomposition of LOS velocities. In this work, the results of ground
vertical displacement calculations for the study area are described, and particular
study-cases are discussed. The first results of this study confirm the very low values of vertical displacements in the area, as confirmed by the known geological
setting. These results can be considered an important value for the proposed Italian
site and the ET infrastructure realization.

Keywords: Einstein Telescope · Sentinel1 · SAR · Persistent Scatterers
Interferometry · Ascending and Descending Combination · Geographic
Information Systems

Supplementary Information The online version contains supplementary material available at
https://doi.org/10.1007/978-3-031-59925-5_3.

E. Borgogno Mondino and P. Zamperlin (Eds.): ASITA 2023, CCIS 2088, pp. 30–47, 2024.
https://doi.org/10.1007/978-3-031-59925-5_3

1 Introduction

The European Strategy Forum on Research Infrastructures (ESFRI), the agency responsible for indicating scientific research priorities to European governments, has added the Einstein Telescope (ET) in the road map of projects deemed valid and to be continued.

ET has been designed to be the largest gravitational wave detector ever built, equipped with a sensitivity of up to ten times more accurate in its measurements than current detectors. It is an underground infrastructure consisting in a new generation detector of gravitational waves, able to explore an area of the universe a thousand times larger in search of gravitational waves, and to detect sources too weak for the current generation of instruments (https://www.et-gw.eu).

An international research group is involved in the project of this new infrastructure, and a special attention is given to the choice of its best localization. Indeed, to observe gravitational waves, ET should be able to measure tiny changes in the length of detector tunnels 200–300 m underground and several kilometres long (https://www.einsteintele scope.nl/en/einstein-telescope/).

A particularly important aspect is therefore the study of disturbances with potential noise effects, one of which can be represented by ground deformations mainly due to tectonic activity. Among all other site-characterization activities, a study on the surficial deformation of the potential site of Sos Enattos has been carried out and described in this study.

SAR interferometry has become a good technique to study land deformation trends with the possibility to measure ground displacements with a very high level of accuracy (1–2 mm/year) slanted towards the Line of Sight (LOS) directions. During last years the temporal and spatial resolutions of sensors and platforms improved with an effective benefit in terms of applications to observations of earth surface dynamics [1–6]. For example in [7] authors uses ENVISAT SAR data to measure ground deformation for the Italian peninsula. The ENVISAT mission covers a long period from 2003 to 2012 but with a temporal resolution of 35 days. Similar studies as [8] applied InSAR data from ENVISAT in order to determine coseismic deformation related to earthquakes in the Northeastern Tibetan Plateau. Moreover it is possible to find some applications with multiplatform (ENVISAT and Sentinel-1) data combination [9] and an increasing number of studies where PSI technique has been adopted for a wide range of applications as tool to detect ground deformations related to landslides [10–15], volcanoes [16, 17], earthquakes [18] and subsidence [19–30].

In the differential SAR Interferometry (InSAR) methodologies, interferogram's stacking has a critical role in the processing chain because this is the most computationally demanding step [31]. In this work, the Persistent Scatterer Interferometry (PSI) technique [16, 17, 19, 32] was applied in order to get the velocity of stable and very high coherent scatterers through the processing of Sentinel-1A satellite data provided by European Space Agency (ESA).

The constellation of Sentinel data has supplied totally free of charge with the possibility to process SAR datasets by means of freely accessible software and tools: ESA has released the Sentinel Application Platform (SNAP) software, supported by a large network of developers and accompanying teams.

Due to low seismicity of Sardinia a general stable setting is expected with minor vertical motions [33]: extremely slow subsidence occurs in the NW while in the central segment of the eastern coast a low rate uplift has been detected [34]. Also, archaeological markers at several locations along the coast indicate a Late Holocene stability or a weak uplift (0.1–0.25 mm/yr) [35]. The high sensitivity of the PSI technique can represent a good tool to evaluate recent vertical movements especially related to anthropogenic elements like buildings and roads.

The relative movement of persistent scatterers can be calculated from the interferograms obtained by SNAP and ingesting them in the Stanford Method for Persistent Scatterers (StaMPS) free tool, as stated in the studies where the PSI method has been carried out by ascending and descending orbits combination [29, 36–38].

In order to derive LOS velocities, the adopted methodology requires a long-time for the processing, mainly due to radar interferograms generation: this is a really resources greedy step. In this study, the opportunity to use a cloud service provided by ESA through the NoR (Network of Resources) initiative has been exploited. With this sponsorship we got access to a cloud computing service for Sentinel-1 provided by Terradue (available at https://www.terradue.com/portal/), and formally called SNAPPING. Finally, LOS velocities derived from SAR images has to been decomposed with a particular approach in order to estimate the vertical motions.

1.1 Study Area

The site of Sos Enattos is located in North-Eastern Sardinia, Italy (Fig. 1). The underground infrastructure should be built with a triangular shape (10 km long sides), whose vertices are positioned between the villages of Lula, Bitti and Onanì.

The geological setting of the area is mainly composed by lithologies of the Varisican basement represented by orthogneiss, micaschists and intrusive units, crossed by regional faults [39].

One of the main reasons in the choice of the area of Sos Enattos, and in general the Sardinia region as international candidate for the ET installation is its low seismicity. The results of the analysis and modelling of earthquakes in Italy demonstrate that Sardinia region is characterized by a very low values of seismicity hazards, as depicted in Fig. 2 [40].

The very low values of the Peak ground acceleration PGA (g) in Sardinia (0.025–0.050) are due to a very few data for the modelling, confirming the low seismicity in the region.

Moreover, some useful data can be extracted from [41]: in this study, a contribution on the actual geodynamics is given using the spatial variations of continuous GNSS series to extract the crustal velocities in the Alpine Mediterranean area. As described in the results, the north-eastern Sardinia show very low/null values of horizontal and vertical velocities.

Fig. 1. Localization of the study area

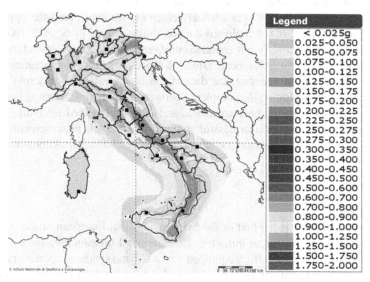

Fig. 2. Seismic hazard model MPS04-S1 (https://esse1-gis.mi.ingv.it/mps04_eng.jsp). The legend represents the values of the Peak ground acceleration.

2   Materials and Methods

2.1   Toolboxes

During the first assessment of this research a dedicated workstation has been prepared with everything needed for SAR data processing using open source ESA SNAP and StaMPS software packages with a set of scripts called *snap2stamps* [29]. In practice it is possible to use a set of scripts that allows a semi-automatic processing by setting some parameters in a configuration file. The *snap2stamps* processing leads to the creation of stacks of single master interferograms defining the bounding box coordinates of a specific area of interest with an integrated atmospheric correction provided by the TRAIN (Toolbox for Reducing Atmospheric InSAR Noise) module [42]. At the beginning, this methodology has been tested with a small area of around 250 square kilometres in Sos Enattos surroundings. In order to evaluate the ground vertical velocities a total amount of 94 radar images (SLC, Single Looking Complex) acquired by Sentinel-1 from January 2021 to July 2022 for both descending and ascending orbits, in number of 46 and 48 respectively, has been processed. We have experienced some constrains: each SAR scene is heavy (around 4 GB for a single image) and even with a relatively powerful workstation equipped with multi core CPUs, good amount of RAM and very performant SSD disks the processing time could reach a lot of hours or days. Due to long processing time related to this methodology to get vertical velocities, we considered the opportunity to use a cloud service. So, we exploited the possibility offered by SNAPPING service provided by Terradue (https://www.terradue.com/portal/), a cloud on-demand computing service for Sentinel-1 Multi-Temporal DInSAR processing, based on integrated SNAP and StaMPS chain. In this service, the dataset can be improved, considering a longer time of acquisition, exploiting the complete Sentinel revisiting time, starting from 2014. The access to this service has been sponsored and supported by the ESA NoR (Network of Resources) initiative after a successful application. With this improvement we were able to investigate a larger surface too, covering around 2500 square kilometers.

2.2   Dataset

Sentinel-1 Data

The Sentinel-1 mission is the first of the five missions that European Space Agency is developing with the Copernicus initiative. The Sentinel-1 mission involves a constellation of two polar-orbiting satellites equipped with a C-band synthetic aperture radar sensor: Sentinel-1A and Sentinel-1B. The analysis has been limited to Sentinel-1A dataset only due to well-known issues related to Sentinel-1B platform that led to the early closure of the mission [43]. However, the Sentinel-1A revisiting time of 12 days can be considered as sufficient in relationship with the expected magnitude of displacements even taking into account the availability of a large number of acquisitions, as well as others works [29].

The chosen ascending and descending Sentinel-1A SLC (Single Look Complex) images are listed in table 1. In order to get a more confident extraction of the vertical movement component, related to acquisition geometry, ascending and descending tracks respectively 88 and 168 have been selected due the comparable incidence angles (around

0.7 rad): by using a combination of similar viewing geometry the vertical motion can be extracted robustly. It should be noted that the number of ascending scenes is half the number of descending scenes: during the processing we get an error due to a system limit on the size of the instructions passing from the portal to the production cluster hosting the processing service. Thus, with the portal support, we made the choice to halving this dataset in order to speed up the processing time avoiding some redundance related to frequent satellite acquisitions.

Table 1. List of Sentinel-1A acquisitions employed for processing.

Orbit	Track	Number of Images	Master Image Date	Time Reference	
				Start	*End*
Ascending	88	196	2015/05/03	2015/05/03	2022/10/29
Descending	168	402	2015/05/09	2015/05/09	2022/10/23

2.3 Processing

SNAPPING - Surface motioN mAPPING application provided by the Geohazard portal https://geohazards-tep.eu/ (Fig. 3) has been used for the data processing. Through an interactive web map interface, it is possible to search and retrieve data of interest without download, avoiding thus transfer time and large local storage availability. Regarding the interferometric processing, the Shuttle Radar Topography Mission (SRTM) 1s HGT has been selected from the options menu, as utilized digital elevation model. Time-processing for the interferogram generation of descending images has requested around 9 h, instead for ascending acquisitions we needed around 3 days of processing due to some adaptions and modifications on configuration processing parameters.

PSI Processing-Chain Description
The StaMPS PSI methodology has been applied in different scenarios with success-ful results [29, 36–38]. In the differential SAR Interferometry (InSAR) methodologies, interferogram's stacking has a primary key role in the processing chain. The first step (Fig. 4) is to select the master scene from the data series: this process is made auto-matically by the software. Therefore, using the master image as reference, in all slaves datasets it is necessary to select the same sub-swath and bursts, in order to guarantee the co-registration between images and the Sentinel orbit files provided by ESA are applied to the whole dataset. The coregistration and the interferogram computation is the most resources-demanding step.

Accordingly with literature, the processing parameters for PSI analysis have been set using the default values: in particular we refer to amplitude dispersion (Da) and to the number of overlapping pixels in the azimuth (na) and range (nr) (Da = 0.4; nr = 50; na = 200). Theses parameters was left as default because no improvements were found changing its value as total number of candidates PS.

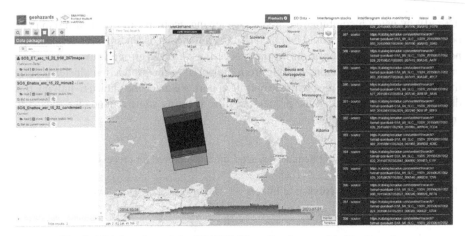

Fig. 3. Web interface of the SNAPPING application provided by Terradue.

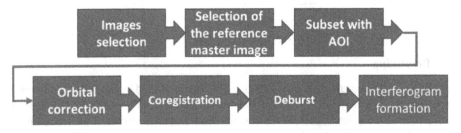

Fig. 4. Workflow of the interferogram formation process.

In order to correctly merge the results from both ascending and descending orbits, the same reference points, referred to a permanent European Reference Frame (EUREF) Permanent Network station (NUOR00ITA) located in the closest station of Nuoro (LON 9,3300 Est, LAT 40,3252 N) were selected. This station appears stable, with extremely very low vertical motion ($V_z = -0.45 \pm 0.1$ mm/yr).

At the end of this processing, we get a LOS velocities file for both acquisition geometries.

Post-processing: The Vertical Velocities
In order to get the vertical displacements, it is necessary to apply a decomposition procedure, related to both ascending and descending LOS velocities calculation and linked to acquisition geometry. Results of both geometries were then combined to compute the actual vertical motion component. For each point it is necessary to consider a couple (ascending and descending) of values. Therefore, for each Persistent Scatter point, the vertical component of the movement is calculated.

Using Eqs. (1) and (2), as described in [44]:

$$\begin{bmatrix} d_{LOS^{asc}} \\ d_{LOS^{desc}} \end{bmatrix} = A \begin{bmatrix} d_{up} \\ d_{hald} \end{bmatrix} \tag{1}$$

with

$$A = \begin{bmatrix} \cos\theta^{asc} & \frac{\sin\theta^{asc}}{\cos\Delta_\alpha} \\ \cos\theta^{desc} & \sin\theta^{desc} \end{bmatrix} \qquad (2)$$

where d_{LOS} is displacement along the LOS, d_{up} is the vertical displacement (Fig. 5), d_{hald} is the projection of horizontal displacement in descending azimuth look direction (ALD), θ is the incident angle, Δ_α is the satellite heading.

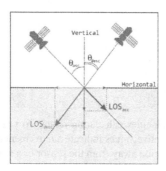

Fig. 5. Descending and ascending decomposition in vertical and horizontal components.

In order to avoid interpolation between measurements, with an increasing of uncertainties by introducing a significant smoothing of the initial PSI measurements, for example with a data rasterization, a vector-based approach has been managed accordingly with [16]. The analysis concerned the identification for each point in one geometry of its closest in the second geometry by means of nearest neighbour vector analysis. In this way the calculation involved only one nearest neighbour point between the two geometries and not an average of several closest points.

Since Permanent Scattered (PS) points are not regularly distributed in space, the distances from their closest neighbour in the opposite geometry can change, in our case with an average of around 30 m. In order to elude the connection with very far points, since they might not be sharing common behaviour of ground displacements, a maximum search radius was introduced. Therefore, this analysis has been restricted within distances shorter than 100 m. To this end, the distance constraint was arbitrary defined as being three times higher than the average distance between PS points. Points failed to meet the above condition were rejected from further analysis.

The achieving of a dataset with the vertical component of the deformation allows to analyse this behaviours in three study-cases: Lula village, SP45 road, Sos Enattos mining site. A buffer zone of 5 m was applied to the roads, in order to consider a reasonable amount of PS points referred to anthropic features.

3 Results

The map of the average PSI LOS deformation rates for both descending and ascending orbits of the study area is in Fig. 6. In the processing, pixels with amplitude dispersion Da < 0.4 were not considered to exclude scatterers with low temporal coherence.

Accordingly, displacement rates have been computed by taking in account a reference point that is supposed to be stable, the Nuoro EUREF station.

Time-series with the deformation data, associated to each measure, are available for each PS point. These series can show linear trends with a dispersion of few millimetres.

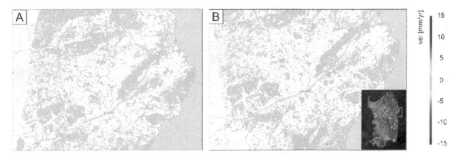

Fig. 6. Line Of Sight (LOS) velocities calculation related to years 2015–2022 for descending (A) and ascending (B) orbits. Positive values indicate a movement toward the sensor or a relative uplift, negative values show a motion away from the sensor or a relative subsidence.

Fig. 7. Average vertical motion rates related to years 2015–2022. Background image centred on 40°30'N and 9°25'E from **Google Earth.** May 16, 2022. Accessed July 2023. Data SIO, NOAA, U.S. Navy, NGA, GEBCO ©

The decomposition of the ascending and descending LOS measurements, gives the vertical deformation rate map shown in Fig. 7. Vertical velocities have been statistically analysed, and the results are given on Table 2.

Table 2. Statistical values calculated for Vertical Velocities points in the whole study area. Max and Min values are the Maximum (positive) and Minimum (negative) velocities with their relative accuracy. The Standard dev. Column is the population standard deviation of the data. The median is the value in the middle of the data set. Q1 and Q3 are respectively the lower and the upper quartiles and the IQR is the Inter Quartile Range, a measure of statistical dispersion.

Max Value (mm/yr)	Min Value (mm/yr)	Standard Dev	Median	Q1	Q3	IQR
5.66 ± 0.1	-7.82 ± 0.1	0.37	-0.02	-0.24	0.21	0.45

Velocities measurement roughly spans from values between -8 mm/yr and + 6 mm/yr with an Interquartile Range (IQR) of 0.45. Positive values have to be interpreted as a relative uplift of the persistent scattered and negative values have to be associated to a relative subsidence motion. It can be realized that various deformation configurations occur: most of the surface appears with no relative motion but it is possible to distinguish some relative subsidence (for example the rocky outcrop of Monte Albo in the Eastern part) or a small uplift in the Orosei surroundings. Roads are clearly visible too, they are a good target for this technique: one reasonable explanation is that the street lamps, stones, and fences distributed along the tracks can be easily and individually identified by the SAR.

We focused then our analysis to infrastructures and buildings in order to investigate their behavior associated with the vertical displacements. The vertical velocities dataset were filtered by intersect the whole dataset with a round-buffer area of 5 m outlined to viability layer. The relative statistics data are shown in the following Table 3.

Table 3. Statistical values calculated for Vertical Velocities points related to viability in the whole study area. Max and Min values are the Maximum (positive) and Minimum (negative) velocities with their relative accuracy. The Standard dev. Column is the population standard deviation of the data. The median is the value in the middle of the data set. Q1 and Q3 are respectively the lower and the upper quartiles and the IQR is the Inter Quartile Range, a measure of statistical dispersion.

Max Value (mm/yr)	Min Value (mm/yr)	Standard Dev	Median	Q1	Q3	IQR
2.82 ± 0.1	-4.04 ± 0.1	0.54	-0.08	-0.37	0.20	0.57

In the roads domain the vertical values are similar to values that has been calculated for the whole area: dispersions values slightly increase but looking at the absolutes values it is possible to notice that they converge towards smaller values. This fact can be interpreted as an indication of a relative greater stability.

3.1   Case-Studies: Roads and Buildings with Time Series

The behaviour of the deformation patterns has been studied in three case-studies associated to the buildings in Lula village and Sos Enattos mine, and to a main road.

Lula Village

In Lula village the concentration of PSs is connected to buildings and small houses (Fig. 8).

Observing at the time series, it is possible to recognize some seasonal variations, with positive and negative oscillation of few millimetres through the years of observations. The linear trend of the velocities has been calculated and showed by the red line.

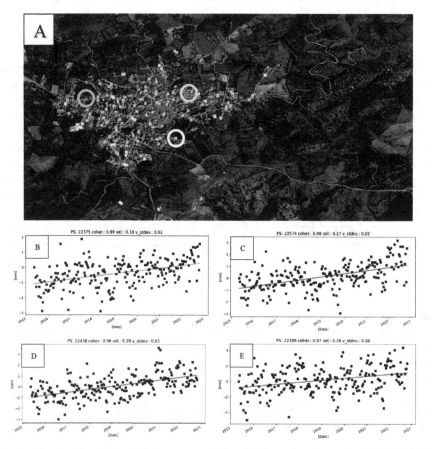

Fig. 8. PS points distribution in Lula town area (A) and deformation time series for PSs 22375 (B - red circle on map), 22574 (C – yellow circle), 22438 (D – orange circle) and 22199 (E – white circle). Background image centred on 40°28'N and 9°29'E from **Google Earth.** May 16, 2022. Accessed July 2023. Data SIO, NOAA, U.S. Navy, NGA, GEBCO ©. (Color figure online)

SP 45 Road

As well as buildings, roads are a good PS as shown in Fig. 9. Generally, the entire road track can be identified with PSI technique. In the chart (Fig. 9), in this case also, it is possible to distinguish some seasonal variations, with positive and negative oscillation of some millimetres.

The temporal trend is flat, demonstrating a general stability.

For the whole track of the road we calculated also statistics related to vertical velocities values, as shown in Fig. 10.

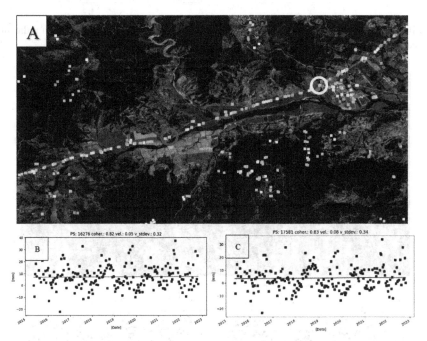

Fig. 9. PS points distribution in SP45 road area (A) and deformation time series for PSs 16276 (B - red circle on map) and 17581 (C – white circle). Background image centred on 40°23'N and 9°26'E from **Google Earth.** May 16, 2022. Accessed July 2023. Data SIO, NOAA, U.S. Navy, NGA, GEBCO ©. (Color figure online)

Sos Enattos Mining Site

As discussed in the introduction, this site is particularly interesting in the framework of the ET infrastructure, and the geodynamic setting has to be considered with special attention [45–48]. The mining activities of Sos Enattos are closed, but tunnels and wells were used in the past and now is used as underground laboratory. So, it is interesting the monitoring of the deformations, starting from this study. The results confirmed the stale trend of the analysed PSs, giving an important information for the choice of this candidate-site. (Fig. 11).

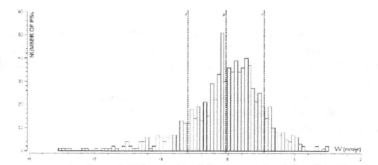

Fig. 10. Histogram of Vertical Velocities values calculated for SP45 road track with indication of mean value (μ) and standard deviation (σ).

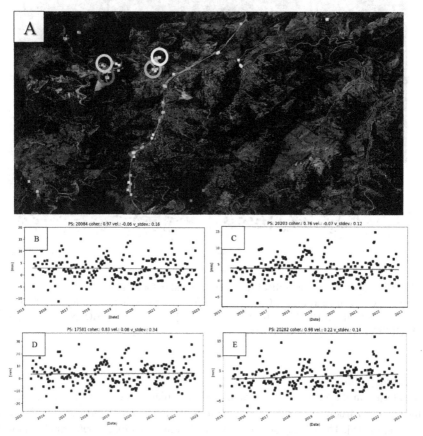

Fig. 11. PS points distribution in Sos Enattos mining site surroundings (A) and deformation time series for PSs 20084 (B - red circle on map), 20203 (C – yellow circle), 17581 (D – orange circle) and 20282 (E – white circle). Background image centred on 40°26'N and 9°27'E from **Google Earth.** May 16, 2022. Accessed July 2023. Data SIO, NOAA, U.S. Navy, NGA, GEBCO ©. (Color figure online)

4 Discussion and Conclusions

For the first time we depicted ground deformation rates in North East Sardinia, covering with a relative continuity a surface or around 2500 square kilometres and extending punctual observations provided by EUREF stations. Time span of measure is covering around 8 years of observations guaranteed by Copernicus Sentinel-1 revisiting time (12 days) with a big amount of data.

The study area shows different deformation configurations, related to different mechanism and phenomena. For most of the situations, the ground deformation can be related to the local geological characteristics. Further and more specific investigations, as detailed geological or geophysical surveys, has required to describe the real deformation trends and their evolution.

In the study area the measured vertical movements seems to be very slight, with a deformation rate of few mm/year, accordingly with previous works [33–35]: from the infrastructures point of view, the area can be considered as reasonably stable with no registration of important movements in last 8 years. In relation to past studies, we expand the area of observation and we improve the time resolution of analysis.

As expected, the highest PS density is located in built-up and rocky areas: PS points hare defined with a strong and constant reflection over a long period.

The proposed case studies show a stable behaviour or irrelevant deformation rates.

In particular, in built-up areas as Lula, we have the possibility to get multiple PS targets within each building: theoretically it can be possible to separate between the deformation of the structures themselves from those connected to soils, but, assumed the uncertainties in the location of the PS points and the resolution of Sentinel-1, this dichotomy of motion should be conducted with particular attention. Moreover, we use only the VV (Vertical Transmit-Vertical Receive) polarization of Sentinel-1: by considering both polarizations (VV + VH, adding Vertical Transmit-Horizontal Receive) an increase of PS targets is reasonably probable. In our study, vertical deformations observed in Lula village shows a positive trend that can be related to general observations of [33]: the measured mean vertical velocities in this area is around +0.1 mm/yr.

Deformation over roads was investigated, with a general confirmation of the surroundings trends of main stability. Locally it is possible to evaluate some relative subsidence or minor uplift and this information can be useful to support engineering designers. The proposed approach allows the identification of the deformation along the entire road track. We inspected in particular the SP45 road, very well detected in every SAR elaboration: the track road roughly follows the SW-NE direction, crossing the whole study area. Time motion series shows a very flattened trend, with a value of the mean vertical velocities of - 0.04 mm/yr. Calculated along the whole track. This confirm the stability and in practice the absence of significant motions that can be associated with dangerous conditions and responsible for cracks in infrastructures. For example, similar works as [49] has detected motions rates along the road network of around – 70 mm/yr. The local scenario is completely different. Finally, the Sos Enattos mining site: it could be reasonably expected to find movements and deformations especially linked to the presence of underground tunnels and galleries and induced slope instability, but looking at the time series of LOS velocities it is possible to find again a flattened trend. Ground subsidence is a common geological phenomenon occurring in mining areas and PSI technique is a good technique to investigate it [50] but the Sardinian context appears very stable. Mean vertical velocities value in this area are very near to zero (-0.02 mm/yr).

InSAR techniques, as stated in literature [51], confirm once again their capability to measure ground movements and the capacity to monitor phenomena by the accessibility of new data.

The ground vertical displacement calculations, composing data from both acquisition orbits, confirm the existing evaluations and extend the current information to the whole study area. Moreover, it will be possible to consider also future acquisition with a continuous monitoring process.

These results can be considered an important value for the proposed Italian site and the ET infrastructure realization.

Supplementary Materials
Sentinel-1 PS LOS displacements rates over the period 2015–2022 are provided in.csv format for both ascending and descending orbits. Each record is descripted by latitude and longitude coordinates, average LOS in mm/yr and relative standard deviation.

Acknowledgments. Project supported by ESA NOR Network of Resources Initiative. Research project with ID 2a20aa: Monitoring land deformation through PSI technique for Einstein Telescope site.

Funding. This research was partly funded in the framework of an agreement between Cagliari and Sassari universities: "Potenziamento del Laboratorio di Fisica della Gravitazione, Sar-Grav, dedicato alla ricerca di base nell'ambito della rivelazione di onde gravitazionali, fisica della gravitazione, geofisica e sue applicazioni (SAR GRAV 2). Art. 3 comma c) "Studio e all'analisi della funzionalità del sito di Lula".

Authors are grateful to Professor Michael Foumelis from Aristotle University of Thessaloniki (Greece) for his availability and his suggestions. The authors would like to thank also Hervé Caumont from Terradue for his excellent support.

References

1. Gabriel, A.K., Goldstein, R.M., Zebker, H.A.: Mapping small elevation changes over large areas: differential radar interferometry. J. Geophys. Res. **94**, 9183 (1989). https://doi.org/10.1029/JB094iB07p09183

2. Massonnet, D., Rossi, M., Carmona, C., et al.: The displacement field of the Landers earthquake mapped by radar interferometry. Nature **364**, 138–142 (1993). https://doi.org/10.1038/364138a0

3. Massonnet, D., Briole, P., Arnaud, A.: Deflation of Mount Etna monitored by spaceborne radar interferometry. Nature **375**, 567–570 (1995). https://doi.org/10.1038/375567a0

4. Massonnet, D., Feigl, K.L.: Radar interferometry and its application to changes in the Earth's surface. Rev. Geophys. **36**, 441–500 (1998). https://doi.org/10.1029/97RG03139

5. Bürgmann, R., Rosen, P.A., Fielding, E.J.: Synthetic aperture radar interferometry to measure earth's surface topography and its deformation. Annu. Rev. Earth Planet. Sci. **28**, 169–209 (2000). https://doi.org/10.1146/annurev.earth.28.1.169

6. Rucci, A., Ferretti, A., Monti Guarnieri, A., Rocca, F.: Sentinel 1 SAR interferometry appli-cations: the outlook for sub millimeter measurements. Remote Sens. Environ. **120**, 156–163 (2012). https://doi.org/10.1016/j.rse.2011.09.030
7. Farolfi, G., Piombino, A., Catani, F.: Fusion of GNSS and satellite radar interferometry: deter-mination of 3D fine-scale map of present-day surface displacements in italy as expressions of geodynamic processes. Remote Sens. **11**, 394 (2019). https://doi.org/10.3390/rs11040394
8. Song, X., Jiang, Y., Shan, X., et al.: A fine velocity and strain rate field of present-day crustal motion of the Northeastern Tibetan plateau inverted jointly by InSAR and GPS. Remote Sens. **11**, 435 (2019). https://doi.org/10.3390/rs11040435
9. Del Soldato, M., Farolfi, G., Rosi, A., et al.: Subsidence Evolution of the Firenze–Prato–Pistoia Plain (Central Italy) Combining PSI and GNSS Data. Remote Sensing **10**, 1146 (2018). https://doi.org/10.3390/rs10071146
10. Solari, L., Raspini, F., Del Soldato, M., et al.: Satellite radar data for back-analyzing a landslide event: the Ponzano (Central Italy) case study. Landslides **15**, 773–782 (2018). https://doi.org/10.1007/s10346-018-0952-x
11. Rosi, A., Vannocci, P., Tofani, V., et al.: Landslide characterization using satellite interferom-etry (PSI), geotechnical investigations and numerical modelling: the case study of Ricasoli Village (Italy). Int. J. Geosci. **4**, 904–918 (2013). https://doi.org/10.4236/ijg.2013.45085
12. Tofani, V., Raspini, F., Catani, F., Casagli, N.: Persistent scatterer interferometry (PSI) tech-nique for landslide characterization and monitoring. Remote Sensing **5**, 1045–1065 (2013). https://doi.org/10.3390/rs5031045
13. Intrieri, E., Raspini, F., Fumagalli, A., et al.: The Maoxian landslide as seen from space: detecting precursors of failure with Sentinel-1 data. Landslides **15**, 123–133 (2018). https://doi.org/10.1007/s10346-017-0915-7
14. Ciampalini, A., Raspini, F., Frodella, W., et al.: The effectiveness of high-resolution LiDAR data combined with PSInSAR data in landslide study. Landslides **13**, 399–410 (2016). https://doi.org/10.1007/s10346-015-0663-5
15. Del Soldato, M., Riquelme, A., Bianchini, S., et al.: Multisource data integration to investigate one century of evolution for the Agnone landslide (Molise, southern Italy). Landslides **15**, 2113–2128 (2018). https://doi.org/10.1007/s10346-018-1015-z
16. Hooper, A., Zebker, H., Segall, P., Kampes, B.: A new method for measuring deformation on volcanoes and other natural terrains using InSAR persistent scatterers. Geophys. Res. Lett. **31**(23), 1–5 (2004). https://doi.org/10.1029/2004GL021737
17. Hooper, A., Segall, P., Zebker, H.: Persistent scatterer interferometric synthetic aperture radar for crustal deformation analysis, with application to Volcán Alcedo. Galápagos. J Geophys Res **112**, B07407 (2007). https://doi.org/10.1029/2006JB004763
18. Tralli, D.M., Blom, R.G., Zlotnicki, V., et al.: Satellite remote sensing of earthquake, volcano, flood, landslide and coastal inundation hazards. ISPRS J. Photogramm. Remote. Sens. **59**, 185–198 (2005). https://doi.org/10.1016/j.isprsjprs.2005.02.002
19. Ferretti, A., Prati, C., Rocca, F.: Nonlinear subsidence rate estimation using permanent scat-terers in differential SAR interferometry. IEEE Trans. Geosci. Remote Sens. **38**, 2202–2212 (2000). https://doi.org/10.1109/36.868878
20. Solari, L., Ciampalini, A., Raspini, F., et al.: PSInSAR analysis in the pisa urban area (Italy): a case study of subsidence related to stratigraphical factors and urbanization. Remote Sens. **8**, 120 (2016). https://doi.org/10.3390/rs8020120
21. Bonì, R., Meisina, C., Cigna, F., et al.: Exploitation of satellite A-DInSAR time series for detection, characterization and modelling of land subsidence. Geosciences **7**, 25 (2017). https://doi.org/10.3390/geosciences7020025
22. Da Lio, C., Teatini, P., Strozzi, T., Tosi, L.: Understanding land subsidence in salt marshes of the Venice Lagoon from SAR Interferometry and ground-based investigations. Remote Sens. Environ. **205**, 56–70 (2018). https://doi.org/10.1016/j.rse.2017.11.016

23. Da Lio, C., Tosi, L.: Land subsidence in the Friuli Venezia Giulia coastal plain, Italy: 1992–2010 results from SAR-based interferometry. Sci. Total Environ. **633**, 752–764 (2018). https://doi.org/10.1016/j.scitotenv.2018.03.244

24. Gao, M., Gong, H., Chen, B., et al.: Regional land subsidence analysis in eastern Beijing plain by InSAR time series and wavelet transforms. Remote Sens. **10**, 365 (2018). https://doi.org/10.3390/rs10030365

25. Hung, W.-C., Hwang, C., Chen, Y.-A., et al.: Land subsidence in Chiayi, Taiwan, from compaction well, leveling and ALOS/PALSAR: aquaculture-induced relative sea level rise. Remote Sens. **10**, 40 (2018). https://doi.org/10.3390/rs10010040

26. Minh, D.H.T., Van Trung, L., Toan, T.L.: Mapping ground subsidence phenomena in Ho Chi Minh City through the radar interferometry technique using ALOS PALSAR Data. Remote Sens. **7**, 8543–8562 (2015). https://doi.org/10.3390/rs70708543

27. Aslan, G., Cakır, Z., Ergintav, S., et al.: Analysis of Secular Ground Motions in Istanbul from a Long-Term InSAR Time-Series (1992–2017). Remote Sensing **10**, 408 (2018). https://doi.org/10.3390/rs10030408

28. Sun, H., Zhang, Q., Zhao, C., et al.: Monitoring land subsidence in the southern part of the lower Liaohe plain, China with a multi-track PS-InSAR technique. Remote Sens. Environ. **188**, 73–84 (2017). https://doi.org/10.1016/j.rse.2016.10.037

29. Delgado Blasco, J., Foumelis, M., Stewart, C., Hooper, A.: Measuring urban subsidence in the Rome metropolitan area (Italy) with Sentinel-1 SNAP-StaMPS persistent scatterer interferometry. Remote Sens. **11**, 129 (2019). https://doi.org/10.3390/rs11020129

30. Melis, M.T., Dessì, F.G., Casu, M.: New remote sensing data on the potential presence of permafrost in the deosai plateau in the himalayan portion of Pakistan. Remote Sens. **15**, 1800 (2023). https://doi.org/10.3390/rs15071800

31. Scheiber, R., Moreira, A.: Coregistration of interferometric SAR images using spectral diversity. IEEE Trans. Geosci. Remote Sens. **38**, 2179–2191 (2000). https://doi.org/10.1109/36.868876

32. Ferretti, A., Prati, C., Rocca, F.: Permanent scatterers in SAR interferometry. IEEE Trans. Geosci. Remote Sens. **39**, 8–20 (2001). https://doi.org/10.1109/36.898661

33. Ferranti, L., Antonioli, F., Anzidei, M., et al.: The timescale and spatial extent of recent vertical tectonic motions in Italy: insights from relative sea-level changes studies. J. Virtual Explor. **36**, 1–34 (2010). https://doi.org/10.3809/jvirtex.2010.00255

34. Ferranti, L., Antonioli, F., Mauz, B., et al.: Markers of the last interglacial sea-level high stand along the coast of Italy: tectonic implications. Quatern. Int. **145–146**, 30–54 (2006). https://doi.org/10.1016/j.quaint.2005.07.009

35. Antonioli, F., Anzidei, M., Lambeck, K., et al.: Sea-level change during the Holocene in Sardinia and in the northeastern Adriatic (central Mediterranean Sea) from archaeological and geomorphological data. Quatern. Sci. Rev. **26**, 2463–2486 (2007). https://doi.org/10.1016/j.quascirev.2007.06.022

36. Cian, F., Blasco, J., Carrera, L.: Sentinel-1 for monitoring land subsidence of coastal cities in Africa using PSInSAR: a methodology based on the integration of SNAP and StaMPS. Geosciences **9**, 124 (2019). https://doi.org/10.3390/geosciences9030124

37. Foumelis, M., Delgado Blasco, J.M., Desnos, Y.-L., et al.: Esa snap - stamps integrated processing for Sentinel-1 persistent scatterer interferometry. In: IGARSS 2018 - 2018 IEEE International Geoscience and Remote Sensing Symposium, pp. 1364–1367. IEEE, Valencia (2018)

38. Mancini, F., Grassi, F., Cenni, N.: A workflow based on SNAP–StaMPS open-source tools and GNSS data for PSI-based ground deformation using dual-orbit Sentinel-1 data: accuracy assessment with error propagation analysis. Remote Sens. **13**, 753 (2021). https://doi.org/10.3390/rs13040753

39. Carmignani, L., Oggiano, G., Funedda, A., et al.: The geological map of Sardinia (Italy) at 1:250,000 scale. J. Maps **12**, 826–835 (2016). https://doi.org/10.1080/17445647.2015.1084544

40. Meletti, C., Montaldo, V.: Stime di pericolosità sismica per diverse probabilità di superamento in 50 anni: valori di ag. Progetto DPC-INGV - S1. http://esse1.mi.ingv.it/d2.html. Accessed 31 Jul 2023

41. Farolfi, G., Ventisette, C.: Monitoring the Earth's ground surface movements using satellite observations - Geodynamics of the Italian peninsula determined by using GNSS networks (2016)

42. Bekaert, D.P.S., Walters, R.J., Wright, T.J., et al.: Statistical comparison of InSAR tropospheric correction techniques. Remote Sens. Environ. **170**, 40–47 (2015). https://doi.org/10.1016/j.rse.2015.08.035

43. Sentinel-1B In-Flight Anomaly Summary Report.pdf. https://sentinels.copernicus.eu/documents/247904/4819394/Sentinel-1B+In-Flight+Anomaly+Summary+Report.pdf. Accessed 31 July 2023

44. Samieie-Esfahany, S., Hanssen, R.F., van Thienen-Visser, K., Muntendam-Bos, A.: On the effect of horizontal deformation on INSAR subsidence estimates (2010)

45. Chiummo, A.: The Einstein telescope: status of the project. EPJ Web Conf **280**, 03003 (2023). https://doi.org/10.1051/epjconf/202328003003

46. Di Pace, S., Mangano, V., Pierini, L., et al.: Research facilities for Europe's next generation gravitational-wave detector Einstein telescope. Galaxies **10**, 65 (2022). https://doi.org/10.3390/galaxies10030065

47. Di Giovanni, M., Giunchi, C., Saccorotti, G., et al.: A seismological study of the sos enattos area—the sardinia candidate site for the Einstein telescope. Seismol. Res. Lett. **92**, 352–364 (2020). https://doi.org/10.1785/0220200186

48. Naticchioni, L., Boschi, V., Calloni, E., et al.: Characterization of the Sos Enattos site for the Einstein Telescope. J. Phys. Conf. Ser. **1468**, 012242 (2020). https://doi.org/10.1088/1742-6596/1468/1/012242

49. Yu, B., Liu, G., Zhang, R., et al.: Monitoring subsidence rates along road network by persistent scatterer SAR interferometry with high-resolution TerraSAR-X imagery. J. Mod. Transp. **21**, 236–246 (2013). https://doi.org/10.1007/s40534-013-0030-y

50. Liu, J., Ma, F., Li, G., et al.: Evolution assessment of mining subsidence characteristics using SBAS and PS interferometry in sanshandao gold mine, China. Remote Sens. **14**, 290 (2022). https://doi.org/10.3390/rs14020290

51. Crosetto, M., Monserrat, O., Cuevas-González, M., et al.: Persistent scatterer interferometry: a review. ISPRS J. Photogramm. Remote. Sens. **115**, 78–89 (2016). https://doi.org/10.1016/j.isprsjprs.2015.10.011

A Low-Cost Three-Cameras Photogrammetric System for Training Students in Physical Simulation of Shallow Landslides

Marco Scaioni[1]([✉]), Karen Lorena Gonzalez Ovalle[2], Rasoul Eskandari[1], and Luca Perfetti[3]

[1] Department of Architecture, Built Environment and Construction Engineering, Politecnico Milano, Via Ponzio 31, 20133 Milan, Italy
{marco.scaioni,rasoul.eskandari}@polimi.it

[2] Lecco Campus, Politecnico Milano, Via Previati 1/C, 23900 Lecco, Italy
karen1.gonzales@mail.polimi.it

[3] Department of Civil, Environmental, Architectural Engineering and Mathematics, Università degli Studi di Brescia, Via Branze 43, 25123 Brescia, Italy
luca.perfetti@unibs.it

Abstract. Simulation of shallow landslides in a scaled-down facility has become a common methodology for investigating slope stability. Multiple parameters may be replicated under different triggering factors, which mainly include water as rainfall or seepage from an artificial basin or pipeline. Landslide simulators are important tools for scientific investigation and to test technical solutions for monitoring and mitigation, but they may also be used for training of students at different education levels. A *Landslide Simulator* (LS) has been established in 2016 on the Lecco Campus of Politecnico Milano, Italy, which is equipped with three different groups of *geotechnical*, *geophysical*, and *imaging/ranging* sensors. This paper is focused on a low-cost Three-Cameras Photogrammetric System (3CPS) recently implemented, based on industrial FLIR cameras mounted on a bar to be placed over the slope in the LS. This is applied during landslide simulation experiments for two purposes: (1) 2D Digital Image Correlation (2D-DIC); and (2) 3D Photogrammetric reconstruction. Two sets of coded targets are located on both sides of the flume to serve as ground control points. Data processing is carried out by students based on two software packages provided by the university: one popular Matlab® code for 2D-DIC, and Agisoft Metashape Professional®. A specific validation study has been developed and illustrated in the paper, together with its application to a couple of landslide simulation experiments.

Keywords: Digital Image Correlation · Landslides · Photogrammetry · Simulation · Training

E. Borgogno Mondino and P. Zamperlin (Eds.): ASITA 2023, CCIS 2088, pp. 48–63, 2024.
https://doi.org/10.1007/978-3-031-59925-5_4

1 Introduction

In recent years the impact of climate change on geohazards has been quite impressive, as reported in many scientific publications [1–3]. This correlation is even higher when considering the attention of the media and the perception of the citizens towards the numerous geohazards depending on climate change [4, 5].

Landslides are natural geohazards that do not make an exception to this trend [6]. Simulation of shallow landslides in a scaled-down simulation facility has become a common methodology for investigating the behavior of different types of slope instabilities [7–9]. Multiple parameters may be simulated (soil type and/or mixture, water content and pressure, slope inclination, surface geometry, and presence of mitigation structures) under different triggering factors. These mainly include water as rainfall or seepage from an artificial basin or pipeline [10, 11], but some experiments where earthquake is simulated can be found in the literature [12].

If landslide simulators are important tools for scientific investigation and to test technical solutions for shallow landslide monitoring and mitigation [13], they also represent useful support during students' training at different education levels. To this purpose, a simulation platform (addressed as "Landslide Simulator" – LS) has been established in 2016 at the Lecco Campus of Politecnico Milano, Italy [14, 15]. Here water-induced [16] landslide simulations are periodically carried out together with students from the MSc. Course on Civil Engineering for Risk Mitigation (CERM) https://www.master-cerm. polimi.it/. The LS is equipped with three different groups of sensors: (1) *geotechnical* sensors (piezometers, osmotic pressure sensors); (2) *geophysical* sensors (geoelectric resistivity [17]); and (3) *2D imaging/3D ranging sensors* (terrestrial laser scanner and digital cameras for image-based deformation measurement [18, 19]). Starting from the simulator start-up, every year the sensor technology has been improved to collect more valuable data and to let students work autonomously.

Here the focus is given to a low-cost Three-Cameras Photogrammetric System (3CPS) implemented in 2021, which is based on three industrial FLIR cameras controlled by means of a self-developed user-interface enabling also non-expert to work (Fig. 1). Cameras are mounted on a bar to be placed over the slope in the LS. A line configuration from the toe to top of the slope is generally adopted, with the chance to change the baselines between cameras.

The 3CPS is applied in LS for three main purposes:

- recording time-lapse images for documentation of the experiments;
- *2D Digital Image Correlation* (2D-DIC) to track surface displacements; and
- *3D photogrammetric reconstruction* based on processing each triplet of contemporary images collected by the 3CPS, after calibration of each camera.

Data processing is carried out by students based on two software packages provided by the university: (a) one popular Matlab® code for 2D-DIC, which has been integrated with some new functions for improving the analysis capability; (b) Agisoft Metashape Professional® for photogrammetric reconstruction.

During the last year, a specific validation study of the 3CPS has been developed, whose outcomes will be illustrated in Sect. 2, which will also present the design and implementation of the system, and the standard procedures adopted for camera calibration and orientation. In Sect. 3 two landslide simulation experiments are shown and discussed with the purpose of describing the performances of the 3CPS. In the end, Sect. 4 will draw some conclusions.

Fig. 1. Top-left: the Three-Cameras Photogrammetric System (3CPS). Bottom-left: 3CPS installed on the Landslide Simulator (LS) at Lecco Campus of Politecnico Milano. Bottom-right: the LS during a landslide simulation experiment.

2   Sensor Technology

2.1   Design of the Three-Cameras Photogrammetric System

The Three-Cameras Photogrammetric System (3CPS) built to complement the Landslide Simulator (LS) was specifically designed to address the size of the facility's structure as well as the conditions of use which determined the choices made regarding the preliminary hardware specifications. The 3CPS is designed to be mounted on the LS frame anchored to the top crossbeams (see Fig. 1), so that the cameras could frame the entire surface of the slope model (i.e., the Area-of-Interest – AoI) in a nadiral or quasi-nadiral direction. In particular, the following objectives were set:

- at least one camera placed nadiral to the AoI;
- at least two cameras placed in stereo (base/distance ratio between 1:1 and 1:2);
- all cameras must frame the entire AoI; and
- to keep the stability of the system in terms of relative and interior orientation for all cameras.

A three-cameras configuration was selected to provide better data redundancy for sensor orientation and photogrammetric reconstruction (see Fig. 1). Cameras are mounted on an extruded aluminium profile mounted at the top of the LS placed in correspondence of the longitudinal axis of the flume. The orientation of the sensors is defined to maximize the coverage of the AoI and frame utilization. A first camera (called Camera

3) is placed centrally and nadiral to the simulator platform, while two other cameras (i.e., Cameras 1 and 2) are placed laterally, slightly tilted toward the center (about 5°). The use of ultra-wide-angle lenses with a horizontal field angle of about 130° ensures that the 3CPS can frame the entire AoI with 100% overlap. The central Camera 3 is a 5 Mpixel FLIR BFS 50S5 CMOS sensor, while the side Cameras 1 and 2 are 3.2 Mpixel FLIR BFS 31S4 CMOS sensors. In most experiments, central Camera 3 is parallel with respect to the slope: for this reason, a larger sensor size allows a higher-resolution image sequence for 2D-DIC.

All three cameras are equipped with color global shutter sensors featuring a squared pixel size of 3.45 μm and mount the same lens (Theia ML183M) with variable focal length (from 1.8 mm to 3 mm), resulting in a horizontal viewing angle from 130° to 105°. As shown in Fig. 2, the focal length of the central Camera 3 must be set to the minimum value to ensure the 130° viewing angle needed to frame the entire AoI. The focal length of the side Cameras 1 and 2, on the other hand, may vary if the aiming direction of the cameras is adjusted. Table 1 summarizes cameras and lens data, while Fig. 3 shows the relationship between the size of the cameras' sensors and the lens projection circle.

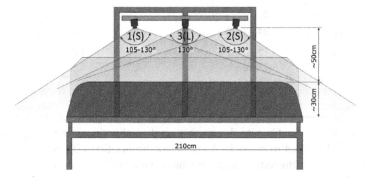

Fig. 2. Scheme of the 3CPS showing the position, rotation angles, and viewing angle of the cameras in relation to the LS structure. The upper part of the facility may be rigidly rotate to incline the slope, while the 3CPS would remain in the same relative position w.r.t. it. The letter after the identifier number of each camera refers to the sensor size: "L" for larger 5 Mpixel FLIR BFS 50S5 CMOS sensor and "S" for smaller 3.2 Mpixel FLIR BFS 31S4 CMOS sensors.

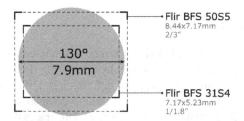

Fig. 3. Scheme of the sensor coverage mounting the Theia lens on the two cameras' type at the shortest focal length.

The 3CPS is connected to a laptop computer via three USB cables that also serve as power supply for the cameras. A desktop application has been developed that enables synchronized image capture in single-shot-on-demand or time-lapse sequence mode.

Table 1. Technical properties of the implemented hardware. The first row describes the configuration used for the central Camera 3, while the second row the configuration for the side Cameras 1 and 2.

			Theia ML183M @f:1.8		Theia ML183M @f:3	
BFS 50S5	Resolution:	2448x2048	Focal length:	1.8 mm		
	Megapixels:	5	FOV (H):	~130°		
	Pixel pitch:	3.45 μm	Imaging circle	7.9 mm		
	Sensor size:	8.44 × 7.17 mm	GSD:	1 mm		
BFS 31S4	Resolution:	2048 × 1536			Focal length:	3 mm
	Megapixels:	3.2			FOV (H):	~105°
	Pixel pitch:	3.45 μm			Imag. Circle	7.9 mm
	Sensor size:	7.17 × 5.23 mm			GSD:	0.6 mm

Image synchronization is provided by hardware triggering: the desktop application controls the master Camera 3, and this sends a shooting electric signal to both side cameras. The effect of possible delay in synchronization [20] between all image sequences has been evaluated. Considering the dynamic of landslide simulation experiments, this delay has been retained negligible since synchronization errors are in terms of milliseconds.

Two sets of coded targets (22 in total) are located on both sides of the flume to be used as ground control points (GCP) for georeferencing in a local topographic reference system. Indeed, coded targets are measured by a total station on occasion of each experiment since the flume of the LS is usually repositioned at a different inclination.

2.2 2D Digital Image Correlation

The term *Digital Image Correlation* (DIC) refers to a non-contact technique able to measure full-field displacements and strains by comparing digital images of the surface material sampled at different stages of deformation. DIC plays a major role in structural monitoring applications, where it is used to compare a series of images of a specimen acquired at different deformation intervals. DIC traces the movement of pixels within the AoI and, using image correlation algorithms, calculates the displacements and deformations by recognizing the same points within different images. *2D-DIC* provides information only in the image plane and is based on a single image sequence. This means that 2D-DIC can be used to track displacements that occur on a planar specimen. *3D-DIC* requires a synchronized stereo-camera system to output 3D information on point displacements [21].

In this application, 2D-DIC is used to evaluate the surface dynamics of the slope and correlate it to the collapse phenomena. A Matlab® code developed by Eberl is used: *Digital Image Correlation and Tracking* [22]. The code works with a fixed grid of points defined on one of the images of the sequence captured by one camera of the 3CPS, usually the one covering the entire surface of the slope to analyze. 2D-DIC provides displacement and velocity of each point of the grid as far as it can be tracked in the image sequence of the experiment. When a fracture occurs on the slope surface, a point located on the detached portion (in general the lower part) cannot be tracked any more.

In this study, some specific software functionalities have been developed to make easier the preparation of the processing of an image sequence recorded in the LS, and to help display the results.

2.3 Camera Calibration

All cameras in the 3CPS need to be calibrated before each experiment [25]. Calibration is strictly necessary for photogrammetric processing, while could be neglected in 2D-DIC [21]. On the other hand, the use of only three different cameras to collect multiple sequences does not allow the application of self-calibration during the *bundle-block adjustment* (BBA) to compute the exterior orientation of all cameras, as typically done in Structure-from-Motion photogrammetry [22, 23].

Camera self-calibration is obtained through a BBA including images of a flat panel (size: 0.9 m x 0.9 m) reporting 38 coded targets (Fig. 4). The entire 3CPS can be removed from the LS and used for recording images of this panel. Coded targets had been previously measured using a high-precision total station to determine their 3D coordinates with submillimeter accuracy. Computed calibration parameters are then applied during successive camera orientation and dense image matching.

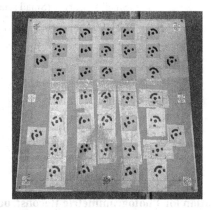

Fig. 4. Panel for camera calibration reporting 38 coded targets.

No tests about calibration stability within time were carried out since students were supposed to repeat the entire photogrammetric pipeline during their experiments. The photogrammetric calibration procedure is applied by using the standard Brown model [24], including principal distance, principal point coordinates, 3 coefficients for radial symmetric distortion, and 2 coefficients for asymmetric distortion.

During the setup of the 3CPS, two different block configurations for self-calibration were tried: (1) three blocks collected with the purpose of independent calibration of each sensor; (2) one block collected with the purpose of contemporary calibration of all sensors. The main difference between these configurations is that in (1) each camera was targeted to collect 16 images of the panel with coded targets from different angles but all aiming at the center of the panel, as discussed in [14]. In configuration (2), the same images were collected with each camera, but at the same time also images recorded by the other two cameras were considered during self-calibration. Camera poses recorded per each configuration have been input in a BBA for self-calibration, run by including GPCs or not. Two different solutions have been tried for configuration (2): (2a) independent BBA per each sensor and (2b) joint BBA including all sensors. Root Mean Squared Errors (RMSE) of 3D residuals with respect to coded targets are shown in Table 2. No distinct results per each coordinate were available in the case of configuration 2b.

The results are quite different per each configuration and camera. Indeed, Camera 3 is equipped with a larger CMOS sensor than Cameras 1 and 2 (see Table 1) but uses the same type of lens. This resulted in a shorter equivalent focal lens motivating the worse RMSE for Camera 3. The best results were achieved when using configuration 2b including GCPs. For this reason, this solution was selected as the standard calibration method for the 3CPS during successive applications in the LS.

Table 2. Comparison of different configurations for camera calibration; results are reported as Root Mean Squared Errors (RMSE) of 3D residuals computed on 38 coded targets (BBA: bundle block adjustment; GCP: ground control point).

Configuration	Configuration name	GCP	Camera 1 (Small sensor)	Camera 2 (Small sensor)	Camera 3 (Large sensors)
Single cameras (indep.) BBA)	1	yes	0.2 pix/1 mm	0.2 pix/1 mm	2.9 pix/9 mm
		no	0.2 pix	0.1 pix	3.5 pix
3 cameras (indep.)	2a	yes	0.2 pix/1 mm	0.2 pix/1 mm	3.4 pix/7 mm
		no	0.2 pix	0.1 pix	7.7 pix
3 cameras (joint BBA)	2b	yes	0.3 pix/1 mm		
		no	pix		

2.4   Camera Configuration for Photogrammetric Reconstruction

A preliminary experiment was carried out to define the ideal configuration of the cameras for generating multi-temporal dense point clouds to be compared within time. Indeed, the purpose of the 3CPS is to reconstruct a surface slope in the LS during an experiment when its shape continuously changes.

To this purpose, the 3CPS was fixed on tripods to ensure the same height in all the acquisitions. Camera baselines were set up to 48 cm to have overlapped images. The target object was a scaled model of a slope providing a realistic test for dense point-cloud generation. Sixteen coded targets were put on two fixed bars aside from the AoI for registration of data collected at different epochs. By ensuring a constant distance between the 3CPS and the object, a total of five images per sequence were captured by shifting the slope model in the direction parallel to the 3CPS baseline (see an example in Fig. 5). Shift was approximately 5 cm in total. Five 3D point clouds were generated and compared to evaluate differences between surfaces.

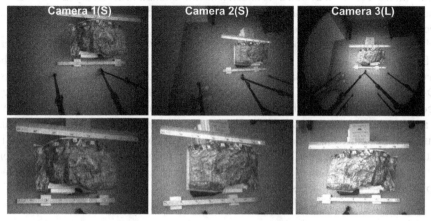

Fig. 5. Example a block of three images recorded by the 3CPS during experiment for testing camera configuration for photogrammetric reconstruction (Subsect. 2.4). The letter after the identifier number of each camera refers to the sensor size (see caption of Fig. 2). The upper row reports the full-size images, and the lower row some zoom-in on the slope model and coded bars.

Data acquisition and processing of each dataset consisted of the following steps:

1. images were imported in Agisoft Metashape Professional® (ver. 1.7.3);
2. cameras were calibrated based on the procedure defined at Subsect. 2.3 and computed camera calibration parameters used in image orientation and dense matching;
3. detection of the coded markers in the images;
4. orientation of the images including coded markers for georeferencing (values obtained from processing Epoch 1 have been used as GCPs in others); and
5. dense point cloud generation.

Obtained point clouds were then imported into CloudCompare software (www.clo udcompare.org) for comparison between different epochs. Some portions of the slope model were not reconstructed in all dense point clouds, preventing the analysis of surface changes. The total amount of missing reconstructed points was, however, lower that 5% of the total surface of the slope model.

A comparison between Epoch 1 and the other epochs was carried out since all of them had been registered in the same reference system. '*Cloud-to-cloud*' ("*C2C*") algorithm was used to compare point clouds [11]. This algorithm takes one point cloud as a reference and compares the closest points in another point cloud. Average distances between point clouds resulted in less than 1 cm, which corresponded to the magnitude of the given shifts. It is possible to conclude from this experiment that 3CPS can be used in the LS to detect sub-centimeter changes of the slope surface shape.

3   Experiments

Some experiments of water-induced landslide simulation were conducted to test the application of the 3CPS as well as to understand limitations and necessary improvements. These experiments were organized and conducted by students from the MSc. CERM at Lecco Campus of Politecnico Milano.

Two experiments are reported here, where slope instability was induced by water: in Experiment 1 (Subsect. 3.1) an artificial rainfall was created; in Experiment 2 (Subsect. 3.2) a water infiltration from a subsurface pipe was used. In both experiments, 2D-DIC was applied to track surface displacements and 3D photogrammetry for surface reconstruction. In the case of Experiment 2, the reconstructed surfaces were compared to a point cloud collected using a medium-range terrestrial laser scanner (TLS). This was used to capture the slope surface before and after the experiment. Here the aim is not to report all results and to give physical interpretations, which should also rely on the concurrent application of geotechnical/geophysical sensors. We limit to show some typical outputs and to discuss them in Subsect. 3.3.

3.1   Experiment 1: Rainfall-Induced Shallow Landslide

In Experiment 1 a slope model was setup in the flume of the LS. The approximate size of the AoI was 200 cm × 80 cm, the latter being the width of the flume. The composition of the slope was sand and the depth in the central part was approx. 25 cm. This setup was prone to a shallow landslide when triggered by an artificial rainfall released by a piping system located at the same height as 3CPS (approx. 80 cm from the slope surface). To protect each sensor from the water, each lens was equipped with a home-made plastic protection (Fig. 1).

2D-DIC. Central Camera 3 was selected for 2D-DIC. Two different grids of points to tracks were initially selected, as shown in Fig. 6: in the central and upper parts of the AoI a larger grid of points with spacing 50 pixels x 50 pixels was chosen in the image space; in the lower part, a denser grid of 25 pixels × 25 pixels was used, since the fractures were mostly expected in this sector of the slope model.

Thanks to a Matlab® function ("*plot_displacement*") developed with the purpose to better investigating the results output by *Digital Image Correlation and Tracking* code [22], it is possible to check both displacement and velocity in correspondence of each point in the defined grids. All points of the grids are displayed in a window and can be queried to show specific plots of displacement and velocity.

In Experiment 1, thirteen fractures were visually detected during the slope failure. By selecting those nodes of the grids closer to each fracture, corresponding plots could be displayed by using another developed Matlab® function ("*DV_graph*"). Figure 7 shows two examples of such plots. Node 120 in Fig. 6 corresponds to the 5th opened fracture, which consisted of two successive phases that were correctly tracked. Node 124 corresponds to the 11th opened fracture, where it is possible to see that, while the point displacement had started before the collapse, the velocity plot helps to locate the event thanks to the sudden acceleration.

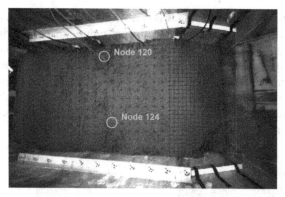

Fig. 6. An image from the sequence recorded by Camera 3 in Experiment 1 overlapped with both grids for tracking surface-point displacements using 2D-DIC.

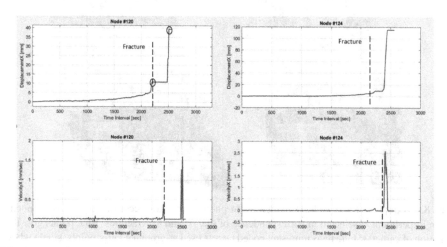

Fig. 7. Windows of the developed Matlab® function "*DV_graph*" to display the node displacement and velocity (in the upper and lower sub-windows, respectively). In the left column, plots related to Node 120 in Fig. 6 are shown, while in the right column is Node 124.

3D Photogrammetric Reconstruction. The reconstruction of the slope surface was possible based on the triplets of contemporary images recorded by the 3CPS. Camera calibration was carried out before each experiment as described in Subsect. 2.3. In theory, each triplet could be used for reconstructing a model, but in general, only the most representative epochs were considered. In general, a time lapse between 5 and 15 s was selected, depending on the expected speed of the experiment. In any case, the number of point clouds that could be reconstructed is much higher than the ones recordable using a TLS. This kind of instrument takes a few tens of seconds to complete the scanning of the entire slope, while each triplet of images is recorded in a synchronous way (see Subsect. 2.1). Photogrammetric processing of the images from Experiment 1 was carried out based on the procedure illustrated in Subsect. 2.4.

In this test, the 3D reconstruction was carried out in correspondence of the 4th and 8th fractures. Textured 3D models obtained from point clouds in Agisoft Metashape Professional® (ver. 1.7.3) are displayed in Fig. 8. As it can be seen, the quality of the reconstruction is quite good, except for the slope toe that is not very clear, because of the low camera coverage. In correspondence of two points (see white circles in both subfigures of Fig. 8) we measured the aperture of corresponding fractures in 3D point clouds and compared them with results from 2D-DIC. The difference between the distances resulted in less than 2 mm, indicating the good quality of 3D models.

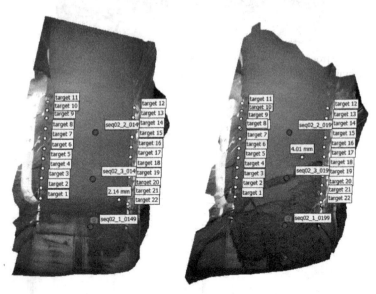

Fig. 8. Examples of textured 3D models from photogrammetric reconstruction of two epochs from Experiment 1, selected in correspondence of the 4th and 8th fractures. Blue points give the location of cameras; blue flags represent coded targets used as ground control points; single white points give the locations where some measurements of fracture apertures were carried out.

3.2 Experiment 2: Shallow Landslide Induced by Water Seepage from a Pipe

In Experiment 2 a pipe was positioned in the upper part of the slope to study the behavior when water rapidly accumulates in the ground and results in a surge of water-saturated earth and debris (see Fig. 9). Acquisition and processing of images were carried out as in Experiment 1. For this reason, here we describe only the comparison of the photogrammetric and TLS point clouds.

Comparison with TLS. A phase-shift TLS Faro Focus s70 has been used during Experiment 2 to record a point cloud describing the slope surface at five epochs from the start to the end. The accuracy and spatial resolution of this instrument at involved distances are in the order of 1 mm and may be considered a reference to check the quality of photogrammetric point clouds. Scanning of the AoI was accomplished in approx. 20 s at each epoch. The first point cloud was georeferenced by using five checkboard targets positioned on the frontal part of the LS's frame. Coordinates of these targets were measured by using a total station and referred to the same reference system adopted for coded targets used for georeferencing photogrammetric data. Successive scans were registered to the first one based on the same checkboard targets. After registration, all point clouds have been edited to remove all points outside the slope. All operations concerning laser scans and point cloud comparison were carried out in CloudCompare ver. 2.14.4 ("*Kyiv*").

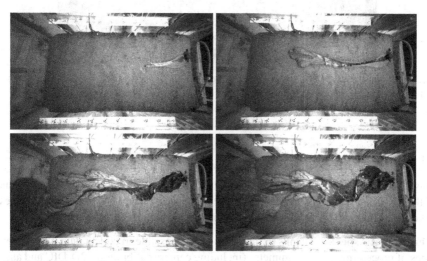

Fig. 9. Four images from the sequence recorded by central Camera 3 during Experiment 2.

To evaluate the quality of the photogrammetric point cloud, the first scan was selected due to the stability of the slope during TLS acquisition. In Fig. 10, both point clouds to be compared are shown. The photogrammetric point cloud has some holes in those regions where texture information is weak, and no matching points could be detected. The TLS point cloud is more complete, but some areas are lacking due to the shadowing effects of some instrument cables. The overall accuracy of the photogrammetric point cloud can be estimated by computing the average distance from the reference TLS point cloud. Due to the smoothness of the latest point cloud with some shadowed areas, a mesh was created as a reference surface. Points from photogrammetric point clouds were compared using the *"Cloud-to-Mesh"* (*"C2M"*) algorithm implemented in CloudCompare [11]. Results from the comparison are discussed in the next subsection.

Fig. 10. Point clouds from photogrammetry (at the top) and terrestrial laser scanning (at the bottom) corresponding to the initial state of the slope model in Experiment 2.

3.3 Discussion

This discussion is organized in three parts. The first part concerns the educational value of the 3CPS for training students in the use of sensing techniques in the Geosciences. Other parts relate to the analyses of both experiments reported in this section.

Educational Aspects. Thanks to the 3CPS it was possible to collect data for different types of processing: photogrammetry (including camera calibration); 2D-DIC and analysis of surface-point displacements correlated to the slope failure providing different types of information; and point comparison between multiple epochs and with respect to TLS data. The simple setup of the system allowed the students to focus more on the preparation of the experiment rather than the sensor implementation as in previous applications described in [14, 15].

Experiment 1. Here the focus was given on the application of 2D-DIC and the photogrammetric reconstruction of the surface slope model. Thanks to the flexibility of the modified code for 2D-DIC, it was possible to tailor a grid of points to track and, after the experiment, to analyze surface displacement and velocity in selected locations corresponding to open fractures. The geometric model applied to transform image coordinates (in pixels) into the object reference system (in metric units) consisted of a simple homogenous scaling. Homography was also tested as a geometric model but with very tiny differences. These were motivated, on one side, by the quite good parallelism between the adopted Camera 3 and the AoI on the slope model. On the other, by the fact that relative displacements are analyzed in 2D-DIC rather than absolute positions. It is important to take care of possible radiometric changes (e.g., due to shadows) in images during the image sequence to be analyzed with 2D-DIC. These effects can be mitigated by using artificial lighting within the 3CPS.

The photogrammetric reconstruction and the texturing process of the derived mesh offered a realistic visualization of some phases of the experiment, as shown in Fig. 8. These 3D models gave the opportunity to better understand the failure process in the slope under rainfall triggering. In addition to the good quality of 3D visualization, a comparison between DIC-2D and photogrammetry was carried out to assess the metric value of reconstructed 3D models. Since 2D-DIC was able to provide sub-millimeter precision relative displacements, it could be considered a good benchmark for validating photogrammetric results. Indeed, differences on some selected points were in the order of a few millimeters.

Experiment 2. In the analysis of this experiment, the comparison between point clouds from photogrammetry and TLS was considered. In fact, the development of Experiment 2 was quite atypical with respect to the usual slope failure process described in Experiment 1. Rather than a retrogressive failure starting from the slope toe upwards due to water seepage flowing down from the entire slope, here a mixture of water-saturated earth and debris surged out from the upper part of the slope. While surface displacements were almost close to zero (as measured using 2D-DIC – results are not reported here), the effect of water was quickly brought to the excavation of a channel in the middle of the slope.

The comparison of point clouds from photogrammetry and TLS was done by considering the initial state of the slope before the experiment started. This analysis allowed to evaluate some problems to cope with both techniques. One of the major problems was due to occlusions in the Field-of-View due to the instruments' connection cable. This problem is clearly visible in Fig. 10, where the TLS point cloud is partially shadowed by a cable, which did not result in any occlusions in photogrammetric output. On the other hand, the latter presents some holes in the central part of the slope: this problem may be due to different reflective areas on the slope surface. The comparison involved 96% of the area covered by both datasets. The average distance computed by $C2M$ method resulted in $+ 0.2$ mm with a standard deviation of 1.4 mm. This outcome indicates a good quality of the photogrammetric point cloud. In addition, we should consider the high-acquisition rate (potentially one per epoch) of photogrammetric point clouds with respect to TLS.

4 Conclusions

In this paper, we have presented the design, implementation, and testing of a Three-Cameras Photogrammetric System (3CPS) to be used in a Landslide Simulation (LS) facility. The 3CPS can provide image sequence to be used for Digital Image Correlation

(DIC) and photogrammetric reconstruction. So far only off-line 2D-DIC has been carried out, but in future developments also real-time processing and output visualization are foreseen to show surface displacement field during a landslide simulation experiment. The presence of three cameras allows to cover the full surface of a slope model, but they could be also used for 3D-DIC based on stereo-images.

After the analyses and preliminary experiments described here, the 3CPS has been introduced in the regular activities carried out with students at the Lecco Campus of Politecnico Milano. The advantages of this new system with respect to previous imaging devices (action cameras – see [14, 15]) consist of the user-friendly interface, the flexible configuration, and the quality of the final outputs. In addition to the improvements of DIC, also the 3D photogrammetric reconstruction process is expected to increase its degree of automation by handling the automatic processing of all available epochs, at least the ones when changes occurred.

Thanks to the 3CPS and the LS, we have already collected several datasets of image, laser scans, geotechnical and geophysical observed data related to several types of landslide simulation experiments carried out in the LS. The policy is to make available recorded data sets after organizing them in an online repository.

Acknowledgements. Grateful acknowledgements go to all colleagues from GAP^2 LAB at Lecco Campus of Politecnico Milano for providing the Landslide Simulator and cooperating with the setup of experiments: Profs. Monica Papini, Luigi Zanzi, Laura Longoni, Azadeh Hojat, and Drs. Monica Corti and Lorenzo Panzeri. We would like also to thank the developers of the CloudCompare software package and the Matlab® code *Digital Image Correlation and Tracking*.

References

1. Van Aalst, M.K.: The impacts of climate change on the risk of natural disasters. Disasters **30**(1), 5–18 (2006)
2. Hallegatte, S.: Natural Disasters and Climate Change, p. 194. Springer, Cham (2016)
3. IPCC. Climate Change 2023: Synthesis Report. Contribution of Working Groups I, II and III to the Sixth Assessment Report of the Intergovernmental Panel on Climate Change. IPCC, Geneva, Switzerland, pp. 35–115 (2023)
4. Pasquaré, F., Oppizzi, P.: How do the media affect public perception of climate change and geohazards? an Italian case study. Global Plan. Change **90–91**, 152–157 (2012)
5. Gioia, E., Casareale, C., Colocci, A., Zecchini, F., Marincioni, F.: Citizens' perception of geohazards in veneto region (NE Italy) in the context of climate change. Geosciences **11**, 424 (2021)
6. Gariano, S.L., Guzzetti, F.: Landslides in a changing climate. Earth Sci. Rev. **162**, 227–252 (2016)
7. Lu, P., et al.: Model test study on monitoring dynamic process of slope failure through spatial sensor network. Environ. Earth Sci. **74**(4), 3315–3332 (2015)
8. Ma, J., Tang, H., Hu, X., Bobet, A., Yong, R., Eldin, M.A.M.: Model testing of the spatial–temporal evolution of a landslide failure. Bull. Eng. Geol. Environ. **76**, 323–339 (2017)
9. Liu, D., Hu, X., Zhou, C., Li, L., He, C., Sun, T.: Model test study of a landslide stabilized with piles and evolutionary stage identification based on thermal infrared temperature analysis. Landslides **17**, 1393–1404 (2020)

10. He, C., Hu, X., Tannant, D.D., Tan, F., Zhang, Y., Zhang, H.: Response of a landslide to reservoir impoundment in model tests. Eng. Geol. **247**, 84–93 (2018)

11. Tavakoli, K., Zadehali, E., Malekian, A., Darsi, S., Longoni, L., Scaioni, M.: Landslide dam failure analysis using imaging and ranging sensors. In: Gervasi, O. (ed.) ICCSA 2021. LNCS, vol. 12955, pp. 3–17. Springer, Cham (2021). https://doi.org/10.1007/978-3-030-87007-2_1

12. Yang, C., Tong, X., Chen, G., Yuan, C., Lian, J.: Assessment of seismic landslide susceptibility of bedrock and overburden layer slope based on shaking table tests. Eng. Geol. **323**, 107197 (2023)

13. Fusco, F., et al.: Susceptibility mapping of shallow landslides inducing debris flows: a comparison of physics-based approaches. Italian J. Eng. Geol. Env. **1**, 63–71 (2023)

14. Scaioni, M., Crippa, J., Longoni, L., Papini, M., Zanzi, L.: Image-based reconstruction and analysis of dynamic scenes in a landslide simulation facility. ISPRS Ann. Photogram. Remote Sens. Spat. Inf. Sci. **4**, 63–70 (2017)

15. Scaioni, M., Crippa, J., Yordanov, V., Longoni, L., Ivanov, V.I., Papini, M.: Some tools to support teaching photogrammetry for slope stability assessment and monitoring. Int. Arch. Photogram. Remote Sens. Spat. Inf. Sci. **42**(34), 453–460 (2018)

16. Ivanov, V., et al.: Investigation on the role of water for the stability of shallow landslides—insights from experimental tests. Water **12**, 1203 (2020)

17. Hojat, A., et al.: Geoelectrical characterization and monitoring of slopes on a rainfall-triggered landslide simulator. J. App. Geophys. **170**, 103884 (2018)

18. Raguse, K., Heipke, C.: Synchronization of image sequences - a photogrammetric method. Photogramm. Eng. Remote Sens. **12**, 535–546 (2009)

19. Scaioni, M., et al.: Analysis of spatial sensor network observations during landslide simulation experiments. Europ. J. Env. Civil Eng. **17**, 802–825 (2013)

20. Feng, T., et al.: Measurement of surface changes in a scaled-down landslide model using high-speed stereo image sequences. Photogramm. Eng. Remote Sens. **82**, 547–557 (2016)

21. Scaioni, M., et al.: Some applications of 2-D and 3-D photogrammetry during laboratory experiments for hydrogeological risk assessment. Geomat. Nat. Haz. Risk **6**, 473–496 (2015)

22. Eberl, C. Digital Image Correlation and Tracking. https://www.mathworks.com/matlabcentral/fileexchange/12413-digital-image-correlation-and-tracking, MATLAB Central File Exchange. Accessed 17 Oct 2023

23. Eltner, A., Kaiser, A., Castillo, C., Rock, G., Neugirg, F., Abellán, A.: Image-based surface reconstruction in geomorphometry – merits, limits and developments. Earth Surf. Dyn. **4**, 359–389 (2016)

24. Granshaw, S.I.: Structure from motion: origins and originality. Photogramm. Rec. **33**, 6–10 (2018)

25. Luhmann, T., Fraser, C.S., Maas, H.-G.: Sensor modelling and camera calibration for close range photogrammetry. ISPRS J. Photogramm. Remote Sens. **115**, 37–46 (2016)

The Italian National Fire and Rescue Service Activity in Forest Fires: The Event in Montegrino Valtravaglia

Onofrio Lorusso and Santo Vazzano[✉]

Italian National Fire and Rescue Service, Department of Firefighters, Public Rescue and Civil Defence, Italian Ministry of Interior, Rome, Italy
{onofrio.lorusso,santo.vazzano}@vigilfuoco.it

Abstract. Every year forest fires spread through the Italian territory causing huge damage to the community and hard consequences on the environment. The fight against this kind of events is one of the purposes of the Italian Fire and Rescue Service (CNVVF), which consists on the extinguishing operations supervision and on the direct extinguishing in case of forest fires involving built environment. In order to achieve increasingly accurate and effective rescue actions, it is therefore essential to conduct a critical analysis and review of the operations in the case of complex real interventions. This action is preparatory to the proper identification of critical issues and problems that are not directly identifiable and solvable during the intervention phase, where the urgent and non-deferrable nature of rescue activities requires swift planning and rapid actions. Managing tools such as the Incident Command System (ICS) well-known in literature and implemented within the CNVVF's organizations with the Note n. 01/2020, provide a useful guide and a valid breakdown of operational actions, facilitating both for the intervention phase and for its subsequent analysis.

Therefore, the paper will focus the events occurred within the Montegrino mountain area, developed at the end of March 2023. In detail, reference will be made to the rescue management models adopted, to the cooperation between the difference state corps and authority intervened, to the role of the national air fleet in the extinguishing and eventually to the use of the innovative drone monitoring techniques in rescue services.

Keywords: Forest fire · Firefighters · Rescue Service · Air fleet · Drones · UAS

1 Introduction

In March 2023, the town of Montegrino Valtravaglia (Varese, Lombardy) faced a forest fire that would leave a significant impact on the local environment, communities, and surrounding areas. Spanning an area of approximately 90 hectares, the fire engulfed vast sections of the dense forest landscape, posing an immediate threat to nearby areas and the residents of Montegrino Valtravaglia. In the aftermath of this natural disaster, efforts were mobilized to understand the extent of the damage, coordinate emergency response

E. Borgogno Mondino and P. Zamperlin (Eds.): ASITA 2023, CCIS 2088, pp. 64–71, 2024.
https://doi.org/10.1007/978-3-031-59925-5_5

actions, and study the effectiveness of various firefighting strategies. This paper delves into the comprehensive analysis of the Montegrino forest fire, focusing on the utilization of aerial forest extinguishers, drone surveys, and the collaboration between regional authorities, the Montegrino mountain community, and the Italian fire and rescue service (CNVVF).

Forest fires represent a worldwide concern, with global warming amplifying the risk, the frequency, and magnitude of such events [1]. The Montegrino forest fire can therefore be useful as a case study for understanding the complexities of these incidents and the importance of an efficient and coordinated response system. Studying this fire allows us to glean valuable insights into the strategies employed to control the blaze and mitigate its impact.

The paper will first focus how the Italian fire and rescue service operates in those events. Before the event, the efforts of the Italian civil protection authorities, of which the CNVVF is one of the main components, were devoted to the prevention culture and territory management [5]. In forest fire scenarios, the CNVVF acts mainly in the management and coordination of emergency events, with exclusive jurisdiction on the interface rescue and extinguishing operations between forests and civilizedl/urbanized areas [4].

Furthermore, the paper will delve into the description of the specific event itself, starting with a brief description of the area and moving on to the motivations and circumstances that led to the escalation of the fire. Such knowledge is crucial for enhancing procedures of civil protection and improving the knowledge of the phenomena evolution in order to prevent future forest fires and better manage rescue operations. One significant approach utilized during the Montegrino forest fire was the use of aerial forest extinguishers, which involves deploying aircraft equipped with specialized firefighting capabilities. Investigating the effectiveness of this strategy can also provide valuable insights into the potential applications of aerial firefighting in future forest fire incidents. Additionally, the paper will explore the utilization of drone surveys in assessing the extent of the damage caused by the fire and the scenario's evolution. Drones equipped with advanced imaging technology have emerged as powerful tools in emergency assessment, enabling responders to access remote and hazardous areas safely. By analyzing the accuracy and efficiency of drone surveys during the Montegrino fire, this study aims to highlight the advantages of integrating this technology into future firefighting and disaster management strategies. Moreover, the success of emergency response efforts depends greatly on the coordination between various stakeholders. At this regard, the research will focus on the collaboration between the Lombardy region, Montegrino Valtravaglia community institutions, and the Italian firefighters (VVF). Understanding the dynamics of this cooperation can provide valuable lessons on how to optimize the coordination between local authorities and central agencies during large-scale emergencies. Ultimately, the findings of this study will be instrumental in developing more robust strategies to combat forest fires and protect vulnerable ecosystems and communities in the face of future calamities.

2 Italian Fire Department in Forest Fire – Lombardy Case

Legislative Decree 177/2016, in terms of forest firefighting (AIB), gives the Italian national Fire and Rescue Service – CNVVF (Art. 9 c.1) the following competencies:

- cooperation with the regions in fighting forest fires with the help of ground and air means;
- coordination of firefighting operations, in agreement with the regions, including the employment of volunteer fire-fighting groups;
- participation in the national coordination structure and regional ones.

Italian law 353/2000 provides that the regions, for the implementation of training and information related to the activities of forecasting, prevention of forest fires, and active fighting, may also make use of the CNVVF (art. 5 art. 7 c. 3 lett. a).

Moreover, Legislative Decree 139/2006 as amended by Legislative Decree 97/2017 (art. 24 c. 9) provides that "without prejudice to the powers of the regions and autonomous provinces and the Department of Civil Protection of the Presidency of the Council of Ministers in the field of extinguishing forest fires,… The central and peripheral structures of the National Corps ensure,… Carry out the tasks that the law assigns to the State in the field of active fight against forest fires".

Program agreements are concluded between the CNVVF and the regions that have an interest in them and must provide, for each territory, the resources, means and personnel of the CNVVF to be made available. The related financial burdens shall be borne by the regions."

Lombardy Region has in fact noted the need to strengthen its own regional arrangements concerning the active fight against forest fires, as well as training and information addressed to citizens and AIB volunteer personnel.

As a result of this, the Region signed in February 2022 a special agreement with the CNVVF for the activities of prevention and active fight against forest fires, valid for three years.

The agreement covers the provision to the region of the following services by the Directorate Lombardy Regional [3]:

a) Coordination of forest fire suppression activities in the region, carried out at the Forest Firefighting Operation Centre (COR AIB) located in Curno (Bergamo) of the CNVVF according to the procedures set forth in this Plan;
b) Strengthening the regional contingent of Directors of Firefighting Operations (DOS) through qualified CNVVF personnel officially recognized as DOS by Lombardy Region, included in the regional list of qualified DOS and called to operate according to employment and rotation criteria provided for in the convention;
c) Organization of firefighters teams dedicated to forest firefighting activated, in availability, at the specific and prior request of the Lombardy Region (SOR PC) through the COR AIB, for an effective operational integration to the resources of the volunteer AIB to which, by established and effective practice of the Region itself, is entrusted with the active fight against forest fires;
d) Support for the coordination of forest firefighting activities in the regional checkerboard carried out by the COR AIB of Curno of the adequately trained, activated at the SS.OO.115 (Operations Rooms of the CNVVF Provincial Commands);

e) Collection, processing and transmission of daily and periodic fire data and establishment and maintenance, on this basis, of an AIB database, according to the indications and needs of the Region. In Lombardy, the organizational structure of the CNVVF is articulated in the VVF Regional Directorate, in the regional capital, which is headed by a Regional Director, and in the Provincial Commands in the various provincial capitals, which are headed by a provincial commander, with the related territorial articulations consisting of permanent and/or volunteer bases.

In addition, the agreement also includes education and training for VVF personnel in Lombardy and AIB Entities. It involves the participation of qualified personnel in the examination boards for AIB unit Chiefs and Directors of Firefighting Operations upon request from the Lombardy Region. The agreement requires qualified involvement in regional coordination structures, preparation of operational guidelines, and standardization of equipment. Additionally, it encompasses AIB evaluation, research, and experimentation activities, aiming to enhance firefighting effectiveness and management systems.

It is worth to be specified that, as expressly stipulated in the Convention, in carrying out the activities indicated above, the tenured personnel of CNVVF remain under exclusive dependence and will refer to the Command of belonging and the CNVVF Regional Directorate of Lombardy. The employment of Firefighters in the activities provided for in the Convention constitutes, for all purposes, institute service.

3   The Event in Montegrino Valtravaglia in March - April 2023

The forest fire in Montegrino Valtravaglia (VA) was triggered after a long dry period and an intense wind day from north in the afternoon of March 27, 2023, near a built-up area. The area is characterized by different interface situation, with high probability of fire propagation from forested areas to civil structures. Firefighters therefore intervened to protect the infrastructure and the residential buildings along the fire front. Contextually, the personnel of the "Comunità Montana delle Valli del Verbano" (the territorially competent institution) and volunteers intervened. Consequently, the COR AIB engaged the DOS. The advanced command post (APC) was established at an accommodation facility near the ignition point. Already from the first hours from fire triggering also the aerial assets intervened. Red Cross arrived too, to manage health issue. To share information about rescuers and institution involved, it was used SITAC (Standardization of Firefighting Tactical Situation Management representation) symbology [6] (Fig. 1).

The fuel of the forest fire object of the present discussion was mainly constituted of fallen leaves and branches and of the softwoods composing the wood. Furthermore, the fire spreading was catalysed by the orography and the huge amount of dry foliage on the ground, Thanks to the first extinguishing activities before the evening the flame front was pushed southward, far from the residential areas. During the first night, firefighters worked to defend homes with four garrisons suitably positioned in order to monitor, confine and promptly intervene in case of need (Fig. 2).

The orography of the west side of Montegrino mountain made the operations inside the forest tough and dangerous to be carried out in low visibility conditions. Remotely piloted aircraft systems were also deployed to monitor the advancing wind-driven flame

Fig. 1. Forest Fire ignition point

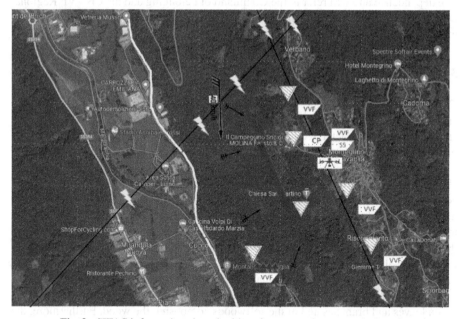

Fig. 2. SITAC information about ignition, forecast and rescuers deployed

front and to build a first estimation of burned areas. The use of drones allowed firefighting teams to maintain high situational awareness. Thanks to the bird's-eye view, it was possible to better deploy firefighting teams in the area while preventing the fire from involving homes. On March 28, thanks to the intervention in force of aerial means, the active fronts were significantly reduced, although in the evening there were some restarts that still engaged the intervening personnel. After a couple of days, the fire was brought under control and was finally-mostly extinguished in early April (Fig. 3).

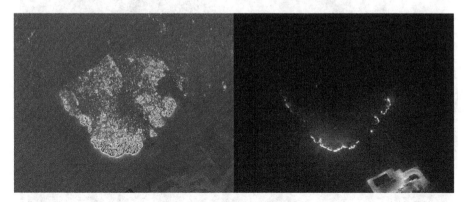

Fig. 3. Optical and thermal view by drones – Flames close to house

This event, which determined a burned area of more than 90ha, was characterized by the synergy put in place by the firefighters of the Varese Command, the AIB Volunteers of the Comunità Montana delle Valli del Verbano and the Municipal Administration of Montegrino Valtravaglia, which supported administratively and logistically the extinguishing activities.

One of the positive elements to be highlighted concerns in particular the establishment of the Advanced Command Post by means of the UCL (Local Command Unit) vehicle of the Varese Fire Department Command, equipped with radios that covering the various bands employed (aviation, VVF and AIB) allowed multi agency communication on the scenario.

In addition, the utilization of drones has proven to be a pivotal asset in controlling and combating forest fires. The deployment of remotely piloted aerial vehicles equipped with advanced thermal imaging technology has emerged as a particularly positive development, especially during times of reduced natural lighting, when ordinary aerial vehicles could not fly to attack the fires.

These drones equipped with thermal payloads facilitated continuous monitoring of the flame front and the identification of hot spots. This continuous surveillance helped not only in enhancing situational awareness, but also allowed the optimization of resource deployment and the strategic planning of interventions.

The above two elements, proper planning and use of technology, were also useful during the mop-up phase. With the drone flights it was possible to recognize hot spot phenomena also in particularly impervious areas, which were then addressed by AIB volunteers with specific high-capacity mop-up equipment for the final extinguishment of the fire (Fig. 4).

Fig. 4. EFFIS burnt area [7]

4 Conclusion

In conclusion, this paper examined the March 2023 Montegrino Valtravaglia (Varese, Lombardy) forest fire, deepening the understanding of the calamitous event and the multifaceted strategies employed to combat its destructive force. The article first focused on the competencies and prerogatives of the various civil protection organisms, with their relevant jurisdictions and competences in population protection against forest fires, detailing the description in the case of Lombardy. Consequently, through an in-depth analysis of the scenario evolution, environmental factors, and aerial firefighting techniques, the study offered some insights into the enhancement of intervention models and proactive measures for forest fire prevention. Furthermore, the synergy between human expertise and technological innovation has been revealed to be an effective and strategic asset. In particular, during the mop-up phase, the integration of drone technology into wildfire control operations extended the operational window during the challenging nocturnal conditions, and also enhanced the overall efficiency and effectiveness of firefighting efforts. The invaluable insights provided by drones can contribute to a more informed decision-making process, ultimately aiding in the protection of lives, property, and the environment in the face of increasingly frequent and intense wildfires. Moreover, the coordination between the Lombardy region, Montegrino Valtravaglia community and municipal institutions, and Italian firefighters highlights the huge importance of cohesive and strict collaboration in mitigating the devastating effects of such disasters, in order to minimize the hazard for the population, minimizing the economic damage, and properly counteract the forest fire phenomenon.

References

1. Khabarov, N., et al.: Forest fires and adaptation options in Europe. Reg. Environ. Change **16**, 21–30 (2016)
2. Feliziani, F., et al.: Progetto di impiego operative dei Sistemi Aeromobili a Pilotaggio Remoto (SAPR) del CNVVF, Atti VGR 2016, Pisa (2016)
3. Lombardy Region Homepage. https://www.regione.lombardia.it. Accessed 31 July 2023
4. Italian Fire Department Homepage. https://www.vigilfuoco.it. Accessed 31 July 2023
5. Italian Civil Protection Department Homepage. https://www.protezionecivile.gov.it. Accessed 31 July 2023
6. CEN CENELEC Homepage, https://www.cencenelec.eu/, last accessed 2023/07/31
7. EFFIS Homepage. https://effis.jrc.ec.europa.eu/. Accessed 31 July 2023

Technological Innovation in Emergency Technical Rescue: The Deployment of CNVVF UAS to Support the Director of Forest Fire Fighting Operations

Franco Feliziani and Onofrio Lorusso(✉)

Italian National Fire and Rescue Service, Department of Firefighters, Public Rescue and Civil Defence, Italian Ministry of Interior, Rome, Italy
{franco.feliziani,onofrio.lorusso}@vigilfuoco.it

Abstract. Over the past few years, partly due to climate change, and the reduction in rainfall, the forest fire season in Italy is expanding and the territory will find itself increasingly subject to extreme natural events. Among the institutional tasks of the National Fire Brigade (CNVVF) is also the contribution in the activities of extinguishing wildfires, particularly when they threaten anthropized areas and in any case for complex events in which the intervention of the air assets of the State fleet is necessary. The search for aids to optimize active firefighting activities has allowed the Corps to experiment and deepen the use of technology in forest firefighting activities.

In particular, the use of remotely piloted aerial systems in support of the Director of Extinguishing Operations (DOS) has been found to be particularly useful because of their ability to acquire data and information that can be used to optimize resources for response to the event. The structured and coordinated deployment of such systems can be particularly useful, especially during the night, to monitor the progress of the flame front and plan for the next morning's activities. In addition, they can be useful to identify "hot spots" or "hot areas" on which to direct the teams assigned to clean-up when active fronts are no longer present.

Data and information acquired by remotely piloted aircraft systems have the advantage of being associated with geographic coordinates, and this allows the creation of mapping databases that can be pooled among the various agencies working together to face the event.

Keywords: Wildfire · Italian Fire Department · UAS · hot spots · georeferenced information · dynamic survey

1 Introduction

In Italy, the framework law on forest fires (n. 353 of November 21, 2000) entrusts the Regions with the responsibility of forecasting, preventing and actively fighting forest fires, while the State is responsible for contributing to the extinguishing activities with the State's aerial fire-fighting fleet. The regions are responsible for the activation of

E. Borgogno Mondino and P. Zamperlin (Eds.): ASITA 2023, CCIS 2088, pp. 72–80, 2024.
https://doi.org/10.1007/978-3-031-59925-5_6

operational rooms to allow the operational activation of teams for the extinction of land and regional air assets (usually helicopters) of forest fires, formed by regional personnel, volunteers and firefighters and, where appropriate, the intervention of civil protection. It is also up to the regions to develop and implement regional plans for forecasting, prevention and intervention updated every year. The Department of Civil Protection, through the COAU - Centro Operativo Aereo Unificato (Unified Aerial Operations Center), is responsible for the coordination of the State's aerial fire-fighting fleet, which consists of Canadair CL-415 and S-64 helicopters owned by the Fire Department, as well as other types of helicopters owned by the Defense Department. The Coau is continuously active 24 h a day throughout the year and is the Command and Control Center of all the aircrafts made available for the State's contribution in the forest fire fighting activity, planning and coordinating the flight activities both nationally and internationally. In the forest fire-fighting activity, the Italian Air Force is in constant contact with the Regional Operations Centers (SOUP) receiving the request for the State air support when the regional forces (teams and helicopters) are not able to face the fire. In order to minimize the time necessary to reach the site of operations, it is essential to plan the ground deployment of available air assets. The fire-fighting aircraft and helicopters of the State air fleet are deployed on the territory taking into account the areas at risk and the weather conditions that make the start of forest fires more likely [3]. Among the institutional tasks of the National Fire Brigade (CNVVF) is also the contribution in the activities of extinguishing wildfires, particularly when they threaten anthropized areas and in any case for complex events. Moreover, Italian Fire Department is experimenting the use of drones (state aircrafts too) to support forest firefighting, taking in account use of airspace in safe way, and acquiring helpful georeferenced information to optimize deployment of resources and teams, and to improve tactical operations [2].

2 Italian Fire Department – Drones Team

Italian Fire Department drone service currently has 15 bases, 150 pilots and has more than 60 drones (both multirotor and fixed wing). As Government Organization, Italian ire Department has specific rules to use drones to support technical rescue operations, as crew of minimum two pilots, pre-flight risk assessment, pre-flight briefing, dynamic risk assessment during operations, post-flight briefing, record of activities; In additions, according the area and the airspace it need to implement mitigation action as air-space observer, hearing aeronautical frequencies, monitoring of FlightRadar24 app and others as consequence of risk assessment. Standard Operations Procedures (POS) and technical guidelines complete the indication of Unmanned Aircraft System (UAS) Operations Manual of Italian Fire Brigades. The drones are covered by specific insurance, have airworthiness certifications, and are maintained according the maintenance instruction and program dawn up by the manufacturer. Drones applications, to support Italian Fire Department Rescue operations, are wide. They may be used in search and rescue operations, in flooding/sliding/avalanches emergencies, earthquakes, hazardous substances emergencies, ordinary technical recue operation outdoor or indoor, and forest firefighting too [1] (Fig. 1).

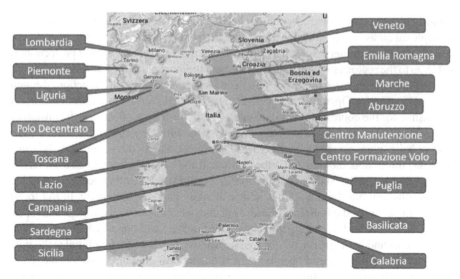

Fig. 1. Italian Fire Department Drones Bases in the Country

3   Use of Italian Fire Department Drones in Forest Fire

In forest firefighting, as aircraft, the use of drones is under coordination of DOS unit, that is in charge of all technical operation for fighting wildfires. The use of drones in these operations is increasing, so it needs to know how drones can be used and what they can be give as product (Fig. 2).

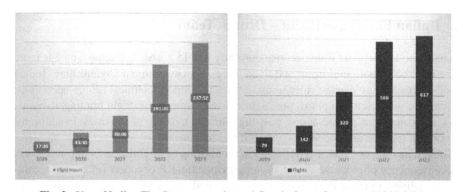

Fig. 2. Use of Italian Fire Department drones' fleet in forest fire (up to 2023/10/23)

The drones fleet of Italian Fire Department is composed by fixed-wing drones (especially used for orthophotogrammetry) end multirotor drone of different dimensions: little drone with MTOM (Maximun Take Off Mass) up to 2 kg and with EO/IR (up to 20 MP/640 × 512) payloads for local inspection and bigger drone (MTOM up to 9,2 kg) with different plug-and-play payloads (EO/IR – 20 MP/640 × 512, Lidar, Photogrammetry Camera (45MP), Night Camera, Laser Telemeter up to 1000 mt, Searchlight of

10.000 lm). These drones can be rapidly deployed in case of emergencies and they are ready to use. However with cited drones it need to take off closed to scenario and then the time to be in operations is affected by distance base-scenario.

Initial Survey

When possible, drones can be used to prevent the forest fire or to recognize early ignition. By years 2022, Italian Fire Department drones are involved in a specific project called "presidi rurali" in some regional and national park really important for environmental characteristics. In 2022, fire departments drones did 264 missions for more than 80 flight hours in 6 areas in Italy. This year the areas are 19 in 13 regions. Dynamic survey drones flight can be useful to acquire updated information on area: access point, availability of path and road, "fuel map", water resources, flight obstacles, etc. This information can be collected by videos and by georeferenced pictures too, that can be elaborated in orthomosaic (Fig. 3).

Fig. 3. Dynamic survey by multirotor drone in Pantelleria Island in 2017

Rapid Deployment After Early Warning

It is possible to deploy immediately drones teams in area where DOS need to be aware-ness with possible risk in fire growing up to deploy the right amount of resources to face the fire. This information can be collected by pictures and by video too, that can be streamed to DOS or remote crisis room. The efficacy of drone deployment is related to time spent by crew to reach scenario, then operational readiness of crews increases effectiveness of using drones (Fig. 4).

Interface Situation

When the forest fire is closed to infrastructure or urban site, the use of drones is very helpful, especially in the night, when the manned aircraft haven't possibility to fight the fire. DOS can have updated information about the velocity and direction of the flame, to improve deployment of ground resources. It can be useful to monitor flame position and velocity for safety of firefighters too. The flight is done with drones with light, with

Fig. 4. Early deployment of multirotor drone in Malnate (VA) Forest Fire in 2022

thermal camera as payload. There is possibility to have a spotlight to illuminate an area or a path to facilitate the movement of rescuers in night conditions (Fig. 5).

Fig. 5. Head of fire monitored by multirotor drone in Angera (VA) wildfire in 2022

Complex Situation and Dynamic Survey

When the wildfires cover a large area, it is helpful for the incident commander have an aerial view to be awareness of complex situation, particularly to have possibility to ensure the safety of the rescuer and the populations. This flight can be done with optical and thermal camera, to capture a video on a large area, and the DOS can have immersive view by goggles. The structured and coordinated deployment of UAS can be particularly useful, especially during the night, to monitor the progress of the flame front and plan for the next morning's activities (Fig. 6).

Fig. 6. Multirotor drone survey in Massarosa (LU) wildfire in 2022

Looking for Hot Spots

When the flames are fight, it is possible to use drones to look for "hot spot" that ground teams may manage to avoid a new ignition. This flight can be done with thermal camera, with possibility to georeference the hot-spot, that can be positioned on a map. So, DOS have possibility to deploy ground teams on a specific target. Helpful is aerial view by drone in case of underground fire affected the area; forestry personnel's knowledge of the territory is very important for interpreting the data acquired by the drone's IR camera (Fig. 7).

Fig. 7. Hot Spot located by drone in Gambarogno (CH) wildfire in 2022

Mapping Burnt Area

When the wildfire is fight, drones can be used for mapping burnt area as orthomosaic. At the end of season, it is possible to have a view of all burnt area in a region. This flight can be done with fixed wing drones, specific for mapping, to cover larger area. Data acquired by drones can be post-elaborated by specific software to obtain 2D or 3D model and points cloud (e.g. Metashape). Normally, in emergencies scenario, 2D model with Ground Sample Distance (GSD) of 5cm/px is enough and reachable (Fig. 8).

Fig. 8. Mapping of burnt area in Albenga (SV) forest fire in 2022, with fixed-wing drone

Locate Point/Area of Interest

Drones can be helpful for to acquire data and information about a specific target too. If there is a specific point of interest, as a church in the forest, or a specific area of interest, as the area of ignition, whit a flight with optical and thermal payloads is possible to collect georeferenced information about it (Fig. 9).

Fig. 9. Burnt area closed to house in Malnate (VA) forest fire in 2022, with multirotor drone

Fast Damage Assessment

When a wildfire affected a large area, it is possible to use drones for a rapid assessment operation on burnt area. Drones can flight over a specific area and to acquire pictures of damaged infrastructure. This georeferenced information may be collected on a map to have awareness about the priority of countermeasures and the critical situations. This offers a great advantage in terms of time compared to the use of ordinary ground teams (who may be unable to view the upper part of the buildings), particularly in those rural areas with a thin road network, with unpaved roads and where there are scattered buildings (Fig. 10).

Fig. 10. Target captured by multirotor drone, for assessment post-wildfire in Oristano in 2021

4   Conclusions

In last years, a lot of wildfire affected Italian territory and all the organization involved in forest firefighting are looking for new instrument to face this emergency. Use of technologies may be helpful but it needs to be organized to support decision of Commander. Italian Fire Department has possibility to deploy, in forest fire, drone teams too. To collect data and information can give to DOS a different "point of view" to manage ground and aerial teams to optimize the fight of wildfires. Otherwise, the possibility to acquire georeferenced data and information may be helpful to increase situational awareness by specific geoportal utility. Use of drones in forest fire is very helpful for firefighter's safety too: Incident Commander can have an aerial view of position and teams deployed and the critical issue they are facing. Nevertheless, drones offer the opportunity to acquire data on the position, development and speed of the flame front during the hours with reduced natural lighting, transforming the night into a period of monitoring and studying the progress of the fire, aimed at acquiring updated information for the attack on the fire the next morning. Furthermore, the support that drones can provide during mop-up operations is very important: through the use of IR camera it is possible to detect hot-spots and provide ground teams, georeferenced information on their position; in this way it is possible to direct the activity on the ground by concentrating it on the points that could present a risk of re-ignition of the fire. Finally, when the fire is fight, the drone can be used to carry out survey of the area burnt, but also to acquire update information for a rapid damage assessment.

References

1. Feliziani, F., et al.: Progetto di impiego operativo dei Sistemi Aeromobili a Pilotaggio Remoto (SAPR) del CNVVF. In: Atti VGR 2016, Pisa (2016)
2. Italian Fire Department Homepage. https://www.vigilfuoco.it. Accessed 31 July 2023
3. Italian Civil Protection Department Homepage. https://www.protezionecivile.gov.it. Accessed 31 July 2023

Platform Prototype for the Prediction of Landslide Susceptibility Through a 4D WebGIS Equipped with Cellular Automata and Neural Networks

Vincenzo Barrile⦿, Francesco Cotroneo, and Emanuela Genovese(✉)⦿

Department of Civil Engineering, Energy, Environment and Materials (DICEAM), Mediterranea University, 89124 Reggio Calabria, Italy
vincenzo.barrile@unirc.it,
emanuela.genovese.728@studenti.unirc.it

Abstract. Climate change and increasing anthropogenic impact in forested areas (logging and fires) have in recent years intensified the Hydrogeological Instability of many mountain slopes in the Italian territory. This leads to greater difficulty in identifying in the short- and long-term well-defined areas of higher priority for preventive intervention to secure inhabited areas and infrastructure. In fact, extreme weather events limited in space and time, together with possible micro-seisms, can make the degree of landslide susceptibility attributable to a given slope change abruptly. In this sense, a WebGIS 4D infrastructure capable of producing susceptibility forecast layers through simulators with emergent properties has been implemented, which will cooperate to create a "digital twin" of the territory and context in being, on which simulations are launched to obtain useful forecasts. The digital twin is created from geo-referenced three-dimensional Cellular Automata (C.A.), which are characterized by states and mutual interactions defined by the phenomenology of that context (moisture diffusion, geologic characterization of the terrain, seismic events…). The states then vary over time as simulation iterations proceed and through data assimilation (e.g., rainfall). An AI with SNN investigates the C.A. states looking for specific patterns, from which to generate the susceptibility index and thus the forecast output. The process can be seen as an immediate downstream update of critical events to susceptibility maps distributed by government agencies (e.g., ISPRA). The application of this method was carried out in South Italy.

Keywords: Landslide susceptibility · Forecasting Model · Susceptibility Maps

1 Introduction

Climate change and the growing human impact on wooded and forested areas have in recent years intensified the Hydrogeological Instability of many mountain slopes in the Italian territory. The assessment of the susceptibility and danger of landslides becomes an aspect to be explored, above all with a view to correct territorial planning and resilient

E. Borgogno Mondino and P. Zamperlin (Eds.): ASITA 2023, CCIS 2088, pp. 81–95, 2024.
https://doi.org/10.1007/978-3-031-59925-5_7

management of the territory. Originally the various methods used were aimed at evaluating stability in static conditions and they were subsequently extended to the case of dynamic stresses through the introduction of statically applied inertia forces. The problem is often analyzed using top-down numerical approaches, the most widespread of which is the method of finite differences. The following research has focused on the application of a bottom-up model and the implementation of a 4D WebGIS infrastructure capable of producing susceptibility prediction layers through emergent property simulators, which cooperate to create a "digital twin" of the territory and of the existing context, on which simulations are launched in order to obtain useful forecasts. The digital twin is created starting from geo-referenced three-dimensional cellular automata (C.A.), which are characterized by states and mutual interactions defined by the phenomenology of this context. The application of this method is carried out in South Italy where there are several landslide susceptibility areas and as a result a 2D/3D/4D WebGIS platform was obtained, capable of launching simulations, creating scenarios and susceptibility maps with a higher predictive precision than the most widespread methodologies today.

The methodology, in particular, is dedicated to increasing precision on the "time" plane downstream of the occurrence of critical events, extreme weather events, land use changes, earthquakes, and microseisms. In Italy, the ISPRA (Superior Institute for Environmental Protection and Research) provides susceptibility maps at very high detail, [1]: some zoning polygons are less than even 1000 square meters and they are classified through a susceptibility index that includes 5 values. The construction of this layer is done using satellite monitoring, the use of classical Geology models, and from analyses of historical events. These types of maps prove to be very useful in the context of medium- and long-term decision support; however, they do not characterize the change in susceptibility to the occurrence of critical events over a given area. The methodology integrated in the platform reported here is intended to offer the possibility of "adjusting" the susceptibility index as soon as a given area being monitored is affected by critical events such as abundant precipitation.

The "perennial" simulation through its digital twin allows tracking the evolution of its integrity status and the critical events it has undergone, if a pattern of variation in the susceptibility index is detected, this promptly goes to "adjust" the classification given by the monitoring agencies.

The paper applies the study of abrupt susceptibility variation to a small study area located in the southern part of the Briga River Basin, along the Ionian coast of Sicily (Italy). In particular, the period prior to October 1, 2009, when the area was affected by an intense rainfall event that triggered abundant slope failures and caused widespread erosion, is simulated, [2].

Finally, the proposed methodology, it will be seen, is very flexible and provides for implementation possibilities with different levels of complexity. The main purpose of the article is to show the goodness of the approach; therefore, it will refer to the possible variants, but will focus on the application of the essential techniques.

2   The Proposed Methodology

The basic idea underlying the operation of the proposed method is the creation of a digital twin representing the terrain/land with its physical and orographic properties. Such creation passes through the use of the 3D component of GIS (orography and DEM) and especially by the representation of the surface and depth volumes of the terrain with the help of 3D cellular automata characterized by appropriate state variables from microphysics rules with which they mutually interact, [3]. This representation is then subjected to computer simulation (computation of microphysics interactions among the cellular automata) with iterations representing a given instant in time (calendar date). Such a system naturally evolves, and each cellular automaton sees the value of its state variables change with each iteration. These variables are analyzed by a Pattern Detector (implemented through a Neural Network) which provides, if detected, the change in the susceptibility index.

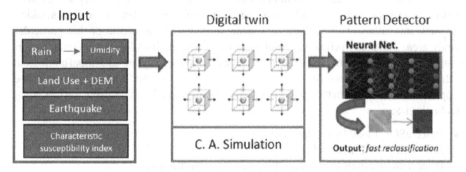

Fig. 1. Process Pipeline.

Figure 1 summarizes the process pipeline exhibited. The input simulation, at a certain time instant, considers/can consider as follows:

1. The surface moisture value (input forcing) calculated from downscaling operations performed by an atmospheric simulator developed by the Geomatics Laboratory of the University of Reggio Calabria [4, 5] from the rainfall value recorded over the area of interest.
2. Land use (forested, croplands, burned areas…) to be coded as an appropriate state variable for superficial cellular automata. In this work it is an input that is not considered.
3. DEM (Digital Elevation Model) information is for the displacement of cellular automata in space (GIS) and for the variable Slope, assigned to surface cellular automata.

4. Earthquakes, events that can change the mechanical properties of soil and rocks. In this work it is an input that is not considered.
5. The characteristic susceptibility index is considered, and it is the susceptibility index provided by ISPRA. It varies along the area considered, of course it also varies over time when the maps are updated by the agency.

This value is taken into account as it brings into the modeling/simulation by inference of the Neural Network the Know-How of the models used by ISPRA. Then, the C.A. Simulation makes the change to the state variables of the cellular automata at each iteration; these values are input to the pattern detector module consisting of a dedicated Neural Network, which has as its output the susceptibility index calculated from the entire pipeline. We can call this index, in line with the above, Fast reclassification index. The index is computed at each iteration and is inherent to the entire attentional front, and thus reports any change in susceptibility by promptly tracking inputs and in particular critical events such as heavy rainfall. The pattern detector is based on a neural network trained using past landslide events in similar areas, assigning them susceptibility scores of 6. Once the network is trained, it will output a new susceptibility index for a new area, taking as input the values of the cellular automata variables characteristic of that particular study area. The study offers an initial insight into the methodology's potential. In this context, future enhancements of the method are planned to integrate additional contextual information derived from geological features, seismic data, and human activities. The implementation of the method was finalized by developing a WebGIS using the following technologies:

- PostgreSQL/PostGIS for data storage
- Java spring for Business Logic
- Html 5 and Cesium JS for the GIS Component on Browser
- Python for CAs
- Tensorflow for A.I.

The AC Modules and A.I. they operate directly on the PostgreSQL / PostGIS database.

3   The Phenomenological Digital Twin, Cellular Automata

The paper applies the study of abrupt susceptibility change on a small study area located in the southern part of the Briga River Basin along the Ionian coast of Sicily (Italy), Fig. 2 shows this area with the ISPRA susceptibility classification.

Figure 3 shows the construction through phenomenological digital twin C.A. The Figure is for illustrative value, in fact the work uses C.A. of 1 m and also the colors are intended to highlight the cubes contours. It shows how the Cellular Automata are prepared to represent the orography of the slope being studied.

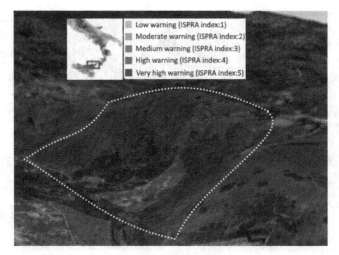

Fig. 2. Briga, Sicily (Italy). ISPRA Susceptibility Classification.

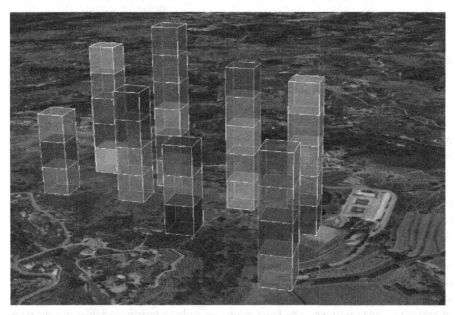

Fig. 3. Briga, Sicily (Italy). Phenomenological Digital Twin using C.A. (the cubes reported are only for illustrative purposes).

Fig. 4. Briga, Sicily (Italy). 3D visualization.

Figure 4 reproduces the representation of Fig. 3 by rendering the satellite basemap in 3D mode using for this purpose the same DEM from which the information for the dislocation of the cellular automata in space and the Slope variable, assigned to the surface cellular automata, were obtained. Figure 4 was included solely to provide a clearer explanation of the methodology used and it shows how the Cellular Automata are adapted to represent the slope's topography under study. In the image, cubes' dimensions, colors, and quantity are for illustrative purposes (it should be note that the graphic rendering operations in relation to the effective real representation of the state-of-art require in general a high-end workstation.) and do not have a specific relationship with the design choices used for the case study and the metrics provided subsequently. In any case, the color of the voxels has no informative value and it is random, as can be observed from Fig. 4 where the representation of the phenomenon does indeed correspond to the case study, and the voxels appear with random colors. It is also worth noting that in the same Fig. 4, the cubes are intentionally oversized (the software allows for setting the size and position of the cubes in the study area) to better illustrate the functioning of the methodology through which they inherit the characteristic ISPRA index. In particular, the image shows how the latter (the surface CAs) inherit an appropriate characteristic susceptibility index. In fact, from the intersection of the susceptibility map with the area of surface cellular automata, the latter adopt, as a characteristic variable, the attribute (susceptibility value) corresponding to the polygon they intersect.

4   Characterization of C.A.

In the specific application, Cellular Automata are characterized by state variables that evolve during the simulation and by the proximity interaction rules (local microphysics) between adjacent cellular automata. It is specified that surface cellular automata, i.e., those that intersect surfaces, have their state variables set by inputs and not by proximity interactions [6]. The C.A. used here, are three-dimensional, georeferenced and have the following dimensions (Fig. 5):

- Width: 1 m.
- Thickness: 1 m.
- Height: 1 m.

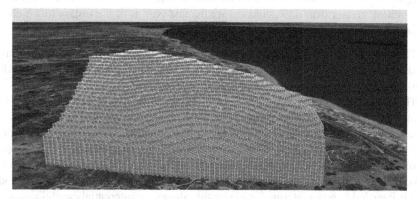

Fig. 5. Briga, Sicily (Italy). Particularization of the Phenomenological Digital Twin using C.A.

The dimensions of the "cube" (of the single automaton) represent a compromise between the precision with which the digital twin is built in the exposed methodology and the necessary computational resources. Compromise born from the experiences built up to now.

It is important to note that exists a strict dependence between dimensions of the individual automaton and the quality and validation of the possible results to be obtained. (in-depth studies must naturally be carried out to investigate this dependence). However, it is immediate to understand that dimensions that are too large (e.g. >5 m) may not be adequate, both due to drift effects during the simulation (propagation of errors in the laws of local microphysics) and because they would likely invalidate the abstraction power of the network neural used as a pattern detector.

In relation to the height of the voxels that represent each of an array of elements of volume that constitute the notional three-dimensional space, especially each of an array of discrete elements into which a representation of a three-dimensional object is divided, it should be note that the number of cubes used to build a single voxel multiplied by the size of the cube must just exceed the altitude of the relief, starting to build the stack from the bottom of the valley. In this way all cellular automata are distributed over the entire three-dimensional domain involved.

State variables are:

- Slope, value in radians. Significant only for surface C.A.
- Characteristic Susceptibility Index. Significant only for surface C.A.
- Degree of Saturation S_r. $S_r = V_w/V_e$. That is, the volume of free water divided by the volume of voids (the spaces between impermeable materials). The value is between zero and one.
- S_n, the number of hours out of the total annual hours (8760) in which the soil had a saturation greater than 30%, considering the last year as of the instant to which the simulation refers. The value is between zero and one.

These dimensions were chosen empirically by observing the evolution of the state variables and choosing the cases that produced "convergent" variations in the humidity diffusion times; and simultaneously analyzing performance.

The choice of such specific variables is motivated by the fact that the output classifying susceptibility is ultimately given by the AI layer that is called upon to infer the law establishing the correlation between the inputs (precipitation), [7], and the output (change in susceptibility index). So, the choice is made to best ensure the typical properties of neural networks. In fact, the pipeline introduced is not intended to totally devolve phenomenological prediction to the C.A. simulator as an alternative to classical methods, but it is intended to be an intermediate layer that allows the inferential capabilities of AI (in particular neural networks) to be best applied in the context under consideration.

Downstream of these considerations, the choice on state variables is better understood. The slope informs the Neural Network of a feature of the orography that conditions landslide events. The characteristic susceptibility index indirectly reports an implicit information content obtained from classical methods (and therefore helps to ensure convergence during the learning phase). The Degree of Saturation covers the role of the geologic parameter that can change abruptly (at each iteration) and naturally affects significantly as the susceptibility value changes because it alters more the stability of the soil and its intrinsic characteristics (e.g., roughness). Finally, the S_n index provides a simple and effective way to inform the Neural Network of the historical evolution of the phenomenology; this avoids the use of Recurrent Neural Networks and their architectural complexities while still including in the overall model the impact of rainfall in a cumulative manner over time.

Only one local interaction law was chosen to be used, and of course it concerns moisture diffusion, or more precisely, the degree of saturation. Each cellular automaton interacts with its neighbors using the Green-Ampt Infiltration Model [8] declined for sand and sandstone type soils as in the case study.

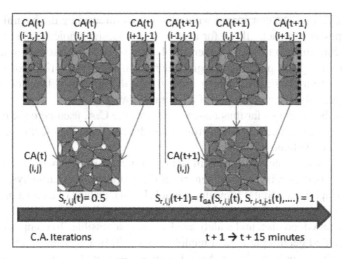

Fig. 6. C.A. Iterations.

Figure 6 shows by way of example (values included) how C.A. change their state variable Sr as iterations vary. For simplicity, the view is in cross section and the index k is not shown. From an information technology perspective, the cellular automata representation used here is a 3-index array (i, j, k), where each cell in these arrays points to a collection of 4 floating-point variables (the states of the C.A. chosen for our model). The simulation thus resolves in exploring all the cells of the array and changing their value according to the values of the states assigned in the previous iteration to the adjacent C.A. Resuming the figure, if we consider the cellular automaton C.A.$_{i,j}$ at time t, we see that its degree of saturation is, for example, 0.5; at the next iteration - that is, when all the other CAs have been processed and we return to automaton (i, j)- the new value is computed using the Green-Ampt method (f_{GA}) by taking into account the S_r values of the adjacent cellular automata, but those cal-culated in the previous iteration.

This is schematized by the following:

$$S_{r,i,j}(t + 1) = f_{GA}\left(S_{r,i,j}(t), S_{r,i-1,j-1}(t), \dots\right) \qquad (1)$$

The function is constructed by weighting characteristic constants such as hydraulic conductivity so that each computer iteration, of calculation, corresponds to 15 simulated minutes, and as mentioned considering sand and sandstone soil type.

In a similar manner, the other state variables are calculated; it should be mentioned that S_n does not consider adjacent C.A. but only the value of itself in the previous iterations. In addition, the states attributed to the surface cellular automata, by the given definition, are not calculated but attributed by the input settings and vary over typically long timescales (of course, this becomes partially true if the area is, for example, actively monitored with remote sensing techniques to update the slope).

This work did not consider other proximity interaction rules such as might have been those aimed at defining the tensional state of the ground represented by the individual cellular automaton. This is because in this work it was chosen that the contribution of such aspects must be considered within the model inferred by the Neural Network. So, the proposed approach allows for a very flexible design choice in this regard, the researcher from time to time can either devolve to the cellular automaton module the contribution of a given phenomenological element through the writing of interaction rules derived from classical models or move this to the inferential layer of the pattern detector (especially when it consists of a Neural Network).

What has been said so far thus underscores how the C.A. used here are profoundly different in use and characterization from other discrete modeling techniques such as may be the finite volume method.

The decision to create a "digital twin" representing the territory with its physical and orographic properties using 3D components of Geographic Information Systems (GIS), such as orography and Digital Elevation Model (DEM), instead of using a geomorphological model, was made because the data obtained from DEM and 3D GIS modeling are highly detailed, precise, and widely available and accessible. To compensate for the lack of a detailed geomorphological model (which will be considered in a subsequent advanced analysis), only the Green-Ampt Law was considered, modulated based on terrain characteristics because it is a well-established law in hydrology and water science. Modulating this law to account for terrain-specific conditions is a valid way to adapt it to a specific area without the need for a detailed geomorphological model at this phase. Furthermore, the focus of the paper, as intended by the authors in this initial phase, wasn't to require a detailed understanding of geomorphological processes (which will be useful in a second phase when the method is optimized). Instead, the primary goal was to test a methodology based on cellular automata, neural networks, and simulators that provide area susceptibility based on simple interaction models among automata. In this first phase, a simplified model was clearly used, and it is the intention to use more complex models in the future, involving expertise from geotechnical professionals who will also utilize geomorphological models.

5 The Pattern Detector

The output of the pipeline is provided by the pattern detector, the values of the state variables of the individual automata come to be the input of the latter module of the susceptibility classification process. The possible classification values are borrowed from the ISPRA data:

- When in the presence of a warning area, the value is 1.0
- When in the presence of moderate warning the value is 2.0
- When in the presence of medium warning the value is 3.0
- When in the presence of high warning the value is 4.0
- When in the presence of very high warning the value is 5.0

  Two possible outputs have been added to this classification:

- When the area is not to be attended to, the value is 0.0; this is also the value assigned to surface C.A. when they do not intersect any ISPRA zoning.
- When there are patterns that have produced landslides in similar situations, the index is 6.0

The pattern detector has only one output, the index classifies the whole area represented by C.A. As anticipated, it is through a Neural Network that the pattern detector was chosen to be implemented for this work. The choice fell on the model called Self-normalizing Neural Networks (SNN) equipped with a layer with an activation function SELUs (Scaled exponential linear units) [10, 11].

This type of activation function has been introduced very recently in the AI landscape and was chosen here mainly because of its high performance in the learning phase and the fact that it does not require any kind of normalization of the input and output data. Other advantages include:

- SELUs does not have vanishing gradient problem
- Compared to ReLUs (Rectified Linear Unit), SELUs' Neurons cannot die
- SELUs learn faster and better than other actuation functions without the need for further processing.

The SNN has 16,800 inputs. It was desired to represent the volume in question with C.A. of 1 cubic meter in volume to have maximum accuracy on the moisture diffusion phenomenon, thus also taking advantage of the accuracy offered by the atmospheric simulator that operates downscaling for precipitation. However, the power of inertness of the neural network type chosen, together with the need to still equalize the number of inputs to be applied to various zones, made it optimal to average the values of the state variables in order to obtain precisely that number of inputs.

The SNN is constructed as follows:

- Input layer (DensData), 16,800 input.
- Layer with Linear Activation Function (16,800 neurons)
- Layer DropOut. With Rate of Activation of 30%. Layer present only during training, helps prevent the phenomenon of overfitting.
- Layer with SELUs Activation Function
- Linear output layer with one output.

The construction of the training set was done by following a strategy consistent with the general layout of the pipeline and the state variables chosen for the automata. In other words, a collection of inputs to the network with relative output was built, the latter reporting the susceptibility classification in the expected intervals (from 1 to 6) while the inputs represent the state values of the ACs. Involved at the moment in which the result is associated. All on sites similar to the one in question, similar in size, geomorphology and lithography. The following steps were followed:

1. Identification of zones similar to the study area in question. Related by lithology, volumetry and shape of the relief group, annual rainfall distribution. Different years were chosen for each zone; at least one landslide event had to be reported during that period, even if it was minor.
2. A simulation with a number of iterations equivalent to one year was operated by taking the rainfall history as input and launching the simulations with these. A reference year is taken because it is essential to populate the S_n variable with the rules given.
3. Periods of maximum rainfall were recorded, at these if there were no reports of landslides during those periods the training set would be constructed with the input

values from C.A. simulation (in the 24 h after rainfall) and as output the ISPRA characteristic susceptibility index was associated.

4. If, on the other hand, there were landslide events even of brave magnitude the values of the C.A. were assigned the index 6.0 (as previously defined).
5. By operating in this way, it was possible to construct a training set that led to convergence during SNN learning, thus obtaining all the modules in the pipeline.

Finally, we note the input of the SNN is not "commutative," so the value of the state variables coming from a surface C.A. has a different contribution from the C.A. placed in depth. It is noted that the two cellular automata are discriminated by the indices i, j, k that identify them and are identically georeferenced. It follows that the spatial location of the C.A. themselves brings information content to the SNN. With the proposed pipeline we also offer a methodology to overcome one of the most important obstacles in applying neural networks to landslide prevention, namely, how to map geographic, orographic, and volumetric information into them. [12–14]. The choice of SELUs was undertaken because it is a variant of RELU, it was built to improve some performance and convergence aspects during learning. The selection of SELUs (Scaled Exponential Linear Units) as the activation function in our methodology was a deliberate choice, driven by several important considerations. SELUs represent a variant of the widely used Rectified Linear Unit (RELU) activation function and were developed to address certain performance and convergence issues that can arise during the training of neural networks. One key reason for opting for SELUs is their ability to mitigate the "vanishing gradient" problem, a common challenge encountered in deep learning. The vanishing gradient problem can hinder the convergence of neural networks, particularly in deep architectures. SELUs, by design, tend to maintain gradients within a certain range, allowing for more efficient training and convergence. Furthermore, the choice of SELUs is well-supported by existing literature and research. They have been extensively studied and have demonstrated their effectiveness in various machine learning and deep learning applications. This established reliability and performance make SELUs a prudent choice for our methodology. In response to the observation, as this is an initial experimentation of the method, further experiments with other networks from the literature will be necessary to verify if similar results can be achieved. However, at this stage, it appears to us to be the most performant solution, [10].

6 Results and Conclusion

Once the pattern detector was obtained through SNN training, the validation activity was performed on the area chosen for the study, an area included in the Briga River Basin, an area subject to landslides over time.It is necessary to note that in the area under study an important landslide event occurred in 2009 and consequently the validation activity was aimed at verifying whether, through the input data relating to a previous year, the proposed system was able to verify in advance (2008) what actually happened in the following year (2009). In this regard, the simulation (operated with the developed software) started with the first iteration mapped on October 1, 2008 (exactly one year before the landslide events (post precipitation). It continued by operating precipitation acquisition throughout the same period. The output after the fourth month of simulation was considered significant; the output index provided averaged 4.25, in line with the ISPRA distribution. The iterations mapped with the date of Oct. 4, 2009, saw the index reach 5.4 and thus signal a significant deviation from ISPRA indices, signaling a worsening of the state of slope stability. Figure 7 summarizes the result obtained.

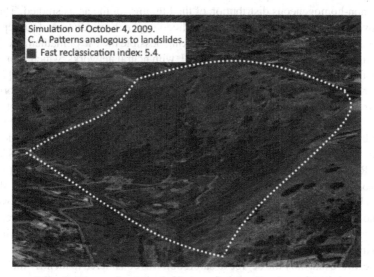

Fig. 7. The result of the simulation related to October 4, 2009.

Precisely the fact that the iteration corresponding to the date of 4 October 2009 returned an index of 5.4 in the platform (Fig. 7) is a useful indicator for the validation of the method precisely because it demonstrates how a priori an increase of the susceptibility index is estimated for a subsequent time period during which a landslide event was actually recorded. In fact, the predicted value (5.4) indicates a significant deviation from the indices provided by ISPRA (4.25), therefore signaling, a priori, a marked worsening of the state of stability of the slopes in 2009, as actually occurred in the same year with the consequent landslide recorded. The results obtained certainly suggest further investigation of the potentiality of the presented technique by validating the approach with a congruent case by comparison with another method already considered reliable.

In particular, it should be noted that the pattern detector used processes its outputs as a function of the states belonging to the entire given domain, and it is on this domain that it applies the inference; therefore, the calculated index must be assigned to the entire domain (this is the reason for the notable dimensions of the output represented in Fig. 7). If there was a need to confine the area to be observed with greater precision, multiple pattern detectors could be used for each area considered (sub domains). This "hybrid" configuration which provides a single simulation domain for the automata and multiple investigation subdomains for the neural networks should be considered as a case study to be addressed in future work.

Although conducting the study on a single location, the validation period of the results was one year, again in line with the expectation. As well as there was an indication of worsening of stability conditions just about the same time as the landslide events. Subsequent investigations must concern both the definition in the micro interactions between C.A. in a more complex manner and, above all, which take into account a complex and non-homogeneous distribution of the lithology of the areas studied. The work aims above all to introduce an innovative methodology in the prediction of susceptibility variation. Method which has the merit of making possible the use of mathematical models with emergent properties and above all A.I. with neural networks, which is presented in the literature as a very complex area in which to apply such methodologies, [11]. We will defer to further refinements of the method to incorporate contextual information derived from geological features of the terrain, seismic data, and the impact of human activities. As regards the construction of the training set, in order to increase the number of candidate areas to acquire information useful for identifying any ongoing deformations, we will rely on monitoring tools for suspect slopes and on SBAS-InSAR and PS-InSAR techniques, associating an estimated susceptibility value so as not to train the network exclusively with boundary values, [15]. Finally, it is underlined that the choice to have a single classification output derived from two considerations: we want to test the goodness of the method in general terms, and we also choose to give, in this work, greater reliability on the time domain than on the space domain, given the same complexity of the model and richness of the training set.

While aware that only the degree of saturation was considered to identify the stability conditions and that the saturation obviously depends on the type of soil formation and the drainage regime of the slope and despite the methodology used by us it therefore refers to an extremely simplified and not completely representative of the instability phenomenon, we believe it is useful to present the tested methodology while waiting to carry out further investigations and studies to obtain a more complete model that takes into account the variables neglected to date.

References

1. Spizzichino, D., Margottini, C., Trigila, A., Iadanza, C.: Landslide impacts in Europe: Weaknesses and strengths of databases available at European and national scale. In: Margottini, C., Canuti, P., Sassa, K. (eds.) Landslide Science and Practice, 73–80. Springer, Heidelberg (2013). https://doi.org/10.1007/978-3-642-31325-7_9
2. Reichenbach, P., Busca, C., Mondini, A.C., Rossi, M.: Land use change scenarios and landslide susceptibility zonation: the briga catchment test area (Messina, Italy). In: Lollino, G., Manconi, A., Clague, J., Shan, W., Chiarle, M. (eds.) Engineering Geology for Society and Territory –Volume 1, pp. 557–561. Springer, Cham (2015). https://doi.org/10.1007/978-3-319-09300-0_104
3. Bhattacharjee, K., Naskar, N., Roy, S., Das, S.: A survey of cellular automata: types, dynamics, non-uniformity and applications. Nat. Comput. **19**, 433–461 (2020)
4. Barrile, V., Cotroneo, F., Iorio, F., Bilotta, G.: An innovative experimental software for geomatics applications on the environment and the territory. In: Borgogno-Mondino, E., Zamperlin, P. (eds.) ASITA 2022. CCIS, vol. 1651, pp. 102–113. Springer, Cham (2022). https://doi.org/10.1007/978-3-031-17439-1_7

5. Bilotta, G., Genovese, E., Citroni, R., Cotroneo, F., Meduri, G.M., Barrile, V.: Integration of an innovative atmospheric forecasting simulator and remote sensing data into a geographical information system in the frame of agriculture 4.0 concept. AgriEngineering **5**(3), 1280–1301 (2023)

6. Hun, L.D., Min, K.D., Mo, J.J.: A unity-based simulator for tsunami evacuation with devs agent model and cellular automata. J. Korea Multimed. Soc. **23**(6), 772–783 (2020)

7. Sachidananda, M., Zrnić, D.S.: Rain rate estimates from differential polarization measurements. J. Atmos. Oceanic Tech. **4**(4), 588–598 (1987)

8. Kale, R.V., Sahoo, B.: Green-Ampt infiltration models for varied field conditions: a revisit. Water Resour. Manage **25**, 3505–3536 (2011)

9. Ciurleo, M., Ferlisi, S., Foresta, V., Mandaglio, M.C., Moraci, N.: Landslide susceptibility analysis by applying trigrs to a reliable geotechnical slope model. Geosciences **12**(18), 1–13 (2022)

10. Klambauer, G., Unterthiner, T., Mayr, A., Hochreiter, S.: Self-normalizing neural networks. In: Advances in Neural Information Processing Systems, vol. 30 (2017)

11. Zhang, D., Yang, J., Li, F., Han, S., Qin, L., Li, Q.: Landslide risk prediction model using an attention-based temporal convolutional network connected to a recurrent neural network. IEEE Access **10**, 37635–37645 (2022)

12. Vacondio, R., et al.: Grand challenges for smoothed particle hydrodynamics numerical schemes. Comput. Part. Mech. **8**(3), 575–588 (2020)

13. Barrile, V., Bilotta, G., Fotia, A.: Analysis of hydraulic risk territories: comparison between LIDAR and other different techniques for 3D modeling. WSEAS Trans. Environ. Dev. **14**, 45–52 (2018)

14. Wang, S., Zhang, K., van Beek, L.P.H., Tian, X., Bogaard, A.: Physically-based landslide prediction over a large region: scaling low-resolution hydrological model results for high resolution slope stability assessment. Environ Model Softw. **124**, 104607 (2021)

15. Yao, J., Yao, X., Liu, X.: Landslide detection and mapping based on SBAS-InSAR and PS-InSAR: a case study in Gongjue County, Tibet, China. Remote Sens. **14**(19), 4728 (2022)

Technological Services for Territory Planning and Management

A Land Monitoring Service for Local Public Administrations: The IRIDE EOS4LPA Lot 3 Project

Antonello Aiello[1]([✉]) [ID], Vincenzo Massimi[1], Nicolò Taggio[1], Raffaele Borrelli[1], Vincenzo Laurino[1], Elisa Filippi[1,2], Paolo Decaro[3], Fabio Lo Zito[4], Peppe D'Aranno[2,5], Maria Marsella[2,5], Dino Quattrociocchi[6], Alessandro Brunetti[7], and Marco Casucci[8]

[1] Planetek Italia srl, Via Massaua,12, Bari, Italy
aiello@planetek.it
[2] Sapienza University Rome, Piazzale A. Moro 5, Rome, Italy
[3] Spark Replay srl, Corso Francia 110, Torino, Italy
[4] Serco Italia SpA, Viale della Tecnica 161, Roma, Italy
[5] Survey Lab srl, Via Eudossiana 18, Roma, Italy
[6] e-GEOS SPA, Via Tiburtina 965, Rome, Italy
[7] NHAZCA srl, Via Bachelet 12, Rome, Italy
[8] EMSEE SPACE for ESA - IRIDE Integrated Project Team, Rome, Italy

Abstract. By addressing the green and digital transition challenges within the Next Generation EU, the Italian PNRR identified an investment in a new "constellation of constellations" of Low Earth Orbit satellites called IRIDE. By the end of 2026, the IRIDE Programme will develop a satellite infrastructure for Earth Observation (EO) to provide services to the Public Administration. Within IRIDE, the EOS4LPA Lot 3 project foresees the development of "Cross-Monitoring of Ground Motion and Hot Spots of Land Cover Change" service for local public administrations (LPA), including regional authorities, municipalities and hydrographic districts. The service will be developed by Planetek Italia (Prime Contractor), together with Serco Italia, Spark Reply, Survey Lab, e-geos and NHAZCA, to provide the following EO-based products by integrating existing operational solutions:

- the thematic grid ground motion (GGM)
- the burnt area map and fire severity map layers (BAM&FSM)
- the land cover change layer (LCC)
- the building stability assessment at the municipality scale (I-MODI).

All involved processing chains will be fed by available open satellite data (e.g., the Sentinels, Landsat, etc.) and monitoring services (e.g., EGMS and other Copernicus Core Services, data available within the LPAs repositories, etc.) until the forthcoming IRIDE data and services are ready.

IRIDE EOS4LPA aims to generate and increase LPA's awareness of the benefits of EO-based services for monitoring the territory. It will demonstrate such solutions' effectiveness and reliability in supporting everyday operations and decision-making processes, attaining their needs and reaching the quality requirements with a cost-effective approach.

E. Borgogno Mondino and P. Zamperlin (Eds.): ASITA 2023, CCIS 2088, pp. 99–108, 2024.
https://doi.org/10.1007/978-3-031-59925-5_8

Keywords: PNRR · EO · IRIDE · satellite service · ground motion · burnt area mapping · fire severity mapping · land cover change · building stability · local public administrations

1 Introduction

The challenges posed by the green and digital transition have prompted the Italian government to prioritise sustainable investments under the ambitious Next Generation EU initiative. As part of the comprehensive Italian National Recovery and Resilience Plan (PNRR), a ground-breaking project named IRIDE has been identified to address these challenges head-on. By the end of 2026, the IRIDE Programme aims to establish a revolutionary satellite infrastructure known as the "constellation of constellations" in the Low Earth Orbit (LEO). This new infrastructure, developed specifically for Earth Observation (EO) purposes, holds tremendous potential to revolutionise services provided to the Public Administration [1].

Within the broader scope of IRIDE, the EOS4LPA Lot 3 project stands out as a pivotal initiative. Its primary objective is to develop an innovative service called "Cross-Monitoring of Ground Motion and Hot Spots of Land Cover Change" for local public administrations (LPAs), including regional authorities, municipalities, and hydrographic districts. The project involves leading organisations such as Planetek Italia (Prime Contractor), Serco Italia, Spark Reply, Survey Lab, e-geos, and NHAZCA. Their collective expertise will integrate existing operational solutions and leverage the power of Earth Observation data to offer a range of essential products to LPAs.

The service provided by IRIDE EOS4LPA Lot 3 encompasses several crucial elements. The first is the development of a thematic grid for ground motion, enabling precise monitoring of terrain displacement. Additionally, the project will deliver comprehensive maps of burnt areas and fire severity, facilitating efficient disaster response and environmental management. The third component entails generating a dynamic land cover change layer to track land-use alterations and facilitate informed decision-making. Lastly, the project aims to conduct building stability assessments at the municipality scale, ensuring urban areas' safety and structural integrity.

To accomplish these objectives, IRIDE EOS4LPA Lot 3 will harness available open satellite data, including information from missions like Sentinels and Landsat and monitoring services like the European Ground Motion Service (EGMS) and the other Copernicus Core Services. Furthermore, the project will tap into the vast LPAs data repositories, establishing a seamless integration with existing resources until the forthcoming IRIDE data and services become available.

The goal of IRIDE EOS4LPA Lot 3 is to enhance the awareness of local public administrations regarding the remarkable benefits of EO-based services for territorial monitoring. By showcasing the effectiveness and reliability of these solutions in supporting everyday operations and decision-making processes, the project aims to meet the specific needs of LPAs and cost-effectively fulfil the stringent quality requirements.

In this conference paper, we will delve into the intricacies of the EOS4LPA Lot 3 project, exploring its objectives, methodologies, and anticipated outcomes. Through this examination, we aim to highlight the transformative potential of Earth Observation-based services for local public administrations, emphasising the value they bring to sustainable territorial management and efficient governance.

2 The "Cross-Monitoring of Ground Motion and Hot Spots of Land Cover Change" Service

The "Cross-Monitoring of Ground Motion and Hot Spots of Land Cover Change" service offers three EO-based products, yearly updated, to address monitoring ground motion and land cover changes. These products include 1) a thematic grid ground motion layer (GGM), 2) a burnt area map and fire severity map layers (BAM&FSM), and 3) a land cover change layer (LCC). To develop this solution, we have integrated and adapted four operational services into a unified Service Point, ensuring comprehensive information access for Champion Users. The integrated services are as it follows: Planetek's Rheticus® Safeland, which provides the thematic grid ground motion product; e-GEOS' FIREO, which offers the burnt area map and fire severity map products; Planetek's land cover changes mapping solution; and Survey Lab's I.MODI solution for building stability assessment at the municipality scale. Additionally, the service can incorporate additional end-user data to enhance the geo-analytics capabilities. All processing chains will utilise available satellite open data (e.g., Sentinels, Landsat) and satellite-based monitoring services (e.g., EGMS and the other Copernicus Core Services) until the upcoming IRIDE data and services become available (Fig. 1).

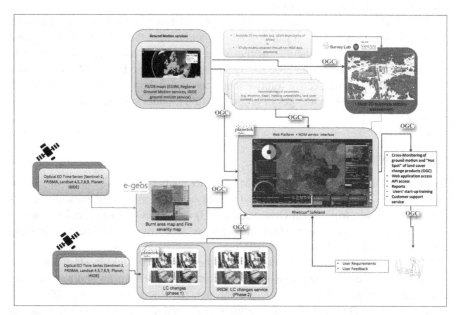

Fig. 1. Schema of the "Cross-Monitoring of Ground Motion and HOts Spots of Land Cover Change" service

2.1 The Involved Champion Users

Within the EOS4LPA Lot 3 project, the end-users, referred to as Champion Users, have already been identified and engaged by the European Space Agency (ESA). The Champion Users encompass Regione Lombardia (including the Comune di Milano, Comune di Bollate, and the Città Metropolitana di Milano), Regione Toscana (including the Comune di San Giuliano Terme), Regione Friuli-Venezia Giulia, Regione Campania, and Comune di Bari.

The project's primary objective is to place the Champion Users at the core of the process, comprehending their needs and providing them with a valuable solution that drives differentiation and impacts their processes. This is accomplished by employing diverse design research techniques to gather insights and identify articulated and unarticulated needs early in the process.

The project emphasises collaboration among the consortium and Champion Users, leveraging their technical capabilities, data lakes and knowledge. This collaboration occurs during the initial stages of the program and continues throughout the implementation phase, following the Agile framework. The approach comprises two main phases: "Create a vision" and "Make it happen". The first phase involves engaging Champion Users, conducting research activities, and employing design thinking to understand their genuine needs and pain points related to the "Cross-Monitoring of Ground Motion and Hot Spots of Land Cover Change". The insights gathered will guide the service's definition and refinement based on existing solutions. After validating the concept with Champion Users, a comprehensive solution is developed by integrating existing services to deliver a seamless and unique user experience.

The paper highlights an iterative process employed throughout the program, ensuring continuous user engagement to gather feedback and evolve the solution. This iterative approach aligns with the principles of the Agile framework, promoting flexibility and adaptability in the development process. By adopting this methodology, the project aims to provide a tailored and effective solution that meets the evolving needs of the Champion Users and addresses the challenges of ground motion monitoring and land cover change detection.

2.2 The Grid Ground Motion Layer

The thematic grid ground motion (GGM) product enables the assessment of ground motion levels by considering various land stability and risk analysis parameters. These parameters, derived from Earth Observation (EO) or non-EO sources, include factors such as morphology (elevation, slope), burnt areas, land cover, landslide and flooding susceptibility, and infrastructure and buildings.

To generate the GGM layer, we employ Rheticus® Safeland, an established and operational web-based solution designed for continuous monitoring and reporting on the stability of a given territory provided through the Rheticus® cloud platform [2]. Using satellite RADAR interferometry, this service evaluates trends and anomalies in surface displacement through mature and robust algorithms presented in the scientific literature [3, 4], assigning a level of concern to each elementary unit within the territory Rheticus® Safeland offers a comprehensive territory view, distinguishing stable regions from those affected by slow-moving landslides and subsidence. It serves as a complementary diagnostic tool, supplementing in-situ monitoring activities.

Through dynamic maps, reports, and alerts, Rheticus® Safeland empowers end-users, particularly Local Public Administrations (LPAs), to easily identify areas with high concern. This enables them to take preventive measures, enhance the organisation of field inspections, and effectively manage the territory while minimising potential damage. By providing accurate information, the service equips planners with the necessary knowledge to mitigate critical issues arising from an incomplete understanding of ongoing phenomena.

The Area of Interest (AoI) of each Champion User is subdivided into hexagonal-shaped elementary units, each covering an approximate area of 5 hectares. Classification of each AoI cell is based on displacement measurements derived from available ground motion maps (e.g., EGMS or regional ground motion services). Additionally, parameters related to land stability, such as morphology (elevation, slope), land cover, burnt areas, landslide and flooding susceptibility maps, and infrastructure and buildings, are considered during the classification process. The GGM layer will be provided with a yearly update frequency.

2.3 The Burnt Area and Fire Severity Layers

Burnt Area Map. Generating the burnt area map at a regional scale involves two main activities. Firstly, an automatic processing pipeline based on the FIREO framework collects satellite data and extracts polygons representing burnt areas. Secondly, a post-processing refinement step is performed to improve the accuracy of the map.

FIREO, the burnt area detection processor, exploits unsupervised analysis of spectral indexes derived from Sentinel-2 and Landsat 8 temporal series data. The project will be leveraged to ingest data from other high-resolution sensors, such as the upcoming IRIDE constellations. The production and potential reanalysis of the BAM requires a computational model based on three key principles: fully automated bulk processing, the processing platform's elasticity and scalability, and the generated products' reliability.

Fire Severity Map. Different approaches to mapping fire severity can be distinguished based on satellite image characteristics. In the EOS4LPA Lot 3 project, satellite optical images with Short-Wave Infrared (SWIR) channels, available as open data (e.g., Sentinel-2 and Landsat 8), are employed for fire severity analysis.

The SWIR channel method is widely used by the US Fire Science community (USFS) [5]. This method relies on the differenced Normalized Burn Ratio (dNBR) index to indicate the ecological impact of a fire on the landscape. Therefore, it is important to maintain consistent terminology. The terms "low severity" and "high severity" do not refer to the intensity of the fire itself but rather indicate the extent of vegetation loss caused by the fire. These severity levels reflect the ecological impact of the fire on the landscape. The severity assessment primarily concerns the extent of environmental transformations brought about by wildfires, specifically their impact on ecological communities. The objective is to gauge the levels of fire severity, including the most severe scenarios where ecological communities are completely devastated and must undergo a regeneration process from the ground up. The BAM & FSM layer will be provided with a yearly update frequency.

2.4 The Land Cover Change Layer

The Land Cover Change (LCC) product offers a valuable data layer that captures land cover changes over two specified periods. This service integrates optical images (e.g., Sentinel-2, Landsat 4, 5, 7, 8, 9, PlanetScope, etc.) and global maps (e.g., Copernicus Global Land Cover (CGLC) [6], ESA World Cover (EWC) [7], and Corine Land Cover (CLC) [8] to compute the precise LCC layer. It enables efficient monitoring of large areas while allowing customisation of the Minimum Mapping Unit (MMU).

The service employs two distinct approaches: a standard approach and a custom approach. In the standard approach, available land cover maps are combined. A post-processing step involving an aggregation module is applied to generate the LCC map as the difference between the two land cover maps.

On the other hand, the custom approach automatically empowers the service to automatically generate an updated LCC map for a specific year with a customised MMU produced by a median aggregation step. If updated land cover maps are unavailable or unsuitable, the service leverages optical multi-band satellite images, existing land cover maps, and a machine learning algorithm (XGBoost) [9]. The system creates the training set using the intersection of existing global land cover maps to apply the XGBoost algorithm. This combination facilitates the automatic generation of highly accurate land cover maps. The generated maps are then merged using a post-processing approach to produce the final LCC layer.

Both approaches offer flexibility in selecting the reference year and the desired MMU, accommodating the specific requirements of the analysis. The LCC layer will be provided with a yearly update frequency.

2.5 The Building Stability Layer

I.MODI structures-monitoring, developed by Survey Lab, offers building classification maps based on risk indicators derived from Differential Interferometric Synthetic Aperture Radar (DInSAR) analysis and qualitative and quantitative damage assessment. Building vector data is sourced from participating local public administrations or as an open-source dataset (e.g., OpenStreetMap). This advanced service evaluates structural behaviour and potential evolution within a single structure [10].

When integrated into the Rheticus® Safeland web app, I.MODI evaluates the risk associated with buildings exposed to natural hazards. By utilising DInSAR-based techniques, it overcomes the limitations of traditional monitoring methods by measuring displacement and deformation trends across numerous targets on the structure surface. This enables effective remote monitoring of entire buildings using satellite sensors, reducing the need for physical access to the structure. Additionally, the availability of extensive DInSAR datasets (spanning over 20 years) facilitates back-analysis studies for calibrating engineering models [11].

The I.MODI levels proposed for integration in the solution are: 1) Classification maps: These maps quantitatively classify buildings using hazard/settlement indicators extracted from DInSAR displacement trends and magnitudes. They provide a comprehensive view, quickly identifying the most critical structures. The maps are accessible through the WebGIS viewer [12]. 2) Single structure analysis level: Preliminary analysis:

DInSAR time series is statistically analysed to obtain reliable assessments of displacement rates on specific structural elements or portions of an aggregated structure. A standardised report, including graphical and numerical outcomes, is delivered through the service interface. 3) Semi-quantitative analysis: This assessment method uses a semi-automatic procedure to evaluate the structural condition and quantify potential damage from ground settlements. It includes a semi-quantitative approach and a comparative analysis against empirical thresholds defined in well-established technical literature. A standardised report is delivered through the service interface. 4) Quantitative analysis: This detailed analysis employs a quantitative approach using finite-element modelling to assess the structural condition and quantify damage at a single structure level. A technical report containing graphical and numerical outcomes is delivered through the service interface. The building stability layer will be provided with a yearly update frequency.

3   The Adoption of IRIDE Data

The IRIDE Program is set to revolutionise satellite Earth Observation with its new end-to-end system. Designed to fulfil the needs of the Italian Public Administration and unlock new commercial opportunities, IRIDE consists of three main components: the multi-sensor constellation for data acquisition and delivery (IRIDE Data), a range of Thematic Services catering to various topics and vertical applications (IRIDE Services), and Digital Twin applications offering scenario simulation capabilities (IRIDE Digital Twin).

Within the overall IRIDE system, IRIDE Data is central, serving as the backbone of the Data Layer for Public Administrations. By adopting IRIDE Data, the EOS4LPA Lot 3 project gains access to an extensive platform effectively linked to multiple supply channels, including IRIDE Data, Services, Digital Twin, and even Third-Party Data/Service/Applications providers. This connectivity ensures a seamless and efficient flow of information, acting as a broker between providers and consumers. As a result, the EOS4LPA Lot 3 project can tap into a wide range of data and services, catering to the needs of various end users and intermediate users across multiple sectors.

Incorporating IRIDE data and services into the project's design phase offers significant benefits. Users are made aware of the potential improvements that can be achieved through this integration. Notably, these improvements manifest in terms of enhanced resolution (both spatial and temporal) and improved thematic accuracy (thanks to advancements in signal-to-noise ratio and spectral resolution, encompassing Very High Resolution (VHR) to multispectral and hyperspectral data).

In particular, the data from the IRIDE constellation is poised to contribute to the grid ground motion (GGM) service by offering unparalleled spatial and temporal resolution, significantly improving the accuracy of land stability assessments. Additionally, its high-resolution imagery will be instrumental in enhancing the detection and analysis of land cover changes (LCC) layer, providing valuable insights into environmental transformations that were previously challenging to detect. Furthermore, integrating IRIDE data will greatly enhance the precision of burnt area mapping and fire severity assessment, improving the service's usefulness in responding to wildfires and managing their aftermath effectively. The IRIDE advancements are crucial in augmenting the existing services and algorithms that heavily depend on data from currently active missions.

This strategic approach ensures smooth and efficient incorporation of EOS4LPA Lot 3 service, minimising disruption and maximising the potential for success.

4 Learning Outcomes from Champion Users Interviews and Workshops

EO technologies have emerged as a valuable asset for public administration, enabling better understanding and management of environmental resources, disaster response, urban planning, and various other applications. However, integrating EO technologies into the existing organisational structures of public administration presents several challenges.

Collaboration and data sharing are fundamental to leveraging the full potential of EO technologies within public administration.

The benefits of open data policies, standardised data formats, and interoperability frameworks enable seamless data exchange and integration. Moreover, the capacity-building initiatives enhance the skills and knowledge of LPA personnel in utilising EO technologies effectively.

The successful integration of EO technologies requires a holistic approach encompassing organisational structures, governance mechanisms, collaboration frameworks, and capacity-building initiatives. By embracing these factors, public administrations can unlock the full potential of EO technologies and leverage them to address societal.

5 Conclusions

In conclusion, the Italian National Recovery and Resilience Plan (PNRR) has recognised the significance of green and digital transitions in the Next Generation EU initiative. As part of this plan, the IRIDE Program has been established to address these challenges and invest in a new network of Low Earth Orbit satellites. The IRIDE Program aims to develop an Earth Observation (EO) satellite infrastructure to provide valuable services to the Public Administration.

Within the IRIDE framework, the EOS4LPA Lot 3 project focuses on developing the "Cross-Monitoring of Ground Motion and Hot Spots of Land Cover Change" service for LPAs. By integrating existing operational solutions, the project aims to provide various EO-based products, including the thematic grid ground motion, burnt area map and fire severity map layers, land cover change layer, and produce a building stability assessment at the municipality scale.

These products will be generated using open satellite data such as Sentinels and monitoring services like EGMS and other Copernicus Core Services.

Additionally, data from LPAs repositories and other sources will be integrated until the forthcoming IRIDE data and services become accessible. The EOS4LPA project seeks to enhance the awareness of LPAs regarding the benefits of EO-based services for effective territory monitoring. It aims to demonstrate the reliability and effectiveness of these solutions in supporting everyday operations and decision-making processes while meeting quality requirements cost-effectively.

In conclusion, the EOS4LPA Lot 3 project stands to gain immensely from the IRIDE constellation's advent. With its comprehensive capabilities, extensive data access, and seamless integration, IRIDE will propel the EOS4LPA Lot 3 project to new heights in satellite Earth Observation, opening doors to unprecedented possibilities for valuable insights and applications.

Implementing the IRIDE Program and, specifically, the EOS4LPA project will contribute to advancing the green and digital transitions within the Next Generation EU framework. By harnessing the potential of Earth Observation and integrating existing solutions, the project will provide valuable insights and tools to local public administrations, enabling them to make informed decisions and efficiently manage their territories.

About the IRIDE Constellation. The IRIDE constellation is a programme of the European Union – NextGenerationEU – PNRR Italia Domani (Fig. 2).

Funded by the European Union – NextGenerationEU

Funded by the Presidency of the Council of Ministries pursuant to Article 1, paragraph 254, of Law 160/2019 Funded by the Presidency of the Council of Ministries from the Complementary Fund

Carried out under ESA Contract No. 4000140733/23/I-EB for the purposes of EO PNRR IRIDE PROGRAMME.

IT PNRR CUP J58G21000010007 (Unique Project Code identifying procurements actions in the frame of Italian PNRR - M1C2.4.2 Earth Observations interventions regarding ESA).

Disclaimer. Views expressed herein cannot be taken to reflect the official opinion of the European Union/European Commission/ESA/Presidency of Council of Ministers of the Italian Republic.

Views and opinions expressed are those of the author(s) only, and the European Union/European Commission/ESA/Presidency of Council of Ministers of the Italian Republic cannot be held responsible for any use which may be made of the information contained therein.

References

1. Piano Nazionale di Ripresa e Resilienza. https://www.italiadomani.gov.it/content/sogei-ng/it/it/home.html
2. Samarelli, S., et al.: Rheticus®: a cloud-based geo-information service for ground instabilities detection and monitoring. In: IGARSS 2018–2018 IEEE International Geoscience and Remote Sensing Symposium, pp. 2238–2240. IEEE (2018)
3. Amoroso, N., et al.: PSI clustering for the assessment of underground infrastructure deterioration. Remote Sens. **12**(22), 3681 (2020)
4. Nettis, A., Massimi, V., Nutricato, R., Nitti, D.O., Samarelli, S., Uva, G.: Satellite-based interferometry for monitoring structural deformations of bridge portfolios. Autom. Constr. **147**, 104707 (2023)
5. Key, C.H., Benson, N.C.: Landscape assessment: remote sensing of severity, the normalised burn ratio and ground measure of severity, the composite burn index. FIREMON: Fire effects monitoring and inventory system Ogden, Utah: USDA Forest Service, Rocky Mountain Res. Station (2005)

6. Copernicus Global Land Cover. https://land.copernicus.eu/global/products/lc
7. ESA World Cover. https://worldcover2020.esa.int/
8. Corine Land Cover. https://land.copernicus.eu/pan-european/corine-land-cover
9. Chen, T., Guestrin, C.: Xgboost: a scalable tree boosting system. In: Proceedings of the 22nd ACM sigkdd International Conference on Knowledge Discovery and Data Mining, pp. 785–794 (2016)
10. Arangio, S., Calò, F., Di Mauro, M., Bonano, M., Marsella, M., Manunta, M.: An application of the SBAS-DInSAR technique for the assessment of structural damage in the city of Rome. Struct. Infrastruct. Eng. **10**(11), 1469–1483 (2014)
11. Zeni, G., et al.: Long-term deformation analysis of historical buildings through the advanced SBAS-DInSAR technique: the case study of the city of Rome, Italy. J. Geophys. Eng. **8**(3), S1–S12 (2011)
12. Orellana, F., D'Aranno, P.J., Scifoni, S., Marsella, M.: SAR interferometry data exploitation for infrastructure monitoring using GIS application. Infrastructures **8**(5), 94 (2023)

Sen4MUN: A Prototypal Service for the Distribution of Contributions to the European Municipalities from Copernicus Satellite Imagery. A Case in Aosta Valley (NW Italy)

Tommaso Orusa[1,2]($\boxtimes$) , Duke Cammareri[2], Davide Freppaz[2], Pierre Vuillermoz[3], and Enrico Borgogno Mondino[1]

[1] Department of Agricultural, Forest and Food Sciences (DISAFA), GEO4Agri DISAFA Lab, Università degli Studi di Torino, Largo Paolo Braccini 2, 10095 Grugliasco, Italy
torusa@invallee.it

[2] IN.VA spa and Earth Observation Valle d'Aosta—eoVdA, Località L'Île-Blonde 5, 11020 Brissogne, Italy

[3] Local Authorities, Aosta Valley Autonomous Region, Piazza/Place Narbonne 3, 11020 Aosta, Italy

Abstract. Recently, the European space program Copernicus' Sentinel missions have allowed to develop several application services. One of them is the Sen4CAP system for the payment of contribution and control in agriculture according to the Common Agricultural Policy in light of the EU regulation (N. 746/2018). Nowadays, the technological transfer offered by remote sensing has permitted to rationalize and rethink many contribution methodologies at different scales. In this regard, to strengthen the use of free satellite data in ordinary administrative workflows, this work aims to evaluate the feasibility and prototypal development of a possible service called Sen4MUN for the distribution of contributions yearly allocated to local municipalities and scalable to all European regions.

The analysis was focused on considering the Aosta Valley Autonomous Region, NW Italy. A comparison between the Ordinary Workflow (OW) and the Sen4MUN approach which is based on yearly Land Cover classification according to EAGLE guidelines was performed by applying a 20 m buffer onto urban class (LC_b). This buffer was performed according to EEA-ISPRA soil consumption guidelines to avoid underestimating some areas that are difficult to map with Sentinel due to sensor limits and spectral mixing issues. The roads were included considering updated GIS databases. In particular, the assessment of the mapped urban anthropic surfaces used to quantify the contribution of adopting the two approaches was realized. An overall MAE of 0.82 km^2 was computed involving LC_b and OW demonstrating the effectiveness of Sen4MUN. The approach developed seems to be capable of providing useful data for contribution purposes to Public Administration.

Keywords: Sen4MUN · Sentinel 1-2 · Earth Observation Data · GIS · Contributions · Municipalities · Aosta Valley · Italy

E. Borgogno Mondino and P. Zamperlin (Eds.): ASITA 2023, CCIS 2088, pp. 109–125, 2024.
https://doi.org/10.1007/978-3-031-59925-5_9

1   Introduction

The European Space program Copernicus with the Sentinels missions has allowed the creation of many research projects (last access 14 July 2023 https://www.copernicus. eu/lv/documentation/project-database?order=title&sort=desc&page=5) and prototypes aiming at developing several services, many of them already available (last access 14 July 2023 https://www.copernicus.eu/en/copernicus-services) based on Earth Observation Data [1–6].

One of them, still under development, and one of the few that aims to use remote sensing in a highly economic key is the Sen4CAP system (last access 14 July 2023 http:// esa-sen4cap.org/) for the payment of contribution and control in agriculture according to the Common Agricultural Policy (CAP) in light of the EU regulation (N. 746/2018) [7, 8]. The CAP of the EU aims at sustainably improving European agricultural productivity while ensuring a decent standard of living for farmers within the EU. With an annual budget of roughly €59 billion, the CAP strengthens the competitiveness and sustainability of agriculture in Europe through a range of measures including direct payments, market measures, and rural development [9]. The largest part of the CAP budget is managed and controlled through its Integrated Administration and Control System (IACS) aiming to safeguard the CAP financials and support the farmers to submit their declarations [10]. The IACS is implemented at the national level through Paying Agencies of each EU member state. The current legal framework of the CAP from 2013 will be reformed by 2020 to modernize and simplify the CAP. In the CAP reform satellite Earth Observation (EO) is seen to take an increasing role in improving the IACS and making it more cost-efficient. It is worth noting that, the role of EO Data has been established as primary importance in this CAP reform, and their adoption is mandatory probably in 2024–2025, including perhaps also future planned missions like IRIDE by the Italian Space Agency in collaboration with European Space Agency. The main role is played by Sentinels missions in particular Sentinel-1 and Sentinel-2. In light of all this, the Sentinels for Common Agricultural Policy - Sen4CAP project aims at providing European and national stakeholders with CAP-validated algorithms, products, workflows, and best practices for agriculture monitoring relevant to the management of the CAP. The project will pay particular attention to providing evidence of how Sentinel-derived information can support the modernization and simplification of the CAP in the post-2020 timeframe. Sen4CAP has been set up by ESA in direct collaboration and on request from DG-Agri, DG-Grow, and DG-JRC [11–15].

Also, other space agencies worldwide like NASA (US), JAXA (Japan), CNES (France), DLR (Germany), and more recently the ASI (Italy) with the ambitious program IRIDE have developed or have planned to strengthen their services addressed to the private and public sector not only for research purposes but to promote technology transfer in many sectors [16–20]. At the same time, in recent years space race has opened up new frontiers of investment for individuals (in particular the large economic giants of the ICT) increasingly interested not only in developing their missions but above all in offering satellite services capable of satisfying numerous needs both for private and public sector. From forest management monitoring to precision agriculture to the management of migratory flows passing through the management of urban areas and planning of smart cities and much more [21–24]. One of the major private players is Google's

Planet, Maxar, or non-American players such as e-Geos in Italy, but new realities are emerging such as Albedo which aims to offer increasingly advanced services even if often without solid scientific validation of the products and offered services. Unfortunately, this bias in the services and products offered sometimes affects also those realized by public agencies leaving room for maneuvering to small research and entrepreneurial realities that have workflows for scientifically based and above all validated products and services [25]. Based on what has been illustrated, the present work aims to create another service at the moment prototypal based on European EO Data about the distribution of contributions intended for municipalities called Sen4MUN where Sen means Sentinels for Municipalities. It is worth noting that in Italy, as in other EU countries, the municipalities receive income from different types according to different criteria [26]. Current incomes of taxes, contributions, and equalization nature are made up of four income items: taxes, duties, and similar income; tax sharing; equalization funds from central administrations; equalization funds from the region or autonomous province. Generally, equalization funds from central administrations and regions or autonomous provinces are the most important and the main core of the approach suggested [27, 28]. Concerning this last income, it is estimated based on two approaches, the first one, is based on the estimated expenditure taking into account the previous year (the more you spend the more you receive money for local development within a budget defined at the regional and governmental level) the second a little more rigorous based on indicators of territorial development (in which, at least in Italy, the more the urbanized area develops, roads, housing units, factories and more in general areas for urban use, the higher the revenues) as a function of the resident population. Without going into the criticisms of the present approaches which certainly should be reviewed from the point of view of environmental sustainability dealing with SDGs goals [29]. Since the second approach permits an exploitation of the possibility offered by EO Data and GIS updated data; a system similar to the idea at the base of Sen4CAP has been suggested in this work. Urbanized components like other territorial bio-physical surfaces can potentially be mapped to the temporal resolution of Sentinels by translating the information produced by a medium-high resolution Land Cover into a datum that can be used by the administrations at an economic level [30]. To date, the monitoring of land cover is carried out only from an environmental point of view (to map the territory or quantify land consumption or for other research purposes), but without up to now deriving any form of economic quantification. To try to bridge this gap the Sen4MUN has been designed.

This approach aims to create a single and standardized approach for the item concerning government revenue or, as in the case of this study, regional revenues for local authorities considering also the environmental issues. Sen4MUN aims to replace the approach currently based on the estimation of territorial indicators obtained from statistical analyzes or very rough estimates used up to now by suggesting a more rigorous, efficient, and objective approach, based on the technology transfer offered by EO Data trying to suggest new approaches by space economy and actual and expected roles of Geomatics within the Next Generation EU framework from Science to Public Services.

In this regard, therefore, to strengthen the use of free European satellite data in Ordinary administrative Workflows such as Sen4CAP, this work has been focused to assess the feasibility and prototypal development of a possible service called Sen4MUN for the distribution of contributions yearly allocated to local municipalities and scalable to all European regions.

The analysis was focused on considering the Aosta Valley Autonomous Region, NW Italy, considered more complex to map with the Sentinels because of its geomorphology. A comparison between the ordinary methodology based on the estimation of territorial indicators (OW) with buffer zone retrieved with statistical surveys and the Sen4MUN approach which is based on yearly Land Cover classification according to EAGLE guidelines has been performed [31, 32]. Finally, due to the fact that some roads cannot be correctly mapped by Sentinels due to a GSD limiting factor, updated GIS geodatabases were included in the Sen4MUN prototypal approach.

2 Material and Methods

2.1 Study Area

The Sen4MUN workflow was developed considering the Aosta Valley Region in NW of Italy. Aosta Valley is a region in northwestern Italy bordering France and Switzerland as reported in Fig. 1. Located in the Western Alps, it is the smallest Italian Region but one of the most complex in terms of geo-morphology [21, 33].

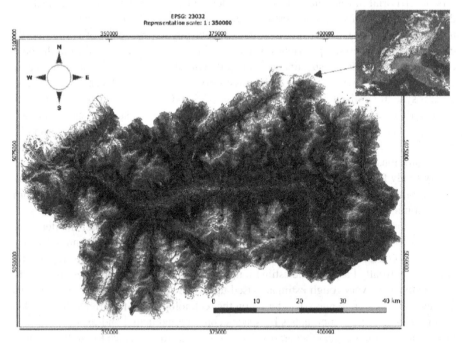

Fig. 1. Area of study, the Aosta Valley Autonomous Region in the NW Italy.

2.2 Ordinary Workflow

As explained in the introduction most Italian and European municipalities receive incomes according to territorial indicators concerning on urban development. This approach adopts statistical data obtained from regional or national offices that starts from building practices or territorial surveys performed within a time range (for example every 5 years) [27]. In the most likely cases, data comes from GIS databases, and the urban components areas and lengths are buffered 10–20 or 30 m (over-estimated) [30]. Anyway, also in the case of GIS geodatabase adoption Earth Observation data is not considered in this approach. In particular, this is the case of the Aosta Valley that follows the Cerutti approach since 1979 which is based on statistical surveys [34, 35]. This approach considered the following patterns: the municipal area, the urban and anthropic areas, the semi-anthropic areas (that includes all vegetated areas cultivated and not cultivated by humans), the sterile areas (that means all land unproductive surfaces, like water bodies and courses, snow and ice, rocks), roads lengths and finally real estate units. All these components are properly weighted and normalized according to financial criteria defined at regional, national, and European levels. It is wort noting that Ordinary Workflow (hereinafter called OW) is based on a simple weighted sum of factors that sum to total land cover. The role of Remote Sensing and GIS is to properly map these areas. Equations 12 and 13 are the core of this approach and each variable cab be obtained weighing each component (representing the input variable) properly mapped. Table 1 shows how each variable was obtained for the only purpose of a complete clarity, although the procedure is as described previously, a simple weighing of weighed remote sensed variables.

Table 1. Equations adopted in the approaches.

Description	Algorithm
Land Cover Areas (LCA)	$d = e + g + I$ (1) where, e = urban and anthropic area, g = semi-anthropic areas i = sterile areas d = municipality's administrative boundaries
LCA Weights	$f = e \times \alpha$ (2) where, e = urban and anthropic area, α = weight (in this case = 3) f = urban weighted area $h = g \times \beta$ (3) where, g = semi-anthropic area β = weight (in this case = 1.5) h = semi-anthropic weighted area $l = i \times \gamma$ (4) where, i = sterile area γ = weight (in this case = 0.5) l = sterile weighted area

(*continued*)

Table 1. (*continued*)

Description	Algorithm
Weighted areas	$m = f + h + l$ (5) where, f = urban weighted area, h = semi-anthropic weighted area l = sterile weighted area $n = \frac{m}{\sum_{i=1}^{n} m} \times 100$ (6) where, m = conventional municipality area $\sum_{i=1}^{n} m$ = sum of all the municipalities in the regional areas n = conventional weighted municipality area $o = n \times \delta$ (7) where, n = conventional weighted municipality area δ = weight (in this case = 50%) o = sub-conventional weighted municipality area
Roads length	$q = \frac{p}{\sum_{i=1}^{n} p} \times 100$ (8) where, p = roads length $\sum_{i=1}^{n} p$ = sum of all the municipalities in the regional areas q = roads weighted length $r = q \times \varepsilon$ (9) where, q = roads weighted length ε = weight (in this case = 30%) r = sub-conventional weighted roads length
Real estate units	$t = \frac{s}{\sum_{i=1}^{n} s} \times 100$ (10) where, s = real estate units $\sum_{i=1}^{n} s$ = sum of all the municipalities real estate units t = real estate weighted units $u = t \times \zeta$ (11) where, t = real estate weighted units ζ = weight (in this case = 20%) u = sub-conventional weighted real estate units

The sub-conventional parameters respectively obtained by Eqs. 7, 9, and 11 are used to obtain the following algorithms. These are adopted by the Regional offices in this case Aosta Valley Autonomous Region to assess the municipality contributions according to the financial budget foreseen annually.

$$v = o + r + u \tag{12}$$

where,

o = sub-conventional weighted municipality area
r = sub-conventional weighted roads length
u = sub-conventional weighted real estate units
v = sum of all sub-conventional weighted parameters

$$z = v \times \eta \tag{13}$$

where,

  v = sum of all sub-conventional weighted parameters
  η = a financial weight in this case 11.50%

2.3 Sen4MUN

The Sen4MUN approach is based on remote sensing and in particular yearly land cover, GIS-updated geodatabases, and deep learning to assess the parameters necessary as input in the OW. In this regard, urban and anthropic areas, semi-anthropic areas, and sterile areas are computed from Aosta Valley yearly Land Cover available at SCT Regional Geoportal and eoVdA webpages (last access 20 July 2023, https://eovda. regione.vda.it/ and https://geoportale.regione.vda.it/download/carta-copertura-suolo/). Road lengths are obtained by GIS viability monthly update geodatabase as well as real estate units including also deep learning. The reference year 2020 was considered. Land cover (LC) complies with EAGLE guidelines and is realized according to [31] and it is based on Sentinels missions (S1-S2) adopting Aosta Valley land cover [32]. Since LC classes are more detailed than those reported in the Cerutti approach, they were aggregated according to the Cerutti's description to integrate the Sen4MUN approach into the OW as follows in Table 2:

Table 2. Comparison between Land Cover EAGLE and Cerutti's classes.

Land Cover EAGLE class	Cerutti class
Urban and anthropic areas	urban and anthropic area
Shrubland and transitional woods	semi-anthropic areas
Woody crops	semi-anthropic areas
Water surfaces	sterile areas
Water courses	sterile areas
Needle-leaved forests	semi-anthropic areas
Broad-leaved forests	semi-anthropic areas
Mixed forests and moors	semi-anthropic areas
Permanent snow and ice	sterile areas
Natural grasslands and alpine pastures	semi-anthropic areas
Lawn pastures	semi-anthropic areas
Bare rocks	sterile areas
Discontinuous herbaceous vegetation of medium-low altitude	semi-anthropic areas
Sparse herbaceous vegetation at high altitudes	semi-anthropic areas
Alpine wetlands	sterile areas

Moreover, real estate units were extracted both from cadastral maps and deep learning adopting open-source libraries and Python scripts integrated with ESRI ArcGIS Pro v.2.8 for object detection and classification. Roads and building footprints were extracted using convolutional neural networks (CNNs) techniques onto the AGEA (Agency for Disbursements in Agriculture) 2020 ortho-rectified imagery, yearly available at the national level. Then from the roads extracted, they were checked with the viability geodatabase, and only municipality roads and areas were considered (as specifically reported in the regional laws) for the road length computation. Then, the land cover areas and roads were buffered 20 m for the following reasons: some sparse urban areas are difficult to map due to the GSD limits of Sentinels, then this threshold is adopted both in OW procedure and ISPRA Land Units in the case of soil consumption estimation [36]. Finally, the areas obtained were used as inputs in the OW equations reported in Table 1.

2.4 Validation

The validation of the Sen4MUN approach and in particular of the surface estimated adopting GIS and Earth Observation Data to retrieve the parameters adopted in the OW was realized by computing the Mean Absolute Error (MAE) according to the equation:

$$\text{MAE} = \frac{\sum_{i=1}^{n} |p_i - o_i|}{n} \tag{14}$$

where pi is the prediction (Sen4MUN component area), oi is the OW component areas estimated without remote sensing methods, and n is the number of municipalities in the Aosta Valley Autonomous Area equal to 74).

3 Results and Discussions

The Sen4MUN approach was validated by computing the MAE compared to the surfaces calculated with the traditional method from statistical surveys. It is worth noting that, for the reference year 2020, the main surfaces and inputs were computed both with OW and Sen4MUN for each municipality within the Aosta Valley. MAEs wre computed for Land cover components, road length and real estate units. A workflow of the Sen4MUN approach is provided in Fig. 2.

Since urban areas play a major role in the present regional regulation in terms of township incomes MAEs involving each municipality were computed also considering their road length and real estate units. The results obtained are reported in Table 3 and a general Table 4 in Supplementary material and in the graphs concerning on the MAEs reported in Fig. 3.

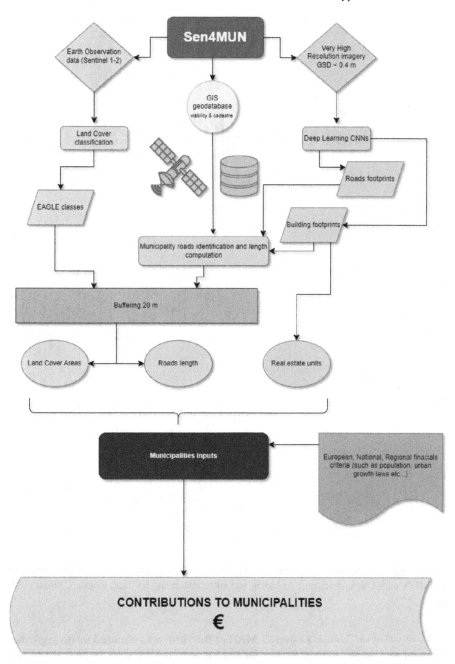

Fig. 2. Sen4MUN workflow.

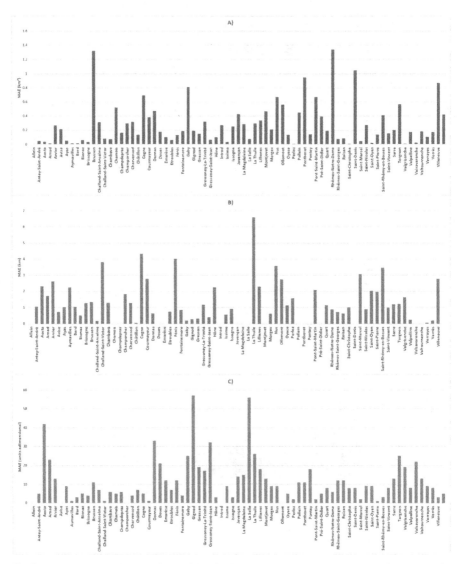

Fig. 3. MAEs computed per each municipality in Aosta Valley Autonomous Region comparing Sen4MUN with OW considering A) Urban and anthropic areas; B) Road length; C) Real estate units.

As reported in Table 3, an overall MAE of 0.16 km^2 was obtained involving Urban and anthropic areas, while 0.81 km for road length and 11 units in the case of real estate units. An overall MAE of 0.82 km^2 was computed involving all EAGLE Land cover classes respecting those computed with Cerutti's approach. It is worth noting that the errors came from Cerutti's approach which overestimate some areas. Furthermore, it is interesting to note that in all the components, for example urbanized areas, road lengths and real estate units, MAEs are associated with municipalities that underwent

Table 3. Overall MAEs and areas computed with both OW and Sen4MUN

Urban & Anthropic areas (km^2)			Road length (km)			Real Estate Units		
Sen4MUN	OW	MAE	Sen4MUN	OW	MAE	Sen4MUN	OW	MAE
103.9	92.1	0.16	1686.7	1626.4	0.81	303049	293214	133

more changes in at least one of the components in the reference year. Unlike what can be derived from the MAEs here computed, the Sen4MUN system is more effective in monitoring territorial changes because it is based on satellite and GIS data updated at a high temporal frequency than the ordinary system. The MAEs obtained allow the transferability of the new approach and possible replacement of the ordinary one even in an Alpine reality such as the one investigated. In fact, MAEs are generally higher in mountains areas than those obtainable in lowland areas due to the limiting factors affecting some remote sensing applications.

The results show the consistency of the methods. Furthermore, the procedure adopts free worldwide coverage data. The creation of Land Covers on an annual, biennial, or monthly basis or even on a time scale of Sentinels (potentially every 5 days) allows continuous monitoring of territorial dynamics. Moreover, this activity is part of the actions that each European country carries out for the monitoring of soil consumption and that the regions or provinces carry out to offer detailed products according to the guidelines of the European Environmental Agency. Furthermore, the availability for the administration of a regional air flight with very higher resolution imagery (like an AGEA flight), albeit for agricultural purposes, allows this type of data to be integrated into other service chains. Such as in the case of Sen4MUN to extract the footprint of buildings and roads thus making public spending more efficient through the expansion of derivable products and services. Naturally, the critical points in the Sen4MUN approach, result in a correct mapping and knowledge of Geomatics and Remote Sensing and their limits. Such as the most suitable approach (hierarchical, single-directed, data fusion, etc.), the classification algorithms, as well as, the input data that best respond to the components to be mapped, etc... Furthermore, the definition of the optimal number of training areas validation sets according to the area to be mapped is crucial in obtaining high accuracies and minimization of errors. Despite this work, a ready land cover has been adopted with an overall accuracy upper than 0.94, the whole procedure considering all these issues has been tackled in previous scientific literature involving the Aosta Valley territory [14, 21, 31–33]. In fact, in the case of a stand-alone and not prototype of this service at an application level not only on a regional or national scale, but on a European scale given the characteristics of the continent, the optimal solution would be to implement a regulated procedure, but which gives a certain degree of freedom in the algorithms and training sets (providing only thresholds) so that chains capable of responding best according to the area to be mapped are developed. Sen4CAP has been excessively standardized also in the algorithms making it less performing in the mountain areas. The need to standardize as much as possible a procedure that moves economic contributions is crucial for large-scale regulation, but this is done with the support of researchers, technicians, and academic experts and after several experiments in UE, to better define the operational leans and freedoms useful for developing consistent products and services for each European reality without creating disparities and differences. The use of the prototypal Sen4MUN Aosta Valley has made it possible to make the procedure for assigning contributions to municipalities more objective through the use of Sentinel data and updated GIS geodatabases, favoring technology transfer and the implementation of a possible new service within the Copernicus program and other future programs such as IRIDE capable of offering increasingly high spatial and temporal resolution data [37–41] useful for direct applications to the public sector.

4 Conclusion

The results obtained show how Sen4MUN can be used as a standard procedure for assigning contributions to municipalities. The procedure is consistent and in line with the Ordinary territorial Workflow based on statistical surveys without the use of Earth Observation Data, Deep Learning, and Geodatabase. Although the system has been tested and used on a prototype level in Aosta Valley, it can be scaled up to other Italian and European regions. The hope is that this service will become operational and spread to all member countries of the European Union as well as other national realities. Sen4MUN could join other services; coming from various Earth observation programs such as Copernicus, favoring an ever more massive technology transfer to the public sector by rationalizing activities and processes with plural activities with a view to the ever-increasing importance of Geomatics in management flows and implementation planners of local, national and European policies. Finally, Sen4MUN seems to be capable of providing useful data for contribution purposes to Public Administration.

Acknowledgments. Thanks to the Regione Autonoma Valle d'Aosta and INVA spa and eoVdA, for having made this work possible, and in particular the head of the Regional Cartographic Office Chantal Tréves, and to Enti Locali e Ufficio finanza e contabilità degli enti locali della Regione Autonoma Valle d'Aosta and in particular, the head Tiziana Vallet, and Stefania Fanizzi, Nicoletta Berno, Emanuela Oro, Alessandra Sibona. Finally, the Geo4Agri DISAFA Lab colleagues and Annalisa Viani for the great support.

Supplementary Material

Table 4. MAEs and areas computed with both OW and Sen4MUN (S4M).

Aosta Valley municipalities	Urban areas (km²)			Roads length (km)			Real estate units		
	S4M	OW	MAE	S4M	OW	MAE	S4M	OW	MAE
Allein	0.28	0.33	0.05	16.37	15.32	1.05	643	638	5
Antey-Saint-André	1.04	1.00	0.04	17.98	15.67	2.31	3250	3208	42
Aosta	9.58	9.57	0.01	106.26	104.55	1.71	65073	65050	23
Arnad	1.68	1.41	0.27	29.34	26.73	2.61	2614	2601	13
Arvier	0.87	0.66	0.21	22.73	22.02	0.71	1970	1971	1
Avise	0.45	0.50	0.05	12.59	11.58	1.00	899	890	9
Ayas	2.84	2.85	0.01	21.28	19.04	2.24	10022	10021	1
Aymavilles	1.37	1.39	0.01	31.05	30.03	1.02	3349	3346	3
Bard	0.26	0.20	0.06	3.04	2.56	0.49	320	315	5
Bionaz	0.55	0.58	0.03	15.22	13.95	1.26	626	622	4
Brissogne	2.11	0.79	1.32	19.78	18.46	1.32	1510	1499	11
Brusson	1.55	1.86	0.31	28.91	28.75	0.16	5229	5222	7
Challand-Saint-Anselme	0.85	0.93	0.08	19.30	15.49	3.81	3231	3230	1
Challand-Saint-Victor	0.63	0.70	0.07	16.93	15.66	1.27	1776	1770	6
Chambave	1.39	0.88	0.52	24.36	25.13	0.77	1804	1799	5
Chamois	0.17	0.33	0.16	3.15	3.15	0.00	568	562	6
Champdepraz	0.94	0.65	0.29	17.60	15.78	1.81	1411	1412	1
Champorcher	0.69	1.00	0.31	22.97	21.72	1.25	2355	2351	4
Charvensod	1.55	1.42	0.13	9.95	9.90	0.05	3897	3890	7
Châtillon	2.97	2.28	0.69	47.63	43.32	4.31	7515	7510	5
Cogne	2.10	1.72	0.38	25.21	22.44	2.78	5528	5527	1
Courmayeur	3.37	2.90	0.47	53.52	52.90	0.62	15334	15301	33
Donnas	1.90	1.72	0.18	26.89	28.21	1.32	4069	4048	21
Doues	0.60	0.70	0.10	24.41	27.03	2.62	1329	1317	12
Emarèse	0.29	0.34	0.06	13.57	12.85	0.72	984	977	7
Etroubles	0.70	0.57	0.13	18.90	14.89	4.01	1314	1302	12
Fénis	1.47	1.28	0.18	27.13	26.30	0.83	3409	3405	4
Fontainemore	0.66	1.47	0.81	26.91	26.74	0.16	1560	1535	25
Gaby	0.61	0.80	0.19	9.51	9.25	0.26	1394	1337	57
Gignod	1.37	1.23	0.15	30.44	30.14	0.30	2692	2673	19
Gressan	2.84	2.52	0.32	27.43	26.26	1.17	8330	8313	17
Gressoney-La-Trinité	0.82	0.88	0.06	4.18	3.80	0.38	1944	1912	32
Gressoney-Saint-Jean	1.86	1.97	0.10	18.56	16.32	2.25	5350	5347	3
Hône	1.16	0.89	0.27	13.00	14.51	1.52	2226	2226	0
Introd	0.56	0.53	0.03	13.87	13.33	0.54	1444	1435	9
Issime	0.77	1.02	0.25	10.47	9.56	0.91	1263	1260	3

(continued)

Table 4. (*continued*)

Aosta Valley municipalities	Urban areas (km²)			Roads length (km)			Real estate units		
	S4M	OW	MAE	S4M	OW	MAE	S4M	OW	MAE
Issogne	1.50	1.08	0.42	26.35	30.83	4.48	2305	2291	14
Jovençan	0.72	0.43	0.28	10.45	13.32	2.87	974	959	15
La Magdeleine	0.28	0.36	0.08	5.46	5.62	0.16	1157	1101	56
La Salle	2.25	1.95	0.29	42.81	36.21	6.59	7445	7419	26
La Thuile	1.77	1.44	0.33	27.23	24.94	2.28	7223	7205	18
Lillianes	0.52	0.98	0.46	19.48	22.28	2.80	1160	1147	13
Montjovet	1.62	1.42	0.21	39.41	38.81	0.60	3271	3262	9
Morgex	2.33	1.66	0.67	22.97	19.41	3.57	6982	6973	9
Nus	2.44	1.88	0.56	54.40	51.67	2.73	5125	5125	0
Ollomont	0.42	0.55	0.13	8.80	7.68	1.12	965	960	5
Oyace	0.27	0.26	0.01	3.50	1.93	1.57	475	473	2
Perloz	0.46	0.91	0.45	19.45	21.95	2.51	1248	1237	11
Pollein	2.11	1.16	0.95	10.27	14.13	3.86	2217	2206	11
Pontboset	0.33	0.47	0.14	10.31	11.32	1.01	809	791	18
Pontey	1.17	0.50	0.67	6.80	4.72	2.07	1296	1294	2
Pont-Saint-Martin	2.00	1.61	0.39	21.39	21.49	0.10	5165	5160	5
Pré-Saint-Didier	1.10	0.91	0.19	20.58	19.46	1.13	5925	5917	8
Quart	3.90	2.56	1.34	59.69	58.83	0.86	6495	6489	6
Rhêmes-Notre-Dame	0.31	0.39	0.08	6.28	5.58	0.70	719	707	12
Rhêmes-Saint-Georges	0.31	0.39	0.08	6.19	5.57	0.62	820	808	12
Roisan	0.66	0.66	0.01	13.44	12.45	0.99	1455	1447	8
Saint-Christophe	2.98	1.93	1.04	44.18	44.32	0.15	5519	5511	8
Saint-Denis	0.49	0.53	0.04	9.98	6.92	3.06	1163	1161	2
Saint-Marcel	1.46	1.19	0.27	34.99	34.13	0.86	2308	2299	9
Saint-Nicolas	0.46	0.48	0.02	19.19	17.17	2.02	1184	1175	9
Saint-Oyen	0.35	0.22	0.14	7.68	5.72	1.96	556	555	1
Saint-Pierre	2.22	1.82	0.41	40.67	37.22	3.45	5225	5222	3
Saint-Rhémy-en-Bosses	0.88	0.73	0.15	19.48	18.51	0.98	1274	1266	8
Saint-Vincent	2.32	2.13	0.20	40.48	39.29	1.19	8956	8943	13
Sarre	2.74	2.18	0.56	41.53	40.33	1.21	6616	6591	25
Torgnon	1.10	1.10	0.00	21.17	19.56	1.61	4332	4313	19
Valgrisenche	0.36	0.54	0.17	14.00	13.78	0.22	859	851	8
Valpelline	0.60	0.62	0.02	13.58	14.25	0.67	1322	1300	22
Valsavarenche	0.48	0.66	0.18	8.46	9.29	0.83	1036	1023	13
Valtournenche	2.76	2.66	0.10	37.56	37.51	0.05	13870	13861	9
Verrayes	1.76	1.59	0.17	26.29	26.12	0.17	3218	3210	8
Verrès	2.14	1.27	0.87	13.50	10.74	2.77	3956	3953	3
Villeneuve	1.43	1.01	0.42	28.31	30.04	1.73	2192	2187	5
TOTAL	103.9	92.1	**0.16**	1686.7	1626.4	**0.81**	303049	293214	**11**

References

1. Matevosyan, H., Lluch, I., Poghosyan, A., Golkar, A.: A value-chain analysis for the Copernicus earth observation infrastructure evolution: a knowledgebase of users, needs, services, and products. IEEE Geosci. Remote Sens. Mag. **5**, 19–35 (2017)
2. Žlebir, S.: Copernicus earth observation program. 40th COSPAR Sci. Assembly **40**, A0-1 (2014)
3. Schroedter-Homscheidt, M., et al.: The Copernicus atmosphere monitoring service (CAMS) radiation service in a nutshell. In: 22nd SolarPACES Conference 2016 (2016)
4. Szantoi, Z., Strobl, P.: Copernicus Sentinel-2 Calibration and Validation. Taylor & Francis (2019)
5. Thépaut, J.-N., Dee, D., Engelen, R., Pinty, B.: The Copernicus programme and its climate change service. In: IGARSS 2018–2018 IEEE International Geoscience and Remote Sensing Symposium, pp. 1591–1593. IEEE (2018)
6. Peuch, V.-H., et al.: The Copernicus atmosphere monitoring service: from research to operations. Bull. Am. Meteor. Soc. **103**, E2650–E2668 (2022)
7. Koetz, B., et al.: SEN4CAP sentinels for CAP monitoring approach. In: Proceedings of the 2019 JRC IACS Workshop (2019)
8. Sarvia, F., De Petris, S., Orusa, T., Borgogno-Mondino, E.: MAIA S2 versus Sentinel 2: spectral issues and their effects in the precision farming context. In: Gervasi, O., et al. (eds.) ICCSA 2021. LNCS, vol. 12955, pp. 63–77. Springer, Cham (2021). https://doi.org/10.1007/978-3-030-87007-2_5
9. Sishodia, R.P., Ray, R.L., Singh, S.K.: Applications of remote sensing in precision agriculture: a review. Remote Sens. **12**, 3136 (2020)
10. Lupia, F., Antoniou, V.: Copernicus Sentinels missions and crowdsourcing as game changers for geospatial information in agriculture. GEOmedia. **22** (2018)
11. Carella, E., Orusa, T., Viani, A., Meloni, D., Borgogno-Mondino, E., Orusa, R.: An integrated, tentative remote-sensing approach based on NDVI entropy to model canine distemper virus in wildlife and to prompt science-based management policies. Animals **12**, 1049 (2022)
12. De Marinis, P., et al.: Supporting pro-poor reforms of agricultural systems in eastern DRC (Africa) with remotely sensed data: a possible contribution of spatial entropy to interpret land management practices. Land **10**, 1368 (2021)
13. Orusa, T., Mondino, E.B.: Landsat 8 thermal data to support urban management and planning in the climate change era: a case study in Torino area, NW Italy. In: Remote Sensing Technologies and Applications in Urban Environments IV, p. 111570O. International Society for Optics and Photonics (2019)
14. Viani, A., Orusa, T., Borgogno-Mondino, E., Orusa, R.: Snow metrics as proxy to assess sarcoptic mange in wild boar: preliminary results in Aosta Valley (Italy). Life **13**, 987 (2023)
15. Orusa, T., Viani, A., Cammareri, D., Borgogno Mondino, E.: A Google earth engine algorithm to map phenological metrics in mountain areas worldwide with landsat collection and Sentinel-2. Geomatics **3**, 221–238 (2023)
16. Amani, M., et al.: Google earth engine cloud computing platform for remote sensing big data applications: a comprehensive review. IEEE J. Sel. Top. Appl. Earth Observ.Remote Sens. **13**, 5326–5350 (2020)
17. Orusa, T., Borgogno Mondino, E.: Exploring short-term climate change effects on rangelands and broad-leaved forests by free satellite data in Aosta Valley (Northwest Italy). Climate **9**, 47 (2021)
18. Orusa, T., Orusa, R., Viani, A., Carella, E., Borgogno Mondino, E.: Geomatics and EO data to support wildlife diseases assessment at the landscape level: a pilot experience to map infectious Keratoconjunctivitis in Chamois and phenological trends in Aosta Valley (NW Italy). Remote Sens. **12**, 3542 (2020)

19. Bagliani, M.M., Caimotto, M.C., Latini, G., Orusa, T.: Lessico e Nuvole: le parole del cambiamento climatico (2019)
20. Caimotto, M.C., Fargione, D., Furiassi, C.G., Orusa, T., Alex, P., et al.: Parlare è pensare. In: Lessico e nuvole: le parole del cambiamento climatico (seconda edizione), pp. 281–284. Università degli Studi di Torino (2020)
21. Orusa, T., Viani, A., Moyo, B., Cammareri, D., Borgogno-Mondino, E.: Risk assessment of rising temperatures using landsat 4–9 LST time series and meta® population dataset: an application in Aosta Valley, NW Italy. Remote Sens. **15**, 2348 (2023)
22. Samuele, D.P., Filippo, S., Orusa, T., Enrico, B.-M.: Mapping SAR geometric distortions and their stability along time: a new tool in Google Earth Engine based on Sentinel-1 image time series. Int. J. Remote Sens. **42**, 9126–9145 (2021)
23. Tartaglino, A., Orusa, T.: Bilancio energetico/Energy Balance in Lessico e nuvole: le parole del cambiamento climatico II ed. Università degli studi Torino. In: Bilancio Energetico, pp. 61–63. Università degli studi di Torino (2020)
24. Borgogno-Mondino, E., Fissore, V.: Reading greenness in urban areas: possible roles of phenological metrics from the copernicus HR-VPP dataset. Remote Sens. **14**, 4517 (2022)
25. Gascon, F., et al.: Copernicus Sentinel-2 mission: products, algorithms and Cal/Val. In: Earth Observing Systems XIX, p. 92181E. International Society for Optics and Photonics (2014)
26. Louvin, R., et al.: Il comitato europeo delle regioni: bilancio e rilancio. In: Il Comitato delle Regioni, Regioni e Regioni alpine: riflessioni ed esperienze sul futuro dell'Unione europea, pp. 61–68. Università degli Studi di Trento. Facoltà di Giurisprudenza (2022)
27. Louvin, R., et al.: Flessibilità fiscale e zone franche. Profili giuridici e finanziari. IUS PUBLICUM EUROPAEUM. NUOVA SERIE **9**, 1–240 (2022)
28. Louvin, R., et al.: L'évolution des compétences communales en Italie: analogies et discordances par rapport au cadre français. In: Quelle (s) commune (s) pour le XXIe siècle?, Approche de droit comparé, pp. 193–216. L'Harmattan (2018)
29. Wunder, S., Kaphengst, T., Frelih-Larsen, A.: Implementing land degradation neutrality (SDG 15.3) at the national level: general approach, indicator selection and experiences from Germany. In: Ginzky, H., Dooley, E., Heuser, I., Kasimbazi, E., Markus, T., Qin, T. (eds.) International Yearbook of Soil Law and Policy 2017, vol. 2017, pp. 191–219. Springer, Cham (2018). https://doi.org/10.1007/978-3-319-68885-5_11
30. Congedo, L., Sallustio, L., Munafò, M., Ottaviano, M., Tonti, D., Marchetti, M.: Copernicus high-resolution layers for land cover classification in Italy. J. Maps **12**, 1195–1205 (2016)
31. Orusa, T., Cammareri, D., Borgogno Mondino, E.: A scalable earth observation service to map land cover in geomorphological complex areas beyond the dynamic world: an application in Aosta Valley (NW Italy). Appl. Sci. **13**, 390 (2022)
32. Orusa, T., Cammareri, D., Borgogno Mondino, E.: A possible land cover EAGLE approach to overcome remote sensing limitations in the Alps based on Sentinel-1 and Sentinel-2: the case of Aosta Valley (NW Italy). Remote Sens. **15**, 178 (2022)
33. Orusa, T., Viani, A., Borgogno-Mondino, E.: Earth observation data and geospatial deep learning AI to assign contributions to European municipalities Sen4MUN: an Em-pirical application in Aosta Valley (NW Italy). Land **13**(1), 80 (2024)
34. Cerutti, P.: Uso del territorio e forme contributive. UTET, Torino (1979)
35. Rosanò, A., et al.: La riforma della legge della Regione Autonoma Valle d'Aosta in materia di attività condotte nell'ambito delle politiche promosse dall'Unione europea. In: Quaderni AISDUE 1/2023, pp. 359–372. Editoriale Scientifica (2023)
36. Strollo, A., et al.: Land consumption in Italy. J. Maps **16**, 113–123 (2020)
37. Viani, A., et al.: R07. 1 Tick's suitability habitat maps and tick-host relationships in wildlife. A one health approach based on multitemporal remote sensed data, entropy and Meta® population dataset in Aosta Valley, NW Italy. In: GeoVet 2023 International Conference (2023)

38. Viani, A., et al.: Bartonella spp. Distribution assessment in red foxes (Vulpes vulpes) coupling geospatially-based techniques. In: Atti SISVet, p. 69. SISVet (2023)

39. Orusa, T., Viani, A., Borgogno-Mondino, E.: IRIDE the Euro-Italian earth observation program: overview, current progress global expectations and recommendations. Perspective **2**, 10 (2023)

40. Latini, G., Bagliani, M., Orusa, T.: Lessico e nuvole: le parole del cambiamento climatico. Youcanprint (2021)

41. Floris, I., et al.: Detection and characterization of zoonotic pathogens in game meat hunted in Northwestern Italy. Animals **14**(4), 562 (2024)

Monitoring and Forecasting Land Cover Dynamics Using Remote Sensing and Geospatial Technology

Alessandro Vitale$^{(\boxtimes)}$ (iD) and Carolina Salvo (iD)

University of Calabria, 87036 Rende, CS, Italy
{alessandro.vitale,carolina.salvo}@unical.it

Abstract. In recent years, the continuous increase in world population has led to a consequent rise in demand for natural resources and living spaces, deteriorating essential environmental services. Therefore, understanding spatiotemporal dynamics in land cover changes has become an essential area of research for scientists to deal with the challenges of making sustainable cities. This study aims to present an innovative methodology based on remote sensing techniques and Geographic Information Systems (GIS) to monitor and predict urban growth and greening transformation patterns. A Cellular Automata model (CA-ANN) is developed to evaluate the driving factors influencing land cover dynamics. The results showed a process of urbanization oriented towards excessive housing dispersion and how a land cover evolution may be more sustainable with scientific spatial plans that consider facilities for people and ecological protection. The proposed method can represent a valid Decision Support System quantifying the land cover dynamics in changing environmental settings and can serve as a helpful tool for sustainable urban development.

Keywords: GIS · Sustainable Development · Land Cover changes

1 Introduction

In recent years, combining multi-temporal data from different satellites and Remote Sensing (RS) techniques have allowed researchers to obtain more comprehensive and accurate information about the Earth's surface with the possibility of extracting valuable information in decision-making [1] and Land Cover (LC) classification [2].

Thanks to free and open data policies, the European Space Agency (ESA), in collaboration with the European Commission (EC), developed the Copernicus program to provide continuous and reliable Earth observation data for environmental monitoring, climate research, disaster management, and sustainable development. The EU's Copernicus Sentinel constellation offers a synthetic aperture radar (SAR) sensor (Sentinel-1 [3]), as well as a multispectral imaging instrument (Sentinel-2 [4–6]) that captures high-resolution optical images of the Earth's land and coastal areas.

Similarly, NASA provides a wide range of satellite products for various applications and research purposes, such as Landsat [7], in collaboration with the United States

E. Borgogno Mondino and P. Zamperlin (Eds.): ASITA 2023, CCIS 2088, pp. 126–140, 2024.
https://doi.org/10.1007/978-3-031-59925-5_10

Geological Survey (USGS), which offers detailed and continuous observations of the Earth's surface, allowing for land cover mapping, change detection, and land surface temperature monitoring.

An accurate assessment of LC maps is crucial for making informed decisions about land use, conservation, urban development, and natural resource management for biodiversity conservation, ecosystem restoration, and assessing the impacts of human activities on the environment [8]. Despite the expanding amount of satellite images and LC data provided by spatial agencies, these are affected by an excessive aggregation level, and often, the satellite images don't have the required spatial and temporal resolution. Therefore, creating an IT platform based on Machine Learning (ML) and Deep Learning (DL) algorithms that can be interfaced with GIS systems allows several advantages, including automated data analysis, improved accuracy, scalability, data integration and interoperability, and real-time processing and predictions.

Using the RS imagery data, Neural Networks can be considered the basis of DL algorithms and have been used in remote sensing applications for many years. Before the development of DL, the remote-sensing research community shifted its attention from neural networks to support vector machine (SVM) and ensemble classifiers, such as random forest (RF), for image classification and other tasks (for example, Land Use change detection). SVM performs in applications characterized by high-dimensionality data and limited training samples. Instead, RF is easy to use and generally has high accuracy. Other classical/traditional algorithms include Mahalanobis distance (MD), hidden Markov models, spectral angle mapper (SAM), radial basis function (RBF), decision tree (DT), fuzzy adaptive resonance theory-supervised predictive mapping (Fuzzy ARTMAP), multilayer perception (MLP), naive Bayes (NB), maximum likelihood classifier (MLC) and fuzzy logic [9–11]. Since 2014, the remote-sensing community has shifted its attention to DL models that can automatically learn features directly from raw satellite imagery, eliminating the need for manual feature engineering and processing large amounts of data. Algorithms such as convolutional neural networks (CNNs), recurrent neural networks (RNNs), and deep neural networks (DNNs) [12–15] guarantee better results and better RS imagery classification and segmentation concerning traditional ML methods. Among the network architectures based on CNNs, the U-Net model is characterized by a U-shaped architecture, skip connections, and multi-resolution feature fusion, contributing to its strengths in semantic segmentation tasks. These characteristics enable accurate and detailed LC classification, making U-Net a popular choice for mapping and monitoring applications [16–21].

Moreover, in recent years, with the combination of the great potential of RS, GIS, and DL techniques like U-Net, researchers and practitioners can benefit from the strengths of each component to improve the accuracy and efficiency of land cover mapping and analysis for a variety of applications, including urban and territorial planning and management, sustainable natural resource management and detecting global change issues [22]. Indeed, DL algorithms can classify and segment thousands of RS images, and GIS enables spatial analysis, allowing users to analyze relationships, patterns, and trends in geospatial data.

Several software programs offering different strengths and capabilities are employed for LC forecasting scenarios, starting from satellite multi-temporal data. For example,

MOLUSCE is an open-source QGIS [23] plugin that uses cellular automata and machine-learning algorithms to model and predict land-use changes. In MOLUSCE, the simulated LC map is developed using a Monte Carlo cellular automata model technique.

Moving from this background, the authors propose an innovative methodology for the survey and the forecast of urban and vegetation cover development changes over time through the spatial analysis of the built-up area and vegetation cover classified and segmented from multitemporal satellite images. The authors applied a U-Net model for each reference year to classify and segment building heritage and vegetation cover. This model is trained and validated using the "Semantic Segmentation of Aerial Imagery" dataset provided by Mohammad Bin Rashid Space Center in Dubai. The classified and segmented elements are imported into the QGIS environment to analyze the urban and vegetation cover changes over time. After the QGIS plugin, MOLUSCE is employed to evaluate the future LC condition and the spatial and temporal transition. Future built-up and vegetation change predictions and spatiotemporal transition probabilities are simulated and modeled for 2044 using a CA-ANN model starting from 2000 to 2022 data and employing spatial driving factors such as altitude and slope, population, employees, distance from the urban center, distance from major roads, distance from streams, distance from railway stations and distance from primary territorial services.

The present study has the following objectives: (i) to analyze built-up and vegetation cover dynamics for the period 2000–2022, classifying and segmenting multi-temporal aerial and satellite images using a DL algorithm; (ii) to identify spatial variables that "drive" LC changes patterns; (iii) to develop a CA-ANN simulation model that, starting from DL model results and considering driving factors which impact on LC changes over time, can predict future LC changes.

The overall methodology is tested in a study area.

This methodology is particularly suitable for quickly processing large amounts of data with a higher level of detail, making results more scalable to many contexts scale applications. Furthermore, it can help decision-makers identify where and when vegetation cover and urban development have grown, as well as the trajectories, potential benefits, and challenges of these forms of development. The proposed integrated spatial and temporal analysis of urban and vegetation cover development can help evaluate and design better urban planning policies.

The structure of this research includes six sections. The first section covers the introduction and the literature review. The second section presents the study area and materials dataset used in the research. The third section is dedicated to methods, while the fourth includes the research results. The fifth section is devoted to results discussions. The sixth and last section provides the conclusions of the research.

2   Study Area and Materials

2.1   Study Area

The proposed method is tested on the municipality of Rende, an urban area in southern Italy that covers a surface of 55 square kilometers and has a population of 36,123 inhabitants (Fig. 1). Considering the urban LC for 2022, the built-up area covers about 1,450 ha (26,3% of the total surface), while the vegetation cover reaches a value of about 2,500 ha (45,4% of the total surface). The remaining 1,550 ha (18,3%) of the total surface is covered by classes (such as bare land, water, etc.) not considered in this study and defined as "unlabeled" categories.

The city experienced significant growth until 2011, following the development of critical territorial services such as the University of Calabria, and reached a very slow growth phase from 2011 until 2022.

During the observation period, from 2000 to 2022, the population slightly increased, going from 34,440 inhabitants in 2000 to 36,123 in 2022 [24, 25].

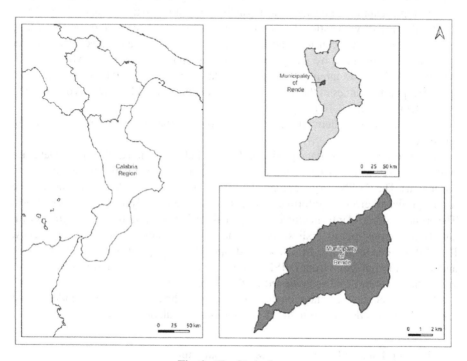

Fig. 1. The Study Area

2.2 Dataset

A combination of RS data and GIS has been used to investigate urban and greening dynamics in the study area.

The training and validation tasks of the U-Net model are developed using the "Semantic Segmentation of Aerial Imagery" dataset provided by the Mohammed Bin Rashid Space Center of Dubai. The dataset is open source and is accessible through a request made on the web portal https://humansintheloop.org/resources/datasets/sema tic-segmentation-dataset-2/ (accessed on 10 January 2023). It comprises 72 RGB (three channels) satellite images with a 70 cm/pixel spatial resolution for each channel and 8 tiles. Each tile has 9 images of various sizes and their corresponding ground-truth segmentation masks for 6 classes, such as building, land, road, vegetation, water, and unlabeled. To overcome the limitation of the small sample, the authors adopted several data augmentation techniques to improve the sufficiency and diversity of sample data, generating a synthetic dataset from the original [26].

The orthophotos used in the study were acquired through a specific request from the Regional Cartographic Center web portal via the following link: http://geoportale.reg ione.calabria.it/ (accessed on 10 January 2023). These are employed to identify the built area and the vegetation cover relating to the year 2000 and are characterized by a pixel size of 1 m. For 2022, Google Earth Pro satellite images of the study area are used.

The representation of the land surface in the study area is made using the Digital Terrain Model (DTM) with national coverage. DTM helps calculate the study area's altitude and average slope, two considered driving factors to model urban and vegetation cover dynamics. It is obtained by interpolating the orographic data from the Military Geographical Institute cartography, defining a regular step matrix of 20 m, whose elements (pixels) report the values of the dimensions. The overall national territory is divided into units (tiles) of 10 km × 10 km.

Road and railway networks are derived from shapefiles in the OpenStreetMap database.

The geo-topographic data produced by the Italian National Synthetic Database (DBSN) is used as the ground truth dataset for identifying the built-up and vegetation cover areas. The DBSN is a geographical database at a national scale level containing the most significant territorial information useful for thematic analysis and representations. The primary source of information is the regional geo-topographic dataset integrated with data from national public bodies, such as the cadastral maps of the Revenue Agency, ISTAT data, data from other Ministries, and Open Street Map data (OSM). The building and vegetation polygons from DBSN referred to 2022, are considered ground truth to verify the accuracy of those predicted by the U-Net model.

The socio-economic dataset on the population and the employees in the industry and services sectors is derived from the ISTAT national population census.

2.3 Driving Factors Identification and Preparation

Physical and socio-economic factors significantly impact and "drive" urban and vegetation cover dynamics over time. These factors are studied by several researchers [27] and include geographical, climatic, proximity, and accessibility factors. In this study, a variety of proximity and physical factors are considered.

The correlation between these factors and urban and vegetation cover changes can be determined using Pearson's correlation [28]. Pearson's correlation, r_p, is calculated by dividing the covariance of the variables and the product of their standard deviations as stated in:

$$r_p(x, y) = \frac{\sum_{i=1}^{n}(x_i - \overline{x}) * (y_i - \overline{y})}{\sqrt{\sum_{i=1}^{n}(x_i - \overline{x})^2 * \sum_{i=1}^{n}(y_i - \overline{y})^2}} \tag{1}$$

$\overline{x}$ and $\overline{y}$ represent the mean of each variable.

Pearson's correlation coefficient values range from −1 to 1. A value of 0 implies no linear association between the two variables. Values 1 and −1 indicate perfect positive and negative correlations between the two variables.

3   Methods

3.1   Classification and Segmentation of Orthoimages and Satellite Imagery

The urban and vegetation cover development analysis is done by quantifying the amount and evaluating the built-up and vegetation cover distribution from 2000 to 2022, analyzing multi-temporal satellite images through the U-Net model.

The U-Net model is trained and validated for classifying and segmenting six features: buildings, vegetation, land, roads, water, and unlabeled. For this study, only buildings and vegetation cover areas are considered.

The accuracy performance of the model in the training and validation stages is determined by considering Precision, Recall, and F1-Score statistics.

Precision, Recall, and F1-Score are calculated by determining True Positive (TP), True Negative (TN), False Positive (FN), and False Negative (FN) instances.

TP are all occurrences predicted positive, which are positive. FP are the instances predicted positive, which are negative. TN are the occurrences predicted negative, which are negative. FN are the instances predicted negative, which are positive.

Precision represents a measure of how many of the positive predictions made by the model are correct (TP) and can be calculated as follows:

$$Precision = \frac{TP}{TP + FP} \tag{2}$$

Recall quantifies how many positive cases the model correctly predicted over all the positive cases in the dataset. It can be calculated as follows:

$$Recall = \frac{TP}{TP + FN} \tag{3}$$

F1-Score is a measure that combines Precision and Recall, generally described as the harmonic mean of the two. This indicator provides a single metric that weights the two ratios (Precision and Recall) in a balanced way. F1-Score can be calculated as follows:

$$F1 - Score = 2 * \frac{Precision * Recall}{Precision + Recall} \tag{4}$$

3.2   Built-up and Vegetation Cover Change Analysis

The trained and validated DL model is then applied to the study area orthoimages for 2000 and satellite images for 2022, obtaining built-up and vegetation cover areas for the two periods. The results are imported and vectorized in the open-source QGIS Desktop software.

To verify and assess the model's accuracy in classifying and predicting built-up and vegetation areas, the authors made a test comparing the building and vegetation polygons predicted by the U-Net model with those derived from DBSN and referred to 2022, determining the F1-Score. This operation is crucial to verify that the spatial autocorrelation between training and testing data is removed. In this case, as the training and validation tasks are based on an imagery dataset of an urban environment considerably different from the case study's spatial and formal characteristics [29], the testing accuracy removed the spatial autocorrelation between the actual and predicted labels. These operations are made all in the QGIS environment.

The Built-up and vegetation cover dynamics are determined by comparing the respective land cover surfaces for the reference period from 2000 to 2022.

3.3 Urban and Vegetation Cover Changes Forecasting

The MOLUSCE plugin in QGIS is employed first to simulate and estimate spatiotemporal changes from 2022 to 2044. Area changes and transition probability matrixes are generated using 2000 and 2022 built-up and vegetation areas determined with the U-Net model. The simulation strategy adopted follows the CA-ANN model architecture.

Considering scientific literature and the general availability of data, this study considers nine driving factors as determinant factors for future urban and vegetation cover prediction. These factors include terrain factors, proximity and accessibility indicators, and distance to territorial services. In the proposed study, the authors considered only the university campus and the railway station as territorial services.

After the CA-ANN simulation model is developed, the simulation results of LC dynamics for 2000–2022 are compared with results obtained through the U-Net model application for the same period (ground truth), and the Root Mean Squared Error (RMSE) is determined.

4   Results

4.1   Built-up and Vegetation Cover Maps and Accuracy Assessment

The U-Net model employed for built-up and vegetation cover classification and segmentation is trained and validated using the IoU-based loss function, achieving a quite good level of accuracy with Precision, Recall, and F1-Score values of 0.63, 0.84, and 0.72, respectively.

Making an independent testing task to assess the accuracy of the trained and validated U-Net model prediction, the actual and predicted built-up area and vegetation cover are compared, using 2022 as the reference period.

The overall accuracy of the U-Net model application to the municipality of Rende is good. Indeed, the F1-Score values for built-up areas and vegetation cover reached 0.87 and 0.74, respectively (Fig. 2).

Once the model's accuracy is determined, it is applied to the case study to classify and segment the built-up and vegetation-covered areas in 2000 (Fig. 3).

Fig. 2. U-Net model classification and segmentation results for 2022

Fig. 3. U-Net model classification and segmentation results for 2000

4.2 Built-up and Vegetation Cover Analysis

After its accuracy evaluation, the U-Net model is applied to the municipality of Rende to predict the built-up and vegetation cover areas for 2000 and 2022 and to evaluate urban and greening changes over these 22 years.

The surface coverage in hectares and the density in percentages of built-up area, vegetation cover, and unlabeled elements for the reference periods are summarized in Table 1.

The classification and segmentation of the natural color orthoimages from 2000 show that most of the study area is covered by vegetation and unlabeled elements, representing 2723.13 ha (49.66%) and 1763.01 ha (32.15%), respectively. The built-up area, instead, covered 997.83 ha with a density rate of 18.19%.

Applying the DL model to the 2022 satellite images, the results showed a built-up area coverage that reached the value of 1458.30 ha, with a density rate of 26.60%. The vegetation cover for 2022 was 2531.15 ha (46.15%), while the unlabeled elements coverage was equal to 1494.61 ha with a density rate of 27.25%.

Considering the 22-year observation period, the built-up area increased by 460.47 ha, with a density increase of 8.41%. In contrast, vegetation cover and unlabeled elements density rate were reduced by 3.51% and 4.90%, resulting in a surface loss of 191.98 ha and 268.40 ha, respectively.

Generally, the results demonstrate a series of urban and greening changes in the study area for the analyzed period (2000–2022), according to which the study area experienced significant built-up area expansion, causing a vegetation cover decline.

Table 1. Built-up and Vegetation cover changes from the U-Net model for 2000–2022.

Land Cover Category	2000 (ha)	2022 (ha)	Change (ha)	2000 (%)	2022 (%)	Change (%)
Built-up	997.83	1458.30	460.47	18.19	26.60	8.41
Vegetation cover	2723.13	2531.15	−191,98	49.66	46.15	−3.51
Unlabeled	1763,01	1494.61	−268,40	32.15	27.25	−4.90

4.3 Driving Factors Analysis

The driving factors selected for the current study are elevation, slope, distance from the main roads, distance from the rivers, distance from the urban center, distance from the university campus, and distance to the railway station. Furthermore, socioeconomic variables such as population and employees are considered.

This study used Pearson's correlation to measure the correlation between variables, as all the variables considered are not categorical. Table 2 indicates that many variables considered are more strongly correlated than other variables. In particular, the variables more strongly correlated are distance to buildings, distance to main roads, distance to the railway, distance to the university campus, elevation, and slope. These variables are considered for developing the simulation and prediction of the CA-ANN model.

Table 2. Pearson's correlation method for the evaluation of correlation among driving factors.

	D. build	D. roads	D. railway	Slope	Elevation	D. rivers	D. univ	Pop	Employees
D. build	–	0.664	0.515	0.356	0.596	−0.134	0.514	−0.203	−0.064
D. roads		–	0.577	0.273	0.753	−0.116	0.609	−0.183	−0.040
D. railway			–	0.641	0.867	−0.195	0.910	−0.042	−0.209
Slope				–	0.631	−0.171	0.540	−0.070	−0.170
Elevation					–	−0.150	0.830	−0.040	−0.217
D. rivers						–	−0.127	0.070	0.187
D. univ							–	0.067	−0.129
Pop								–	0.046
Employees									–

4.4 Built-up and Vegetation Cover Prediction and Simulation Using CA-ANN Model

The artificial neural network (ANN) and cellular automata (CA) machine learning algorithm employs the multilayer perception (MLP) approach, considering previously recorded built-up and vegetation cover changes and driving factors (explanatory variables) for determining LC modifications. In this study, the built-up and vegetation cover for 2000 and 2022 and six driving factors, including distance to buildings, distance to main roads, distance to the railway, distance to the university campus, elevation, and slope, are considered as inputs for the simulation model using the MOLUSCE plugin in QGIS.

Starting from the modifications in built-up and vegetation cover for 2000–2022, the simulation model is developed, and verification is performed considering 2022. Actual and simulated changes for 2022 are reported in Table 3.

Table 3. Actual and simulated built-up and vegetation cover changes for 2022.

Land Cover Category	Actual (ha)	Simulated (ha)	Actual (%)	Simulated (%)	RMSE (ha)
Built-up	460.47	498.42	8.41	9.15	26.83
Vegetation cover	−191.98	−201.51	−3.51	−3.70	6.74
Unlabeled	−268.40	−296.91	−4.90	−5.45	20.16

From Table 4, a good correspondence in terms of RMSE between actual and simulated changes in built-up and vegetation cover areas can be seen. This good result is also valid for unlabeled elements.

4.5 Built-Up and Vegetation Cover Prediction for 2044

As the CA-ANN simulation model developed provides good results, a prediction of built-up and vegetation cover changes for 2044 is performed. In Table 4 are reported simulation results.

It can be noted that from 2022 to 2044, there is a very slow growth of built-up areas that amount to 2.19 ha with a decrease in vegetation cover areas of 0.89 ha. The average increase/decrease rate of built-up and vegetation cover is 0.44%. This result appears very realistic. The simulation of LC changes from 2022 to 2044 is represented in Fig. 4.

Table 4. Built-up and Vegetation cover changes for the period 2022–2044.

Land Cover Category	2022–2044 (ha)
Built-up	2.19
Vegetation cover	−0.89
Unlabeled	−1.31

5 Discussions

The application of the proposed methodology to the municipality of Rende indicates that significant urban and greening cover changes occurred during the observation period from 2000 to 2022.

These results are obtained starting from two different methodological assumptions based on different validation tasks to determine the accuracy level of the overall methodology. In the first instance, the study area's built-up and vegetation cover changes are determined through the classification and segmentation of multi-temporal satellite imagery using a DL approach. The considered model is based on a U-Net architecture trained and validated on the "Semantic Segmentation of Aerial Imagery" dataset provided by the Mohammed Bin Rashid Space Center of Dubai. The training and validation stages demonstrated good accuracy, reaching Precision, Recall, and F1-Score values of 0.63, 0.84, and 0.72, respectively. The model can classify and segment six categories of features, but only built-up and vegetation cover areas are considered for this study. The other features are classified as unlabeled. Although the training and validation tasks are based on an imagery dataset of an urban environment considerably different from that of the case study in terms of spatial and formal characteristics, the testing task on the municipality of Rende demonstrated good levels of accuracy both in the classification and segmentation of built-up and vegetation cover areas. Considering 2022 as the reference year, the testing stage of the model produced an F1-Score value of 0.87 for

Fig. 4. CA-ANN model classification and segmentation predictions for the period 2022–2044

built-up areas and 0.74 for vegetation cover areas. These results indicate that spatial autocorrelation between the actual and predicted labels is removed. Given that, the DL model is applied to classify and segment the orthoimages from 2000, identifying and determining land cover changes from 2000 to 2022.

Applying this first methodological approach, it is possible to highlight that, in the municipality of Rende, during the 22-year analyzed period, the built-up area density increased by 8.41%, while the vegetation cover density decreased by 3.51%. This research finding indicates that the study area experienced a growing urbanization phenomenon, which generated pressure on the environment with a decline in vegetation cover.

The second part of the methodology, starting from the results obtained from the multitemporal analysis of the satellite images, is dedicated to investigating the reasons and causes of this urban growth at the expense of vegetation cover, identifying the driving factors that have determined the patterns of these land cover changes. Starting from a first set of nine factors, six factors most correlated to urban growth are selected employing Pearsons' correlation analysis. The selected factors are distance to buildings, distance to main roads, distance to the railway, distance to the university campus, elevation, and slope.

Once the key factors driving the land cover changes from 2000 to 2022 have been identified, the CA-ANN algorithm is applied to determine the built-up and vegetation cover dynamics simulation. The aim is to verify the convergence with the results obtained from applying the U-Net model to orthoimages and satellite images and to predict LC dynamics for 2044. The results demonstrate a very good accuracy of CA-ANN simulation model predictions concerning the results obtained from applying the U-Net model with low values of RMSE. Indeed, according to the simulation model, during the 22-year analyzed period, the built-up area density increased by 9.15%, while the vegetation cover density decreased by 3.70%, and the unlabeled features decreased by 5.45%. These results confirm the dynamic evolution of the LC in the municipality of Rende both qualitatively and quantitatively.

Starting from these assumptions, the CA-ANN simulation model is employed to predict for 2044. The results show a very slow urban development, around 0.44%, with a consequent reduction of the vegetation cover equal to the same value. These results appear very realistic considering the urban development analyses obtained from 2000 to 2022.

6 Conclusions

The proposed methodology, based on the integration between the DL technology, GIS techniques, and CA-ANN models, can be employed not only as a rapid system to estimate the built-up area and the vegetation cover with a good level of accuracy quantitatively but, thanks to the CA-ANN simulation model, it provides valuable information about actual and future land use dynamics patterns, helping planners and decision-makers to realize sustainable land management. It can be used as a rapid tool to quantify and visualize the actual and future consumption of natural resources, such as vegetation and soil, in a semi-automatic way.

The methodology using Satellite and aerial images from UAS flights ad-hoc planned can guarantee higher spatial resolution than most land cover maps provided by National Space Agencies, often based on aggregated data from various sources. This allows for more detailed and precise delineation of features. Image segmentation algorithms, such as the U-Net model applied to this study, can be tailored to specific tasks and regions, identifying custom LC classes that may not be present in standard LC maps. This flexibility is valuable for specialized applications, such as environmental monitoring, urban planning, and precision agriculture. Furthermore, Satellite and aerial images can be acquired frequently, allowing near-real-time monitoring processes of land cover changes. This is particularly useful for detecting rapid changes in urban areas and natural disasters.

On the other hand, LC maps provided by reputable spatial agencies are subject to rigorous validation and are based on consistent classification methods. This ensures a standardized and reliable representation of land cover across large areas.

The choice between segmenting satellite images and using land cover maps provided by spatial agencies depends on the specific objectives of the analysis. Satellite image segmentation offers higher spatial resolution, customization, and real-time monitoring capabilities, while land cover maps from spatial agencies provide consistency, historical data, and expert validation. Combining both approaches can benefit comprehensive land cover analysis, monitoring, and forecasting.

The spatiotemporal LC simulation results, obtained by applying the CA-ANN simulation model, will aid policymakers in analyzing the changes in LC intensity, considering the socio-economic elements that influence it, and promoting environmental conservation and sustainable development policies and planning strategies. Furthermore, it can also be used as an early warning system to identify land cover changes occurring without authorization or permission.

The proposed research work may be improved by increasing the satellite images for the training and validation stages of the U-Net model to provide better accuracy. Moreover, other DL architectures will be tested to achieve better performances in building and vegetation cover prediction. To increase the monitoring and forecasting capabilities of the proposed methodology, other socio-economic and environmental indicators will be introduced to analyze the drivers and the impacts of the urban and vegetation cover development over time and space.

References

1. Hecheltjen, A., Thonfeld, F., Menz, G.: Recent advances in remote sensing change detection– a review. In: Land Use and Land Cover Mapping in Europe: Practices & Trends, pp. 145–178 (2014)
2. Chughtai, A.H., Abbasi, H., Karas, I.R.: A review on change detection method and accuracy assessment for land use land cover. Remote Sens. Appl. Soc. Environ. **22**, 100482 (2021)
3. Marzahn, P., Mermoz, S., Quegan, S.: The Sentinel-1 mission: new opportunities for SAR remote sensing observations. Remote Sens. Environ. **120**, 13–24 (2012)
4. Drusch, M., et al.: Sentinel-2: ESA's optical high-resolution mission for GMES operational services. Remote Sens. Environ. **120**, 25–36 (2012)
5. Phiri, D., Simwanda, M., Salekin, S., Nyirenda, V.R., Murayama, Y., Ranagalage, M.: Sentinel-2 data for land cover/use mapping: a review. Remote Sens. **12**, 2291 (2020)
6. ESA: Sentinel-2 Missions-Sentinel Online, ESA, Paris, France (2014)
7. Chen, X., et al.: Estimating global gross primary productivity with satellite data using deep learning. Ecol. Indicat. **117**, 106535 (2020)
8. McCarthy, M.J., et al.: Satellite remote sensing for coastal management: a review of successful applications. Environ. Manag. **60**, 323–339 (2017)
9. Giordano, S., Bailly, S., Landrieu, L., Chehata, N.: Improved crop classification with rotation knowledge using Sentinel-1 and -2 time series. Photogramm. Eng. Remote Sens. **86**, 431–441 (2020)
10. Ma, L., Liu, Y., Zhang, X., Ye, Y., Yin, G., Johnson, B.A.: Deep learning in remote sensing applications: a meta-analysis and review. ISPRS J. Photogramm. Remote. Sens. **152**, 166–177 (2019)
11. Shih, H.C., Stow, D.A., Tsai, Y.H.: Guidance on and comparison of machine learning classifiers for Landsat-based land cover and land use mapping. Int. J. Remote Sens. **40**, 1248–1274 (2019)
12. Carranza-García, M., García-Gutiérrez, J., Riquelme, J.C.: A framework for evaluating land use and land cover classification using convolutional neural networks. Remote Sens. **11**, 274 (2019)
13. Shafaey, M.A., Salem, M.A.M., Ebied, H.M., Al-Berry, M.N., Tolba, M.F.: Deep learning for satellite image classification. In: Proceedings of the International Conference on Advanced Intelligent Systems and Informatics, Cairo, Egypt (2018)
14. Helber, P., Bischke, B., Dengel, A., Borth, D.: Eurosat: a novel dataset and deep learning benchmark for land use and land cover classification. IEEE J. Sel. Topics Appl. Earth Observat. Remote Sens. **12**, 2217–2226 (2019)
15. Pires de Lima, R., Marfurt, K.: Convolutional neural network for remote-sensing scene classification: Transfer learning analysis. Remote Sens. **12**, 86 (2019)

16. Mohajerani, S., Saeedi, P.: Cloud-Net: an end-to-end cloud detection algorithm for Landsat 8 imagery. In: Proceedings of the IGARSS 2019, IEEE International Geoscience and Remote Sensing Symposium, Yokohama, Japan, 28 July–2 August 2019, pp. 1029–1032. IEEE, Piscataway (2019)

17. Ye, H., Liu, S., Jin, K., Cheng, H.: CT-UNet: an improved neural network based on U-net for building segmentation in remote sensing images. In: Proceedings of the 2020 25th International Conference on Pattern Recognition (ICPR), Milan, Italy, pp. 166–172 (2021)

18. He, N., Fang, L., Plaza, A.: Hybrid first and second order attention Unet for building segmentation in remote sensing images. Sci. China Inf. Sci. **63**, 140305 (2020)

19. Hou, Y., Liu, Z., Zhang, T., Li, Y.: C-Unet: complement UNet for remote sensing road extraction. Sensors **21**, 2153 (2021)

20. Francini, M., Salvo, C., Vitale, A.: Combining deep learning and multi-source GIS methods to analyze urban and greening changes. Sensors **23**, 3805 (2023)

21. Francini, M., Salvo, C., Viscomi, A., Vitale, A.: A deep learning-based method for the semi-automatic identification of built-up areas within risk zones using aerial imagery and multi-source GIS data: an application for landslide risk. Remote Sens. **14**, 4279 (2022)

22. Mohan, S., Giridhar, M.V.S.S.: A brief review of recent developments in the integration of deep learning with GIS. Geomat. Environ. Eng. **16**, 21–38 (2022)

23. QGIS. 2023 QGIS User Guide. https://docs.qgis.org/3.22/it/docs/user_manual/. Accessed 5 June 2023

24. ISTAT (2001) 14° Censimento della Popolazione e delle Abitazioni. http://www.istat.it/it/censimento-popolazione/censimento-popolazione-2011

25. ISTAT (2011) 15° Censimento della Popolazione e delle Abitazioni. http://www.istat.it/it/censimento-popolazione/censimento-popolazione-2011

26. Yang, S., Xiao, W., Zhang, M., Guo, S., Zhao, J., Shen, F.: Image data augmentation for deep learning: a survey. In: Proceedings of the Computer Vision and Pattern Recognition Conference (CVPR), New Orleans, LA, USA (2022)

27. Akdeniz, H.B., Sag, N.S., Inam, S.: Analysis of land use/land cover changes and prediction of future changes with land change modeler: case of Belek, Turkey. Environ. Monit. Assess. **195**, 135 (2023)

28. Rodgers, J.L., Nicewander, W.A.: Thirteen ways to look at the correlation coefficient. Am. Stat. **42**, 59 (2008)

29. Spasov, A., Petrova-Antonova, D.: Transferability assessment of open-source deep learning model for building detection on satellite data. In: Proceedings of the 16th GeoInfo Conference, New York City, NY, USA (2021)

The QGIS Platform for LABMET Observatory. The Experience of the Metropolitan City of Cagliari (MCC)

Nicolò Fenu[1,2](✉) [iD] and Valentina Talu[3]

[1] ESOMAS, University of Turin, Turin, Italy
nicolo.fenu@unito.it
[2] SARDARCH Spin Off, Cagliari, Italy
[3] UNISS Università degli Studi di Sassari, Sassari, Italy

Abstract. The MCC- Metropolitan City of Cagliari has significantly promoted spatial policy initiatives by implementing the Metropolitan Strategic Plan. LABMET, also known as the "Laboratorio Metropolitano d'Innovazione," operates as the Urban Agency of the Metropolitan City of Cagliari. It serves as both a digital and physical hub for sharing and popularizing urban issues, functioning as an effective tool for land development while fostering a community of open discussions accessible to all, guided by the principles of open government. One of the most significant action of LABMET is The MCC GIS Observatory. It is a dedicated program within the Metropolitan City of Cagliari aimed at collecting, managing, analyzing, and disseminating geographical data. Its primary objective is to monitor and comprehend territorial dynamics through GIS tools. In pursuit of its objectives, the Observatory undertakes essential tasks, such as collecting, selecting, organizing, and disseminating data and information, thus progressively enriching the shared knowledge base. This collective epistemic foundation supports decision-making in the public interest. It is critical in advancing and administering the processes of gathering, filtering, systematizing, and circulating information and data and territorial dynamics through GIS tools.

Keywords: qgis · città metropolitana di Cagliari · digital geography · LABMET

1 Introduction

Geographic information systems (GIS) continues to be an increasingly important component in the planning support system, facilitating data-driven decision-making and enabling planners to identify patterns and assess relationships between geographic features [19].

GIS offer a versatile and effective framework for planning and analysis, particularly in scenarios involving the management of extensive and dynamic spatial data [15].

GIS has gained significant popularity in planning agencies worldwide, including developed and developing countries. Many planning departments have transitioned from traditional mapping systems to GIS due to its user-friendliness, increased functionality,

E. Borgogno Mondino and P. Zamperlin (Eds.): ASITA 2023, CCIS 2088, pp. 141–151, 2024.
https://doi.org/10.1007/978-3-031-59925-5_11

and affordability. The integration of GIS with planning models, visualization, and the internet has further enhanced its usefulness in urban planning Even though the extensive availability of (GIS) within local government has yet to be fully utilized as a planning tool. The context of planning departments, the utilization of GIS continues to be hindered by various obstacles of technological, organizational, and institutional nature. Among these obstacles, challenges related to training, funding, and data emerge as the most prominent, impeding the wider adoption of GIS for planning purposes; organizational and institutional factors play a more critical role than technological barriers in limiting the full potential of GIS in planning applications [11].

However, the main challenges in utilizing GIS in urban planning are not technical in nature but rather the availability of data, organizational change, and staffing [3] [19]. Despite these constraints, the advent of cloud computing around 2010 has led to a transformative web GIS pattern, which has matured over the years. Today, more than 350,000 GIS organizations are globally catering to millions of users who utilize GIS in various domains and industries [23]. In recent years, GIS has undergone a significant transformation with the advent of cloud computing and the development of web GIS patterns. This platform allows users to access and share a vast amount of information items, including maps, apps, analytical models, and data tables. These items go beyond raw data and encompass interactive maps, functional information layers, and even implementations of machine learning and artificial intelligence [13]. The convergence of the Internet and cloud computing is significantly reshaping the approach taken by software companies in delivering their services, consequently exerting a profound influence on the methods employed by end users in performing their tasks [4]. Cloud computing has enabled the creation of comprehensive and community-based [13].

According with Alfaqih Cloud GIS *is the combination of running GIS software and services on cloud infrastructure and accessing GIS capabilities using the web. In the literature review, section divided the GIS cloud into four area as (Geospatial Information, A spatial web portal (SWP), Emergency Management, Social Media)* [1].

INSPIRE (Infrastructure for Spatial Information in Europe)

INSPIRE (Infrastructure for Spatial Information in Europe) is a European Commission project that aims to create an infrastructure for interoperable spatial information within the European Community. The INSPIRE directive, which came into force in 2007 and was implemented in Italy by Legislative Decree 32/2010, establishes a legal framework for the implementation of national spatial data infrastructures. The goal of INSPIRE is to facilitate the formulation, implementation, monitoring and evaluation of EU policies at various levels and to provide information to citizens. Each EU member state is to implement its own spatial data infrastructure, coordinating subnational levels and making geographic data, metadata and services available. These national infrastructures will form the nodes of the European spatial infrastructure, with access to services provided through the INSPIRE geoportal. Member states may also develop national geoportals to provide access to spatial data [8].

There are both positive and negative conclusions to the INSPIRE Directive initiative and its implementation. Positively, the INSPIRE Directive is an important and necessary initiative to establish a unified standard for Spatial Data Infrastructure in Europe. [3]. More important is the evolution about Inspire: "*the INSPIRE Directive should be interpreted not as one of a set of legal requirements within a legislative framework but rather as one where the adoption of high standards of principles and practice is a matter of course. The objective should not simply be about meeting legal obligations but of putting in place policies, processes and systems that result in continuous development and improvements in the capture of geospatial environmental data as well as the sharing and provisioning of geospatial products among MS. It is submitted that the INSPIRE Directive should be perceived as a set of processes that results in improvements in data integration, data quality and value-adding arising from interoperability and transferability of information. INSPIRE as an infrastructure for geospatial environmental data, should aspire towards a sharing information society that drives key benefits for the whole community"* [6].

Italy is virtuous regarding the implementation of inspire; the results of the annual INSPIRE monitoring for 2022 that is carried out on the basis of metadata published in national search services accredited to the European geoportal. For Italy, the reference search service is the National Directory of Spatial Data (RNDT) [5, 7].

For the Italy results highlight: a conspicuous increase in resources documented for INSPIRE purposes: for datasets from 4864 in 2021 to 7447 in 2022 (+53.1%), for series from 78 to 224 (+187.2%), and for services from 1920 to 2231 (+16.2%); a confirmation of the excellent performance with regard to metadata compliance, which stands at 98.8% for datasets and 95.6% for services; an increase/decrease of less than 10 percent in the accessibility of datasets through network services: although this is still a low value at the percentage level, it should be pointed out that this still corresponds to an increase in absolute terms because, as pointed out earlier, the total number of documented resources (thus the denominator of the related indicators) has increased; Stationary values, however low, for the other dimensions (data and service compliance) [5, 22].

2 Materials and Methods. The Case Study of Labmet Observatory

This research employed a structured case studies analysis approach [14], the present contribution analyzes the case study of Gis Labmet Observatory in the Metropolitan City of Cagliari in Sardinia. In this sense, the case study of Labmet Observatory can highlight the advantages of a gis observatory in urban agency.

2.1 Study Area

The Metropolitan City of Cagliari (MCC) is a vast territorial entity established in 2016, assuming its responsibilities from the Province of Cagliari as of January 1, 2017, as per the Resolution of the Regional Council October 25, 2016, No. 57/12. In addition to the capital city, it comprises sixteen municipalities, encompassing both conurbation areas and a portion of those in the hinterland. The Metropolitan City currently has a population of 419,399 and covers an area of 1,248 km^2 (Fig. 1).

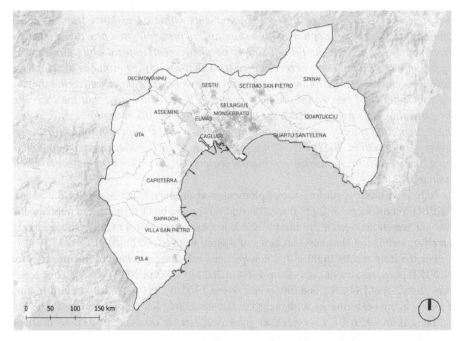

Fig. 1. 17 municipalities of Metropolitan City of Cagliari

The Metropolitan City has been entrusted with several fundamental functions critical to its effective governance and development. Among these functions, a significant one is a formulation and regular update of a three-year Strategic Plan for the metropolitan territory. This Strategic Plan serves as a comprehensive policy framework, guiding the actions and responsibilities of the municipalities falling under its jurisdiction.

Another crucial function of the Metropolitan City is its role in overall spatial planning, which encompasses various elements such as communication facilities, service networks, and infrastructure within its jurisdiction. This function involves establishing constraints and objectives to ensure coordinated and harmonious development among the municipalities in the metropolitan area. By actively engaging in spatial planning, the Metropolitan City strives to promote sustainable growth and equitable distribution of resources while fostering efficient communication and service provision throughout the region. The Metropolitan City assumes responsibility for organizing and managing public services of general interest that extend beyond the boundaries of individual municipalities. Collaborating with the concerned municipalities, it undertakes various tasks, including preparing tender documents, contracting services, monitoring service contracts, and organizing competitions and selection procedures. Moreover, the Metropolitan City plays a crucial role in mobility and road management, ensuring compatibility and consistency in urban planning across the entire metropolitan area. This involves promoting efficient transportation systems and fostering sustainable development practices. Facilitating and coordinating economic and social development constitutes another critical function of the Metropolitan City. It actively supports and fosters innovative economic and research activities that align with the strategic plan of the territory. Additionally, the Metropolitan City is actively involved in promoting and coordinating the implementation of computerization and digitization systems throughout the metropolitan area. The Metropolitan City of Cagliari (MCC) has initiated the implementation of the Metropolitan Strategic Plan, aiming to establish a comprehensive and cohesive approach to various urban development and governance initiatives. The plan envisions a strategic and organic vision for a range of actions that will significantly transform the urban structure through urban redevelopment and improved governance practices.

2.2   MCC Strategic Plan

The MCC has significantly promoted spatial policy initiatives by implementing the Metropolitan Strategic Plan. This plan lays out a comprehensive and cohesive vision for a series of actions that will bring about profound changes in urban planning, particularly concerning urban redevelopment and governance.

The formulation and implementation of the strategic plan have been pivotal in fostering awareness regarding the inherent issues in urban development and planning. Notably, it has emphasized the importance of systemic land management as a critical aspect to address.

Throughout the construction process of the strategic plan, an ideal condition has emerged, facilitating the promotion of spatial policy initiatives that encompass the entire metropolitan territory. This inclusive approach involves active participation from local authorities and stakeholders of diverse backgrounds, which is a fundamental foundation for establishing an effective urban planning agency.

The collaborative atmosphere nurtured by this condition encourages the alignment of common interests around shared projects and policies. Consequently, a conducive context has been created, propelling the emergence of a territorial political will. As the strategic plan outlines, this political will find its practical expression and implementation through "Project 45 - Urban Lab of the Metropolitan City of Cagliari," which aims to foster citizen participation and proposal in various urban projects.

The strategic plan incorporates a significant initiative known as the LABMET Metropolitan Innovation Lab; a digital platform dedicated to collaborative sharing. During its initial phase, LABMET focuses on establishing an observatory and data collection, deemed essential activities.

2.3   LABMET

LABMET, also known as the "Laboratorio Metropolitano d'Innovazione," operates as the Urban Agency of the Metropolitan City of Cagliari. It serves as both a digital and physical hub for sharing and popularizing urban issues, functioning as an effective tool for land development while fostering a community of open discussions accessible to all, guided by the principles of open government. LABMET translates these principles into tangible actions, thus becoming a mechanism for developing and guiding public spending with a strong emphasis on inclusivity, participation, transparency, and accountability.

Notably, LABMET was initially established as a pilot project under the 4th National Action Plan for Open Government, receiving funding through FSC (Fondo di Sviluppo e Coesione) from the Cagliari Metropolitan City's Development and Cohesion Plan within the 2014–2020 programming cycle. Moreover, it has already been recognized as a strategic project of the Regional Plan of the Autonomous Region of Sardinia, securing ERDF (European Regional Development Fund) funds for the 2021–2027 programming cycle [9, 20, 21].

Labmet's initial activities will encompass a startup phase characterized by specific tasks, including re-drafting the feasibility study. This process will facilitate the identification of primary challenges in the area through collaboration with stakeholders. Additionally, shared expectations and strategies will be outlined, allowing for the formulation of envisaged scenarios. These scenarios will define crucial aspects, such as the territorial perimeter, governance arrangements, legal framework, agency missions, required resources (including human, technical, and material) and financing arrangements. The feasibility study will be pivotal in envisaging scenarios for establishing an urban agency.

Building effective governance is a fundamental element in establishing the agency, necessitating prior decision-making by all stakeholders. During this stage, the affected territory's perimeter is precisely defined based on the willingness of the involved actors to participate in the process. This definition also serves as the basis for determining the means and missions of the agency.

Labmet will engage in these critical activities throughout this first year of activation, laying the foundation for its subsequent endeavours to promote effective urban development and governance.

Labmet is envisioned as a device in its start-up phase, wherein research activities play a crucial role in raising questions concerning its identity as an urban agency. Additionally, these inquiries delve into matters at the core of contemporary debates, thereby contributing to the shaping of Labmet's strategic vision. Simultaneously, all activities integrated into the agency during this initial phase can be considered validation operations for the assumptions outlined in the Strategic Plan and Labmet's conceptual framework. The first year of experimentation establishes the necessary groundwork, preparing the conditions for more robust and effective efforts in subsequent stages of the agency's development.

The activities aim to achieve a comprehensive objective of establishing the partnership framework and governance structure, which involves the establishment of both a technical monitoring committee and a scientific committee. The work program encompasses three distinct components: partnership development, conjunctural initiatives, and perennial activities. Creating a proficient team responsible for conducting studies and effective management is essential and will be supported by adequate local and material resources. Implementing specific tools like a geographic information system and a dedicated website will enhance communication and streamline operations.

2.4 MCC Gis Observatory

The MCC GIS Observatory is a dedicated program within the Metropolitan City of Cagliari aimed at collecting, managing, analyzing, and disseminating geographical data. Its primary objective is to monitor and comprehend territorial dynamics through GIS tools.

In pursuit of its objectives, the Observatory undertakes essential tasks, such as collecting, selecting, organizing, and disseminating data and information, thus progressively enriching the shared knowledge base. This collective epistemic foundation supports decision-making in the public interest. It is critical in advancing and administering the processes of gathering, filtering, systematizing, and circulating information and data and territorial dynamics through GIS tools.

To achieve adequate documentation and portrayal of urban and spatial transformations at different scales, the Observatory employs open-source GIS software called QGIS. This platform facilitates the storage, updating, and analysis of georeferenced data, enabling the creation of practical decision-making and management tools for planning activities.

The activities of the GIS Observatory encompass the following key aspects:

(I) Data collection and integration: the Observatory gathers geographical data from diverse sources, including public entities, government agencies, research institutes, and remote sensors.

(II) Spatial analysis: The Observatory uses spatial analysis tools to understand the spatial relationships among various datasets.

(III) Monitoring and forecasting: The Observatory continuously monitors changes in the territory over time and provides forecasts based on models and trends. This monitoring may extend to environmental changes, urbanization, land use, and infrastructure development.

(IV) Indicator creation and reporting: To better understand social, economic, environmental, and demographic dynamics in a specific area, the Observatory generates meaningful territorial indicators.

(V) Data and information dissemination: the Observatory makes geographical data and information accessible through online platforms or interactive tools, ensuring that valuable insights are available to stakeholders and the public.

The first phase of the project will deal with the design of the Observatory based on the indications that will be provided by the municipalities. Specifically, the most effective tools, methodologies and operational procedures for documenting and representing urban and territorial transformations at different scales will be identified through the use of data. In particular, the open-source application QGis will be used, which, in addition to allowing the storage and updating of georeferenced data and information, enables the construction of real tools to support decision-making and management and planning activities. The experimental phase of the observatory is focused on carrying out a comprehensive mapping of public green spaces within the metropolitan area. This mapping exercise also includes schoolyards of secondary schools. The primary objective of this exercise is to build a reliable cognitive framework for the current and potential green areas of the metropolitan territory. This framework will serve to support the planning of interventions for the recovery or transformation of these spaces. The working group will define a set of spatial attributes that will be used to achieve this objective.

In the second phase of the project, on an experimental basis, we will experiment with selecting an in-depth topic to be used in the construction of an initial pilot project of the Observatory.

Taking into account the conditions of feasibility, scalability, immediate usability of the outcomes by the Authority and the potential ability to stimulate and accompany paths of involvement of relevant actors and citizenship, a mapping of public green spaces in the metropolitan territory is created, including the schoolyards of secondary schools (managed by the Metropolitan City of Cagliari). This mapping is aimed at the construction of a robust cognitive framework related to the current and potential green areas of the metropolitan territory that can be used to support the planning activity of interventions of recovery or transformation of these spaces, based on a set of spatial attributes that will be defined by the working group.

the GIS project that will be elaborated will allow the Authority to have a useful tool not only to archive a very large and diversified set of data and georeferenced information on the green spaces of the Metropolitan City of Cagliari and its constituent municipalities, including the open spaces pertaining to the 25 School Institutes of the Metropolitan City of Cagliari, but also and above all to support choices and facilitate planning activities regarding the reorganization/rehabilitation of the mapped spaces and to build policies and projects aimed at improving and increasing the relationships between them and their reference contexts, with particular reference to the issues of urban forestation and, more generally, sustainable transformations (e.g., *depaving* interventions, creation of educational gardens, etc.).

The structure of the geodatabase will also be designed so that it can be easily adapted, both to extend the survey to schools of all grades in the area and to include other public spaces (Fig. 2).

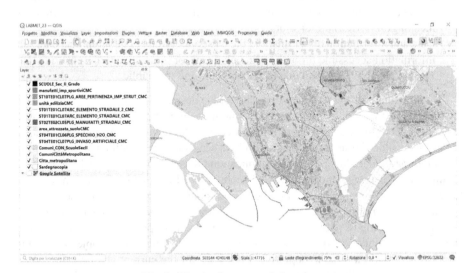

Fig. 2. Geodatabase green infrastructure

Finally, the choice to focus on green spaces will facilitate the possibility of engaging target communities (in the case of schoolyards, and school communities) in participatory activities aimed at data integration or co-design of transformative solutions. The outcomes of the work carried out by the Observatory will inform and feed the research and training activities, engagement processes and initiatives to support territorial trans-formations that Labmet will promote, and will contribute to integrating the cognitive framework of reference of the consultations promoted within the platform of public participation under the Metropolitan City of Cagliari.

The GIS database will support decision-making processes and facilitate planning activities relating to the reorganisation and rehabilitation of mapped spaces. It will also enable policymakers to develop projects aimed at enhancing the relationships between green spaces and their associated contexts, with a focus on urban forestation and sustain-able transformations. The geodatabase structure is designed to be easily adapted, either to extend the survey to schools of all grades in the area or to include other public spaces (Fig. 3).

Fig. 3. Map of green areas of the city of Cagliari

The outputs of this activity encompass the following:

1. Guidelines for the Observatory, which include specific operational objectives, allocation of resources, expertise requirements, and internal organizational structure.
2. The design and execution of the Geographic Information System (GIS) project using the open-source application QGis, as it relates to the pilot project mentioned earlier.
3. The compilation of a comprehensive dataset and the processing of information, along with the creation of cartographic representations derived from the GIS project mentioned above.

4. The preparation of a comprehensive document detailing the conditions under which the developed tool can be replicated and the specification of the models to be employed in constructing data and information elaborations and cartographic representations.

3 Discussion and Conclusion

The pilot project serves the dual purpose of archiving a vast and heterogeneous dataset, replete with georeferenced information concerning green spaces within the metropolitan area. Additionally, it is designed to provide critical support for decision-making processes, streamline programmatic activities about the revitalization of the delineated spaces, and formulate policies and initiatives directed at enhancing and fostering synergistic associations between these spaces and their respective environmental contexts. This endeavor focuses on themes such as urban afforestation and broader sustainable transformations.

Although the project is still in its experimental phase, we can trace the prospects and potential of the project. The MCC QGIS platform offers a wide range of applications beyond urban planning. By involving municipal technical offices, the project improves the quality and accuracy of geographic and cartographic data for MCC municipalities. Training interventions enable officials to effectively utilize GIS for data and cartography production in urban planning and construction. This, in turn, enhances decision-making and planning in the region. The MCC GIS platform enables municipalities to make informed decisions through spatial data analysis and visualization [17]. It aids in identifying suitable locations for infrastructure development, land use planning, and environmental conservation. By leveraging GIS, administration and planners can assess the potential impact of decisions and make more effective choices. Additionally, GIS empowers MCC citizens to enhance resource management capabilities, monitor natural resource utilization, and implement sustainable management strategies. It promotes effective decision-making, long-term environmental and economic sustainability, and citizen participation in community affairs. GIS also plays a crucial role in environmental conservation by monitoring and managing natural resources and ecological systems. It helps identify environmentally sensitive areas and develop conservation strategies. GIS further assists in infrastructure development planning and management by analyzing transportation networks, optimizing routes, and identifying areas in need of improved infrastructure [2, 12, 18]. Overall, GIS empowers communities by providing valuable spatial information and analysis, enabling evidence-based decision-making, and fostering active community participation. By harnessing the power of GIS, communities can address their specific needs, enhance resilience, and create sustainable futures [10, 16].

Funding. This research received no external funding.

References

1. Alfaqih, T.: GIS cloud : integration between cloud things and geographic information systems (GIS) (2016)
2. Al-Hader, M., Rodzi, A.: The smart city infrastructure development & monitoring. Theor. Empir. Res. Urban Manag. **4**(211), 87–94 (2009)

3. Bartha, G., Kocsis, S.: Standardization of geographic data: the European inspire directive. Eur. J. Geogr. **2**, 2 (2011)
4. Bhat, M.A., et al.: Cloud Computing: A solution to Geographical Information Systems (GIS). **3**, 2 (2011)
5. Centre, E.C.-J.R.: INSPIRE Geoportal. https://inspire-geoportal.ec.europa.eu/srv/eng/cat alog.search. Accessed 31 July 2023
6. Cho, G., Crompvoets, J.: The INSPIRE directive: some observations on the legal framework and implementation. Surv. Rev. **51**(367), 310–317 (2019). https://doi.org/10.1080/00396265. 2018.1454686
7. European Commission. Joint Research Centre.: Establishing a new baseline for monitoring the status of EU spatial data infrastructure: experiences and conclusions from INSPIRE 2019 monitoring and reporting. Publications Office, LU (2020)
8. European Parliament: Directive 2007/2/EC of the European parliament and of the council. https://eur-lex.europa.eu/legal-content/EN/TXT/PDF/?uri=CELEX:32007L0002. Accessed 05 July 2023
9. Fenu, N.: Citizen E-participation: the experience of LABMET in the Metropolitan City of Cagliari. In: Gervasi, O., et al. (eds.) Computational Science and Its Applications – ICCSA 2023 Workshops, pp. 646–656. Springer, Cham (2023)
10. Ghose, R., Elwood, S.: Public participation GIS and local political context: propositions and research directions. URISA J. **15**, 17–22 (2003)
11. Göçmen, Z.A., Ventura, S.J.: Barriers to GIS use in planning. J. Am. Plann. Assoc. **76**(2), 172–183 (2010). https://doi.org/10.1080/01944360903585060
12. Jain, K., Y.V.S.: Site suitability analysis for urban development using GIS (2007). https://doi. org/10.3923/jas.2007.2576.2583
13. Mennecke, B.E., West, L.A., Jr.: Geographic information systems in developing countries: issues in data collection, implementation and management. J. Global Inf. Manag. **9**(4), 44–54 (2001)
14. Priya, A.: Case study methodology of qualitative research: key attributes and navigating the conundrums in its application. Sociol. Bull. **70**(1), 94–110 (2021). https://doi.org/10.1177/ 0038022920970318
15. Saleh, B., Sadoun, B.: Design and implementation of a GIS system for planning. Int. J. Digit. Libr. **6**(2), 210–218 (2006). https://doi.org/10.1007/s00799-005-0117-0
16. Steinmann, R., Krek, A., Blaschke, T.: Can online map-based applications improve citizen participation? In: Böhlen, M., Gamper, J., Polasek, W., Wimmer, M.A. (eds.) TCGOV 2005. LNCS (LNAI), vol. 3416, pp. 25–35. Springer, Heidelberg (2005). https://doi.org/10.1007/ 978-3-540-32257-3_3
17. Stevens, D., et al.: ICity: A GIS–CA modelling tool for urban planning and decision making. Environ. Model. Softw. **22**(6), 761–773 (2007). https://doi.org/10.1016/j.envsoft.2006.02.004
18. Strachan, N., et al.: Soft-linking energy systems and GIS models to investigate spatial hydrogen infrastructure development in a low-carbon UK energy system. Int. J. Hydrogen Energy **34**(2), 642–657 (2009). https://doi.org/10.1016/j.ijhydene.2008.10.083
19. Yeh, A.G.: Urban planning and GIS. Geogr. Inf. Syst. **2**(877–888), 1 (1999)
20. LABMET – Laboratorio Metropolitano di Innovazione. https://laboratoriometropolitanocag liari.it/. Accessed 29 July 2023
21. Percorso pilota della Città Metropolitana di Cagliari | Italia Open Gov. https://open.gov.it/per corso-pilota-citta-metropolitana-cagliari. Accessed 29 July 2023
22. RNDT - Monitoraggio INSPIRE 2022, conformità dei metadati quasi al 100%. https:// geodati.gov.it/geoportale/notizie/497-monitoraggio-inspire-2022-conformita-dei-metadati-quasi-al-100. Accessed 31 July 2023
23. United Nations World Data Forum. https://unstats.un.org/unsd/undataforum/blog/geography-in-implementing-the-SDGs/. Accessed 31 July 2023

The Digital Twin of the Metropolitan Area of Milan: Quality Assessment of Aerial and Terrestrial Data

Marica Franzini[1]([⊠]) [iD], Vittorio Casella[1] [iD], and Bruno Monti[2]

[1] Department of Civil Engineering and Architecture, University of Pavia, 27100 Pavia, Italy
{marica.franzini,vittorio.casella}@unipv.it

[2] Technological and Digital Innovation Department, Data Interoperability Area, Municipality of Milan, 20123 Milan, Italy
bruno.monti@comune.milano.it

Abstract. Digital twins have emerged as a promising technology for city planning and management, paving the way for the development of smart cities. Milan, Italy, has set an impressive example by planning to create a digital twin of its entire Metropolitan Area, covering a vast expanse of 1500 km^2. In late 2020, a tender was issued to collect aerial nadir and oblique images, LiDAR, and terrestrial mobile mapping data. The project will generate advanced products such as true orthophoto, classified LiDAR point cloud, DTM, DSM models, MMS point clouds and spherical depth images, and a database of 22 urban objects. To ensure the accuracy and consistency of the datasets, complex GNSS and terrestrial LiDAR measurements have been included for ground control and quality checks. The surveying activities were completed, and the data were delivered in mid-2023. The paper provides an overview of the quality assessment of aerial and terrestrial data, describes the datasets, analyzes image resolution, and discusses the accuracy and precision of acquired dataset, LiDAR, and imagery.

Keywords: City digital twin · hybrid sensor · LiDAR data · imagery · quality assessment

1 Introduction

Digital twins are an up-and-coming technology for creating smart cities in terms of planning and management [1–4]. Numerous authors have highlighted their potential applications, including investigating energy consumption [5], enhancing security [6], analyzing healthcare [7], and improving mobility [8].

Several cities across the world have created digital twins, including Zurich [9], Vienna [10], Helsinki [11], and Singapore [12]. Milan project shares similarities with two initiatives: the Netherlands' 3D digital model [13, 14] (which uses the same technologies mentioned in this paper) and Germany's digital twin [15] (which is being created using single photon LiDAR and is promoted by BKG - Bundesamt für Kartographie und Geodäsie – to cover the entire country).

E. Borgogno Mondino and P. Zamperlin (Eds.): ASITA 2023, CCIS 2088, pp. 152–171, 2024.
https://doi.org/10.1007/978-3-031-59925-5_12

Cities are intricate systems that change over time due to modifications in their physical structures, economic and political activities, and social and cultural aspects [16]. Defining digital twins can be complex as different parties may have their interpretations, as stated in [17]. However, this paper defines a digital twin in a geomatic sense, specifically referring to its geometric aspect.

From this perspective, a city digital twin is the geospatial, or geometric, layout that is the foundation for integrating other information with associated positions [18]. Besides, over the past few years [19, 20], there has been an increasing demand for more accurate and detailed data. As a result, having a high-quality base layer that reflects as many aspects as possible in all three spatial dimensions is essential. This trend leads to the necessity of reliable methods for verifying the quality of the gathered data [21, 22].

In the field of geomatics, assessing data quality is a frequent task. Many scientific papers suggest solutions for aerial photogrammetry [23–29], LiDAR [30–32], and MMS [33–35]. However, with the increasing use of hybrid sensors and integrated surveys, it is crucial to develop new methods for evaluating multiple data sources contemporarily. Milan project fits perfectly within this context; the paper will outline its characteristics, the data collected, the ground control network designed explicitly for its evaluation, and the quality assessment conducted so far.

1.1 Milan Digital Twin Project

Milan is situated in the Lombardy region of Northern Italy, as shown in Fig. 1. The city has initiated a project to obtain a comprehensive city digital twin of the Metropolitan Area. A tender invitation was released in late 2020 to acquire aerial nadir and oblique images, LiDAR, and terrestrial mobile mapping data. The tender was awarded to a temporary joint venture consisting of four companies:

- CGR S.p.A. is an Italian company based in Parma, near the airport, and operates its aircraft fleet from there. It is a top player in photogrammetry and remote sensing in Italy and Europe, utilizing the latest digital sensor-based technologies, including LiDAR, multispectral sensors, and photogrammetry.
- CycloMedia is a Netherlands-based company that provides comprehensive visualizations of environments through 360° panoramic photographs, also known as Cycloramas and LiDAR data. The company utilizes specialized technology to capture and store imagery of large public areas in an online database.
- ESRI Italia S.p.A. is a member of the ESRI One Company and serves as the official distributor of its products in Italy. The company is a top geospatial solutions provider, offering comprehensive services and support across various application areas where geoinformation data is crucial. ESRI Italia S.p.A. has successfully executed numerous projects and system integrations for several Italian Municipalities and Metropolitan Areas.
- S.I.T. S.r.l. is an Italian company recently acquired by MERMEC Engineering. They specialize in topographic and cartographic sectors, covering everything from surveying to geodata processing and cartography production to geodatabase creation.

Each company participation in the project was based on its unique set of skills. CGR was responsible for surveying and processing all aerial data, while CycloMedia had the same responsibilities for MMS activities regarding surveying and data processing. ESRI Italia managed the resulting data, and S.I.T. was tasked with creating and measuring the ground control network. The Laboratory of Geomatics at the University of Pavia was responsible for analyzing the data quality. This institution has extensive experience in land and aerial surveying and geographical information, spanning more than four decades.

The project began in 2022 and involved gathering different data types, including nadiral and oblique aerial images, LiDAR points, terrestrial mobile mapping data, and providing both traditional and innovative products. The aerial surveying aspect comprises true orthophoto (RGB and CIR - meaning Color InfraRed imagery), classified lidar point cloud, and DTM and DSM models. The terrestrial mobile mapping component includes point clouds, spherical depth images, and a database that contains information about 22 urban objects: traffic light systems, light poles, wire poles, driveways, barriers, dehors, kiosks, road traffic area materials, gates, road signs, commemorative plaques, commercial shop windows, public billboard systems, advertising systems, shelters, ramps, public clocks, tramway tracks, house numbers, panels, vertical and horizontal road signs. The database will consist of approximately 1.2 million elements, identified, located, and characterized using artificial intelligence directly by CycloMedia.

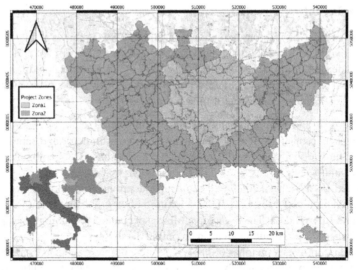

Fig. 1. The Metropolitan Area of Milan covers an area of 1776 km^2 (datum UTM32N-RDN2008 (EPSG: 7791)). The colors represent the area subdivision in two zones: Zona1 in green and Zona2 in blue. In the overview maps, the location of the site within the Lombardy region and Italy is displayed (Color figure online).

The metropolitan area is split into Zona1, which encompasses Milan and its surrounding municipalities, and Zona2, which covers the remaining territory. Figure 1 depicts the division, highlighting Zona1 in green and Zona2 in blue. The larger polygon at the center represents the Municipality of Milan. The project includes 133 municipalities, including the exclave of San Colombano al Lambro (the polygon in the lower-right corner).

The technical specifications for the tender outline the parameters for acquiring data according to different areas. The entire region must be captured with nadir imagery and LiDAR, with a resolution of 5 cm and a density of 20 points per square meter (details on the quality required by the tender technical specifications will be given in the following sections). Oblique images are only necessary for Zona1, while the MMS survey covers roads in the Municipality of Milano. However, the joint ventures have decided to acquire the same aerial data types for Zona1 and Zona2, resulting in both areas having oblique and nadiral imagery.

The aerial survey was conducted using the Leica CityMapper-2, a hybrid system described in detail in the following section, and covered an area of 1776 km². The MMS survey was conducted using CycloMedia's system, covering approximately 2555 km. To ensure that all datasets have consistent geometry and quality, the planned activities include using advanced GNSS and terrestrial LiDAR measurements; these features will serve as ground control and rigorous, independent quality checks.

Finally, the tender technical specification requires software tools to be supplied, allowing users to access complex datasets seamlessly. Two main tools are envisioned: a web app that will be particularly useful for sharing data with all the municipalities of the metropolitan area and a plugin of the ESRI ArcGIS™ environment.

All the surveying activities, aerial and terrestrial, were already concluded, and the processing is still in progress; all the data were delivered in mid-2023. The already available information has been allowed to quantify data consistency, as reported in Table 1.

Table 1. Consistency of the project acquisitions.

Data Type	Parameters	Values
Photogrammetry	Number of missions	23
	Strips acquired	429
	Strips total length	8999 km
	Overall flying time (without transfers)	37 h 55 min
	Shots performed	88781
	Images acquired	433905
	Storage occupation[a]	43.10 TB
LiDAR	Point cloud file number	9617
	Number of surveyed points (up to 15 returns)	$2.2 \cdot 10^{11}$
	Point cloud files storage occupation	9 TB
MMS	Surveyed streets	2555 km
	Image storage occupation[a]	9 TB
	Point cloud files storage occupation	1 TB
	Urban objects database storage occupation	0.5 TB

[a] Stored in JPEG format.

1.2 Aerial and Terrestrial Sensors

Aerial Acquisition System. Different data types, such as imagery and LiDAR, are necessary to create digital twins. The most efficient way to collect this information is through aerial sensors that can gather it simultaneously [36, 37]. In 2016, Leica Geosystems introduced the first hybrid sensor, the Leica CityMapper, and in 2021, they released its updated version, the CityMapper-2 [38].

The optical system consists of two nadir 150 MP cameras (RGBN) and four oblique 150 MP cameras at a 45° angle (only RGB). Three focal length options (71, 112, and 146 mm) exist for low, standard, and high-altitude operations. Milan project used the second configuration, which allows for achieving a ground sampling distance (GSD) of 5 cm flying at an altitude of approximately 1500 m Above Ground Level (AGL).

The LiDAR system uses a Leica Hyperion2+ unit with a pulse repetition rate of up to 2MHz (compared to 700 kHz in the previous version). It can handle up to 15 returns (up to 35 Multiple-Pulse-in-the-Air) and operate at altitudes between 300 and 5500 m AGL. The theoretical vertical accuracy is less than 5 cm at 1000 m AGL, with an aircraft speed of 60 m/s. The Leica CityMapper-2 system uses a scanning method called the Palmer scanner [38], which rotates a scan wedge with a tilted axis. This method produces a spiral-shaped scan pattern on the ground, allowing the system to scan under overpasses or bridges and potentially get more returns from building facades. It also allows the system to survey objects from different viewpoints by enabling a backward and forward look along the same scan strip. This scanning mechanism causes an inhomogeneous point distribution with a much higher density on the border than the strip center [39].

MMS Acquisition System. The terrestrial datasets consist of two sources of data: panoramic images, also known as "Cycloramas", and point clouds generated from a LiDAR system. CycloMedia owns the Digital Cyclorama Recorders (DCR) acquisition system, which includes five cameras with fisheye lenses, a LiDAR scanner, an Inertial Measurement Unit (IMU), and a GNSS antenna. An electronic system synchronizes the cameras, LiDAR, and IMU/GNSS [40, 41].

The Cyclorama is a high-resolution image with 14400×7200 pixels and provides a full panoramic view of 360° horizontally and 180° vertically. It has a ground sampling distance (GSD) of approximately 0.5 cm at 10 m from the capture location. Cycloramas are captured every 5 m on all public roads accessible to vehicles.

The Velodyne HDL-32E is used to capture street LiDAR, which has the following capabilities: 32 distinct beams, up to 695,000 pulses emitted per second, and a maximum recording distance of 70 m in all directions. The speed of the recording vehicle influences the density of points per square meter, the location and position of the surface, and the number of reflections per pulse. In built-up areas, while moving at 40 km/h, the point density on the ground can be between 2250 to 2540 points per square meter, while on building facades, it can range from 1570 to 2100 points per square meter.

2   The Ground Control Network

Milan digital twin project has notable features regarding extension and data collected. Among the others, a ground control network serves the dual purpose of aiding the temporary joint venture in data processing and providing the project validation team with reliable and accurate quality checks.

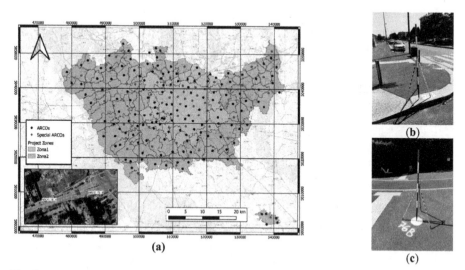

Fig. 2. (a) The map displays the locations of 200 ARCOs (Special ARCOs are depicted in red); the smaller frame provides an example of the position of the two types of ARCO benchmarks, consistent with those shown on the right. Specifically: (b) TypeA benchmark wedged in a large concrete curb; (c) TypeB photogrammetric marker placed in a flat area without any obstacles or changes in slope within a 2-m radius (Color figure online).

The main characteristic is the presence of 200 control areas, referred to as ARCO (short for "ARee di COntrollo" in Italian). The distribution of these areas can be seen in Fig. 2a; each ARCO consists of two benchmarks approximately 100 m apart. Markers "A" (Fig. 2b) are stable topographic nails firmly stuck into concrete structures like curbs; markers "B" (Fig. 2c) are photogrammetric points constituted by white circles with a radius of 15 cm that are directly painted onto the ground (e.g., asphalt, paver blocks); such a kind of artificial marker has already been tested by the authors with promising results [42]. The terrain surrounding each TypeB marker is flat without any obstacles or varying slopes, at least 1 m in radius, but it is recommended to be 2 m; this characteristic makes the area around the markers useful for LiDAR vertical quality assessment and density estimation.

GNSS measurements were employed for benchmark surveying; the aerial imagery 5 cm ground sampling distance (GSD) required a static network for optimal results. The Italian datum UTM32N-RDN2008 (EPSG: 7791) served as the framework for the network, which was established through connections to the SPIN3 GNSS permanent network [43] of Lombardy, Piedmont, and Valle D'Aosta Regions.

Figure 3 displays the static network structure, which is a two-level system. The first level consists of long baselines (shown in black), which link the SPIN3 stations with eight well-distributed ARCOs; the second level comprises short bases that connect all the TypeA ARCOs (shown in blue in Fig. 3 and Fig. 4a). TypeB benchmarks were also connected in a static approach to the two "A" vertices closer, as shown in red in Fig. 4b. According to this strategy, ARCOs-A achieves a relative redundancy of 3 to 5, whereas Type B ARCOs attains 2.

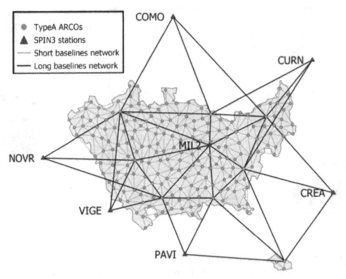

Fig. 3. General schema of the GNSS network: SPIN3 stations are represented by red triangles, and blue dots denote TypeA ARCOs. Long baselines are depicted in black, whereas short ones are in blue (Color figure online).

GNSS network compensation was subdivided into the following steps:

1. Performing minimum constraints adjustment for the short-baseline network, taking into account both TypeA and TypeB vertices;
2. Performing minimum constraints adjustment for the long-baseline network, involving SPIN3 GNSS stations and the eight chosen TypeA benchmarks;
3. Estimating a rigid transformation between the two networks, using the eight points that are common to both;
4. Estimating a rigid transformation between the obtained network and the SPIN3 using the adjusted and the official GNSS permanent station coordinates.

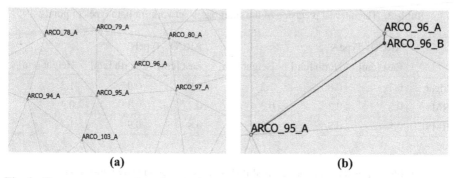

Fig. 4. Here are two examples of network connections: (a) The short-base network connecting TypeA ARCOs; (b) TypeB connections to two "A" benchmarks (Color figure online).

The two tables below illustrate the quality achieved during the first and fourth steps. Table 2 presents the inner precision of the short-base network. The stats are divided into TypeA and TypeB, with TypeB having slightly lower quality due to its lower redundancy. The main statistical figures have been reported indicating that the quality achieved is sufficient to evaluate the accuracy of aerial data. Specifically, the horizontal component is consistently less than 1 cm, and the vertical component is less than 1.5 cm. The tender technical specifications require a maximal value of 15 mm for the horizontal components and 22 mm for the vertical one; the network compensation fulfills both requirements. Table 3 shows the overall accuracy of the GNSS measurements further down the global rigid transformation. The east and north components have achieved satisfactory outcomes (less than 1 cm), whereas the height component performance is slightly lower (just above 2 cm). This could be due to using a simplified antenna model for some SPIN3 stations during network adjustment. Despite this, there is a good agreement between the survey conducted for the project and the official datum. RMS and RMSE have been determined according to the formulas specified by the U.S. Geological Survey (USGS) lidar base specification [44].

To analyze LiDAR data, 50 out of 200 ARCOs were surveyed using a Terrestrial Laser Scanner (TLS). The selected ARCOs, called Special-ARCOs (red dots in Fig. 2), were chosen for the presence of valuable elements in evaluating the precision of point clouds' horizontal and vertical components (Fig. 2a). Indeed, each Special-ARCO location contains one or more manufactured structures, such as buildings, garages, or bus shelters, with at least two vertical perpendicular sides. Additionally, there are flat areas at different elevations from the street level and well-preserved large road markings, like zebra crossings. Since data checking is ongoing, the paper will only cover the use of TypeB ARCOs for LiDAR assessment and will not include Special-ARCOs.

Table 2. The internal precision of the short bases network for both types of points.

	ARCOs-TypeA			ARCOs-TypeB		
	East [cm]	North [cm]	Height [cm]	East [cm]	North [cm]	Height [cm]
Mean	0.7	0.8	1.2	0.8	0.9	1.3
RMS	0.2	0.2	0.3	0.2	0.3	0.4
RMSE	0.7	0.8	1.2	0.8	0.9	1.3

Table 3. Residuals on the seven SPIN3 stations after rigid body transformation.

	Empirical results		
	$|\lambda E|$ [cm]	$|\lambda N|$ [cm]	$|\lambda h|$ [cm]
Maximum residual	0.6	0.8	2.3

Evaluating mobile mapping datasets to ensure accuracy and consistency with other information is also essential. Since topographic activities and MMS surveys were conducted simultaneously, ARCOs were not present during terrestrial data acquisition. Furthermore, the analysis would be inadequate due to insufficient benchmarks, as the MMS survey only covered the Municipality of Milan. As a result, 2000 additional points were measured along the city main road using photogrammetry after block adjustment processing was completed (these points are not displayed in Fig. 2a for readability reasons). These coordinates were compared to those from the MMS survey to determine their accuracy and consistency with the aerial dataset.

3   Quality Assessment of Aerial and Terrestrial Data

Milan city digital twin will be created by managing data from various sources coming from aerial and terrestrial systems. The Leica CityMapper2 hybrid sensor has captured aerial imagery and LiDAR data, whereas CycloMedia's system has generated the MMS datasets. The previous section introduced the ground control network created to ensure data consistency using the ARCOs (Type A, Type B, and Special) and the 2000 photogrammetric points. This section will show how this data has been used to evaluate the accuracy of both aerial and terrestrial datasets.

3.1   Aerial Imagery

Aerial images are a key data source, and the project aims to evaluate various factors related to the collection of photogrammetric blocks and the results of bundle block adjustment.

Photogrammetric Blocks Parameters. The tender specifications require the assessment of the appropriate image acquisition parameters to guarantee the prescribed level of precision and accuracy. Multiple factors were considered, such as ground sampling distance (GSD), longitudinal and transversal overlapping, and sun elevation. The paper highlights the main results of the assessment, which was conducted in a MATLAB R2022b environment using custom codes to manage, visualize, and analyze all data. Furthermore, all analyses were completed automatically.

Ground Sampling Distance. The nominal GSD is 5 cm, but the tender specifications state that the average GSD of each image should not exceed 6 cm. To determine this parameter, a digital terrain model and the exterior orientation parameters of the imagery can be used; the footprint of each image was determined, and then the average GSD was calculated. The analysis results are displayed in Fig. 5, where the green and orange dots depict the average GSD for the whole area. Green dots represent images with a GSD of less than 5 cm, while orange dots represent images with a GSD between 5 and 6 cm. It is worth noting that none of the images exceeded the GSD limit.

Longitudinal and Transversal Overlaps. When planning aerial photogrammetry flights, it is expected to establish fixed percentages for longitudinal and transversal overlapping. These percentages control the multiplicity of points, which refers to the number of images in which a point is visible and the ability of the images to capture the ground and building facades in urban areas (this assumption is mainly connected to traditional nadir imagery). However, this assumption is only partially valid due to the camera's varying focal lengths and sensor sizes on the market. Blocks planned with the same overlapping could have different susceptibility to perspective obstructions caused by different camera parameters. This susceptibility is ultimately determined by the Field of View (FOV), and it is indicated by the phenomenon of "building leaning" or "apparent inclination of buildings" resulting from the shadow cast by obstacles or perspective obstructions. Determining the ideal overlap based on the camera characteristics is important to achieve the best results. Based on this principle, the tender documentation did not specify general overlaps. Instead, it suggested determining the ideal value based on the system used. For the Leica CityMapper-2, the ideal values for longitudinal and transversal overlapping are 70% and 50%, respectively. However, the analysis has shown that the actual image acquisition positions generate a longitudinal overlap ranging from 79.6% to 84.6% (Fig. 6a) and a transversal overlap ranging from 55.1% to 69.8% (Fig. 6b).

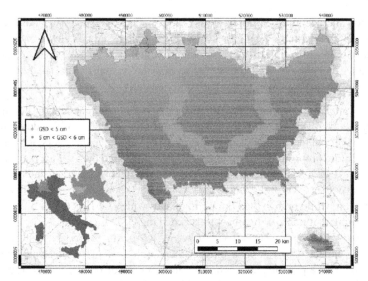

Fig. 5. Green and orange dots depict the average GSD across the Milan Metropolitan area. The green dots represent images with a GSD of less than 5 cm, while the orange dots represent images with a GSD between 5 and 6 cm (Color figure online).

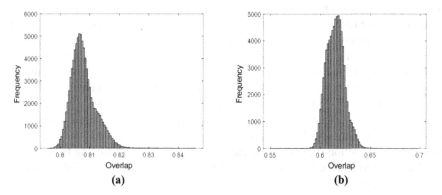

Fig. 6. The histograms for the longitudinal (a) and transversal (b) overlaps.

Sun Elevation. According to the tender specifications, the images must be taken when the sun is at an elevation greater than 35°. Using the external orientation parameters, the metadata containing the date and time for each image, and a sun elevation model, it can be verified whether the images comply with this requirement.

The sun angle changes between 26° and 68° (Fig. 7). Of all the images, only 1378 (around 1.5%) were taken when the sun was below the required angle. A subset of these images underwent a visual inspection to confirm their quality.

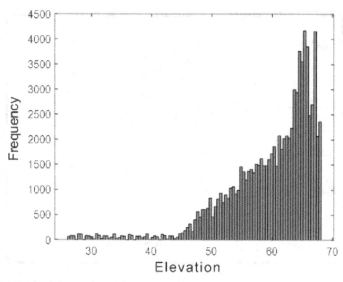

Fig. 7. Histogram of the sun elevation

Bundle Block Adjustment. Due to the extension of the project area, aerial triangulation can be performed by subdividing the processing into sub-blocks with regular shapes, including an adequate number of ARCOs and 500 m of overlap between them. The entire region has been divided into five sub-blocks, with four covering the main area (as depicted in Fig. 8) and the fifth covering San Colombano al Lambro. Considering the overlapping between each block, their extensions are similar, corresponding to about 400 km^2. Each photogrammetric sub-block has two categories of ARCOs: Control ARCOs and Check ARCOs. Control ARCOs are dispersed evenly throughout the area and support aerial triangulation. Check ARCOs serve for quality assessment and must consist of at least 15 points, except for San Colombano.

The aerial data was processed by CGR using the Leica HxMap suite. The University of Pavia received its principal outputs and log files for analysis, which were then investigated through custom codes in MATLAB R2022b.

The accuracy of bundle block adjustment was determined by comparing photogrammetric and topographic coordinates. Table 4 presents the key findings of this analysis. The RMSE of residuals demonstrates excellent performance, considering Control or Check ARCO. The horizontal components are less than half the nominal GSD of 5 cm, while the height slightly exceeds the half-GSD.

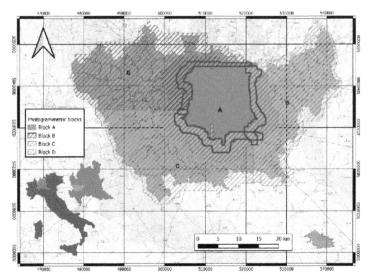

Fig. 8. Four photogrammetric blocks were utilized for aerial triangulation. It should be noted that there is a fifth block for San Colombano Municipality, although it is not identified with a letter.

Table 4. Control and Check ARCO accuracy achieved by comparing photogrammetric and topographic coordinates.

	Control ARCOs			Check ARCOs		
	East [cm]	North [cm]	Height [cm]	East [cm]	North [cm]	Height [cm]
Mean	−0.1	0.1	1.2	−0.4	0.1	1.9
RMS	1.4	1.5	2.7	1.8	1.5	3.2
RMSE	1.4	1.5	2.9	1.8	1.5	3.7

3.2 Aerial LiDAR

The project foresees to evaluate the vertical and horizontal components of aerial LiDAR data using TypeB-ARCOs and Special-ARCOs. The point cloud density will also be analyzed. However, only TypeB benchmarks and the vertical component will be utilized and discussed in this paper; height accuracy and precision are crucial to DTM generation and, therefore, a significant aspect to investigate. The tests were performed in a MATLAB R2022b environment with custom codes developed to handle, visualize, and examine all the data obtained. Additionally, all analyses are completed automatically.

Point Clouds Density. Point cloud density and its variations inside a block influence derived products, such as DSM or DTM, and must be evaluated [39]. The LiDAR datasets were delivered as overlapped strips, and for this study, the density has been assessed by analyzing each strip individually, as well as the entire dataset as a whole. By conducting a dual investigation, we can thoroughly investigate the impact of both the circular oblique scanning pattern used for acquisition and the level of overlapping in the data.

The density of the LiDAR point cloud has been measured by utilizing the terrain around each TypeB ARCOs. A 4-square meter area is chosen to determine the relative density, counting the number of internal points. According to the technical specifications, a density of at least 20 points per square meter is required. When analyzing each strip individually, the density varies from 25 points per square meter to 190 points per square meter. The diversity observed in the density is caused by the circular acquisition pattern, leading to a noticeable variation from the center to the edges of the strips. The median density is approximately 33 points per square meter.

When utilizing the hybrid Leica CityMapper-2, there is a significant overlap between strips due to the prioritization of photogrammetric planning over LiDAR. If we apply the same analysis above to the entire dataset, the median score increases from 33 points per square meter to 77 points per square meter. However, this increased density can only be fully utilized if the strips are consistent.

Vertical Accuracy Assessment using TypeB ARCOs. When assessing LiDAR data, three key attributes are taken into account. Firstly, the accuracy of point clouds is evaluated based on their proximity to ground truth. Secondly, the precision of the data is assessed by examining any noise present in the point clouds. Finally, the congruency between adjacent strips is analyzed. It is worth noting that accuracy and precision are used in their conventional sense, with accuracy referring to how closely a measurement matches the actual value and precision referring to how closely multiple measurements match each other. TypeB ARCOs can be valuable tools for assessing all of these characteristics.

When analyzing these benchmarks, the terrain within a 2-m radius is considered flat. The data points within a 4-square meter area are then isolated, and a plan is fitted onto them; using a plan allows us to consider any possible terrain slope.

The MSAC (Mestimator SAmple Consensus) algorithm proposed by [45] as a variant of RANSAC is used for the fitting purpose. After determining the threshold for identifying outliers, the algorithm proceeds to estimate the parameters for the geometric model of the plane, as well as the indices for the inlier and outlier points. Additionally, it calculates the mean error of the distance between the inlier points and the model. The threshold for the outlier has been set at 18 cm, which is three times the maximum Mean Square Error mentioned in the tender documents. Once the plane has been identified, it is shifted until the TypeB marker rests on it. After this, the perpendicular distances between each inlier point belonging to the LiDAR cloud and the shifted plane are calculated. To determine the vertical component of the estimated perpendicular distance, the slope of the plane has been considered [30, 46]. The statistical figure for the vertical accuracy obtained is presented in the first line of Table 5, showing good results with an RMSE of approximately 4.5 cm.

The estimated plans have also been utilized to assess the precision of the LiDAR point clouds. This was done through the MSAC algorithm, which measures the average distance error between inlier points and the model itself. The technical specification for the tender requires this value to be no more than 6 cm. All the plane is significantly lower than this requirement (the maximum value is about 4.8 cm), with an RMSE of only 1.4 cm (second line of Table 5).

Finally, since the strips are significantly overlapped, 82 markers are visible in two strips; the distance between their planes can then be used to estimate their consistency. Although the two plans could be tilted relative to each other, this should be neglected given the small size of the tested areas (only 4 sqm). The average distance between adjacent strips is 1.2 cm, with an RMSE of 1.3 cm (third line of Table 5).

Table 5. Summary of vertical assessment of aerial LiDAR datasets

	ARCOs-TypeB		
	Vertical accuracy [cm]	Vertical precision [cm]	Strips' vertical consistency [cm]
Mean	3.4	1.1	1.2
RMS	3.3	0.9	0.4
RSME	4.8	1.4	1.3

3.3 MMS Data

The MMS data acquisition is a crucial part of the Milan digital twin project, as it supports creating the city digital model and extracting the urban object database. The paper will focus on evaluating the geometric contents only, including the evaluation of point cloud density, panoramic image resolution, and horizontal and vertical accuracy. The urban object database was compiled by CycloMedia using artificial intelligence, and the Municipality of Milan is currently reviewing its contents. Instead, the geometric analysis has been completed and will be described in the following sections. The tests were conducted through visual inspection and custom codes written in the MATLAB R2022b environment.

Point Cloud Density and Panoramic Image Resolution. The MMS survey focuses exclusively on the Municipality of Milan. The collected data was evaluated based on the density of the point cloud and the resolution of panoramic images. To conduct the first analysis, 100 well-distributed test areas containing at least one vertical planar surface of 2 × 2 square meters, such as building facades, were selected; the surfaces must be about 10 m from the vehicle path. The point density was then calculated and compared to a threshold of 1500 pt/sqm as required by the tender technical specifications; all test areas exceeded this limit. Furthermore, the same building facades were used to evaluate the image resolution, which must be equal to or smaller than 8 cm/pixel according to the tender technical specifications. The dimensions of the facades were obtained from the point cloud, and the corresponding pixel dimensions were determined from the panoramic images. The test results were positive, with the resolution always meeting the minimum requirement.

Horizontal and Vertical Accuracy. In Sect. 2, it was mentioned that 2000 points were measured using photogrammetry to evaluate the accuracy of MMS (the tender does not require analysis on precision). These points were observed along the city main roads and included visible details like manhole covers and road markings. The coordinates of these points were compared to those observed on the MMS survey to estimate their accuracy and consistency with the aerial dataset. The statistical figures derived from the residuals obtained are shown in Table 6. While the values are slightly higher than previous results, it is important to note that they incorporate both the uncertainty of photogrammetric processing and MMS data elaboration. The results are satisfactory, and the two datasets can be used together.

Table 6. Summary of horizontal and vertical assessment of MMS datasets.

	2000 MMS benchmarks		
	East [cm]	North [cm]	Height [cm]
Mean	−0.6	0.0	5.7
RMS	7.6	7.3	12.9
RMSE	7.6	7.3	14.1

4 Conclusion

Milan has invested in creating a complex dataset to generate a digital twin for the Municipality and Metropolitan Area. This dataset comprises information from various sources, including aerial photogrammetry, LiDAR, and terrestrial mobile mapping surveys. To ensure accurate and reliable geometric data, it is crucial to evaluate the quality of the information gathered and ensure that they are consistent. To achieve this goal, Milan has established a ground control network that is innovative and dependable, with numerous valuable features that guarantee redundancy and precision. The ARCO network was surveyed using static GNSS measurements that ensure the best accuracy for a reliable photogrammetric processing evaluation. Indeed, the achieved precisions (Table 2) guarantee an optimal assessment of the bundle block adjustment, considering that the GSD of 5 cm.

Creating a digital twin is a challenging process that begins with acquiring data and continues with assessing its precision and accuracy. The second step, faced in the paper, is crucial to generate reliable outcomes, including true-orthophotos, digital models (DTS/DTM), and tools for city management (e.g., solar potential, green maintenance, pollution analysis). The final goal to generate a photorealistic 3D city model combining aerial and terrestrial data, including imagery and point cloud, requires high-quality information and mutual coherence.

The paper shows promising results in accomplishing these further scheduled tasks (product generation and 3D city model). Specifically, the image resolution and point density meet or exceed the standards outlined in the technical documents provided for the project. The bundle block adjustment for the aerial acquisition reports excellent RMSEs of residuals [47]: horizontal components are less than half the nominal ground sampling distance (GSD) of 5 cm, while the height slightly exceeds the half-GSD. Aerial LiDAR was tested only for the vertical component, showing promising results [46, 48]: the accuracy RMSE is about 5 cm, whereas the cloud noise is less than 1.5 cm. Also, MMS data reports positive outcomes [34, 49], ranging from 7.5 cm of the horizontal components to 14 cm of the vertical one.

Careful consideration must be made regarding the vertical components of the datasets analyzed. The results obtained from the aerial triangulation are excellent for both the ground and check ARCOs without showing any significant systematisms. This outcome is reasonable since the coordinates of the check ARCOs are included in the bundle block adjustment. However, the aerial LiDAR and MMS data processing was carried out independently of the ARCOs using the SPIN3 GNSS network, guaranteeing consistency between all the analyzed datasets. As mentioned earlier, the results are very satisfactory. Nonetheless, it is worth highlighting that both datasets present a non-zero value for the altimetric averages. This result could be linked to the vertical residual reported in Table 3. Therefore, a part of the RMSE obtained could be due to this aspect, thus further underlining the high quality of the values obtained.

A final remark must be made on the tender technical specifications requirements that specify only the thresholds for the maximal allowable error and the 95-percentile one. Reporting only the former, the thresholds for aerial triangulation (for check ARCOs only) are 7.5 cm and 15 cm for horizontal and vertical components, respectively; 24 cm for LiDAR vertical accuracy, and 72 cm for 3-dimensional residuals in the MMS survey. All the datasets passed the tests, presenting values below the reported thresholds. Standard statistical figures, like mean, RMS, and RMSE, have been inserted in the paper because they are more understandable and representative of the achieved quality.

The following steps in the quality checks involve analyzing the quality of the horizontal components of LiDAR datasets and assessing the final products, including true-orthophotos and digital models such as DSM and DTM. The resolution of data in imagery and point clouds, along with their geometric quality, serves as the foundation for creating the digital twin and the connected various applications that the Milan municipality is either launching or planning to launch soon. For instance, these applications include analyzing building roofs to identify the flat ones that can be converted into green roofs (improving the temperatures in the city) or identifying pitched roofs that are optimal for installing photovoltaic systems (ensuring that they are clear of obstructions such as dormer windows or chimneys). The data is also used to verify land use compliance from a tax perspective and to identify ramps or stairs for accessibility purposes. All these applications require high-quality precision and data resolution, and the results obtained from the analysis give hope for their effective implementation.

References

1. Botín-Sanabria, D.M., Mihaita, S., Peimbert-García, R.E., Ramírez-Moreno, M.A., Ramírez-Mendoza, R.A., Lozoya-Santos, J.J.: Digital twin technology challenges and applications: a comprehensive review. Remote Sens. **14**, 1335 (2022). https://doi.org/10.3390/RS14061335
2. Enders, M., Enders, M.R., Hoßbach, N.: Dimensions of digital twin applications-a literature review. Completed Research (2019)
3. Shahat, E., Hyun, C.T., Yeom, C.: City digital twin potentials: a review and research agenda. Sustainability **13**, 3386 (2021). https://doi.org/10.3390/SU13063386
4. Deng, T., Zhang, K., Shen, Z.J.: A systematic review of a digital twin city: a new pattern of urban governance toward smart cities. J. Manag. Sci. Eng. **6**, 125–134 (2021). https://doi.org/10.1016/J.JMSE.2021.03.003
5. Francisco, A., Asce, S.M., Mohammadi, N., Asce, A.M., Taylor, J.E., Asce, M.: Smart city digital twin–enabled energy management: toward real-time urban building energy benchmarking. J. Manag. Eng. **36** (2020). https://doi.org/10.1061/(ASCE)ME.1943-5479.0000741
6. Kim, J., Kim, H., Ham, Y.: Mapping local vulnerabilities into a 3D city model through social sensing and the CAVE system toward digital twin city. In: Computing in Civil Engineering 2019: Smart Cities, Sustainability, and Resilience - Selected Papers from the ASCE International Conference on Computing in Civil Engineering 2019, pp. 451–458 (2019). https://doi.org/10.1061/9780784482445.058
7. Laamarti, F., Badawi, H.F., Ding, Y., Arafsha, F., Hafidh, B., El Saddik, A.: An ISO/IEEE 11073 standardized digital twin framework for health and well-being in smart cities. IEEE Access. **8**, 105950–105961 (2020). https://doi.org/10.1109/ACCESS.2020.2999871
8. Shiqing, D., Zhang, H., Yanqin, Z., Wang, A., Xiong, Y., Jingmeng, Z.: Research on construction of spatio-temporal data visualization platform for GIS and BIM fusion. noa.gwlb.de. (2020). https://doi.org/10.5194/isprs-archives-XLII-3-W10-555-2020
9. Schrotter, G., Hürzeler, C.: The digital twin of the city of Zurich for urban planning. PFG – J. Photogramm. Remote Sens. Geoinf. Sci. **88**, 99–112 (2020). https://doi.org/10.1007/S41064-020-00092-2/FIGURES/14
10. Lehner, H., Dorffner, L.: Digital geoTwin Vienna: towards a digital twin city as geodata hub. PFG - J. Photogram. Remote Sens. Geoinf. Sci. **88**, 63–75 (2020). https://doi.org/10.1007/S41064-020-00101-4
11. The Kalasatama Digital Twins Project. https://www.hel.fi/static/liitteet-2019/Kaupunginkanslia/Helsinki3D_Kalasatama_Digital_Twins.pdf. Accessed 05 Apr 2023
12. Virtual Singapore. https://www.nrf.gov.sg/programmes/virtual-singapore. Accessed 05 Apr 2023
13. Hexagon's HxDR to host 3DNL, Cyclomedia's Digital Twin of the Netherlands. Leica Geosystems. https://leica-geosystems.com/it-it/about-us/news-room/news-overview/2021/04/cyclomedias-digital-twin-of-the-netherlands. Accessed 05 Apr 2023
14. Jalonen, M.: Smart Cities in Smart Regions Conference Proceedings (2022)
15. Hopfstock, A., Hovenbitzer, M., Knöfel, P., Lindl, F., Lenk, M.: Auf dem Weg zu einem Digitalen Zwilling von Deutschland. ZfV - Zeitschrift für Geodäsie, Geoinformation und Landmanagement (2021). https://doi.org/10.12902/ZFV-0379-2021
16. Yencken, D.: Creative cities. In: Space Place and Culture, pp. 1–21 (2013)
17. Barricelli, B.R., Casiraghi, E., Fogli, D.: A survey on digital twin: definitions, characteristics, applications, and design implications. IEEE Access **7**, 167653–167671 (2019). https://doi.org/10.1109/ACCESS.2019.2953499
18. Liu, X., Wang, X., Wright, G., Cheng, J.C.P., Li, X., Liu, R.: A state-of-the-art review on the integration of Building Information Modeling (BIM) and Geographic Information System (GIS). ISPRS Int. J. Geoinf. **6**, 53 (2017). https://doi.org/10.3390/IJGI6020053

19. Ketzler, B., Naserentin, V., Latino, F., Zangelidis, C., Thuvander, L., Logg, A.: Digital twins for cities: a state of the art review. Built Environ. **46**, 547–573 (2020). https://doi.org/10.2148/BENV.46.4.547

20. Kalogianni, E., van Oosterom, P., Dimopoulou, E., Lemmen, C.: 3D land administration: a review and a future vision in the context of the spatial development lifecycle. ISPRS Int. J. Geo-Inf. **9**, 107 (2020). https://doi.org/10.3390/IJGI9020107

21. Shojaei, D., Olfat, H., Quinones Faundez, S.I., Kalantari, M., Rajabifard, A., Briffa, M.: Geometrical data validation in 3D digital cadastre – a case study for Victoria, Australia. Land Use Policy **68**, 638–648 (2017). https://doi.org/10.1016/J.LANDUSEPOL.2017.08.031

22. van Nederveen, G.A., Tolman, F.P.: Modelling multiple views on buildings. Autom. Constr. **1**, 215–224 (1992). https://doi.org/10.1016/0926-5805(92)90014-B

23. Casella, V., Franzini, M., Kocaman, S., Gruen, A.: Geometric accuracy assessment of ADS40 imagery under various network configurations. In: International Archives of the Photogrammetry, Remote Sensing and Spatial Information Sciences - ISPRS Archives (2008)

24. Honkavaara, E., et al.: A permanent test field for digital photogrammetric systems. Photogramm. Eng. Remote Sens. **74**, 95–106 (2008). https://doi.org/10.14358/PERS.74.1.95

25. Schiewe, J.: Status and future perspectives of the application potential of digital airborne sensor systems. Int. J. Appl. Earth Obs. Geoinf. **6**, 215–228 (2005). https://doi.org/10.1016/J.JAG.2004.10.011

26. Honkavaara, E., et al.: Digital airborne photogrammetry—a new tool for quantitative remote sensing?—A state-of-the-art review on radiometric aspects of digital photogrammetric images. Remote Sens. **1**, 577–605 (2009). https://doi.org/10.3390/RS1030577

27. Cramer, M.: Performance of medium format digital aerial sensor systems. Int. Arch. Photogram. Remote Sens. **35**, 769–774 (2004)

28. Casella, V., et al.: Initial results of the Italian project on direct georeferencing in aerial photogrammetry. In: International Archives of the Photogrammetry, Remote Sensing and Spatial Information Sciences, pp. 881–886 (2004)

29. Casella, V., Franzini, M.: Experiences in GPS/IMU calibration. Rigorous and independent cross-validation of results. In: Proceedings of ISPRS Hannover Workshop 2005, High-Resolution Earth Imaging for Geospatial Information (2005)

30. Casella, V., Spalla, A.: Estimation of planimetric accuracy of laser scanning data. Proposal of a method exploiting ramps. In: International Archives of the Photogrammetry, Remote Sensing and Spatial Information Sciences - ISPRS Archives (2000)

31. Höhle, J.: The assessment of the absolute planimetric accuracy of airborne laserscanning. Int. Arch. Photogram. Remote Sens. Spatial Inf. Sci. **38**, 145–150 (2012)

32. Liu, X.: Accuracy assessment of LiDAR elevation data using survey marks. Surv. Rev. **43**, 80–93 (2013). https://doi.org/10.1179/003962611X12894696204704

33. Toschi, I., Rodríguez-Gonzálvez, P., Remondino, F., Minto, S., Orlandini, S., Fuller, A.: Accuracy evaluation of a mobile mapping system with advanced statistical methods. Int. Arch. Photogram. Remote Sens. Spatial Inf. Sci. **XL-5-W4**, 245–253 (2015). https://doi.org/10.5194/ISPRSARCHIVES-XL-5-W4-245-2015

34. Al-Durgham, K., Lichti, D.D., Kwak, E., Dixon, R.: Automated accuracy assessment of a mobile mapping system with lightweight laser scanning and MEMS sensors. Appl. Sci. **11**, 1007 (2021). https://doi.org/10.3390/APP11031007

35. Elhashash, M., Albanwan, H., Qin, R.: A review of mobile mapping systems: from sensors to applications. Sensors **22**, 4262 (2022). https://doi.org/10.3390/S22114262

36. Toschi, I.: Airborne oblique imaging: towards the hybrid era. Cartography Remote Sens. **31**, 2391–9477 (2019). https://doi.org/10.2478/apcrs-2019-0002

37. Toschi, I., Remondino, F., Rothe, R., Klimek, K.: Combining airborne oblique camera and LiDAR sensors: investigation and new perspectives. Int. Arch. Photogram. Remote Sens.

Spatial Inf. Sci. **XLII–1**, 437–444 (2018). https://doi.org/10.5194/isprs-archives-XLII-1-437-2018

38. Bacher, U.: Hybrid aerial sensor data as basis for a geospatial digital twin. https://doi.org/10.5194/isprs-archives-XLIII-B4-2022-653-2022

39. Petras, V., Petrasova, A., McCarter, J.B., Mitasova, H., Meentemeyer, R.K.: Point density variations in airborne LiDAR point clouds. Sensors **23**, 1593 (2023). https://doi.org/10.3390/s23031593

40. Joosten, F., Verbree, E.: Map supported point cloud registration a method for creation of a smart point cloud (2018)

41. Alsadik, B.: Multibeam LiDAR for mobile mapping systems feasibility of using aerial images to improve the positioning accuracy of mobile mapping systems. View project hybrid adjustment of UAS-based LiDAR and image data view project

42. Casella, V., Galetto, R., Franzini, M.: An Italian project on the evaluation of direct georeferencing in photogrammetry. In: Proceedings Eurocow 2006 (2006)

43. SPIN3 GNSS – Servizio di Posizionamento Interregionale GNSS. https://www.spingnss.it/. Accessed 10 July 2023

44. Heidemann, H.K.: Lidar base specification. In: Techniques and Methods (2012). https://doi.org/10.3133/TM11B4

45. Torr, P.H.S., Zisserman, A.: MLESAC: a new robust estimator with application to estimating image geometry. Comput. Vis. Image Underst. **78**, 138–156 (2000). https://doi.org/10.1006/cviu.1999.0832

46. Hodgson, M.E., Bresnahan, P.: Accuracy of airborne lidar-derived elevation: empirical assessment and error budget. Photogram. Eng. Remote Sens. **70**, 331–339 (2004). https://doi.org/10.14358/PERS.70.3.331

47. Maset, E., Rupnik, E., Pierrot-Deseilligny, M., Remondino, F., Fusiello, A.: Exploiting multi-camera constraints within bundle block adjustment: an experimental comparison. Int. Arch. Photogram. Remote Sens. Spatial Inf. Sci. **XLIII-B2-2021**, 33–38 (2021). https://doi.org/10.5194/ISPRS-ARCHIVES-XLIII-B2-2021-33-2021

48. Khanal, M., Hasan, M., Sterbentz, N., Johnson, R., Weatherly, J.: Accuracy comparison of aerial lidar, mobile-terrestrial lidar, and UAV photogrammetric capture data elevations over different terrain types. Infrastructures **5**, 65 (2020). https://doi.org/10.3390/INFRASTRUCTURES5080065

49. Bos, K.: Analyzing deformation of buildings using LiDAR point clouds obtained by a Mobile Laser Scanning System (2023). https://repository.tudelft.nl/islandora/object/uuid%3Ac545eb66-b1aa-43dd-b3ad-eebcf5f03ec6

On the Role of Geomatics and Official Regional Cartography in the Interconnected Nord-Est Innovation Ecosystem

Eleonora Maset$^{(\boxtimes)}$ (ID), Domenico Visintini (ID), and Alberto Beinat (ID)

Polytechnic Department of Engineering and Architecture (DPIA),
University of Udine, Udine, Italy
{eleonora.maset,domenico.visintini,alberto.beinat}@uniud.it

Abstract. The paper presents the expected role of geomatics within the *Interconnected Nord-Est Innovation Ecosystem* (iNEST), a research and innovation project funded by the Italian National Recovery and Resilience Plan and involving universities, companies and territorial institutions of the Triveneto macro-region. The iNEST ecosystem aims to extend the beneficial effects of digitalization to the key specialization areas of *Nord-Est*, including technologies for the marine and mountain environment, smart agri-food, architecture, tourism and cultural heritage. In fields such as these, where knowledge of the territory is paramount, up-to-date regional cartographic products are essential. Therefore, this work also gives us the opportunity to provide a comprehensive overview of the cartographic products available for Friuli Venezia Giulia, one of the regions included in the iNEST project.

Keywords: Geomatics · Official Cartography · Interconnected Nord-Est Innovation Ecosystem · Italian National Recovery and Resilience Plan · Friuli Venezia Giulia region

1 Introduction

As outlined in the National Recovery and Resilience Plan (NRRP), Italy's post-pandemic recovery from COVID-19 is based on the digitalization of products, processes and services, and requires measures to improve the quality of life and environmental safety. It is clear that this is a multidisciplinary challenge that can be tackled by bringing together different skills and technologies, with a key role for data of various kinds, including geographic information. Nowadays, geospatial data is indeed central to many business models sustaining the digital transition and user demand for geographic information is growing like never before [1]. Geomatics can support other disciplines by providing up-to-date, complete and accurate three-dimensional geometric and semantic data of both the natural

E. Borgogno Mondino and P. Zamperlin (Eds.): ASITA 2023, CCIS 2088, pp. 172–183, 2024.
https://doi.org/10.1007/978-3-031-59925-5_13

environment and artificial objects, which could serve as a basis for the simulation, understanding and monitoring of complex phenomena [2,3]. The transversal involvement of geomatics is acknowledged also in the development of Smart Cities, where geographic information is essential in the management and decision tools [4,5].

In this context, it is worth mentioning the high quality, reliable and certified official cartography produced by public administrations [1], that seems to be essential, especially for projects covering large areas. The spatial information accessible through regional geoportals can be one of the starting points for institutions, companies and researchers to carry out the activities envisaged to achieve the objectives of the NRRP. In addition, NRRP projects are expected to be implemented in a very short time frame, so the immediate availability of regional cartographic products is another strength of these data sources.

The aim of this paper is two-fold. In Sect. 2, we present the *Interconnected Nord-Est Innovation Ecosystem* (iNEST), a project funded within the NRRP to extend the advantages of digitalization to the main specialization areas of Northeast Italy, and highlight the activities that will significantly benefit from geographic data and surveying techniques. The paper should be regarded as a preliminary report providing an overview of the pervasiveness of geomatics in various planned activities. In future research, challenges and problems encountered in the use of geospatial technologies will be analyzed in depth. On the other hand, some of the topics addressed by iNEST and its interregional nature make the importance of public cartographic products evident. We therefore describe in Sect. 3 the ambitious cartographic program launched by the Friuli Venezia Giulia (FVG) region in 2017, whose features place it at the forefront of Italian regional databases.

2   Interconnected Nord-Est Innovation Ecosystem

According to the definition given by the European Commission, innovation ecosystems are ecosystems that bring together different actors whose goal is to enable technology development and innovation [6,7]. The NRRP is funding within the Mission 4 – "Education and research", Component 2 – "From research to business", innovation ecosystems born to strengthen the cooperation among universities, businesses and territorial institutions, with the aim of involving also the local community in digitalization and sustainability issues.

The iNEST ecosystem is one of 11 financed projects, built on the Smart Specialization Strategies of the northeastern Italian territory, in compliance with the industrial and research missions of the Triveneto macro-region. The territory, that includes the Regions of Friuli Venezia Giulia and Veneto and the two Autonomous Provinces of Trento and Bolzano, is characterized by a variety of vocations, from industry to agri-food, from tourism to cultural heritage. This wealth of key sectors has been transferred to the project by setting up nine interconnected spokes, each led by one of the nine universities of Northeast and devoted to a different theme (Fig. 1). The planning of the activities carried out by each spoke is detailed in [8].

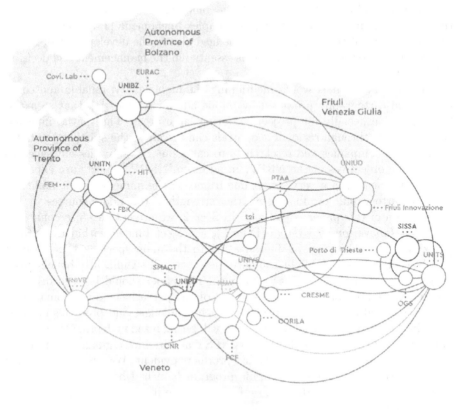

Fig. 1. Partners of the iNEST ecosystem [8].

The iNEST project can be considered as an opportunity to establish synergies not only between different partners (universities, companies, local authorities), but also between disciplines and technologies. Within this framework, geomatics techniques can assist in carrying out many activities, as they can be used in different application contexts. In particular, the role of geomatics is most significant within spoke 1 and 8, which deal with mountain and marine ecosystems, respectively.

Improving the resilience of mountain areas to the risks of climate change and geo-hydrological hazards is one of the research and technology transfer actions carried out in spoke 1, led by the Free University of Bolzano. The *Topography, remoTe sensing, and Mobile mapping systems* (ToTeM) Laboratory of the University of Udine, together with the *HydroLab uniUD* group, is currently involved in the development of a reference framework aimed at optimizing the effectiveness of risk prevention measures and structures in mountain basins. The activities employ both current and legacy cartographic data, to monitor the evolution of torrents and sediment-related phenomena at a regional scale, as well as high-resolution topographic surveys (mainly based on photogrammetry and laser scanning techniques) to locally assess the interaction between sediment dynamics and channel control works. The overall goal is to define a protocol of operational techniques for remote sensing surveys and geographic data processing, that allows quantifying the problems at different scales and could be profitably applied in the future not only by researchers, but also by practitioners and local authorities.

The aim of spoke 8 (led by the University of Trieste) is the creation of the North Adriatic Digital Twin, in cooperation with spoke 9 (coordinated by the International School for Advanced Studies – SISSA). Among the activities currently carried out, we can find the production of high-quality, certified, harmonized, accessible and reusable georeferenced data.

The survey and assessment of existing buildings, as well as the realization of Building Information Models (BIM), can be one of the inputs for some of the actions carried out by spoke 4, led by Iuav University of Venice and focused on the construction and design sectors. The activities related to the sustainable development and management of the territory also benefit from topographic geodatabases and Geographic Information System (GIS) tools.

On the other hand, geomatics techniques, from laser scanning to photogrammetric 3D modeling, are supportive technologies in the field of culture and creative industries (spoke 6, led by the University Ca' Foscari of Venice), especially for realizing virtual experiences involving heritage sites, allowing also the collection of 2D and 3D data for precision agriculture (spoke 7, coordinated by the University of Verona).

Although less prominent, geomatics methods and surveying techniques can provide metrology solutions to support disciplines such as robotics and artificial intelligence, which are crucial in the areas of digital health (spoke 2, coordinated by the University of Trento), advanced manufacturing (spoke 3, led by the University of Udine), and Industry 5.0 (spoke 5, supervised by the University of Padova).

The topics and activities described above require to resort to regional cartographic products. Therefore, the following section provides a comprehensive overview of the recent mapping program developed by the Autonomous Region of Friuli Venezia Giulia, one of the territories involved in the iNEST project.

3   Friuli Venezia Giulia Regional Cartography

The history of regional cartography in Friuli Venezia Giulia dates back to 1970, when the production of the first technical map at a scale of 1:5,000 started. Although limited in size (it is the fifth smallest region of Italy, covering an area of approximately 7,900 km^2), the region is characterized by a great variety of landscapes, ranging from coastal plains to hilly and mountainous alpine terrain. Moreover, Friuli Venezia Giulia has been subject to intense seismic and hydrological events in the last decades. In such a scenario, an accurate knowledge of the changing territory is essential, which has led the regional administration to carry out partial updates of the technical map over the years [9].

The breakthrough came in 2017 when, after a successful test in some municipalities of the Isonzo area, a major and ambitious program was launched to completely renew the regional geodatabases [10]. Thanks to the use of state-of-the-art instruments and advanced processing methods, new cartographic products are now freely available and can be accessed via the geoportal *Eagle.fvg* [11].

According to the Ministerial Decree 10.11.2021, "Adoption of the National Geodetic Refence System", all the data are expressed in the RDN2008 reference system, which is the Italian realization of the ETRF2000 frame, and the cartographic coordinates are represented according to the UTM system, Zone 33N. It is worth mentioning that the cartographic products are distributed both in GRS80 ellipsoidal heights and in othometric heights, the latter referring to the mean sea level and computed according to the geoid undulation model provided by the Italian Military Geographic Institute (IGM). The adoption of such technical specifications promotes the interoperability with European datasets.

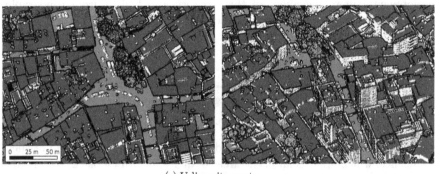

(a) Udine city center.

(b) Mountain village.

Fig. 2. Top view (left) and 3D view (right) of classified airborne LiDAR point clouds. Classes: *ground* (orange), *low and medium vegetation* (dark green), *high vegetation* (light green), *roof* (red), *power line* (blue), *other* (white). (Color figure online)

3.1   Laser Scanning Data

The first product delivered was the airborne laser scanning survey. The entire region was mapped using a Riegl LMS-Q780 Light Detection and Ranging (LiDAR) sensor, able to register the full-waveform of the backscattered signal. Up to 9 echoes for each emitted pulse could be retrieved by the instrument, maximizing ground point density and vegetation penetration. The flights were planned to ensure an average density of 16 points/m^2 in areas below 1,000 m above seal level (asl), and 10 points/m^2 for higher altitudes. A flight altitude of 500 m above ground level (agl) was thus used, also guaranteeing a 30% overlap between adjacent strips. As a result, more than 300 billion points were acquired, with an accuracy of better than 10 cm in elevation.

To associate semantic information with the point cloud, useful also for data interpretation and the subsequent generation of digital elevation models, a novel deep learning algorithm was implemented to efficiently and accurately classify the data [12,13]. Figure 2 shows some examples where points are colorized in accordance with the identified classes: *ground, low, medium and high vegetation, building roof, power line, water* and *other* (e.g., walls and cars). As can be seen in the figure, the high density of the survey allowed the reconstruction of thin objects such as low-voltage electricity network, chimneys, and fences.

The labeled point cloud was then used to derive raster maps at 0.5 m/pixel resolution, including the Digital Terrain Model (DTM), obtained from the *ground* class (Fig. 3a), and the Digital Building Model (DBM), in which *ground* and *roof* points are considered (Fig. 3b). The Digital Surface Model is derived from all the first returns (i.e., the first echoes registered by the instrument for each pulse emitted, corresponding to the higher points), obtaining the so-called DSM*first* (Fig. 3c), whereas the DSM*last* (Fig. 3d) takes into account all the last returns (i.e., the last echoes registered by the instrument for each pulse emitted, corresponding to the lower points).

3.2   True Orthophoto

The 3D LiDAR point cloud is complemented by a high-precision orthomosaic of the entire region, characterized by a resolution of 10 cm/pixel and a planimetric accuracy of better than 20 cm. To obtain these results, a large-format Vexcel UltraCam Eagle digital camera was used (panchromaic image size of 20,010 × 13,080 pixel, color image size 6,670 × 4,360 pixel), capturing 4 bands (RGB and NIR channels) at an average flight altitude of 1,300 m agl. The strips were planned to ensure a frontal overlap of 80% and a side overlap of 60%, values that allowed the subsequent precise orthorectification process.

It is worth underlying that the result produced is a *true* orthophoto, i.e., a highly detailed and accurate photogrammetric-derived DSM was used in the rectification process, rather than a DTM. The differences and advantages over a traditional orthophoto are clearly shown in Fig. 4: the accurate planimetric position of all objects can be measured in the true orthophoto (Fig. 4a), whereas in the standard orthophoto there is a significant displacement of tall structures (Fig. 4b).

(a) Digital Terrain Model.

(b) Digital Building Model.

(c) Digital Surface Model (first returns).

(d) Digital Surface Model (last returns).

Fig. 3. Digital models at 0.5 m/pixel resolution, obtained from the airborne LiDAR survey.

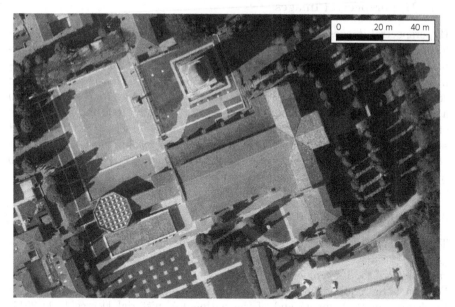

(a) True orthophoto.

(b) Traditional orthophoto.

Fig. 4. True orthophoto (a) of the Basilica of Aquileia (Udine) compared to a traditional orthophoto (b). Significant displacement of tall structures (bell tower and church walls) is visible in (b).

3.3   Hyperspectral Images

Hyperspectral images of entire regions are usually acquired using satellite platforms. Instead, the Friuli Venezia Giulia administration commissioned an airborne survey at an average flight altitude of 1,500 m agl to reduce the radiometric distortion caused by the atmosphere and increase the spatial resolution compared to satellite imagery. Hyperspectral rectified images were obtained with a resolution of 1 m/pixel, covering the spectral range 400–1000 nm. For the area of the Province of Trieste, hyperspectral data were acquired with a CASI 1500H sensor from ITRES, characterized by a radiometric resolution of 125 bands at 14 bits. The rest of the region was surveyed employing a HySpex VNIR-1800 sensor from NORSK Elekto Optikk, which collected 186 bands at 16 bits.

3.4   Topographic Database

The previously described datasets were the basis for the creation of the Topographic Database (DBT*fvg*) of the main municipalities of the FVG region, a valuable tool for its geometric structure, semantic content and metric quality. Following the requirements of the INSPIRE Directive (Directive 2007/2/EC of the European Parliament) and of the national Ministerial Decree 10.11.2011, "Technical rules for the definition of the content specification of the geotopographic databases", the DBT*fvg* is structured according to the GeoUML standard, based on ISO specifications.

The reference element is the *class*, which contains objects that share common properties and is associated with a predefined number of strictly coded attributes. Classes of similar objects are grouped into *themes*, which in turn are organized in *layers*. For instance, the classes *natural water course*, *channel* and *water pipeline* belong to *hydrographic network*, that is one of the four themes grouped in the *hydrography* layer.

It should be noted that most of the objects were obtained from photogrammetric restitutions, while each roof was modelled in 3D using the LiDAR point cloud as a reference. The complexity and high level of detail of the novel DBT*fvg* can be seen in Fig. 5a.

The geometric features of the DBT*fvg* make it a GIS-oriented product, since each object is fully defined and topological consistency is guaranteed. On the contrary, in the previous digital regional technical cartography (CTRN), some elements are implicitly defined by the geometry of adjacent objects, making spatial analyses far more complex.

The first experiment of the DBT*fvg* was carried out in the years 2012–2014 for the area of Monfalcone (scale 1:2,000), and then it was realized at a scale of 1:1,000 for the city of Trieste, and of 1:5,000 for extra-urban areas of the nearby province. In 2021 the DBT*fvg* was extended to the municipalities of Udine, Gorizia and Pordenone, adopting a scale (and, thus, the corresponding nominal tolerance) of 1:2,000. In the near future, the DBT*fvg* will cover also the remaining municipalities with more than 15,000 inhabitants.

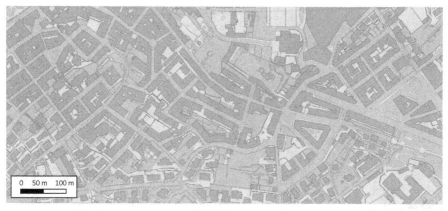

(a) DBT*fvg*.

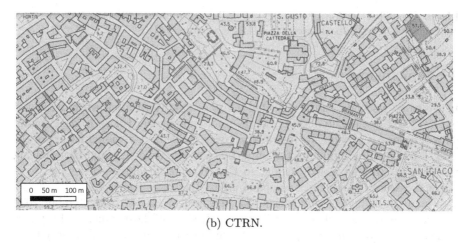

(b) CTRN.

Fig. 5. (a) The DBT*fvg* for an area of the city of Trieste. (b) Representation of the corresponding CTRN.

Due to the difficulties and long lead times required to produce a map as detailed as the DBT*fvg*, the regional administration is adopting a cost-effective solution for updating the regional cartography in the remaining areas. A simplified version of the DBT (called DBT*sped*, Fig. 6) is currently being developed, taking into account only the classes of major interest (i.e., *building*, *road*, *bare soil*, *green or agricultural area*, *forest*, and *water courses*) and directly using the true orthophotos as input data to localize the footprints of the desired object classes. As with the classification of LiDAR data, the use of artificial intelligence algorithms proves essential to automate the process.

Fig. 6. Simplified version of the DBT (DBT*sped*), obtained directly from the true orthophoto. Only the most interesting classes are retrieved.

4 Conclusion

In this work, we analyzed the expected role of geomatics within the topics covered by the iNEST project, underlining at the same time the need of up-to-date spatial data in order to carry out the planned activities. The inter-regional nature of the iNEST consortium highlights the importance of standardizing and harmonizing the data produced by each region, so that the methodologies developed by a regional research group can be applied across the ecosystem.

Finally, it should be emphasize that the project started in September 2022 and the activities described are still at an early stage of development. This paper is therefore a preliminary report: at the end of the project, which is scheduled for December 2025, it will be interesting to analyze what role geomatics has actually played and the problematic and innovative aspects connected to the use of geospatial data, emerged from the research works. It will also be useful to understand which cartographic data have been most commonly used, and to point out any difficulties that have arisen in integrating data provided by different regions.

Acknowledgement. This study was carried out within the Interconnected Nord-Est Innovation Ecosystem (iNEST) and received funding from the European Union Next-GenerationEU (Piano Nazionale di Ripresa e Resilienza (PNRR) – Missione 4 Componente 2, Investimento 1.5 - D.D. 1058 23/06/2022, ECS00000043). This manuscript reflects only the authors' views and opinions, neither the European Union nor the European Commission can be considered responsible for them.

References

1. United Nations Committee of Experts on Global Geospatial Information Management: Future trends in geospatial information management: the five to ten year vision. Third Edition, August 2020. https://ggim.un.org/meetings/GGIM-committee/10th-Session/documents/Future_Trends_Report_THIRD_EDITION_digital_accessible.pdf
2. Beani, E., et al.: The 3D metric survey for the digital cartographic production to support the knowledge of the new municipality of Mappano. In: Brunetta, G., Lombardi, P., Voghera, A. (eds.) Post Un-Lock. LNCS. The Urban Book Series, pp. 153–168. Springer, Cham (2023). https://doi.org/10.1007/978-3-031-33894-6_12
3. Avtar, R., Aggarwal, R., Kharrazi, A., Kumar, P., Kurniawan, T.A.: Utilizing geospatial information to implement SDGs and monitor their progress. Environ. Monit. Assess. **192**, 1–21 (2020)
4. Daniel, S., Doran, M.A.: geoSmartCity: geomatics contribution to the smart city. In Proceedings of the 14th Annual International Conference on Digital Government Research, pp. 65–71 (2013)
5. Lim, T.K., Rajabifard, A., Khoo, V., Sabri, S., Chen, Y.: The smart city in Singapore: how environmental and geospatial innovation lead to urban livability and environmental sustainability. In: Smart Cities for Technological and Social Innovation, pp. 29–49. Academic Press (2021)
6. European Union: Regulation (EU) 2021/695 of the European Parliament and of the Council of 28 April 2021 establishing Horizon Europe - the Framework Programme for Research and Innovation, laying down its rules for participation and dissemination, and repealing Regulations (EU) No 1290/2013 and (EU) No 1291/2013 (2021). https://eur-lex.europa.eu/eli/reg/2021/695/oj
7. Amitrano, C.C., Tregua, M., Russo Spena, T., Bifulco, F.: On technology in innovation systems and innovation-ecosystem perspectives: a cross-linking analysis. Sustainability **10**(10), 3744 (2018)
8. Interconnected Nord-Est Innovation Ecosystem (iNEST): Planning of activities (2022). https://www.consorzioinest.it
9. Crosilla, F., Picech, G., Beinat, A.: Fifty years of the Friuli Venezia Giulia regional technical map: a best practice in the Italian cartographic context. Appl. Geomat. **13**(3), 437–452 (2021)
10. Beinat, A., Basso, M.,Viero, E.: The new geospatial data of the Friuli Venezia Giulia Region (Italy): a geomatic challenge. In: Abstracts of the International Cartographic Association, vol. 3, p. 27. 30th International Cartographic Conference (2021)
11. Eaglefvg Webgis. https://eaglefvg.regione.fvg.it/eagle/main.aspx?configuration=guest. Accessed 31 July 2023
12. Zorzi, S., Maset, E., Fusiello, A., Crosilla, F.: Full-waveform airborne LiDAR data classification using convolutional neural networks. IEEE Trans. Geosci. Remote Sens. **57**(10), 8255–8261 (2019)
13. Maset, E., Padova, B., Fusiello, A.: Efficient large-scale airborne LiDAR data classification via fully convolutional network. Int. Arch. Photogramm. Remote Sens. Spat. Inf. Sci. **43**(B3), 527–532 (2020)

Methodological Advancements in Data Analysis and Processing

Biodiversity-Proof Energy Communities in the Urban Planning of Italian Inner Municipalities

Alessandra Marra[✉]

Department of Civil Engineering (DiCiv), University of Salerno, 84084 Fisciano, SA, Italy
almarra@unisa.it

Abstract. Renewable Energy Communities (RECs) are considered a promising instrument for the achievement of carbon neutral settlements and a possible area-based strategy to counter the depopulation of inland areas. The connection with local energy systems from renewable sources poses the need for their optimal location to respect the territorial heritage, which is particularly rich in inner areas. This work focuses on the protection of biodiversity, an aspect scarcely investigated in the scientific literature on the topic of RECs in urban planning. To this end, a fast method is proposed to build the Map of Ecological Connectivity on an urban scale, starting from the data available from the early stages of the planning process. The model is applied to the municipal territory of Roccabascerana, belonging to the inner areas of Campania Region (Italy), in the context of studies and research for the formation of the Municipal Urban Plan. The results achieved allowed the recognition of potential flow corridors in areas with higher connectivity, supporting the spatial identification of areas unsuitable for the RES plants localization.

Keywords: Renewable Energy Communities · Urban Planning · Inland areas · Biodiversity · Ecological Connectivity

1 Introduction

In a global context in which it is necessary to significantly reduce climate-changing emissions and the cost of energy, Renewable Energy Communities (RECs) represent an important tool for promoting the transition to carbon neutrality and reducing energy poverty, as evidenced by numerous experiences conducted at international level [1–6].

In Directive EU/2001/2018, also known as "RED II", the European Commission defines RECs as "coalitions of citizens, small and medium-sized enterprises and local authorities, including municipal administrations, which are able to produce, consume and exchange energy produced from renewable sources, with the main aim of providing environmental, economic or social benefits to the community itself or to the local areas in which it operates". With the same directive, the Member States are required to carry out an assessment of the existing obstacles and the RECs development potential in their territories, as well as to provide an adequate support framework capable of promoting and facilitating them [7].

E. Borgogno Mondino and P. Zamperlin (Eds.): ASITA 2023, CCIS 2088, pp. 187–200, 2024.
https://doi.org/10.1007/978-3-031-59925-5_14

In Italy, Legislative Decree 199/2021 transposed this directive, updating the previous national regulatory framework on the RECs subject. According to current Italian legislation, an economic incentive is paid with reference to the amount of energy shared by plants and consumption users connected under the same primary substation, i.e. the high voltage substation. The aforementioned areas have a municipal or infra-municipal dimension in urban and metropolitan areas, while they occupy inter-municipal areas in inland areas [8].

Given the spatial link of RECs with the areas in which they operate, urban and regional planning can play an important role in their promotion. In fact, the benefits recognized to RECs can overlap with planning objectives to promote the carbon neutrality of urban and territorial systems, in a socially, economically and environmentally sustainable manner [9–11]. However, RECs have received little attention in planning practice and have only recently come to the interest of researchers [12]. This is a matter of particular concern in Italy, where the complexity of the planning system, generally not updated on the subject, can make the RECs authorization process difficult and slow down their rapid diffusion [13, 14]. Furthermore, in the European inland areas, energy self-sufficiency through the RECs can be a lever for the fight against demographic desertification which severely characterizes these areas also in Italy [15]. In fact, this strategy is already included in the National Recovery and Resilience Plan (Next Generation Italy), which provides an investment channel to encourage the formation of Renewable Energy Communities in municipalities with a population of less than 5,000 inhabitants, mainly present in inland areas [16].

Since the technical feasibility of the RECs depends on the spatial proximity to plants for the energy production from renewable sources (RES), there is a need to make these objectives converge with the protection of the historical-architectural, naturalistic, ecological, landscape and environmental resources of which the entire national territory boasts a significant presence on the international scene. This takes on relevance in inner areas, where the aforementioned territorial values have been better preserved by the limited anthropic impact.

2   Objectives of the Work

In this scenario, this work pays attention to the relationship between the promotion of RECs and the protection of biodiversity in the urban planning of municipalities belonging to Italian inner areas. Biodiversity, in addition to being fundamental for the continuity of life, is linked to the functionality of ecosystems, to their resilience with respect to natural and anthropic hazards, thus influencing the quality of the services they offer [17]. Encouraging the design of ecological networks, such as green and blue infrastructures, in order to promote the increase in biodiversity and develop the offer of essential ecosystem services for resident populations, is among the measures proposed for updating the National Strategy for Biodiversity (SNB) towards the "SNB 2030", especially to face the consequences of climate change [18]. The construction of the ecological network on a regional, provincial and municipal scale is essential to discourage the drafting of territorial and urban planning instruments responsible for the loss of biodiversity. This assumption is now incorporated into the Regional Laws of Territorial Government and acquired in planning practice [19].

As mentioned, RECs are still little investigated in urban planning, therefore the relationship between user networks that can be aggregated in a REC and ecological networks represents a new line of research.

However, the reference to the protection of biodiversity is already present in the legislation that defines the general criteria for the location of areas unsuitable for the installation of RES plants, the Ministerial Decree 10 September 2010, and in some regional regulations on the same issue. More precisely, the national legislation mentions the "areas that perform decisive functions for the conservation of biodiversity, such as areas of connection and ecological-functional continuity between the various natural and semi-natural systems" [20].

On an infra-urban scale, the source for the detailed spatial identification of these areas is represented by a specific draft of the Municipal Urban Plan (PUC), representing the project of the Municipal Ecological Network. Nevertheless, in ordinary planning activities, open data that allow access to this information is generally not available, as it is a work produced in the context of specialized studies, specifically commissioned by the municipal administrations. Moreover, it is frequent that the aforementioned elaboration is made available in the final phase of the planning process. It precludes the possibility to share an overall knowledge of the existing obstacles to the RECs formation from the early stages of the formation of the municipal planning instrument (PUC Preliminary), in order to accelerate their rapid diffusion, as well as to promote their formation without harming local biodiversity. If this approach is generally acceptable, it is particularly important in inland areas, where there is no excessive fragmentation of the wooded and agricultural landscape, which typically occurs in the territorial contexts closest to the urban poles. Therefore, the wealth of natural resources that characterizes the inland areas favours a high level of biodiversity, the protection of which is essential, also due to the compensatory role that these areas play compared to the metropolitan ones, in which the biological variety is severely compromised.

In this theoretical reference framework, the specific objective of this contribution is to present a model for the identification of spatial constraints to the diffusion of RECs on a local scale, with reference to the areas for biodiversity conservation. To this end, the present work proposes a rapid methodology for constructing the Map of Ecological Connectivity on an urban scale, starting from data available from the early stages of the urban planning process.

The method presented in the paper is applied to the municipal territory of Roccabascerana, belonging to the context of the inland areas of Campania Region (Italy).

3 Study Area

The municipality of Roccabascerana, which extends for 12.46 km^2, is located in the historic district of Irpinia in the Province of Avellino, on the border with the provincial territory of Benevento (Fig. 1).

Similarly to many municipalities belonging to Italian inner areas, the analysis of the demographic trend shows a progressive decrease in the population, which from 3,962 units after the Second World War has 2,366 inhabitants in 2011 and 2,319 at the ISTAT census of 31 December 2021 [21]. Therefore, the municipality is eligible as a beneficiary of the funds for the creation of RECs that the Next Generation Italy addresses to municipalities with a population of less than 5,000 inhabitants.

Despite the administrative and management difficulties that characterize the small municipalities of Southern Italy, the Municipality under study has completed the drafting of the new Municipal Urban Plan (PUC), with the technical and scientific support of the Department of Civil Engineering of Salerno University, within the framework of an Institutional Agreement between the local authority and the department[1].

From the analyses conducted in force of this agreement, it emerges that the Campania Regional Territorial Plan (PTR) includes the municipal territory of Roccabascerana in the Development Territorial System (STS) predominantly naturalistic "A8 Partenio", for which it identifies the defense of biodiversity as a strategy of primary importance[2].

In the Regional Ecological Network Roccabascerana is located in a barycentric position between two Regional Parks, that of Partenio and the Taburno Park, located to the south-west and north-west of the municipal area, respectively.

The Provincial Territorial Coordination Plan (PTCP) inserts Roccabascerana in the "Città Caudina" city system[3], as the main inhabited centre, with its 417 m above sea level, rises in the Caudina Valley, close to the Apennine slopes. These features make the municipal area rich in naturalistic, ecological, geomorphological and environmental values of notable interest. The Provincial Ecological Network identifies the "Ecosystems and elements of ecological and faunal interest" in the area under study, which cannot be the subject of urban expansion forecasts, or, in the case of already urbanized areas falling within them, PUCs must promote interventions to mitigate the impacts on the ecosystems concerned. These ecosystems mostly correspond to the extensive wooded areas present in the municipality in question, which are not contiguous to each other, as they are fragmented by areas of more direct interference from the settlement and infrastructural elements. Therefore, the protection of the wooded areas alone is not sufficient to preserve biodiversity effectively. In fact, defining the Ecological Network at the provincial level, PTCP refers the definition of the local network to the PUC, in order to ensure the continuity of the habitats at a more detailed level. In particular, for the

---

[1] The scientific responsible of the activities envisaged by the Agreement is Prof. Roberto Gerundo, while the author has supervised the research and application aspects connected to the promotion of Renewable Energy Communities through the Municipal Urban Plan, the subject of this contribution.

[2] With the term Territorial Development Systems, the Regional Territorial Plan identifies inter-municipal areas for which to outline shared development strategies. The STS, identified in number of 45 on the entire regional territory, are classified according to territorial dominants, in particular the following: naturalistic, rural-cultural, rural-manufacturing, urban, urban-industrial, landscape-cultural.

[3] The PTCP means "City Systems" made up of aggregates of neighbouring municipalities for which a common vision of strategies for the development and organization of the territory is recognizable, as well as a coordinated municipal planning is desirable, with the purpose of avoiding the persistence of the phenomenon of depopulation.

municipality in question, the municipal planning guidelines regard the need to guarantee a high degree of continuity of the local ecological network, in order to favor the transversal relationships between the Partenio and the Taburno, especially in the light of existing productive settlements and planned road infrastructures [22]. In fact, in the north-western portion of the municipal territory there is an extensive production area, which represents an industrial center of reference, also for the neighboring municipalities. The value of the production plant will probably be strengthened, as the municipal territory is affected by the construction of an inter-municipal connection axis, intended to connect the Industrial Development Areas (ASI) of Paolisi (BN) and Pianodardine (AV). Therefore, the Municipality of Roccabascerana can be assumed as an optimal case study in the light of the topic addressed in this contribution.

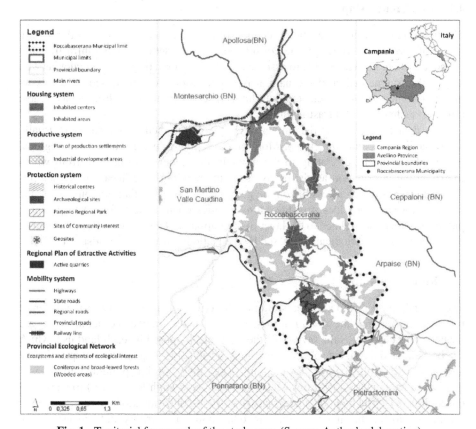

Fig. 1. Territorial framework of the study area. (Source: Author's elaboration).

4   Methodological Proposal

The methodology aims to spatially map the inter-patch ecological connectivity, i.e. the degree to which the territorial matrix facilitates or prevents the exchange of individuals of a species between patches of habitat[4], in order to guide the design of the Municipal Ecological Network [25].

The construction of the Ecological Connectivity Map passes through four phases, aimed at the elaboration of the following thematic maps, respectively: i) Interferences Map; ii) Resistance Map; iii) Map of Proximity to primary elements; iv) Ecological Connectivity Map.

4.1   Interference Map

The first phase concerns the spatial location of potential interference with the natural transit of species. Interferences are considered to be the settlement and infrastructural elements, where it is reasonable to assume that the anthropic pressure is greater, as well as that the fragmentation of the natural flow corridors is compromised. The following interferences are then selected: buildings, inserted or not in built-up areas; roads; railways; technological infrastructures.

The data necessary for the implementation of this methodological step usually accompanies the planning activity. More precisely, they can be found in the regional topographical database relating to the municipality under investigation, from which to extract the information levels, or layers, of the buildings and linear infrastructures. This database is freely accessible on the geoportals of some Italian Regions, while the Campania Region provides it to the Municipalities upon request, for urban planning purposes. Other data, related to the layer of built up-areas, can be found from the dataset of inhabited areas, periodically released by the National Institute of Statistics (ISTAT).

4.2   Resistance Map

The second phase is aimed at mapping the ability of organisms to travel the different types of soil through the territorial matrix in which the fragmented habitat units are located. This capacity is the inverse of the resistance opposed by each land use, which can be estimated through a variety of methods, attributable to qualitative or quantitative approaches [26–30]. However, for the purposes of the work, it is preferable to assign a qualitative value (Very low, Low, Medium, High, Very High Resistance) to each land cover class [31]. The input data necessary to carry out the evaluation are represented by the information on the land use belonging to the municipal territory under investigation, which can be inferred from the Agricultural Land Use Map. The latter is a specialized

---

[4] Following the publication of the insular biogeography theory [23], a *patch* of *habitat* is intended to be a natural area where the variety of species, the abundance and presence of individual species vary according to the size and isolation of the single *patch* with respect to the others. The isolation of the various *patches* increases with the increase of a fragmentation process, due to natural, semi-natural or anthropic causes, which intervenes on a pre-existing distribution of *habitats* without solutions of continuity, i.e. interruptions [24].

elaboration whose drafting is mandatory for the adoption of the PUC according to the national and regional legislation in force. In the absence of such a document in the initial planning stages, it is alternatively possible to achieve the input data from the Corine Land Cover (CLC) at the third hierarchical level [32], deemed adequate for the investigated spatial scale.

4.3 Map of Proximity to Primary Elements

The third phase concerns the definition of the proximity to the primary elements, indicative of the maximum distance that the species are willing to cover when crossing the territorial matrix, during the transit from one primary habitat to another.

By 'primary element' we mean a more or less extensive territorial area, which has not been substantially modified by anthropic intervention, so it is suitable for the natural diffusion of a species. The threshold value relating to the practicable distance varies according to the species populating the area under study, but also to the location of the possible interferences present in the territorial matrix. This value is attested, depending on the different species, along the minimum distance free of interference that connects two patches of primary habitat. The maximum distance that can be covered, thus identified, is divided into five intervals of equal values, corresponding to the classes defined for the map referred to in the previous phase (Very Low, Low, Medium, High, Very High Proximity).

4.4 Ecological Connectivity Map

The fourth and last phase allows to get the Ecological Connectivity Map, intersecting the thematic map of Proximity to primary elements with that of Resistance. For this purpose, a specific matrix is proposed (Tab. 1), in application of which the Ecological Connectivity will vary according to the five classes already identified for the previous maps: "Very Low"; "Low"; " Medium"; "High"; "Very High".

Table 1. Matrix for assessing the degree of Ecological Connectivity (Source: Own elaboration).

Ecological Connectivity		Resistance				
		Very high	High	Medium	Low	Very Low
Proximity	Very high	Very Low	Very Low	Low	Medium	High
	High	Very Low	Very Low	Low	Medium	High
	Medium	Very Low	Low	Medium	High	Very high
	Low	Very Low	Low	Medium	High	Very high
	Very Low	Very Low	Low	Medium	High	Very high

5 Application to the Study Area

5.1 Data Processing

The application of the proposed methodological path to the study area is carried out with the aid of Geographic Information Systems (GIS). Using the ArcGis commercial software (Esri, US), a geodatabase is built, in order to collect the input data, as described in the methodological steps in relation to each map to obtain.

The Interference Map is constructed simply by overlaying the georeferenced input data of the selected interferences, requiring no further operations in a GIS environment.

The Resistance Map is reached starting from the spatial data of land uses, which derive from the CLC classification for the study area, in the absence of more detailed data available in the planning process. These uses, limited to the territory of the municipality in question, are assigned different scores, in accordance with the reference literature [31], as reported in Table 2.

Table 2. Resistance values for land uses in the municipality under study (Source: Own elaboration)

Land Use (Corine Land Cover, Third level)	Score	Resistance
Deciduous forests	1	Very Low
Areas mainly occupied by agricultural crops with the presence of important natural spaces	2	Low
Temporary crops combine with permanent crops	3	Medium
Complex cropping systems and parcels	4	High
Discontinuous urban fabric	5	Very High

This operation requires an extension of the attribute table associated with the polygonal land use layer, creating the two new fields "Score" and "Resistance". The latter is populated through an Arcade calculation expression, which relates the degree of resistance (string) to the previously attributed score (number).

The Proximity Map to primary elements requires the identification of primary habitat patches and the definition of the maximum distance that the species are willing to travel. Patches of primary habitat are identified in wooded areas, which the PTCP recognizes as those with the highest degree of naturalness (Fig. 1). As regards the maximum distance, reference can be made to the threshold value identified in the study preceding this work, in which a municipality belonging to the same geographical context and populated by similar species is examined [25]. So, the maximum distance is set on 250 m, depending on which the subsequent values are defined: 200, 150, 100 and 50 m.

Using the "Multiple ring buffer" tool, it is possible to indicate the threshold values mentioned above and deduct the five intervals corresponding to the classes Very Low, Low, Medium, High and Very High.

Since it is assumed that the transit of the species is severely hindered in correspondence with the interferences identified in the Interference Map, from the Resistance Map and the Proximity Map it is necessary to exclude the areas identified as interferences, using the "Erase" tool. The two resulting thematic maps, classified according to the five classes mentioned above, constitute input data to obtain the Ecological Connectivity Map. The latter is made by implementing the matrix referred to in Table 1 through a raster analysis.

5.2 Mapping Ecological Connectivity

The data processing is resulted in the elaboration of the thematic maps necessary for the construction of the Ecological Connectivity Map: i) Interference Map (Fig. 2,a); ii) Resistance Map (Fig. 2,b); (iii) Map of Proximity to primary elements (Fig. 2,c).

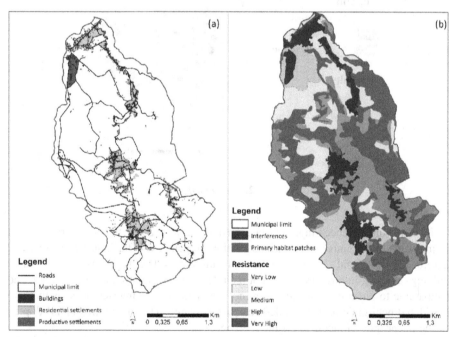

Fig. 2. Interference Map (a) and Resistance Map (b) obtained for the study area. Map of Proximity to primary elements (c) obtained for the study area (Source: Author's elaboration).

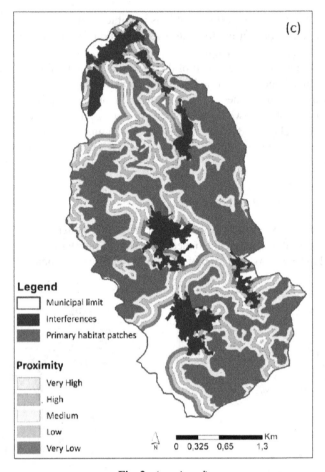

Fig. 2. (*continued*)

From the Interference Map, it can be seen that interferences are mostly represented by the main inhabited centre and its various fractions, together with the industrial settlement, therefore by polygonal elements. In the application carried out in this work, the isolated buildings existing in rural areas, i.e. not included in the discontinuous urban fabric and comparable to punctual obstacles, were not listed among the interferences, as they are considered negligible on the detailed scale investigated. The same rationale is adopted for the linear interferences, so for the road network.

The Ecological Connectivity Map (Fig. 3) has allowed the recognition of potential flow corridors in areas with higher connectivity, supporting the spatial identification of areas unsuitable for the RES plants localization, corresponding to High and Very High Connectivity. Ultimately, the Ecological Connectivity Map can represent the source for a survey of the areas that perform crucial functions for the conservation of biodiversity at a local scale, in the context of identifying the spatial constraints on the diffusion of RECs at this level of investigation.

This aspect is not intended to represent a limit to the rapid diffusion of Renewable Energy Communities. On the contrary, one of the main strengths of the RECs is that they allow renewable energy production plants to be located where it is most appropriate, without excluding potential members whose buildings are located in areas not suitable for the installation of RES plants. The only limit, in the light of the technical specifications imposed by current legislation, is that potential users of a REC receive economic incentives if the buildings and systems are located within the perimeter of the same primary substation. However, this spatial constraint can easily be overcome in inner areas, where the networks served by the primary substations have an inter-municipal dimension.

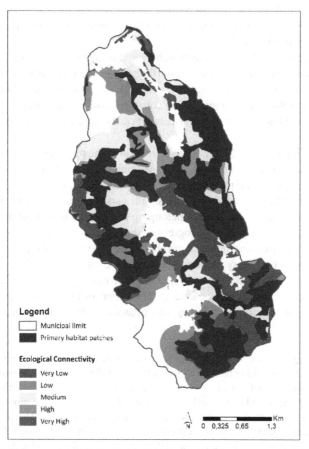

Fig. 3. Ecological Connectivity Map obtained for the study area (Source: Author's elaboration).

6   Conclusion

In-depth knowledge of unsuitable areas for the development of plants by Renewable Energy Sources, on a local scale, is essential for orienting urban planning towards choices that promote socially, economically and environmentally sustainable Renewable Energy Communities spatial configurations. In this direction, this work has focused on the protection of biodiversity, an aspect scarcely investigated in the search for optimal spatial configurations of RECs, at an infra-urban scale, in the scientific literature on the subject.

It is appropriate to specify how the proposed model can be improved, in order to guide planning choices through a more detailed cognitive framework. An expansion of the contribution can be considering neglected factors, such as linear interferences. In this direction, the Interference Map can be enriched by pre-existing energy infrastructures, which in inland areas can be found in an extensive form, even if this is not the case of the municipality examined here.

Similarly, the Resistance Map can be achieved starting from a more detailed perimeter of the agricultural land use, as it is ordinarily done in the integrative agronomic study of the municipal urban plan, in compliance with the legislation. This study was not yet available in the preliminary planning, therefore the Corine Land Cover was used, since it is considered adequate in the initial phase, but it can be approximate to support definitive planning choices.

Finally, the input data useful for the application of the proposed methodology, which fall within the knowledge framework of the Municipal Urban Plan, are freely accessible from the early stages of the planning process, as they derive from periodically updated databases and officially released by public entities and bodies. Therefore, the model can be easily applied to other case studies belonging to the territorial context of inner areas, which represents another possible progress of the work.

In largely urbanized and infrastructural contexts, the search for possible ecological connections between primary habitats is not possible on a local scale, but it requires a different level of analysis, corresponding to the inter-municipal or vast area scale, due to the greater distance of the primary elements. This aspect offers insights regarding the role of inter-municipal planning in fulfilling this objective, which is a further development of the work.

Acknowledgments. This contribution represents an extended version of a work by the same author: Marra A., Comunità Energetiche Rinnovabili a prova di biodiversità. Un modello a supporto della pianificazione urbanistica nelle aree interne, LaborEst, 26 s.i., 2023. The methodological path retraces and integrates a model proposed by the research Group in Urban Planning and Techniques (GTPU) of the University of Salerno, to which the author is associated. The model, applied to another study case, is described in the following article: Fasolino I., Gerundo R., Grimaldi M., Un approccio GIS-based per la costruzione della rete ecologica alla scala locale, In Sessa S., Di Martino F., Cardone B. (eds.) GIS DAY 2014 - Il Gis per il governo e la gestione del territorio, pp. 199–207, Aracne, 2015.

Disclosure of Interests. The author has no competing interests to declare that are relevant to the content of this article.

References

1. Brummer, V.: Community energy – benefits and barriers: a comparative literature review of Community Energy in the UK, Germany and the USA, the benefits it provides for society and the barriers it faces. Renew. Sustain. Energy Rev. **94**, 187–196 (2018). https://doi.org/10.1016/j.rser.2018.06.013

2. McCabe, A., Pojani, D., van Groenou, A.B.: Social housing and renewable energy: community energy in a supporting role. Energy Res. Social Sci. **38**, 110–113 (2018). https://doi.org/10.1016/j.erss.2018.02.005

3. Koltunov, M., Bisello, A.: Multiple impacts of energy communities: conceptualization taxonomy and assessment examples. In: Bevilacqua, C., Calabrò, F., Della Spina, L. (eds.) NMP 2020. SIST, vol. 178, pp. 1081–1096. Springer, Cham (2021). https://doi.org/10.1007/978-3-030-48279-4_101

4. Tarpani, E., et al.: Energy communities implementation in the European Union: case studies from pioneer and laggard countries. Sustainability **14**, 12528 (2022). https://doi.org/10.3390/su141912528

5. Dolores, L., Macchiaroli, M., De Mare, G.: Financial impacts of the energy transition in housing. Sustainability **14**, 4876 (2022). https://doi.org/10.3390/su14094876

6. Macchiaroli, M., Dolores, L., De Mare, G., Nicodemo, L.: Tax policies for housing energy efficiency in Italy: a risk analysis model for energy service companies. Buildings **13**, 582 (2023). https://doi.org/10.3390/buildings13030582

7. European Commission, EU: Directive (EU) 2018/2001 of the European Parliament and of the Council of 11 December 2018 on the Promotion of the Use of Energy from Renewable Sources (2018)

8. E-distribuzione: Mappa delle aree servite dalle cabine primarie (2023). https://www.e-distribuzione.it/a-chi-ci-rivolgiamo/casa-e-piccole-imprese/comunita-energetiche.html. Accessed 5 Apr 2023

9. Fasolino, I., Coppola, F., Grimaldi, M.: A model for urban planning control of the settlement efficiency: a case study. Archivio di Studi Urbani e Regionali **127**, 181–210 (2020)

10. Fasolino, I., Grimaldi, M., Zarra, T., Naddeo, V.: Implementation of integrated nuisances action plan. Chem. Eng. Trans. **54**, 19–24 (2016)

11. Sebillo, M., Vitiello, G., Grimaldi, M., Buono, D.D.: SAFE (Safety for Families in Emergency). In: Misra, S., et al. (ed.) ICCSA 2019. LNCS, vol. 11620, pp. 424–437. Springer, Cham (2019). https://doi.org/10.1007/978-3-030-24296-1_34

12. Gerundo, R., Marra, A.: Renewable energy communities: urban research and land use planning. BDC. Bollettino del Centro Calza Bini **22**(2), 160–311 (2022)

13. Ministero dello Sviluppo Economico, Ministero dell'Ambiente, della Tutela del Territorio e del Mare, Ministero delle Infrastrutture e dei Trasporti: Piano Nazionale Integrato per l'Energia e il Clima (PNIEC) (2019). https://www.mise.gov.it/images/stories/documenti/PNIEC_finale_17012020.pdf. Accessed 5 Apr 2023

14. De Lotto, R., Micciché, C., Venco, E.M., Bonaiti, A., De Napoli, R.: Energy communities: technical, legislative, organizational, and planning features. Energies **15**(5), 1731 (2022). https://doi.org/10.3390/en15051731

15. Dipartimento per le Politiche di Coesione della Presidenza del Consiglio dei Ministri, DPS: Strategia Nazionale per le Aree Interne: definizione, obiettivi, strumenti e governance, Documento tecnico collegato alla bozza di Accordo di Partenariato 2014–2020 trasmessa alla CE il 9 dicembre 2013. DPS (2014)

16. Governo Italiano: Piano Nazionale di Ripresa e Resilienza (PNRR). Next Generation Italy (2021). Available at: https://italiadomani.gov.it/it/home.html. Accessed 5 Apr 2023

17. Oliver, T.H., et al.: Biodiversity and resilience of ecosistem functions. Trends Ecol. Evol. **30**, 673–684 (2015)
18. Ministero della Transizione Ecologica, MITE: Strategia Nazionale per la Biodiversità 2011–2020. Rapporto Finale Conclusivo. Mite, Roma (2021)
19. Istituto Superiore per la Protezione Ambientale, ISPRA: Le reti ecologiche nella pianificazione territoriale ordinaria ISPRA, Roma (2010)
20. Ministero dello Sviluppo Economico: Decreto Ministeriale 10 settembre 2010. Linee guida per l'autorizzazione degli impianti alimentati da fonti rinnovabili. https://www.gazzettauffi ciale.it/eli/id/2010/09/18/10A11230/sg. Accessed 31 Apr 2023
21. Istituto Nazionale di Statistica, ISTAT: Dati sulla popolazione residente al 31 dicembre di ogni anno nei Comuni Italiani. Available at: https://demo.istat.it/ (Last accessed: 5/04/2023)
22. Provincia di Avellino: Piano Territoriale di Coordinamento Provinciale (PTCP), Schede dei Sistemi di Città. Indicazioni per la pianificazione comunale coordinata, Città Caudina. Provincia di Avellino (2014)
23. MacArthur, R.H., Wilson, E.O.: The Theory of Island Biogeography. Princeton University Press, Princeton (1967)
24. Battisti, C.: Frammentazione ambientale, connettività, reti ecologiche. Un contributo teorico e metodologico con particolare riferimento alla fauna selvatica. Provincia di Roma, Assessorato alle politiche ambientali, Agricoltura e Protezione civile, Roma (2004)
25. Fasolino, I., Gerundo, R., Grimaldi, M.: Un approccio GIS-based per la costruzione della rete ecologica alla scala locale. In: Sessa S., Di Martino F., Cardone B. (eds.) GIS DAY 2014 - Il Gis per il governo e la gestione del territorio, pp. 199–207. Aracne (2015)
26. Patrono, A., Saldana, A.: Modeling with neighbourhood operators. ILWIS 2.1 Application Guide. ILWIS Department-ITC, Enschede (1997)
27. Marulli, J., Mallarach, J.M.: A GIS methodology for assessing ecological connectivity: application to the Barcelona Metropolitan Area. Landsc. Urban Plan. **71**(24), 243–262 (2005). https://doi.org/10.1016/j.landurbplan.2004.03.007
28. Beier, P., Spencer, W., Baldwin, R.F., McRae, B.H.: Toward best practices for developing regional connectivity maps. Conserv. Biol. **25**, 879–892 (2011)
29. Caoa, Y., Rui Yanga, R., Carverc, S.: Linking wilderness mapping and connectivity modelling: a methodological framework for wildland network planning. Biol. Cons. **251**, 108679 (2020). https://doi.org/10.1016/j.biocon.2020.108679
30. Zhao, Z., et al.: A protected area connectivity evaluation and strategy development framework for post-2020 biodiversity conservation. Land **11**, 1670 (2022). https://doi.org/10.3390/land11 101670
31. Ziółkowska, E., Ostapowicz, K., Radeloff, V.C., Kuemmerle, T.: Effects of different matrix representations and connectivity measures on habitat network assessments. Landsc. Ecol. **29**(9), 1551–1570 (2014). https://doi.org/10.1007/s10980-014-0075-2
32. ISPRA – Istituto Superiore per la Protezione e la Ricerca Ambientale: Dati CLC - Corine Land Cover - per il territorio italiano. ISPRA, Roma (2018). https://groupware.sinanet. isprambiente.it/uso-copertura-e-consumo-di-suolo/library/copertura-del-suolo/corine-land-cover/clc2018_shapefile. Accessed 5 Oct 2023

GIS Analysis for Urban "Anti-fragility" to Climate Change

Alessandro Seravalli[1], Paola Caselli[2], Andrea Lugli[1(✉)], Fabio Bologna[1], Beatrice Giorgi[1], Luca Galeotti[1], and Davide Magurno[1]

[1] Sis.Ter/GeoSmart Lab, Via Emilia 69, Imola, Italy
a.lugli@sis-ter.it
[2] UP Urban Planning, Via Emilia 67, Imola, Italy

Abstract. This paper aims at illustrating the methodology adopted for the elaboration of the Diagnostic Knowledge Framework (in accordance with the Regional Law of Emilia-Romagna Region L.R. 24/2017) in the metropolitan context of Bologna. Through this methodology it was possible to define appropriate sites for soil adaptation actions, taking into account soil permeability (physical dimension), transformation capacity through public facilities (functional dimension), and the possibility of fostering new natural ecosystem connections (environmental dimension). Furthermore, this approach aims at fostering connections between green and blue infrastructures in the urban context in order to build upon biodiversity and regulating ecosystem services, as well as to enhance the capacity of the urbanized areas to adapt to climate change.

Keywords: Urban Planning · Climate Change · GIS Analysis

1 Introduction

In the last fifteen years many paradigms have changed. Within the framework of geographical information application, web mapping systems have become more pervasive, due to both the possibility to access to them without specific technical skills, and the considerable amount of geolocated data acquired in consumer markets and available in the web in various forms. GeoSpatial and georeferencing are now part of our daily life. As for other academic contexts in which information technology play an important role, digital abuse has led to many distortions and confusion. It is easy to observe previous similar dynamics. Digital photography that made famous smartphones, enabled an exponential growth of photos by ego-photographers that became self-displaying. Similarly, the use of GPS on vehicles or for outdoor activities made geographical technologies ordinary tools. Analog photography was planned and chosen. The digital one is consumed, instinctive and cumulative[1] [6]. The same occurs for geolocated information. A simplistic approach, devoid of knowledge, increasing according to ease and accessibility

---

[1] "The smartphone is the main infoma of our time. It not only makes many things superfluous, it derealises the world by reducing it to information".

E. Borgogno Mondino and P. Zamperlin (Eds.): ASITA 2023, CCIS 2088, pp. 201–217, 2024.
https://doi.org/10.1007/978-3-031-59925-5_15

of use, twists the information return fostering the excess of available information and the inability to assimilate and critically thinking: it is a cultural flattening that make vain even digitalization processes themselves[2]. This automated production leads to an inability to translate information into knowledge that can support decisions through synthesizing forms which represent intervention strategies, above all in the field of territorial planning. The availability of much information does not imply the automation of making good choices, as Isaac Asimov said "If knowledge can create problems, it is not through ignorance that we can solve them". Nevertheless, knowledge is not accumulation of data and information, but the synthesis and elaboration of them. There are several experiences of decisions taken on the basis of few but significant observations of the world.

Therefore, it is clear how automation processes represent methods and tools to ease man activity, as well as any technology. Artificial Intelligence itself is based on data, learns from data accumulation and, in this sense, it may be predictive but not forward-looking, as only human thinking can be. The paradox arosed is that the more technology and data availability increase, the more man contribution should be strategic and exclusive. Data synthesis is an exercise itself, strategic data reading through several criteria is not neutral but requires vision, culture, history and identity. Nowadays, this is the challenge coming from digital transition that fosters methods and tools of data elaboration that man has at disposal for the first time and that represent a kind of accountability to face new challenges of climate change and energy transition. Climate change requires new skills related to project elaboration that need to be concrete forms of decision-making, not only projections.

From this particular point of view, information synthesis is translated into planning. It has to be read as: urban planning aimed at making city morphology more adaptable to tackle its vulnerabilities, mainly consequences of urbanization, and territory protection to strengthen natural and eco-systems, in order to gradually make territory more antifragile[3]. In this way, integrated planning restores the reciprocity between urban and rural.

In Italy, urban drift[4] [2, 5], does not reach the results of global city model, in part due to its morphology. Only 45 out of 7.904 cities have more than 100.000 inhabitants and around 5.800 of them have less than 5.000 inhabitants (among them 50% are subject to abandonment). This spread system, rich of human biodiversity, encouraged sprawl growth, mainly in the Po River Valley favouring a strong anthropization of natural environment.

Soil sealing, deriving from the building system of the last sixty years, represents a weakness and a vulnerability that intensifies the impact of urban heating, even with dramatic effects, enhancing phenomena like surface runoff and low level of drainage in case of heavy rainfall, including the permeable soil within the cities. These factors

---

[2] Suffice it to say that the growth of accumulated data is much faster than the time it takes humans to assimilate it, bring it to synthesis and thus make it useful.

[3] Following N.N. Taleb's definition, resilience is the ability to react to a shock, antifragility is the ability to resist but also reap the benefits. [8]

[4] Measured as the percentage of the population living in urban areas, is growing by 0.2% each year.

make urban system even more fragile. Many cities, mainly in Europe, face the challenge of radically re-thinking their identity and position within national and regional contexts, because of the "new urban issue" characterized by population increasing and climate change. The analysis of territory vulnerabilities is based on the observation and understanding of complex phenomena, which are consequences of urban drift (urban heat islands, deforestation, energy needs, congestions, pollutants concentration, etc.). These events can be easily analysed through geomatics tools to understand natural and anthropic causes.

Urban drift and climate change consequences lead to social, environmental and economic repercussions (increasing of urban poverty, structural inefficiencies, temperature and extreme meteorological events, scarcity of water resources, impacts on health, energy consumption). Urban planning must inevitably face these consequences and vulnerabilities in a systemic way that translate observations and evaluations into concrete projects. GIS solutions offer several possibilities to build tools for decision-making support, as in the case of General Urban Plan (in Italy: Piano Urbanistico Generale PUG, Emilia-Romagna Region regional law 24/2017, from now on L.R. RER 24/2017) oriented to strategic and monitoring actions to make cities and territories antifragile.

Urban planning, in its modernist evolution, has always been linked to urban development. Environment itself has been considered as an anthropocentric context, not natural, a concept that gradually evolved in the last fifty years. Over time, the attention to contain the level of urban consumption arose, together with the awareness of the need to preserve the natural ecosystem from which our defences come from (ecosystem services). Therefore, it is important not to interfere with natural ecosystem that is our source of life, but also cause of death (it has been proven by extreme events in which nature takes back its space, taken by man over time). This awareness leads to the restoration of the balance in the Italian landscape between urban and rural.

2 Context and Use Case

The methodology explained in this document has been developed and applied in a specific territorial context within Bologna metropolitan area, within the framework of the "Quadro Conoscitivo Diagnostico". It is a part of new tools for territorial and urban planning (L.R. n. 24/2017) that provide an organic representation and evaluation of the territory conditions and evolutive processes that characterized it, with particular attention to the effects linked to climate change. It is an essential reference to define goals and specifications of the plan[5]. In fact, thanks to new tools, the new regional law aims to achieve specific goals such as fighting soil consumption, urban and territorial regeneration, landscape and biodiversity preservation. These are pursued through a strategy for ecological and environmental biodiversity, that in turn is declined into policies and actions aimed to enhance territory adaptability and resilience to climate change (Fig. 1).

The geographical context of reference, on which the methodology here explained has been applied, extends for more than 400 sqkm, of which around 95% being rural and composed of these three ecosystems: plain, hills and mountains. On the other hand,

---

[5] Art.22 c.1, L.R. 24/2017.

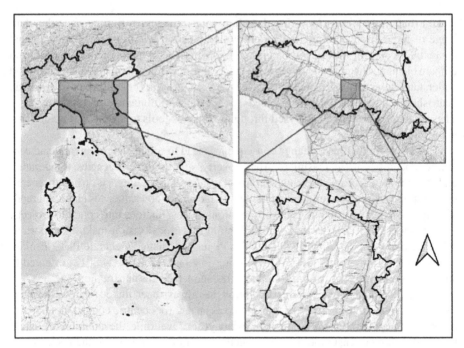

Fig. 1. Area of interest, located in the Province of Bologna, Northern Italy.

the urban part is mainly on the plain, where urban centres are densely populated and services and productive areas are located. It is interesting to observe urbanized areas on hills and mountains, where centres are more rarefied and strewn, a sort of archipelago or, in some cases, island of built zones. From an urban resilience point of view, one of the strong points of the area analysed is the existence of natural ecosystems, knots and green corridors: they represent an opportunity if adequately connected to green and blue infrastructures also within built areas in urban centres. Conversely, big road infrastructures on the plain and valley floor together with extended industrial areas are a threat to these interesting opportunities of enlarging and connecting the already existing ecological network.

Therefore, in the territory analysis for the "Quadro Conoscitivo Diagnostico" through the methodology here exposed, the main aspects examined have been: green and blue infrastructures in urban centres, ecological networks in rural areas, high biodiversity zones, heat islands and soil sealing. It has been observed that the last two elements are quite common and penalizing above all in the industrial areas. The studies conducted, together with a further analysis on urban pattern and public equipment (intended as elements of potential urban transformation), have generated the starting framework to strategically face challenged related to adaptability to climate change, heat islands, territory security and safeguard of ecosystems as sources of important services for the territory.

3   GIS Analysis Implementation to Define a Scalable Method

The methodology has been developed through a geographical analysis performed over a grid of squared cells according to Eurostat grid scheme, easily transferable and replicable also in different context and nations. This type of analysis has been conducted in several scopes becoming a widespread approach[6] [1, 7] characterized by its invariance over time[7], ability of updating and integrating heterogeneous information, ability to read and elaborate through multiple criteria that foster understanding, diagnosis and planning of territory systems adaptability.

The method applied to this use case consists of the division of the studied area into squared cells and, for each of them, the calculation of an index that recaps multiple variables used to describe the phenomenon analysed [3, 4]. The result is a new information polygon layer that with a single attribute is able to describe complex phenomena and that allows to generate thematic cartographies immediately understandable by decision-makers. Through periodic updating of the index, the grid may be applied also to the monitoring of territory, providing appropriate feedback. The area subdivision in cells is created with the overlapping of a square grid, which can be generated especially for the analysed area or may be originated from grids with higher extension/dimension: in order to ensure the method scalability and its application to any portion of Italian territory, a 500 m module has been chosen from Eurostat grid census 2021 [12]. The variables used in the index calculation derive from geodata point, line or polygon features and can be 'geometric' variables, such as the count of point geodata, the length of a linear geodata or the extent of a polygonal geodata, or corresponding information or even variable numerical values of a raster, such as the altitude of a Digital Terrain Model. Therefore, the system represents a database with its own territorial taxonomy [7].

In order to obtain the values to be used in the index calculation, an operation of "intersection" has been carried out between the acquired geographical data and the grid itself, achieving a new level of vector information with the following characteristics according to the type of geometry of the start point:

- point → point feature in which to each point is associated an identificative code of the cell where it is located, which becomes a new field in the attributes table;
- line/polygon → line or polygon feature in which each element is divided into fragments according to the number of cells in which it falls (e.g., an area falls into 2 cells → it is divided and two new geometries with the same attribute values are generated) and each fragment is assigned the identification code of the cell in which it falls, which becomes a new field in the attribute table.

The approach applied is Tomlin's [13] Map Algebra declined on geographical informative mixed type levels, raster and vector. Starting from the feature attribute table obtained with the intersection operation, a pivot table is generated considering as row values the grid cell codes and as column values the count, sum, average etc. of the

---

[6] Several Authorities use grid for monitoring thematic territorial phenomena, In Italy for example ISTAT for demography, ISPRA for soil consumption or permeability monitoring.

[7] As Mark Twain said when discussing about the meridians and parallels of the Atlas State at the Rockefeller centre, it is like a big fishing net where everything underneath can vary.

values of a field in the feature attribute table. The resulting pivot chart, with as many lines as grid cells, is exported as a CSV file (*Comma-Separated Values*). In case of geographical data in raster format it is possible to obtain a CSV file to be used to calculate the index calculating zonal statistics from the grid: for each grid cell, the pixels of the raster falling within it are identified and from them basic variables such as sum, mean, maximum value, etc. are calculated Later, a left join is done between the grid and the above-mentioned CSVs using a key for the linking them. The values of the fields of the expanded attribute table thus obtained are re-scaled so that they are non-dimensional and fall within the range 0–1 (min-max normalisation): in this way they can be combined with each other even if they have different starting units of measurement or absolute values that differ by several orders of magnitude. The re-scaled values are, thus, combined applying the formulas defined according to experts' knowledge on the field related to the phenomenon studied. These formulas may range from an easy linear combination to advanced statistical methods. More specifically, an analysis has been carried out in order to identify areas with higher hydrogeological vulnerability, to plan territory security, and with higher biodiversity level, to enlarge already existing ecological net and ecosystemic services.

3.1 Hydrogeological Vulnerability Grid

The hydrogeological vulnerability is elaborated from the hydrogeological instability map, from where the following variables are considered[8]:

– Geology/cover of the quaternary grouped according to lithology
– Active and quiescent landslides
– Slopes (from DTM)

These variables are combined together with a "category" approach, not with a mathematical formula: according to the recorded morphological characteristics within the grid cells, values of hydrogeological criticality are assigned. These values are derived from a synthesis by the multidisciplinary experts of the group of work and they are reported in the following table, where geology and landslides are in columns and slopes are in rows (Table 1).

Table 1. Table of the values used for analysis.

Slope [degree]	Rocks	Flysh	Sunstone	Marl	Clay/AES/quiescent landslides	Active landslides
0°–15°	0	0	0	0	0	18
15°–24°	0.5	1	1.5	2	2.5	18
>24°	3	6	9	12	15	18

---

[8] This work deepens the previous activities in the 30 municipalities in the Province of Forlì-Cesena [14].

A thematic map is obtained by computing the hydrogeological vulnerability for each grid cell.

Data sources are listed in the following table (Table 2):

Table 2. Table of the data sources for the hydrogeological vulnerability and instability map.

	RAW Data	RAW Data Source
Geological units grouped into macro-groups according to lithologies	Geological database at the scale 1:10.000 Geological units	minERva [10]
Active and quiescent landslides and quaternary cover (AES)	Geological database, 1:10,000 - Landslides, slope deposits and alluvial deposits - 1:10.000	minERva [10]
Land slopes (by DTM)	DTM Emilia Romagna Region 5 × 5 m	Geodata Regional Portal [9]

The hydrogeological criticality was accompanied by an in-depth study on hydraulic hazard that worked on the following geodata:

– PGRA (Flood risk management plan) hazard maps related to the Rhine (UOM ITI021) and Po (ITN008) basins, containing the perimeter of the areas that could be affected by floods according to the three scenarios.

   (a) low probability of floods or extreme event scenarios (P1, low hazard);
   b) infrequent floods (P2, medium hazard);
   c) frequent floods (P3, high hazard);

– depressed areas obtained from the 5 × 5 m DTM.
   For each grid cell, the degree of hazard was estimated by combining weights that express the hazard from the point of view of the individual geodata mentioned above. These weights follow the following general criteria:

– hydraulic hazard areas (subdivided into P1, P2 and P3): it is sufficient that there is a portion of surface area within the cell in the higher hazard category (high hazard P3, medium hazard P2, low hazard P1) for the cell to acquire the weight of the higher class (Fig. 2).

– presence of depressed areas: only depressed areas with an extension greater than 20 sqm are considered and these areas are distinguished on the basis of their overlap with P3, P2, P1 areas (also in this case the overlap with the higher hazard class prevails).

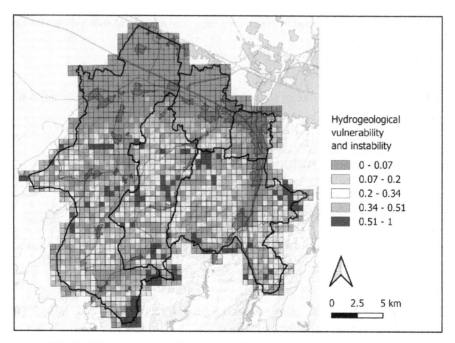

Fig. 2. Elaboration map of the hydrogeological vulnerability and instability.

The weights of the various cases and the hydraulic hazard values resulting from their combination are shown in the following table (Table 3):

Table 3. Table of the weights of the various cases.

		Depressed areas in PGRA P3	Depressed areas in PGRA P2	Depressed areas in PGRA P1	Depressed areas outside PGRA areas or absent
		1	**0.9**	**0.8**	**0.7**
Area P1	0.35			0.28	0.25
Area P2	0.6		0.54	0.48	0.42
Area P3	1	1.00	0.90	0.80	0.70

Finally, a correction coefficient was applied according to the percentage of the area falling within the highest hazard band (Px), so that cells only partly affected by high hazard bands took on a slightly lower weight:

- Px > 50% → 1
- 25% <= Px <= 50% → 0,95
- Px < 25% → 0,9

By calculating the hazard values for each grid cell, it was possible to generate the following map (Fig. 3 and Table 4).

Table 4. Table of the data sources for the summary thematic map on hydraulic hazard.

	RAW Data	RAW Data Source
PGRA hazard maps [11] for the Rhine (UOM ITI021) and Po (ITN008) basins	Poligonal feature of PGRA (shp)	Water authority Po river basin
Depressed areas derived from the DTM	DTM ReR 5x5m	Geodata Regional Portal [9]

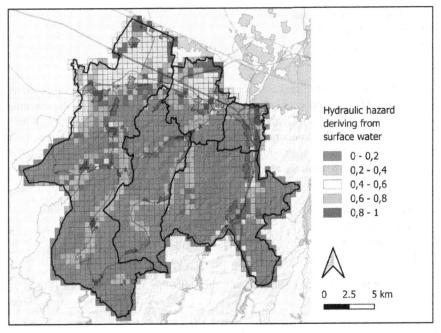

Fig. 3. Specific summary thematic map on hydraulic hazard (work on behalf of the Reno-Lavino Samoggia Union).

3.2 Expansion Potential of the Ecological Network

The analysis, elaborated from the biodiversity grid, aims at identifying those areas with the highest expansion potential of the ecological nodes and corridors. This is derived from the combination of 2 different grids which allow to evaluate the ecological treasure of a territory: the naturality grid, evaluating the flora, and the nesting potential grid, evaluating the fauna and, in particular, identifying those areas which are appropriate for some key bird species nesting. The creation of these grids was possible thanks to the collaboration with experts[9].

Naturality Grid

Wood and forest areas are updated by cross-checking forest maps and land use maps. Twelve naturality classes are identified to describe the territory, gathered into four main categories:

– Anthropogenic vegetation
– Semi-natural vegetation
– Sub-natural vegetation
– Natural vegetation

The data are put on the grid and, for each cell, the naturality level is computed as a percentage. At first, within each cell, the involved surface is multiplied for the maximum value of naturality (i.e., 12). Then, the surface fraction for each class is multiplied for its naturality value (i.e., the number of the class), and the results are summed per cell. The score is finally scaled on the naturality potential, to obtain the naturality percentage per cell. Five naturality percentage classes are then defined:

– Class 0: 1–10%
– Class 1: 10–25%
– Class 2: 25–40%
– Class 3: 40–55%
– Class 4: 55–100%

By assigning a class to each grid cell, the following map is obtained (Fig. 4 and Table 5):

---

[9] Ecosistema Scrl http://www.ecosistema.it/ecosistema/index.asp.

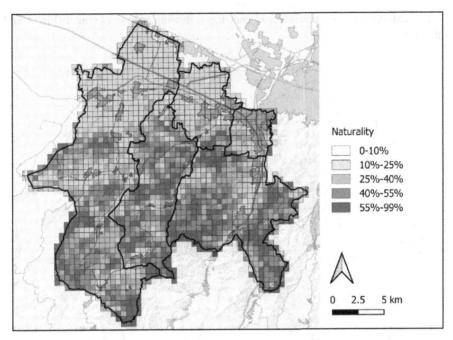

Fig. 4. Elaboration map of the percentage of naturality.

Table 5. Table of the data sources for the percentage of naturality map.

Data	Data Source
Land use detail – 2020 Edition	minERva [10]
Forest area – 2014 Edition	Geodata Regional Portal [9]

Nesting Potential Grid

Based on the bird observations that are in the area of interest, we have selected 28 species whose conservation importance has been stated by European Union laws. For each of them, the needs for nesting are identified. According to these needs, the land use polygons are classified to define their level of suitability for each species. Only those areas with highest suitability are put on the grid, then, the number of potentially nesting species per cell is counted. Values range from 0 to 21 species in a single cell. Based on these values, five classes are considered:

Class 0: 0 species
Class 1: 1 to 5 species
Class 2: 6 to 10 species
Class 3: 11 to 15 species
Class 4: 15 to 21 species

By assigning a class to each grid cell, the following map is obtained (Fig. 5 and Table 6):

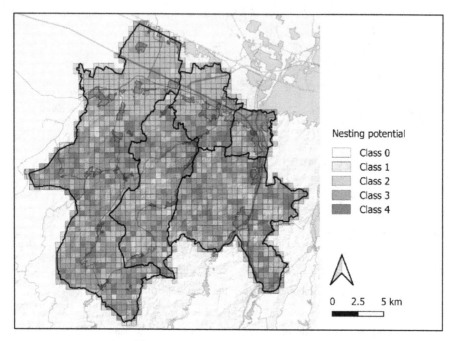

Fig. 5. Elaboration of nesting potential.

Table 6. Table of the data sources for the nesting potential map.

Data	Data Source
Land use detail – 2020 Edition	Geodata Regional Portal [9]
Bird Observation in the territory – 2018 Edition	Ecosistema s.c.r.l. http://www.ecosistema.it/eco sistema/index.asp

Biodiversity Grid (suitability and naturality)

The aggregation of the data into a single map is obtained by summing the previous two grids, obtaining values ranging from 0 to 8, where 8 corresponds to maximum biodiversity (suitability-naturality from now on). These values were then aggregated into 4 classes with class 0 corresponding to the minimum level of biodiversity (values 0, 1, 2) and class 3 corresponding to the maximum level of biodiversity (values 7, 8) (Fig. 6).

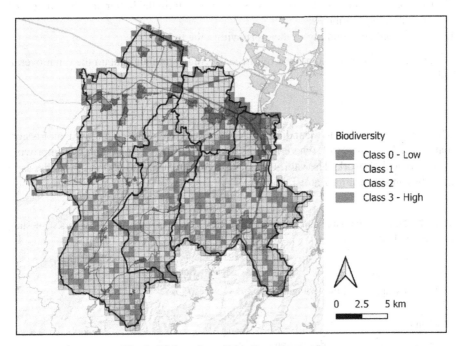

Fig. 6. Elaboration of identity and naturalness.

3.3   Grid of the Expansion Potential of the Ecological Network

The grid about the ecological network results from the analysis of the cells with the highest suitability-naturality values falling outside the ecological networks already identified by the province urban plan (in Italian, Piano Territoriale Metropolitano – PTM). To perform the analysis, we computed:

– The centroids of the cells (c-nat from now on), whose attribute is the value of the suitability-naturality in the cell
– The centroids of the cells containing elements of the existing ecological network (c-eco from now on), whose attribute is the percentage coverage of the network within the cell
– The centroids of the cells containing a urban area (c-urb from now on)

A buffer with a radius equal to twice of the cell diagonal is created around each c-nat, to analyse the first and the second ring of cells nearby it. The c-nats, c-ecos, and c-urbs falling inside the buffer are then identified. Thus, for each c-nat, a number of indicators are considered:

A. The suitability-naturality value;
B. The normalized product of the c-nats counting within the buffer and the sum of the corresponding attributes;
C. The normalized product of the c-ecos counting within the buffer and the sum of the corresponding attributes;
D. The normalized counting of the c-urb within the buffer

These indicators are combined by the following formula to obtain the c-nat overall indicator:

$$A * (B + C + D)$$

where each letter refers to the indicator listed above. Finally, the overall indicator is normalized in the range 0 to 1, where 1 corresponds to the maximum potential of improving the ecological network. The values are mapped to the 500 m × 500 m grid cells, as in the following map (Fig. 7 and Table 7):

Table 7. Table of the data sources for the summary classification of the biodiversity, nesting potential and naturalness.

Data	Data Source
Polygonal shapefiles of the ecological network elements:	
ZSC and ZPS	
Regional and provincial parks, natural reserves, natural and semi-natural protected landscape	
Multi-functional ecological corridors of the waterways	
Crossings and discontinuities	
- Geosites	Metropolitan Territory Plan (PTM [15])
Polygonal shapefile of the regional ecological connections	Environment portal of the Region Emilia Romagna [16]
Polygonal shapefiles of the urban area	PTCP [17]
Biodiversity grid	See above

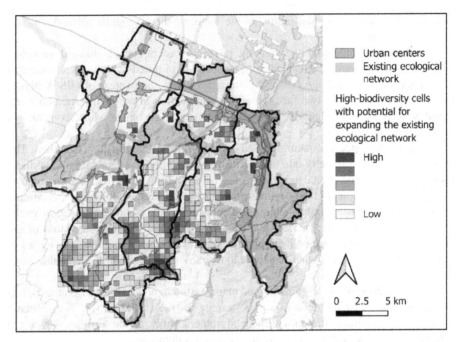

Fig. 7. Summary classification of biodiversity - Nesting potential and naturalness.

4   Conclusions

Choosing a common language for an inter-municipal approach constitutes a decision-making aspect for understanding natural themes and their correlations. Nature does not follow administrative limits. To build a matrix to focus on priorities aimed at mitigating the impacts of disasters deriving from the hydrogeological instability of a fragile territory subjected to climate change, it is necessary to cross-reference the different types of natural risks and seize the opportunities at a systemic level. Having information on the morphology of the territory is a fundamental knowledge condition to define mitigation activities. The various layers aimed at understanding the interferences, characteristics and opportunities have been added above the Digital Terrain Model (DTM), building the output synthesis to support the actions and strategies.

The steepness (slope) and lithology maps, together with the landslide risk drawn up by the Emilia Romagna Region, constitute the levels identified to develop a summary of observation of the fragilities resulting from instability. Some recent events have had consistent feedback with the summary on instability fragility developed, highlighting how the steepness combined with the type of superficial lithological layer can more easily trigger sliding or detachment phenomena with negative impacts both on the landscape and on the natural system ecosystem and man.

Similar methodology involved the coverage overlay on hydraulic risk, in particular using the datasets developed by the PGRA of the basin authority. This synthesis feeds a descriptive approach of the critical issues which was accompanied with the elaboration, according to the same spatial metric of the Kmq, of the ecological network and the potential naturalness.

The data available and with which the research was conducted, although georeferenced, are sector-specific. This leads to specialized but limited readings. Knowledge in the context of territorial analysis and more generally in the context of GIS Analysis, is not simply the sum of two factors but the construction of a new information level, possibly deriving from algebraic formulas of existing data but in whose content it is generated something new.

Then, in the aspects of naturalness, the availability of initial data is even less. The analysis must therefore enter into the merits of the cognitive domain with a multidisciplinary approach. The choice to identify five classes of representation for each processing is aimed at bringing out the portions of territory with values falling into the extreme classes because it favors understanding and correlation between the information levels. In the case of the development of maps on naturalness or nesting, the values of the classes and their ranges are defined with the support of naturalists. This activity led to the creation of a replicable and scalable biodiversity map based on the available input data.

The correlation of the aforementioned maps is used to build a general synthesis map aiming at supporting the definition of a strategy for the L.R. 24/2017. The thematic visualization highlights the criticalities and vulnerabilities of the territory, which are actually experienced after natural events. Some considerations:

- A taxonomic database is able to provide a synthetic representation of a phenomenon, as well as constituting a monitoring instrument to evaluate strategy actualization over time, by iterating the method with new and more integrated data
- The elaboration is a strong support instrument to urban planning
- The identification of vulnerabilities and criticalities favour a systemic approach, not only additional and punctual, aware of the connections, dependencies and waterfall consequences on a natural environment (butterfly effect)
- The territorial systems, both anthropic and natural as in our case study, are highly complex systems that must be analysed at different levels. The word "complexity" itself is linked to unitary vision, wrapping, keeping together. Is there such a strong complexity and interdependence between phenomena, geographies, environment and human actions, that a systemic approach is fundamental. There is no sustainability that is not systemic.

Definitely, there is a critical aspect in transferring and adapting the model according to a specific context, both spatial and morphological. The GIS analysis shown here has proved to be an extremely useful instrument, if supported by a multidisciplinary team of specialists. Indeed, the consistency and effectiveness of the weights attributed to the different levels result from the knowledge and former experience on similar territories in the regional context.

Also, the importance of geomatics, intended as a set of tools, is further highlighted in the planning path by the many levels of information reading and interpretation, which are needed to transform output evidences into strategic planning choices.

References

1. Seravalli, A.: La città adattiva – strumenti e metodi di analisi del grado di eterogeneità urbana. In: Murgante, B., Pede, E., Tiepolo, M. (a cura di), Innovazione tecnologica per la riorganizzazione spaziale, pp. 75–80, Planum Publisher, Milano (2021)
2. Preti, M.: La città del XXI secolo. In: Urban Design Magazine, no. 15, pp. 10–37 (2021)
3. Seravalli, A.: Misurare l'eterogeneità urbana. In: Urban Design Magazine, no. 12, pp. 6–9 (2019)
4. Seravalli, A.: GIS Teorie e applicazioni, La Mandragora (2011)
5. ISPI. https://www.ispionline.it/it/pubblicazione/2030-global-cities-cinesi-motore-del-mondo-22759. Accessed 31 July 2023
6. Byung-Chul Han, Le non cose, Einaudi (2022)
7. Seravalli, A., Amadio, L.: Taxonomic model for visualization and monitoring of actual liquid cities. In INPUT 2018
8. Taleb N.N.: Antifragile, Prosperare nel disordine, Il Saggiatore (2013)
9. GeoData Portal. https://geoportale.regione.emilia-romagna.it/. Accessed 31 July 2023
10. MinERva. https://datacatalog.regione.emilia-romagna.it/catalogCTA/. Accessed 31 July 2023
11. PGRA. https://ambiente.regione.emilia-romagna.it/it/suolo-bacino/sezioni/piano-di-ges tione-del-rischio-alluvioni/mappe-pgra-secondo-ciclo. Accessed 31 July 2023
12. Eurostat. https://ec.europa.eu/eurostat/web/gisco/geodata/reference-data/population-distri bution-demography/geostat. Accessed 31 July 2023
13. https://www.urbanit.it/wp-content/uploads/2018/10/BP_Serravalli.pdf. Accessed 31 July 2023
14. Seravalli, A.: La Smart Land come paradigma per un approccio sistemico e adattivo, in Conoscenza materiale e immateriale e gestione delle informazioni Atti XXIV Conferenza Nazionale SIU, Volume 02, pp. 20–27 (2022)
15. PTM. https://www.ptmbologna.it/ptm_approvato. Accessed 31 July 2023
16. Environment Portal of the Region Emilia Romagna. https://ambiente.regione.emilia-romagna. it/it/parchi-natura2000/consultazione/dati. Accessed 31 July 2023
17. PTCP. https://cartografia.cittametropolitana.bo.it/catalogo/. Accessed 31 July 2023

Next Pandemic Preparedness: A Focus on Health Data Standardization and Readiness for Spatial Enablement

Marica Teresa Rocca$^{(\boxtimes)}$ ⓘ and Vittorio Casella ⓘ

Università degli Studi di Pavia, DICAR, Pavia, Italy
{maricateresa.rocca,vittorio.casella}@unipv.it

Abstract. Within the EU H2020 PERISCOPE Project (Pan-European Response to the Impacts of COvid-19 and future Pandemics and Epidemics), the authors have dealt with several data sources related to the COVID pandemic, focused on health, socioeconomics, and policies. In the present paper, some lessons learned are presented, focused on the ECDC (European Centre for Disease Prevention and Control) repository and, more precisely, on the spatial enablement of the COVID-related data. The paper illustrates the inconsistencies the authors found, and the strategies depicted to fix them. The paper also proposes some modification to the ECDC repository, to make its data easier and quicker to integrate and analyze. Finally, some graphs are shown, highlighting how interesting and powerful the full integration of the whole ECDC Covid-related archive can be.

Keywords: PERISCOPE Project · COVID-19 · Pandemic Response

1 Introduction

The year 2020 saw the rapid worldwide spread of the COVID-19 pandemic, a very contagious and potentially lethal virus, never previously identified in humans. As of 14 June 2023, according to the World Health Organization (WHO) [1], over 767 million confirmed cases and over 6.9 million deaths have been reported globally.

In this framework the PERISCOPE project [2], acronym of *Pan-European Response to the ImpactS of COvid-19 and future Pandemics and Epidemics*, aims analyzing COVID-19 impacts in a broad scale, involving a consortium of 32 European institutions.

To evaluate the pandemic impacts, attention was paid at different areas as:

- Public health and public health systems [3];
- Socioeconomics [4];
- Policies [5].

The main activity of the authors has been devoted to planning and developing the *Atlas*, a *Web-based tool able to show and analyze spatio-temporal data* connected to the three aforementioned areas.

E. Borgogno Mondino and P. Zamperlin (Eds.): ASITA 2023, CCIS 2088, pp. 218–242, 2024.
https://doi.org/10.1007/978-3-031-59925-5_16

The *Atlas* integrates data the users can access and analyze in a flexible and powerful way. Data originate from various sources: ECDC for health [6], CoronaNET for policies [7], OECD for socioeconomics [8].

The present paper is focused on the lessons learned from the integration and spatial enablement of the ECDC data, as the authors met several difficulties and had to spend significant time in their harmonization before they could effectively use them.

We present the actual organization of the downloaded data, the strategies we implemented to integrate them and some recommendations on how their structure can be modified to speed up their integration and make them quickly available to analysis and advanced visualization. The value of the recommendations is not limited to COVID obviously but aims at being a significant contribution to the next pandemic preparedness.

The paper is organized as follows. Section 2 describes the materials provided by ECDC repository, the availability of base maps and the coding system employed for the unique identification of countries; in Sect. 3, we present the strategy outlined to overcome the numerous challenges encountered and describes the enormous work of data harmonization to create a stacked table structure for the spatial enablement of the downloaded data, Sect. 4 reports the results of these efforts, while Sect. 5 begin a discussion of the findings. Finally, Sect. 6 provides a comprehensive summary of the work done.

1.1 The EU H2020 Periscope Project

PERISCOPE is a large-scale research project funded by the European Commission under the Horizon 2020 research program; its ID number is 101016233. It has 32 partners listed in Table 1.

The initiative is coordinated by Paolo Giudici, full professor at the University of Pavia. The project's website address is https://periscopeproject.eu/.

Its aim is the analysis of the behavioral and socio-economic short and long-term impacts of COVID -19 to propose policy and technology measures to prepare Europe for eventual future epidemics.

The main goals are the creation of an accessible COVID-19 *Atlas* that allows spatiotemporal analysis of data, useful predictions related to the disease, and identify the best policies adopted locally, potentially extendable to a wider level and used to respond to possible future similar events. Furthermore, the project assessed policies and their impact on different sectors of society.

Periscope's activities are broken down into 15 Work Packages, which are in turn aggregated into 4 clusters named DIG (Data, Impacts, and Government response), BEAM (Behavior, Experiments, Atlas, and Modelling cluster), GIG (Governance, Innovation, and Guidance cluster) and TED (Testing, Education, and Deployment). The clusters are further grouped into two areas eloquently called Learn and Respond.

Project's general organization and interrelations between the work packages are summarized in the PERT chart shown in the following Fig. 1 and in Table 2.

The activities linked by the dotted lines are connected and interdependent operations, called dummy activities, useful for setting up a logical and consequential workflow.

Table 1. Consortium's Partners.

N	Name	Country
1	Università degli Studi di Pavia	Italy
2	Centre for European Policy Studies	Belgium
3	Sociedade Portuguesa de Inovacao Consultadoria Empresarial e Fomento da Inovacao Sa	Portugal
4	Fédération Européenne des Académies de Médecine	Belgium
5	Johann Wolfgang-Goethe-Universität Frankfurt Am Main	Germany
6	Technische Universiteit Delft	Netherlands
7	Politecnico di Milano	Italy
8	London School of Economics and Political Science	Great Britain
9	Università degli Studi di Trento	Italy
10	Universidad Politecnica de Madrid	Spain
11	Assistance Publique Hôpitaux de Paris	France
12	Fondazione IRCSS Policlinico San Matteo	Italy
13	Istituto per l'Interscambio Scientifico	Italy
14	Technische Universität München	Germany
15	European Regional and Local Health Authorities Asbl	Belgium
16	Fédération Européenne des Hôpitaux et des Soins de Santé	Belgium
17	Agencia de Qualitat i Avaluacio Sanitaries de Catalunya	Spain
18	Preduzeće za Informacione Tehnologije i Elektronsko Trgovanje Belit Doo	Serbia
19	Modefinance Srl	Italy
20	Genegis Gi Srl	Italy
21	Forum des Patients Européens	Belgium
22	Ecole des Hautes Etudes en Santé Publique	France
23	Mental Health Europe - Santé Mentale Europe	Belgium
24	Národní Ústav Duševního Zdraví	Czech Republic
25	Agora Sa	Poland
26	Karolinska Institutet	Sweden
27	Handelshögskolan i Stockholm	Sweden
28	Università della Svizzera Italiana	Switzerland
29	Universiteit Gent	Belgium
30	Institut National de la Santé et de la Recherche Médicale	France
31	Institut für Höhere Studien - Institute for Advanced Studies	Austria
32	Institutul de Virusologie Ştefan S. Nicolau	Romania

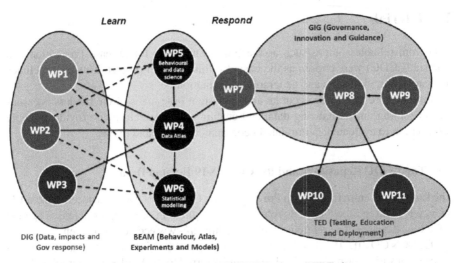

Fig. 1. Workplan of PERISCOPE Project - PERT chart

Table 2. Workplan

	Cluster	Work Package
LEARN	DIG	WP1 – Socio economic impacts
		WP2 – Impact on mental health
		WP3 – Impact on health systems
	BEAM	WP4 – Data Atlas
		WP5 – Behavioral and data science analysis
		WP6 – Statistical modeling
RESPOND	GIG	WP7 – Innovative public policies
		WP8 – Holistic policy
		WP9 – Multi-level governance
	TED	WP10 – Testing and deployment
		WP11 – Training and education
		WP12 – Ethics and data governance
		WP13 – Project management
		WP14 – Dissemination
		WP15 – Ethics requirement

2 Materials

Data from reliable sources such as the European Centre for Disease Prevention and Control (ECDC) were chosen as the basis for this research project. This data includes relevant health indicators and geographic information.

Furthermore, acquiring accurate and consistent base maps of the borders is essential for joining and visualizing data, and enabling spatial analysis to provide valuable information to evaluate health-related geographic patterns and trends.

2.1 The ECDC Repository and the COVID-19 Related Data

The European Centre for Disease Prevention and Control (ECDC) is a decentralized EU agency located in Stockholm; its role is the strengthening of Europe's defenses against infectious diseases. The reference website is https://www.ecdc.europa.eu/en.

ECDC's COVID-19 related activities include the collection of a large amount of data focused on various aspects of the disease and referred to the EU/EEA geographical area (Europe Union and European Economic Agreement).

Covid related data are supplied in eight tables, whose content is described in the following sections. We underline that the tables do not have a name, according to ECDC: there is a sort of a title (or short description) where they are listed on the website, while the name of the downloaded file is *"data.csv"*, invariably. There is no indication of the contents of the downloaded table, out of the eight variables, no reference to the date of transfer (since the documents are constantly updated), nor specification of the source of the files.

Within the paper, for the sake of clarity, the tables have been given a name, such as "ECDC_Table_1". This denomination is reported at the beginning of the heading of the following subsections. The rest of the heading corresponds to the *title* used by ECDC on its website. As an example, the table already mentioned has the title "14-Day Notification Rate of New Covid-19 Cases and Deaths".

Basic Concepts and Terminology about Tables

Before describing the structure of the ECDC tables, it is worth recalling basic concepts and terminology on the structure of data tables. If there were only one significant indicator, say the number of new cases per week per country, the considered data could be stored in a 3-column table reporting in each row the time the assessment is referred to, the country and the actual value; the header of such columns could be *time_ID, country_ID* and, *value*. If there were two indicators, say the number of new cases per week per country and the number of deaths, a further column should be added; the headers could be: *time_ID, country_ID, new_cases_value, deaths_value*. For the sake of clarity, an example is shown of the depicted structure, in Table 3.

Table 3. Example of depicted table

Time_ID	Country_ID	new_cases_value	deaths_value
2021–11	AUT	21074	246
2021–12	AUT	22296	216
...	...	...	...
2021–11	BEL	29329	178

An alternative way to store the same data is to stack the previous table; this means that the indicators' values are all stored in the fourth column and the third one specifies what indicator the row is referred to. The previous table would become as shown in Table 4.

Table 4. Example of stacked table

Time_ID	Country_ID	Indicator	value
2021–11	AUT	new_cases	21074
2021–11	AUT	Deaths	246
2021–12	AUT	new_cases	22296
2021–12	AUT	Deaths	216
...	...	...	...
2021–11	BEL	new_cases	29329
2021–11	BEL	Deaths	178

The first example shown can be defined as an unstacked structure; the second is stacked instead. The first one is more readable but needs a structure change when a new indicator is inserted into the database. The second one is less readable (but filtering can help) but has the advantage of being able to store as many indicators as needed in the same 4-column structure.

The ECDC tables generally implement a mixed structure i.e., they are stacked and unstacked at the same time. This poses significant harmonization problems when the downloaded table must be further processed. Figure 2 shows an example of such mixed concept.

country	ISO3	continent	population	indicator	week_count	year_week	rate_14_day	cumulative	source	note
Austria	AUT	Europe	8978929	cases	21074	2021-11	437.602302	510902	TESSy COVID-	
Austria	AUT	Europe	8978929	cases	22296	2021-12	483.019745	533198	TESSy COVID-	
Austria	AUT	Europe	8978929	deaths	246	2021-11	51.2310544	11093	TESSy COVID-	
Austria	AUT	Europe	8978929	deaths	216	2021-12	51.4537981	11309	TESSy COVID-	
Belgium	BEL	Europe	11617623	cases	29329	2021-11	435.407484	835677	TESSy COVID	
Belgium	BEL	Europe	11617623	cases	33998	2021-12	545.094293	869675	TESSy COVID	
Belgium	BEL	Europe	11617623	deaths	178	2021-11	30.0405685	22618	TESSy COVID-	
Belgium	BEL	Europe	11617623	deaths	188	2021-12	31.5038627	22806	TESSy COVID-	

Fig. 2. Extract of 14-Day Notification Rate of New COVID-19 Cases and Deaths table

ECDC_Table_1 – 14-Day Notification Rate of New COVID-19 Cases and Deaths

The table contains weekly COVID-19 data related new cases and deaths, grouped by country. Moreover, it stores the 14-day rate of newly reported cases per 100,000 population and the 14-day notification rate of reported deaths per million population. The 14-day rate is calculated by considering the total events of the considered week and of the previous one.

The table organization can be summarized as follows (more details in Table 6 in the Appendix):

- Spatial granularity: *country*;
- Temporal granularity: *week;*
- Format of the time tag: *year's week number with the format "yyyy-ww";*
- Country key: *3-letter ISO code;*
- Stacked indicators: *cases_weekly_count, cases_rate_14_day, cases_cumulative_count, deaths_weekly_count, deaths_rate_14_day, deaths _cumulative_count*;
- Unstacked indicators: *country, ISO3, continent, population, year_week;*
- Scope: *till June 2022, the whole world; EU only afterwards.*

ECDC_Table_2 – 14-Day Age Specific Notification rate of New COVID-19 Cases

The downloadable data file contains information on the 14-day notification rate of newly reported COVID-19 cases per 100,000 population by age group, week, and country.

The table organization can be summarized as follows (more details in Table 7 in the Appendix):

- Spatial granularity: *country*;
- Temporal granularity: *week;*
- Format of the time tag: *year's week number with the format "yyyy-ww";*
- Country key: *2-letter ISO code;*
- Stacked indicators: *age_group, new_cases, rate_14_day_per_100k*;
- Unstacked indicators: *country, ISO2, year_week, population;*
- Scope: *till December 2020, the whole world; EU only afterwards.*

ECDC_Table_3 – Daily Number of New COVID-19 Cases and Deaths in EU/EEA

The downloadable data file contains information on newly reported COVID-19 cases and deaths in EU/EEA countries. Each row contains the corresponding data for a certain day and per country.

The table organization can be summarized as follows (more details in Table 8 in the Appendix):

- Spatial granularity: *country*;
- Temporal granularity: *daily;*
- Format of the time tag: *date with the format "dd/mm/yyyy";*
- Country key: *2 and 3 -letter ISO code;*
- Stacked indicators: *daily_cases, daily_deaths;*
- Unstacked indicators: *date, day, month, year, country, ISO2, ISO3, population, continent;*
- Scope: *till October 2022, then the daily count is archived.*

ECDC_Table_4 – Hospital and ICU Admission Rates and Occupancy for COVID-19

The downloadable data files contain information about hospitalization and Intensive Care Unit (ICU) admission rates and current occupancy for COVID-19 by date and country.

The table organization can be summarized as follows (more details in Table 9 in the Appendix):

- Spatial granularity: *country*;
- Temporal granularity: *daily;*
- Format of the time tag: *date with the format "yyyy-mm-dd";*
- Country key: *country name;*
- Stacked indicators: *daily hospital occupancy, daily ICU occupancy, Weekly new hospital admissions per 100k, Weekly new ICU admissions per 100k*;
- Unstacked indicators: *country, date, year_week.*

ECDC_Table_5 – Vaccination in the EU/EEA

The downloadable data files contain the data on the COVID-19 vaccine rollout mentioned above and each row contains the corresponding data for a certain week and country.

The table organization can be summarized as follows (more details in Table 10 in the Appendix):

- Spatial granularity: country, regions (just some countries);
- Temporal granularity: weekly;
- Format of the time tag: year's week number with the format "yyyy-Www";
- Country key: 2-letter ISO code;
- Stacked indicators: TargetGroup, Vaccine.
- Unstacked indicators: YearWeek, ISO2, population number doses received, number doses exported, FirstDose, FirstDoseRefused, SecondDose, DoseAdditional1, DoseAdditional2, UnknownDose.

This table is really complex, as it simultaneously contains age groups, type of vaccine, and number of doses administered. To simplify its structure in a stacked table, despite knowing that we have lost information, we decided to summarize the number of vaccinated by age target, and the number of vaccines by type.

ECDC_Table_6 – Testing for COVID-19 by Week and Country
The downloadable data file contains information about testing volume for COVID-19 by week, country, and subnational region (where available).

The table organization can be summarized as follows (more details in Table 11 in the Appendix):

- Spatial granularity: *country*;
- Temporal granularity: *weekly;*
- Format of the time tag: *year's week number with the format "yyyy-Www";*
- Country key: *2-letter ISO code;*
- Stacked indicators: *new_cases, tests_done, testing_rate, positivity_rate;*
- Unstacked indicators: *country, ISO2, year_week, level, country, population, testing_data_source.*

ECDC_Table_7 – SARS-CoV-2 Variants in the EU/EEA
The downloadable data file contains information about the volume of COVID-19 sequencing, the number and percentage distribution of Variants Of Concern (VOC) by week and country.

The table organization can be summarized as follows (more details in Table 12 in the Appendix):

- Spatial granularity: *country*;
- Temporal granularity: *weekly*;
- Format of the time tag: *year's week number with the format "yyyy-ww";*
- Country key: *2-letter ISO code*;
- Stacked   indicators: *new_cases, number_sequenced, percent_cases_sequenced, variant, number_detections_variant, number_sequenced_known_variant, percent_variant;*
- Unstacked indicators: *country, ISO2, year_week.*

ECDC_Table_8 – Country Response Measures to COVID-19
The data on non-pharmaceutical measures are based on information available from official public sources. The data on response measures has several limitations: there is substantial heterogeneity in physical distancing policies and their implementation, for some countries data are no longer available on official websites.

The table organization can be summarized as follows (more details in Table 13 in the Appendix):

- Spatial granularity: *country*;
- Temporal granularity: *date start/date end*;
- Format of the time tag: *date with the format "yyyy-mm-dd";*
- Country key: *country name;*
- Stacked indicators: *response_measure;*
- Unstacked indicators: *country, date_start, date_end.*

2.2   Issues with ECDC Data Tables

As anticipated, several issues were met in downloading and integrating ECDC data, preventing their quick utilization. The main issues met are illustrated in the following.

1. **Meaningless names of the downloaded files**. As already mentioned, the name of the downloaded file will be "*data.csv*", invariably. This doesn't account of which table has been accessed, out of the eight available; of the time the table was downloaded, as data are updated very often; and of the source of the data, ECDC. As an example, keeping on Table 1, the downloaded file could be named "ECDC_COVID19_Table1_2021_07_05".
2. **Inhomogeneous choice for the country_ID**. As documented in detail in previous Sections, the eight considered tables implement three different choices for the country ID. Indeed, the ISO3 key is adopted in Table 1 and Table 3; the ISO2 code is adopted in others: Table 2, Table 3, Table 5, Table 6, and Table 7; the country clear name is used in Table 4, and Table 8 instead.
3. **Inhomogeneous structure for the time_ID.** The considered data generally have the weekly time granularity. Unfortunately, the considered tables implement different ways to administer year weeks. Some tables (Table 1, Table 2, Table 7) use the structure as "*yyyy-ww*" (e.g., 2020–01); others (Table 5, Table 6) use the format "yyyy-Www" (e.g., 2020-W01).
4. **Mistakes in the ISO codes used**. Some simple mistakes were met, in ISO codes. For instance, Greece's ISO2 Code is GR and not EL, as reported in ECDC data, in Tables 2, 3, 5, 6, and 7.
5. **Inhomogeneous spatial granularity**. While data are normally aggregated at the country level, Table 5 contains information at a finer spatial resolution for just a few countries: Finland, France, Italy, and Poland.

2.3   On the Availability of Suitable Base Maps

The availability of open and standardized boundary maps plays a crucial role in various fields, including geography, cartography, and data analysis. Standardization is an important aspect for these maps: boundary maps use international standards such as ISO codes, which provide unique identifiers for countries and their subdivisions. These codes establish a common language, allowing the communication and integration of data from various sources. The harmonization and standardization enhance the interoperability with geospatial dataset, such as the ones analyzed in this document. Their availability is useful to ensure consistency to allow communication across different systems and platforms.

Base maps of nations and their first-level subdivisions were downloaded from GADM website [9], which provides freely available shapefiles of country borders for academic use. However, the ID_codes of the countries do not always correspond with the ISO-codes, which we have chosen as the standard system for recognizing nations.

Considering that most of the countries are correctly identified according to ISO.org standards, for consistency it was decided to make corrections to those not corresponding to the values indicated by the aforementioned website. This included adjustments for nations such as China, Estonia, Greece, Morocco, Montenegro, the Netherlands, and

Poland. Regarding the ID_codes related to the subdivisions of Great Britain, these are not ISO-codes but BS-codes, as they fall within the British Standard BS 6879.

Some subnational subdivisions are being progressively updated: the number of counties in Norway has gone from 18 to 11 in 2020, and the same goes for South Sudan, where the original shapefile of the borders has been changed by merging the Jonglei and Lakes regions. Some islands of Portugal do not have ISO-codes.

Furthermore, dealing with the geographic boundaries of countries and their first-level subdivisions presents integrity challenges. The political issues and tensions related to the recognition of national borders are complex and always evolving, which leads to difficulties in establishing the respective ISO-code.

One example is the occupation of some districts in Azerbaijan by Armenian forces since 1993, despite Azerbaijan reclaiming them on December 1, 2022. In the case of Kosovo, we had to edit the original subdivisions' shapefile, in order to use ISO-codes, which consider it part of Serbia. We combined Sevastopol with the Russia shapefile, starting with the ISO-code of Ukraine (UA-40) and changing it to RU-40, preserving the uniqueness of the codes.

2.4   Keys for Countries and Their Political Subdivisions

ISO Code

ISO 3166 country codes [10] are globally recognized codes identifying each country and its subdivisions. They are published by the International Organization for Standardization (ISO). Using these codes helps prevent errors that can occur due to variations in country names in different languages. These codes have practical purposes as: national postal organizations, internet domains, and money transfers between banks.

The ISO code consists of two parts: country and subdivisions codes. Country codes are represented by a two-letter code (alpha-2) or a three-letter code (alpha-3).

The ISO code repository is an Online Browsing Platform (OBP) [11] available at the following link: https://www.iso.org/obp/ui/#home.

NUTS Code

NUTS (Nomenclature of Territorial Units for Statistics) is a classification system used to divide the economic territory of the EU and the UK into hierarchical regions for statistical purposes. For each EU country, Eurostat has established a three-level hierarchy of the NUTS code.

The current NUTS 2021 classification [12], valid from 1st January 2021, includes 92 regions at first level, 242 regions at second level, and 1166 regions at third level.

This classification has multiple purposes, such as collecting, developing, and harmonizing regional statistics in Europe, conducting socio-economic analyses, and framing EU regional policies. Note that the NUTS subdivisions do not always align with administrative divisions within the country.

The NUTS code consists of a two-letter country code, followed by one or more numbers to represent its subdivisions.

NUTS code repository (GISCO: geographical information and maps) [13] can be found at the following link: https://ec.europa.eu/eurostat/web/gisco/geodata/reference-data/administrative-units-statistical-units/nuts.

3   The Method Depicted at the Laboratory of Geomatics

Within the PERISCOPE Project, the main purpose of the Laboratory of Geomatics of the University of Pavia is the collection and harmonization of data.

The goal of data harmonization is to achieve, or improve, compatibility of data collected from similar but independent sources in order to enable pooling or sharing of information [14]. In our case data harmonization plays a key role in facilitating the joining of tabular and geographical data and the visualization of the information within the Atlas, enhancing spatial analysis capacity.

ECDC COVID-19 data, as already mentioned, presents numerous challenges, making it difficult to draw meaningful insights; an update of the original tables, with the listed problems resolved, could simplify their visualization.

However, by organizing these different data sources into a harmonized stacked structure, we are able to obtain a useful tool for efficient data management and analysis.

Harmonization not only simplifies the data integration process, but also improves the quality of visualizations within the Atlas, enabling a representation of spatial patterns and relationship. Ultimately, it fosters a deeper understanding of geographic data and provides a solid foundation for informed decision-making.

Table 5. Stacked table structure

Variable	Definition
Country	
ISO_L1_A3	3-letter ISO code
ISO_L1_A2	2-letter code
Year	
Week	
time 1	Start date
time 2	End date
Total population	
What	
Value	
Measure	
GK	Grand Key: unique name

Having multiple data sources to download makes essential to transform, harmonize and organize data. The eight original tables were reorganized into a twelve-columns format, shown in Table 5 below, so that all significant health data could be merged into one stacked table. The structure of a stacked table is a sort of database system particularly useful for answering management-related queries: a well-structured table allows the storage, retrieval, and analysis of large volumes of data organized differently and coming from different sources. The organization of this type of structure requires the implementation of a logical scheme capable of adapting to all the data examined.

3.1 The Lookup Table

To ensure the accuracy and consistency of the data contained in the originally downloaded tables, a key aspect of our approach involved creating an ISO alpha-3/alpha-2 code lookup table. This lookup table plays an important role in verifying the integrity of our dataset evaluating the uniqueness of the data associated with each country.

The lookup table consists of three columns: the country name, the 3-letter ISO code (ISO_L1_A3), and the 2-letter ISO code (ISO_L1_A2). By cross-referencing the data obtained from the downloaded tables with the ISO codes, we could not only ensure the accuracy and consistency of the information, but also establish a direct link between the data and its respective country. In the event that the ISO codes present in the original tables do not match any of the entries whithin the lookup table, an automatic warning system is activated, serving as a detection mechanism for potential data errors or inconsistencies. These anomalies are then subject to further investigations, which require careful examination of the source data tables.

4 Results

We developed a bespoke MATLAB script that allows the extraction of chosen data directly from the European Centre for Disease Prevention and Control (ECDC) website.

This effort was made necessary by the variations in the structural composition of each table we encountered during the data acquisition process. Our custom-designed system was designed paying particular attention on the conversion of the weeks of the year into corresponding start and end dates.

To ensure consistent organization of the data within our chosen stacked structure, we conducted a harmonization process across the eight distinct tables, outlined in Sect. 2. This harmonization step involved standardizing the format and structure of the data, making it amenable to comprehensive analysis and interpretation.

Consider Fig. 3, which effectively illustrates an excerpt of rows 18 to 33 from our entire dataset, offering a glimpse of the structured data and their information.

As of October 12, 2022, the latest data processing produced a complete data archive, consisting of 865,923 rows and spanning 12 columns. This comprehensive archive effectively includes all the data extracted from the previously analyzed tables, strengthening the robustness of our data repository and being able to store all needed the indicators.

1 country	2 ISO_L1_A3	3 ISO_L1_A2	4 Year	5 Week	6 time1	7 time2	8 Total_Population	What	9 Value	10	11 Measure	12 GK
Austria	AUT	AT	2020	6	03-Feb-2020	09-Feb-2020	893266	cases_cumulative_count		0	<undefined>	"AUT_2020_6_cases_cumulative_count"
Austria	AUT	AT	2020	7	10-Feb-2020	16-Feb-2020	893266	cases_weekly_count		0	<undefined>	"AUT_2020_7_cases_weekly_count"
Austria	AUT	AT	2020	7	10-Feb-2020	16-Feb-2020	893266	cases_rate_14_day		0	<undefined>	"AUT_2020_7_cases_rate_14_day"
Austria	AUT	AT	2020	7	10-Feb-2020	16-Feb-2020	893266	cases_cumulative_count		0	<undefined>	"AUT_2020_7_cases_cumulative_count"
Austria	AUT	AT	2020	8	17-Feb-2020	23-Feb-2020	893266	cases_weekly_count		0	<undefined>	"AUT_2020_8_cases_weekly_count"
Austria	AUT	AT	2020	8	17-Feb-2020	23-Feb-2020	893266	cases_rate_14_day		0	<undefined>	"AUT_2020_8_cases_rate_14_day"
Austria	AUT	AT	2020	8	17-Feb-2020	23-Feb-2020	893266	cases_cumulative_count		0	<undefined>	"AUT_2020_8_cases_cumulative_count"
Austria	AUT	AT	2020	9	24-Feb-2020	01-Mar-2020	893266	cases_weekly_count		12	<undefined>	"AUT_2020_9_cases_weekly_count"
Austria	AUT	AT	2020	9	24-Feb-2020	01-Mar-2020	893266	cases_rate_14_day		0.1343	<undefined>	"AUT_2020_9_cases_rate_14_day"
Austria	AUT	AT	2020	9	24-Feb-2020	01-Mar-2020	893266	cases_cumulative_count		12	<undefined>	"AUT_2020_9_cases_cumulative_count"
Austria	AUT	AT	2020	10	02-Mar-2020	08-Mar-2020	893266	cases_weekly_count		114	<undefined>	"AUT_2020_10_cases_weekly_count"
Austria	AUT	AT	2020	10	02-Mar-2020	08-Mar-2020	893266	cases_rate_14_day		1.4106	<undefined>	"AUT_2020_10_cases_rate_14_day"
Austria	AUT	AT	2020	10	02-Mar-2020	08-Mar-2020	893266	cases_cumulative_count		126	<undefined>	"AUT_2020_10_cases_cumulative_count"
Austria	AUT	AT	2020	11	09-Mar-2020	15-Mar-2020	893266	cases_weekly_count		873	<undefined>	"AUT_2020_11_cases_weekly_count"
Austria	AUT	AT	2020	11	09-Mar-2020	15-Mar-2020	893266	cases_rate_14_day		11.0493	<undefined>	"AUT_2020_11_cases_rate_14_day"
Austria	AUT	AT	2020	11	09-Mar-2020	15-Mar-2020	893266	cases_cumulative_count		999	<undefined>	"AUT_2020_11_cases_cumulative_count"

Fig. 3. Example of the stacked table organization (rows from 18 to 33).

As an example of the work carried out, this paper shows the comparison between two of the indicators of the stacked table: the weekly cases count, and the 14-day notification rate of reported cases per 100,000 population. The rate, considering the number of people, simplifies the comparison between countries that may have different demographic sizes.

The following Fig. 4 shows the weekly cases count for some European countries. E.g., Great Britain reported about two million and five hundred thousand cases in January 2022, whereas Italy recorder slightly fewer than one million cases in the same period.

The 14-day notification rate of reported cases (per 100,000 population), as shown in Fig. 5 shows a rate of cases about seven thousand in Great Britan and about four thousand in Italy in the same period.

The graphical representation of the data simplifies the interpretation of the large table created, allowing a quick comparison of the data for the different European Countries.

Data harmonization allows tabular data to be joined with the base map of countries, simplifying the understanding and visualization of the chosen indicators. This finding is summarized in Fig. 6, an excerpt from the Atlas data, where COVID-19 cases, counts, and rates (per 100,000 population) are graphed. The Atlas features a time slider, which allows users to dynamically track and evaluate changes in chosen indicators over time.

This tool empowers researchers and decision makers, providing a basis for informed choices.

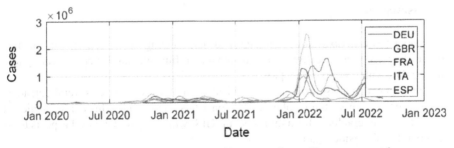

Fig. 4. Comparison of the cases weekly count of some European countries.

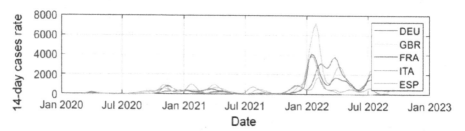

Fig. 5. Comparison of the 14-day rate of reported cases per 100,000 population.

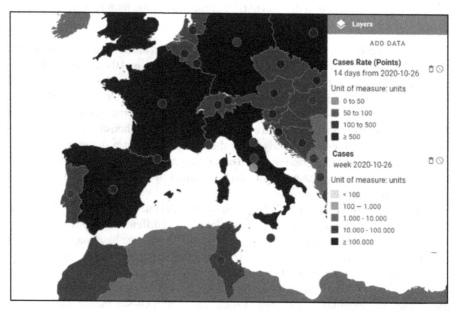

Fig. 6. Extract of Atlas data – week 26/10/2020 – Comparison of the 14-day rate of reported cases per 100,000 population (points) and the cases weekly count.

5   Discussion

This paper has described how managing and harmonizing very large amount of data from different sources is a significant challenge, but fundamental for collaborating and sharing data with other partners [15].

Improving a database from a geographical point of view involves several considerations as enhancing spatial resolution and consistency is crucial. This can be achieved thanks to the geographic information system (GIS) which allows temporal aspects to be incorporated alongside spatial ones [16].

Our main goal was to optimize the database for spatial queries and analysis, which involves implementing spatial indexing.

Starting from the original data downloaded from the European Centre for Disease Prevention and Control (ECDC) website [3], sorted into eight differently organized tables, we managed to standardize and harmonize the data in a structured and unaltered format, encompassing all available data.

The stacked table created, is not easy to read, and the graphic result makes it easy to visualize and compare data across different countries and over time. The join of the tabular data with the base map of the country borders further improves understanding.

Despite this progress, several challenges persist, as the need for standardized data formats and interoperability is fundamental.

6 Conclusions

The global COVID-19 pandemic has taken the world by surprise, leaving countries unprepared for the scale of its impacts in many areas.

In the field of public health, the pandemic has highlighted the vulnerabilities of health systems, testing the resilience of medical infrastructures and the ability to respond to a sudden health emergency. The socio-economic realities of individuals and communities have borne the brunt of the crisis. Furthermore, the policies adopted in response to the pandemic have been very different, reflecting the diverse approaches and strategies adopted by governments to mitigate its effects.

Within this context, PERISCOPE project's aim is to analyze the impacts of COVID-19 on the aforementioned areas:

- Public health;
- Socio economic realities;
- Policies adopted.

With this goal the Geomatics Laboratory of the University of Pavia is working on the development of an accessible Atlas that allows the spatiotemporal visualization of data, useful for the decision-making process.

In the present paper we have focused in particular on the ECDC repository, which collects a large amount of health data related to COVID-19 referring to the EU/EEA geographical area.

Specifically, the data analyzed are listed below:

- 14-days new COVID-19 cases and deaths;
- 14-days age specific COVID-19 new cases;
- Daily new COVID-19 cases and deaths;
- Hospital and ICU admission rates;
- Vaccination;
- Testing for COVID-19;
- SARS-CoV-2 variants;
- Country response measure.

Downloading such heterogeneous data, we encountered several challenges, the main one being the identification value of each country, which differs from table to table.

The other non-negligible problem concerned dealing with the different time granularity and format. To solve these problems and the others mentioned above, harmonization has been resorted to, using standardization techniques.

We developed custom MATLAB scripts to extract and standardize data from the ECDC web link, resulting in harmonized tables. These harmonized datasets were subsequently structured into a stacked table format, adaptable to all the examined data, thus improving the efficiency of data management.

Leveraging the stacked table structure, we further devised MATLAB scripts for data visualization, enabling graphical representations that offer valuable insights and facilitate indicator comparisons.

In summary, starting from the original data from the ECDC website, our harmonization efforts and the creation of a comprehensive table have laid the foundation for seamless integration with the shapefiles of national borders within the Atlas of PERISCOPE project. This integration, in turn, facilitated the visualization and analysis of spatiotemporal data.

Acknowledgements. The present paper has been prepared under the umbrella of the EU H2020 Periscope Project, grant number 101016233, in the framework of PhD course XXXVIII cycle.

Appendix

Table 6. ECDC_Table_1 – 14-Day Notification Rate of New COVID-19 Cases and Deaths.

Variable	Definition
Country	
country_code	3-letter ISO code
Continent	
Population	Eurostat
Indicator	Cases, Deaths
weekly_count	
year_week	
rate_14_day	14-day notification rate of reported COVID-19 cases per 100,000 population OR 14-day notification rate of reported deaths per 1,000,000 population
cumulative_count	
Source	Epidemic intelligence, national weekly data

Table 7. ECDC_Table_2 – 14-Day Age Specific Notification Rate of New COVID-19 Cases.

Variable	Definition
Country	
country_code	2-letter ISO code
year_week	
age_group	Age group of cases in years
new_cases	Weekly number of new confirmed cases. Numbers under 5 are suppressed
Population	Age-specific population for the country
rate_14_day_per_100k	Age-specific 14-day notification rate of reported COVID-19 cases per 100,000 population
Source	TESSy

Table 8. ECDC_Table_3 – Daily Number of New COVID-19 Cases and Deaths in EU/EEA.

Variable	Definition
dateRep	Date of reporting "dd/mm/yyyy"
Day	
Month	
Year	
Cases	Number of newly reported cases
Deaths	Number of newly reported deaths
countriesAndTerritories	Name of the country or territory
geoId	2-letter code
countryterritoryCode	3-letter ISO code
popData2020	Eurostat 2020 data
continentExp	Name of the continent reporting

Table 9. ECDC_Table_4 – Hospital and ICU Admission Rates and Occupancy for COVID-19.

Variable	Definition
Country	
indicator	Daily hospital occupancy, Daily ICU occupancy, Weekly new hospital admissions per 100k population, Weekly new ICU new admissions per 100k population
date	Date for daily occupancy indicators
year_week	
value	Number of patients or new admissions per 100,000 population
source	Categorical source of data: TESSy, Country_API, Country_Github, Country_Website, External_Github, JRC, Surveillance, Other_Website
url	URL of data source

Table 10. ECDC_Table_5 – Vaccination in the EU/EEA.

Variable	Definition
YearWeekISO	Date when the vaccine was received/administered "yyyy-Www"
ReportingCountry	2-letter ISO code
Denominator	Population for target groups (total population and age-specific population from Eurostat/UN). Denominator reported by countries for specific Target Groups: HCW (Health Care Workers) and LTCF (residents in Long-Term Care Facilities).
NumberDosesReceived	Number of vaccine doses distributed by the manufacturers to the country during the reporting week.
NumberDosesExported	Number of vaccine doses donated or sold by the country during the reporting week.
FirstDose	Number of first dose vaccine administered to individuals during the reporting week.
FirstDoseRefused	Number of individuals refusing the first vaccine dose.
SecondDose	Number of second dose vaccine administered to individuals during the reporting week.
DoseAdditional1	Number of first additional vaccine doses administered after a complete standard primary course to individuals during the reporting week.
DoseAdditional2	Number of second additional vaccine doses administered after a complete standard primary course to individuals during the reporting week.
DoseAdditional3	Number of third additional vaccine doses administered after a complete standard primary course to individuals during the reporting week.
UnknownDose	Number of doses administered during the reporting week where the type of dose was not specified.
Region	As a minimum, data should be reported at national level (country code).
TargetGroup	ALL = Overall adults (18+)
	Age<18 = Overall adolescents and children (0-17 yo)
	HCW = Health Care Workers
	LTCF = residents in LongTerm Care Facilities
	Age0_4 = 0-4 yo
	Age5_9 = 5-9 yo
	Age10_14 = 10-14 yo
	Age15_17 = 15-17 yo
	Age18_24 = 18-24 yo
	Age25_49 = 25-49 yo
	Age50_59 = 50-59 yo
	Age60_69 = 60-69 yo
	Age70_79 = 70-79 yo

(*continued*)

Table 10. (*continued*)

Variable	Definition
	Age80+ = 80 years and over
	AgeUnk = Unknown age
	1_Age<60 = adults below 60 years of age and above 17
	1_Age60+ = adults 60 years and over
Vaccine	AZ = AstraZeneca - Vaxzevria
	BECNBG = Beijing CNBG - BBIBP-CorV
	BHACOV = Bharat - Covaxin
	CHU = Chumakov - Covi-Vac
	CAN = CanSino - Convidecia
	COM = Pfizer BioNTech - Comirnaty
	COMBA.1= Pfizer BioNTech - Comirnaty Original/Omicron BA.1
	COMBA.4-5 = Pfizer BioNTech – Comirnaty Original/Omicron BA.4/BA.5
	COMBIV = Pfizer BioNTech – Comirnaty (Original/Omicron BA.1 or Original/Omicron BA.4/BA.5)
	CVAC = Curevac - CVnCOV
	HAYATVAC = Julphar- Hayat-Vax
	JANSS = Janssen - Jcovden
	MOD = Moderna - Spikevax
	MODBA.1 = Moderna - Spikevax Bivalent Original/Omicron BA.1
	MODBA.4-5 = Moderna - Spikevax Bivalent Original/Omicron BA.4/BA.5
	MODBIV = Moderna - Spikevax Bivalent (Original/Omicron BA.1 or Original/Omicron BA.4/BA.5)
	NVX = SII – Covovax
	NVXD = Novavax – Nuvaxovid
	QAZVAQ = RIBSP - QazVac
	SGSK = Sanofi GSK - Vidprevtyn
	SIICOV = SII - Covishield
	SIN = Sinovac - CoronaVac
	SPU = Gamaleya - Sputnik-V
	SPUL = Gamaleya - Sputnik-Light
	SRCVB = SRCVB - EpiVacCorona
	UNK = UNKNOWN
	VLA = Valneva – VLA2001
	WUCNBG = Wuhan CNBG - Inactivated
	ZFUZ = Anhui ZL - Zifivax
Population	Age-specific population for the country

Table 11. ECDC_Table_6 – Testing for COVID-19 by Week and Country.

Variable	Definition
country	
country_code	2-letter ISO code
year_week	"yyyy-Www"
level	National or subnational level data
region	2-letter ISO code where level is national. Nuts code (or alternative) for subnational region
region_name	Country name where level is national or name of region where level is subnational
new_cases	Number of new confirmed cases
tests_done	Number of tests done
population	
testing_rate	Testing rate per 100,000 population
positivity_rate	Weekly test positivity (%): 100 x Number of new confirmed cases/number of tests done per week
testing_data_source	Country API, Country GitHub, Country website, Manual web scraping, Other, Survey, TESSy: data provided directly by Member States to ECDC via TESSy

Table 12. ECDC_Table_7 – Variants in the EU/EEA

Variable	Definition
country	
country_code	2-letter ISO code
year_week	"yyyy-ww"
source	Data source, either GISAID EpiCoV database or TESSy
new_cases	Weekly number of new confirmed cases. Set to zero in the event that countries have negative case counts due to retrospective correction of data
number_sequenced	Weekly number of sequences carried out
percent_cases_sequenced	100 x new_cases/number_sequenced
valid_denominator	GISAID data: TRUE TESSY data: FALSE if there are discrepancies in the data reported for a given week, such as where the sum of number_detections_variant across all variants exceeds number_sequenced (aggregate data), or where no sequences have been reported that are coded as 'wild type' (case-based data)
variant	Each VOC, Other or UNK
number_detections_variant	Number of detections reported of the variant
percent_variant	100 x number_detections_variant/ number_sequenced. Np value given if valid_denominator = = FALSE

Table 13. ECDC_Table_8 – Country Response Measures to COVID-19

Variable	Definition
Country	
Response_measure	StayHomeOrder: Stay-at-home orders for the general population; RegionalStayHomeOrder: Regional stay-at-home orders for the general population at least in one region; StayHomeGen: Stay-at-home recommendations for the general population; StayHomeRiskG: Stay-at-home recommendations for risk groups or vulnerable populations; SocialCircle: Social circle/bubble to limit social contacts; PrivateGatheringRestrictions: Restrictions on private gatherings; ClosDaycare: Closure of educational institutions (daycare or nursery); ClosPrim: Closure of educational institutions (primary schools); ClosSec: Closure of educational institutions (secondary schools). ClosHigh: Closure of educational institutions (higher education). MassGatherAll: Interventions are in place to limit mass/public gatherings; BanOnAllEvents: Interventions are in place to limit all indoor/outdoor mass/public gatherings; IndoorOver50: Interventions are in place to limit indoor mass/public gatherings of over 50 participants; IndoorOver100: Interventions are in place to limit indoor mass/public gatherings of over 100 participants; IndoorOver500: Interventions are in place to limit indoor mass/public gatherings of over 500 participants; IndoorOver1000: Interventions are in place to limit indoor mass/public gatherings of over 1000 participants; OutdoorOver50: Interventions are in place to limit outdoor mass/public gatherings of over 50 participants; OutdoorOver100: Interventions are in place to limit outdoor mass/public gatherings of over 100 participants; OutdoorOver500: Interventions are in place to limit outdoor mass/public gatherings of over 500 participants; OutdoorOver1000: Interventions are in place to limit outdoor mass/public gatherings of over 1000 participants ClosPubAny: Closure of public spaces of any kind; EntertainmentVenues: Closure of entertainment venues; ClosureOfPublicTransport: Closure of public transport: GymsSportsCentres: Closure of gyms/sports centres; HotelsAccommodation: Closure of hotels/accommodation services; NonEssentialShops: Closures of non-essential shops; PlaceOfWorship: Closure of places of worship;

(continued)

Table 13. (*continued*)

Variable	Definition
	RestaurantsCafes: Closure of restaurants and cafes/bars
	MasksVoluntaryAllSpaces: Protective mask use in all public spaces on voluntary basis;
	MasksVoluntaryClosedSpaces: Protective mask use in closed public spaces/transport on voluntary basis;
	MasksMandatoryAllSpaces: Protective mask use in all public spaces on mandatory basis;
	MasksMandatoryClosedSpaces: Protective mask use in closed public spaces/transport on mandatory basis;
	Teleworking: Teleworking recommendation;
	AdaptationOfWorkplace: Adaptation of workplaces;
	WorkplaceClosures: Closures of workplaces;
	StayHomeOrderPartial: Stay-at-home orders for the general population – partially relaxed measure;
	RegionalStayHomeOrderPartial: Regional stay-at-home orders for the general population at least in one region – partially relaxed measure;
	StayHomeGenPartial: Stay-at-home recommendations for the general population – partially relaxed measure;
	StayHomeRiskGPartial = Stay-at-home recommendations for risk groups or vulnerable populations – partially relaxed measure;
	SocialCirclePartial = Social circle/bubble to limit social contacts – partially relaxed measure;
	PrivateGatheringRestrictionsPartial: Restrictions on private gatherings – partially relaxed measure;
	ClosDaycarePartial: Closure of educational institutions (daycare or nursery) – partially relaxed measure;
	ClosPrimPartial: Closure of educational institutions (primary schools) – partially relaxed measure;
	ClosSecPartial: Closure of educational institutions (secondary schools) – partially relaxed measure
	ClosHighPartial: Closure of educational institutions (higher education) – partially relaxed measure
	MassGatherAllPartial: Interventions are in place to limit mass/public
	Gatherings – partially relaxed measure;
	BanOnAllEventsPartial: Interventions are in place to limit all indoor/outdoor mass/public gatherings – partially relaxed measure;
	IndoorOver50Partial: Interventions are in place to limit indoor mass/public gatherings of over 50 participants – partially relaxed measure;
	IndoorOver100Partial: Interventions are in place to limit indoor

(*continued*)

Table 13. (*continued*)

Variable	Definition
	mass/public gatherings of over 100 participants – partially relaxed measure;
	IndoorOver500Partial: Interventions are in place to limit indoor mass/public gatherings of over 500 participants – partially relaxed measure;
	IndoorOver1000Partial: Interventions are in place to limit indoor mass/public gatherings of over 1000 participants – partially relaxed measure;
	OutdoorOver50Partial: Interventions are in place to limit outdoor mass/public gatherings of over 50 participants – partially relaxed measure;
	OutdoorOver100Partial: Interventions are in place to limit outdoor mass/public gatherings of over 100 participants – partially relaxed measure;
	OutdoorOver500Partial: Interventions are in place to limit outdoor mass/public gatherings of over 500 participants – partially relaxed measure;
	OutdoorOver1000Partial: Interventions are in place to limit outdoor mass/public gatherings of over 1000 participants – partially relaxed measure;
	ClosPubAnyPartial: Closure of public spaces of any kind – partially relaxed measure;
	EntertainmentVenuesPartial: Closure of entertainment venues – partially relaxed measure;
	ClosureOfPublicTransportPartial: Closure of public transport – partially relaxed measure;
	GymsSportsCentresPartial: Closure of gyms/sports centres – partially relaxed measure;
	HotelsAccommodationPartial: Closure of hotels/accommodation services – partially relaxed measure;
	NonEssentialShopsPartial: Closures of non-essential shops – partially relaxed measure;
	PlaceOfWorshipPartial: Closure of places of worship – partially relaxed measure;
	RestaurantsCafesPartial: Closure of restaurants and cafes/bars – partially relaxed measure;
	MasksVoluntaryAllSpacesPartial: Protective mask use in all public spaces on voluntary basis (general recommendation not enforced) – partially relaxed measure;
	MasksVoluntaryClosedSpacesPartial: Protective mask use in closed public spaces/transport on voluntary basis – partially relaxed measure;

(continued)

Table 13. (*continued*)

Variable	Definition
	MasksMandatoryAllSpacesPartial: Protective mask use in all public spaces on mandatory basis – partially relaxed measure;
	MasksMandatoryClosedSpacesPartial: Protective mask use in closed public spaces/transport on mandatory basis – partially relaxed measure;
	TeleworkingPartial: Teleworking recommendation or workplace closures – partially relaxed measure;
	AdaptationOfWorkplacePartial: Adaptation of workplaces – partially relaxed measure;
	WorkplaceClosuresPartial: Closures of workplaces – partially relaxed measure.
date_start	Start date of the intervention/response measure "yyyy-mm-dd"
date_end	End date of the intervention/response measure (NA indicates a measure that is still active on the date of the file/end date in the future) "yyyy-mm-dd"

References

1. World Health Organization. https://www.who.int/emergencies/diseases/novel-coronavirus-2019/. Accessed 14 June 2023
2. PERISCOPE Project Homepage. https://periscopeproject.eu/. Accessed 29 June 2023
3. Singh, J., Singh, J.: COVID-19 and its impact on society. Electron. Res. J. Soc. Sci. Humanit. **2** (2020)
4. Delardas, O., et al.: Socio-Economic impacts and challenges of the coronavirus pandemic (COVID-19): an updated review. Sustainability **14**(15), 9699 (2022)
5. Berardi, C., et al.: The COVID-19 pandemic in Italy: policy and technology impact on health and non-health outcomes. Health Policy Technol. **9**(4), 454–487 (2020)
6. European Centre for Disease Prevention and Control. https://www.ecdc.europa.eu/en/covid-19/data. Accessed 29 June 2023
7. CoronaNet Research Project. https://www.coronanet-project.org/. Accessed 29 June 2023
8. OECD.Stat – Key Short-Term Economic Indicators. https://stats.oecd.org/Index.aspx?DataSetCode=KEI. Accessed 29 June 2023
9. GADM Homepage. https://gadm.org/. Accessed 29 June 2023
10. ISO.org, https://www.iso.org/iso-3166-country-codes.html, last accessed 2023/06/28
11. ISO OBP. https://www.iso.org/obp/ui/#home. Accessed 29 June 2023
12. Eurostat NUTS classification. https://ec.europa.eu/eurostat/web/nuts/background. Accessed 28 June 2023
13. Eurostat NUTS GISCO. https://ec.europa.eu/eurostat/web/gisco/geodata/reference-data/administrative-units-statistical-units/nuts. Accessed 29 June 2023
14. Doiron, D., et al.: Facilitating collaborative research: implementing a platform supporting data harmonization and pooling. Norsk Epidemiologi **21**(2) (2012)
15. Doiron, D., Burton, P., Marcon, Y., et al.: Data harmonization and federated analysis of population-based studies: the BioSHaRE project. Emerg. Themes Epidemiol. **10**, 12 (2013). https://doi.org/10.1186/1742-7622-10-12
16. Rushton, G.: Public health, GIS, and spatial analytic tools. Annu. Rev. Public Health **24**(1), 43–56 (2003)

Towards a Spatial Decision Support System for Hydrogeological Risk Mitigation in Railway Sector

Giada Varra[1]([✉]) [iD], Luca Cozzolino[1] [iD], Renata Della Morte[1] [iD], Mario Tartaglia[2] [iD], Andrea Fiduccia[3] [iD], Ivan Agostino[4] [iD], and Alessandra Zammuto[4] [iD]

[1] University of Naples Parthenope, 80133 Naples, Italy
{giada.varra,luca.cozzolino,renata.dellamorte}@uniparthenope.it
[2] Ferrovie dello Stato Italiane Spa, Staz. Santa Maria Novella Binario 2, 50123 Florence, Italy
m.tartaglia@fsitaliane.it
[3] Ferrovie dello Stato Italiane Spa, Piazza della Croce Rossa 1, 00161 Rome, Italy
a.fiduccia@fsitaliane.it
[4] Rete Ferroviaria Italiana Spa, Piazza della Croce Rossa 1, 00161 Rome, Italy
{i.agostino,a.zammuto}@rfi.it

Abstract. Railway systems are exposed to the impacts of climate change weather-related events, such as landslides and flooding due to intense rainfall. To maintain resilient infrastructure and operations, railway owners face the challenging task of identifying and prioritizing adaptation interventions, which is exacerbated by railways spatial extent and by uncertainties in future weather events. Given the distributed structure of railways and their interaction with the surrounding territory, the optimal approach is to integrate a Geographic Information System (GIS) with predictive models to analyze multiple scenarios, resulting in a Spatial Decision Support System (SDSS). A SDSS provides a systematic approach for railways adaptation, assessing their exposure and vulnerability to hydrogeological hazards, and facilitating the identification of effective structural and non-structural interventions for resilience enhancement. By combining management experiences in railway infrastructure with scientific advancements, this research proposes a conceptual framework for developing a SDSS that can support strategic decision making. First, an inventory of adaptation measures for railways to hydrogeological hazards was produced in the context of the Italian National Adaptation Plan (PNACC, [1]). The subsequent step investigated the cause-and-effect relations between hydrogeological hazards and damage to railway in a specific case study. The GIS component of the SDSS allows to integrate heterogeneous data sources from different information systems related to the examined railway track, with the aim of identifying a set of geographic data sources applicable at the national scale. The SDSS prototype is implemented, in parallel with the framework development, in the Strategic Information Management System (SIMS) of the Italian FS Group.

Keywords: Railways · Geographic Information System · hydrogeological hazards

E. Borgogno Mondino and P. Zamperlin (Eds.): ASITA 2023, CCIS 2088, pp. 243–256, 2024.
https://doi.org/10.1007/978-3-031-59925-5_17

1 Introduction

Functional and efficient infrastructures such as railway networks play a fundamental role for the economic and social development of a country, while also contributing to anthropogenic climate change mitigation due to their relatively small environmental impact [2]. Linear transport infrastructures often cross very heterogeneous environments, from a geological and geomorphological point of view, which may involve different kinds of hazardous events, spanning from rock falls and soil slips to floods and bank erosion [3]. Railway systems are highly exposed to the impacts of hydro-meteorological hazards, such as landslides and flooding due to intense rainfall, which may severely affect its infrastructure and operations, causing accidents, damages, delays, and interruptions, with significant direct and indirect socio-economic losses [4]. Nearly 7700 km of the Italian railway network extend through hilly and mountainous areas, potentially susceptible to landslides, and the remaining nearly 9000 km cross urban floodplains that may potentially be affected by hydraulic phenomena [5]. As the magnitude and frequency of extreme weather events is expected to increase due to global climate change, damage, and disruption to transport infrastructure, together with the related costs, are also expected to increase [6]. These factors contribute to the creation of a rather unsettling scenario for railway operators, which are not even directly responsible for the conditions arising in the catchment areas outside their own jurisdiction.

The process of adapting linear transport infrastructures entails the assessment of potential risks and consequences, alongside the identification of opportunities for sustainable development [7]. By integrating the identified vulnerable and susceptible areas into the decision-making process, it becomes feasible to avert or minimize potential damage and disruption to infrastructure and operations. Consequently, there is the necessity to develop a methodological framework for evaluating hydrogeological hazards in railway networks, enabling the identification of high-risk elements, and facilitating efficient planning for maintenance and adaptation measures. To maintain resilient infrastructure and operations, railway owners face the challenging task of identifying and prioritizing adaptation interventions, which is exacerbated by the spatial extent of railway networks and by the uncertainties in future weather events [2]. Given the distributed structure of railway systems and their interaction with the surrounding territory, the optimal approach is to integrate a Geographic Information System (GIS) with predictive models to analyze multiple scenarios, resulting in a Spatial Decision Support System (SDSS).

SDSSs evolve from Decision Support Systems (DSSs), which have been extensively used in diverse domains to effectively manage environmental issues and address complex decision problems. Their growing significance in recent years in the domain of natural hazard risk reduction arises from the substantial impact of these hazards on communities and economies, with anticipated future increases in disaster-induced losses [8]. SDSSs are defined as integrated computer systems that support decision makers in addressing complex spatially related problems in an interactive and iterative way, providing a framework for integrating (i) spatial and non-spatial data management, (ii) analytical and spatial modelling capabilities, (iii) decision support utilities such as scenario analysis, and (iv) effective data and information display functionalities [9]. In practice, a SDSS can be seen as a combination of mathematical models, GIS functionalities (that are commonly used to create, manage, visualize, and analyze spatial data allowing for a more spatial approach to adaptation planning) and other decision support tools that facilitate decision-making for risk-reduction and adaptation [9–12].

The present work originates from a collaboration with Ferrovie dello Stato Italiane (FSI), the parent company of the Italian national railway infrastructure manager Rete Ferroviaria Italiana (RFI), as part of the ARFEC (Advanced Resilience Framework for Enhancing Climate adaptation in railway systems) project, which is co-funded by the European Union under the Next Generation EU program. The scope of the present paper is to outline a conceptual framework for building a SDSS, hereinafter ARFEC-SDSS, which can aid railways in identifying effective adaptation measures to hydrogeological hazards in a context of high uncertainty resulting, among the various things, from climate change. The ARFEC-SDSS is conceived as a module of the Strategic Information Management System (SIMS) of FSI. The SIMS is a DSS aimed at supporting (i) the strategic decision-making processes of the Holding Company FSI and the other FS Group companies and (ii) the collection, storing and processing of official data of the FS Group [13].

The first steps of the methodology are tested using a case study concerning a main railway track in a Southern Italy area that recently suffered performance failures and intense damages due to an extreme hydro-meteorological event, which produced multiple effects on the territory such as flooding, run-off soil erosion, and landslides. Interestingly, railway damages resulted from a combination of an overflowing main river and overland flow phenomena triggered by heavy rainfall, which appear to be occurring more frequently due to anthropogenic climate change in combination with uncontrolled urban growth and land development. Although the SDSS methodology is developed to analyze a specific case study, it can be adapted to different cases.

The paper is organized as follows: firstly, Sect. 2 focuses on conceptualizing the methodological framework for the construction of the ARFEC-SDSS and its implementation inside the SIMS system architecture. Then, Sect. 3 provides a detailed description of the selected case study for testing the methodology application, along with the data, methods and models exploited for the analysis. Finally, preliminary conclusions are drawn.

2 Conceptual Framework

In the following, it is provided a step-by-step account of the methodology for the construction of the ARFEC-SDSS and its implementation inside the SIMS system architecture of FSI. The proposed methodology develops through the following main steps:

1. An inventory of adaptation measures specifically tailored to address hydrogeological hazards (with a focus on floods and landslides) for railways is developed [14] extending the conceptual framework of the Italian National Adaptation Plan (PNACC, [1]). This stage includes a comprehensive review of existing literature, technical guidelines, and best practices in railway infrastructure resilience and adaptation. The inventory serves as a basis for identifying potential interventions to be integrated into the ARFEC-SDSS.

2. A case study approach is adopted to investigate the cause-and-effect relationships between hydrogeological hazards and railway damage. Historical data on incidents, such as landslides and flooding, are collected for a specific case study and analysed to understand the patterns and factors contributing to infrastructure vulnerability. This analysis provides valuable insights into the critical areas and vulnerabilities that need to be considered within the ARFEC-SDSS. A main railway track in Southern Italy, which recently suffered performance failures and intense damages due to an extreme hydro-meteorological event, is selected for the analysis.

3. The GIS component of the ARFEC-SDSS is developed to integrate heterogeneous data from various information systems and public agencies related to the railway track under examination. This stage includes the exploitation of the SIMS Geodatabase storing geological, hydro-meteorological and hydrological data, topographic information, land use and land cover data, and infrastructure details. The GIS module allows storage and visualization of maps and geospatial data, providing functions for spatial analysis, and is supported on the full GIS stack of SIMS (ESRI ArcGIS and HEXAGON GeoMedia Desktop GIS and HEXAGON M.App Enterprise for the WebGIS component). The GIS component is essential for conducting a comprehensive assessment of railway exposure and vulnerability to hydrogeological hazards from a local scale to a national scale.

4. Predictive models are run to simulate the behaviour of hydrogeological hazards under different scenarios. These models, which consider rainfall patterns, soil properties, topographic information, geometric characteristics of the infrastructure and other relevant factors, provide insights into potential future hydrogeological risks and can assist in identifying areas where adaptation measures are most needed. Flooding phenomena related to intense rainfall can be simulated using two-dimensional (2D) flood propagation models. In the context of the present procedure, the 2D HEC-RAS (Hydrologic Engineering Center's River Analysis System) hydrologic-hydrodynamic model, hereinafter called 2DHR, is selected for flooding simulations. The 2DHR software can be freely downloaded from a dedicated page of the Hydrologic Engineering Center's website (https://www.hec.usace.army.mil/software/hec-ras/). The selection of the type of modelling to be carried out is essential for the success of the analysis and must be carefully conducted starting from the specific case study. Here, we adopt a *non-classical* approach in which rain data are imposed directly as input in the 2D hydrodynamic model for simulating the runoff generation and the subsequent inundation processes (fluvial flooding and overland flows), as will be better illustrated in Sect. 3.1.

5. Qualitative hydrogeological susceptibility and vulnerability infrastructures indicators are developed and applied to the specific case study for identifying the critical segments of the railway track that are prone to floods and landslides and in which adaptation measures are needed to reduce the risk. These indicators, which are built by intersecting the relevant territorial information and hazard maps with the topographical and geometrical characteristics of the railway infrastructure, allows the identification and prioritization of interventions.

6. The ARFEC-SDSS is designed and implemented, incorporating the inventory of adaptation measures, cause-and-effect relations, GIS data integration, predictive model outputs and qualitative indicators. The ARFEC-SDSS provides a user-friendly interface for decision-makers to explore different scenarios, identify the most effective adaptation interventions, and make informed decisions regarding resilience enhancement in railway systems.

At this stage, the structure of the ARFEC-SDSS subsystem consists of the following main components: (i) database management system, (ii) simulating and predicting model (2DHR), (iii) GIS application for managing and analyzing hydro-meteorological, inundation data and other relevant information. Figure 1 illustrates the implementation of the ARFEC-SDSS subsystem inside the SIMS system architecture [13].

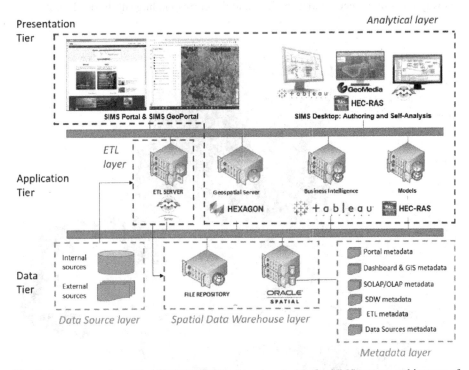

Fig. 1. Implementation of the ARFEC-SDSS sub-system inside the SIMS system architecture of FSI [13].

3   Case Study and Methods

A case study is used to test the applicability of the methodology at the local scale and the viability of ARFEC-SDSS implementation. Clearly, the application of the methodology to the specific case study is strictly dependent on data availability. The study area is in the Benevento province of Campania region (Southern Italy) and includes a portion of the

Calore Irpino River (Fig. 2). This area has been recently affected by a destructive flood induced by an extreme rainfall event occurred on 14th–15th October 2015. The intense meteorological event caused two victims, extensive damages to infrastructures, buildings, agricultural areas, and produced multiple effects on the territory such as flooding, run-off soil erosion, and landslides [15–17]. It should be noted that the area of Benevento province has experienced many similar events in the past [16]. The case study railway track, which belongs to the Napoli-Bari route, develops parallel to the Calore Irpino River (Fig. 2) and passes through 3 stations (Ponte Casalduni, San Lorenzo Maggiore and Solopaca). The 14th–15th October 2015 rainfall event and the subsequent flooding caused severe economic damages and impacts to the railway line, also leading to a six-day service disruption. The hydrologic-hydrodynamic modelling application for the storm-event hazard assessment involved the Calore River reach that flows parallel to the railway line, immediately adjacent to it, and the corresponding sub-basin (Fig. 2).

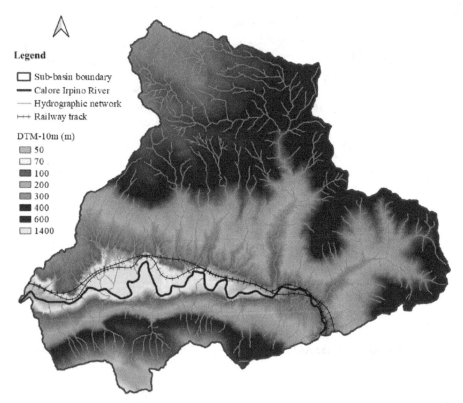

Fig. 2. Study area in the Benevento province of Campania region (southern Italy). Representation of the terrain elevation, hydrographic network, and selected railway track. Red line indicates the sub-basin boundary. (Color figure online)

3.1 Data Collection and Processing

Several thematic data, organized in raster and vector feature classes, were exploited for the analysis of flood hazard along the selected railway segment using the GIS platform. The available topographic, hydro-meteorological, land use, and geological data collected from several public agencies were made homogeneous to create a proper geodatabase. Some of the most relevant data and information layers exploited in the present study are described in the following. The description should be understood as indicative and not exhaustive.

Railway Network. The national coverage of railway network was retrieved from the National Summary Database (Database di Sintesi Nazionale, DBSN), which is a vector database containing the most significant territorial information for conducting thematic analyses at the national level. Data can be freely downloaded (upon registration) from a dedicated page of the Italian Military Geographic Institute (IGM) website (https://www.igmi.org/it/dbsn-database-di-sintesi-nazionale) in the geodatabase format (.gdb). IGM is an Italian governmental mapping agency with a central role in the production and management of official cartographic products and started the DBSN release in September 2022.

Terrain Data. Two different topographic sources were employed in the present work. (i) The first one is a Digital Terrain Model (DTM) of the whole Italian territory [18] produced by the National Institute of Geophysics and Vulcanology (INGV), which is freely available for download from a dedicated page of the INGV website (https://tin italy.pi.ingv.it/) as a 10 m-cell size grid (in GeoTIFF format) in the UTM WGS 84 zone 32 projection system. This dataset, called hereinafter DTM-10m, was analyzed by means of GIS tools to determine the catchment boundary of the study area (Fig. 2). (ii) The second topographic source is a DTM with ground resolution of 1 m derived from airborne LIDAR (Light Detection and Ranging) scanning, provided by the Italian Ministry of Environment (Ministero dell'Ambiente e della Sicurezza Energetica, MASE) upon request. This dataset, hereinafter DTM-1m, exclusively encompasses the river network and coastal areas of Campania Region, and therefore, it does not provide a complete coverage of the considered sub-basin (see Fig. 3). While this is not a constraint when conducting river flood simulations, as they should account for the river floodplain and the immediate adjacent zones, it may represent a significant limitation when conducting pluvial flood simulations, which should consider the entire extension of the basin (or sub-basin) for accurate results.

Hydrographic Network. The regional hydrographic network employed in the present study (Fig. 2) is freely available for download from a dedicated page of the Campania region website (https://sit2.regione.campania.it/node) in vector polygon format.

Hydrologic-Hydrodynamic Modelling for Flood Mapping. The most common type of flooding is known as fluvial (or riverine) flooding, which occurs when intense rainfall causes water levels in rivers to rise and overflow onto the adjacent low-lying areas. The standard method for simulating fluvial flood events is the well-established approach that involves two sequential steps based on separate models: (i) firstly, a discharge hydrograph related to individual runoff events is computed by means of established hydrological rainfall-runoff models, (ii) then, the computed hydrograph is imposed as upstream boundary condition in a 2D hydrodynamic model [19, 20], as schematically illustrated in Fig. 4 (left).

Fig. 3. Area covered by the DTM-1m dataset. Red line indicates the case study sub-basin boundary. (Color figure online)

However, there is an increasing recognition of various other flood types that appear to be occurring more frequently due to anthropogenic climate change in combination with uncontrolled urban growth and land development [21]. These hazardous *non-fluvial* floods stem from heavy rainfall and are often referred to as flash or pluvial floods [22]. Flash floods usually affect small watersheds, and are characterized by high flow velocities that may lead to debris flows, significant erosion and sediment transport [23, 24]. On the other hand, pluvial flooding can be broadly defined as flood arising from rainfall-generated overland flow and ponding before the runoff finds its way into any watercourse, drainage system, sewer, or when it cannot enter these systems due to full capacity [25]. For modeling this kind of rainfall *non-fluvial* floods, the present study employs the direct rainfall modelling (DRM) approach, also known as rain-on-grid (RoG) modelling. The DRM is an increasingly popular approach in the context of flood risk management and consists in modelling the hydrological and hydrodynamic flood processes entirely within a single 2D hydrodynamic model, rather than using two separate models [19, 20] (Fig. 4, right). The integrated hydrologic-hydrodynamic 2DHR model is used here for simulating a historic storm event in the case study area and identifying the corresponding flood extension in the computational domain. To reach a reasonable compromise between computational time and results accuracy, several computational grids were tested for the storm-event simulation with varying elements size.

The simulated rainfall event lasted from 08:00 pm, 14th October 2015, to 07:00 am, 15th October 2015. In a first preliminary stage, precipitation data from 11 rain gauges operated by the regional Civil Protection Department were interpolated by means of the Thiessen Polygon approach inside the 2DHR model. The transformation of rainfall to flood runoff was made by using the well-known original Soil Conservation Service (SCS, [26]) curve number (CN) method (one of the three available infiltration methods in

HR2D), which assigns to different areas in the computational domain a CN dimensionless value theoretically ranging from 0 to 100 based on the soil type, land use, vegetation cover and antecedent moisture conditions.

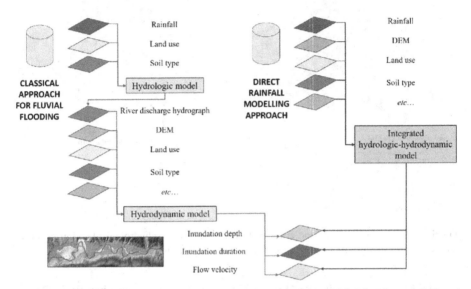

Fig. 4. Schematic framework of the standard method for simulating fluvial flood events (left) and of the direct rainfall modelling (DRM) approach (right).

Land Cover and Land Use. The study area was classified into different land cover and use types, including green land and crops, urbanized surfaces, and water bodies, to set up the infiltration rate and the Manning's roughness parameters in the flood numerical 2DHR model. In a preliminary stage, land cover and use data from the regional map of rural soil use, edited in 2009 by the National Institute of Agricultural Economics (INEA), were used. The regional map, known as CUAS (Carta di Utilizzazione Agricola dei Suoli) map, is freely available for download from a dedicated page of the Campania region website (https://sit2.regione.campania.it/node) in vector polygon format. 23 different land cover and use classes were identified in the study area, as shown in Fig. 5a.

Soil Type. Different soil textures and types have various infiltration capacities and a specific impact on surface runoff, influencing the susceptibility of an area to flood hazard. The SCS method subdivides the various soil types into four hydrologic groups (A, B, C, and D), characterized by different infiltration rate and runoff potential (group A has the lowest runoff potential while group D has the highest). The hydrological soil groups in the study area (Fig. 5b) were determined, according to the soil classification groups in the SCS method [26], by analyzing the regional map of soil features, 1:250000 scale, which is freely available for download from a dedicated page of the Campania region website (https://sit2.regione.campania.it/node) in vector polygon format.

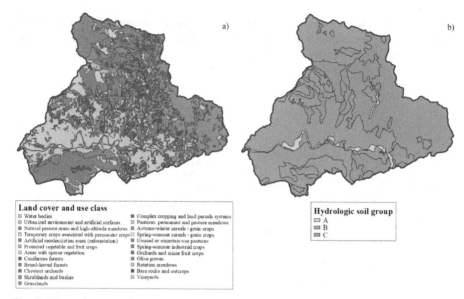

Fig. 5. Thematic maps of (a) land cover and use classes, and (b) hydrological soil groups used for the storm-event hazard assessment with the 2D HEC-RAS model.

Official Flood and Landslides Hazard Maps. In Italy, the seven River Basin District Authorities produce flood inundation hazard maps that, according to the European Floods Directive 2007/60/EC (transposed into the Italian Legislative Decree no. 49/2010 [27]), provide a delimitation of the areas that could be potentially affected by riverine flood events for three different hazardous scenarios: (i) H1 for rare events (with return period, also called recurrence interval, ranging in the interval T = 200–500 years), (ii) H2 for frequent events (with T = 100–200 years) and (iii) H3 for very frequent events with (T = 20–50 years).

The River Basin District Authorities also produce hazard maps related to landslides and hydraulic instabilities, which are contained in the River Basin Plans for the hydrogeological territory arrangement (known as Piano di Assetto Idrogeologico, PAI), according to the Legislative Decrees 180/1998 [28] and 152/2006 [29]. These multiple datasets were merged in two national mosaics of hazard zones (one for flood hazard and the other for landslide hazard) by the Italian Institute for Environmental Protection and Research (ISPRA). The two datasets have been lastly updated in 2021 [30] and are freely available for download from a dedicated page of the ISPRA website (https://idrogeo.isprambie nte.it/app/page/open-data) in vector polygon format and in the WGS 84 UTM zone 32 projection system. ISPRA has generated the landslide hazard mapping using a harmonized legend with five classes for the entire national territory: very high hazard (H4), high hazard (H3), moderate hazard (H2), low hazard (H1), and areas of attention (AA). Figure 6 shows the official flood and landslide hazard maps covering the study area extension, visualized inside the SIMS system.

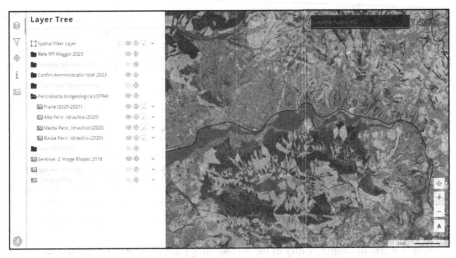

Fig. 6. Official flood and landslides hazard maps visualized in the SIMS environment. Blue colors refer to flood hazard maps, while red, green and yellow colors refer to landslide hazard maps. (Color figure online)

Susceptibility Evaluation. In Fig. 7, the inundated areas and the maximum flood depth related to the flooding event simulated with 2DHR including the effect of rainfall is represented for the case study under examination. Other types of spatial representations involve the flow velocity and the flow momentum.

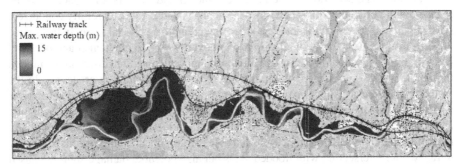

Fig. 7. Inundated areas simulated in the 2D HEC-RAS model with the direct rainfall modelling (DRM) approach.

Notably, this type of representation allows to individuate the portions of infrastructure that intersect with the flooded areas, leading to potential damage. The inclusion of the rainfall effects allows to individuate the tributary creeks along which rapid flows may occur, with possible damage that is not currently incorporated into the maps produced by the River Basin District Authorities (see Fig. 6), which generally account for the overflowing of main rivers. In addition, these representations allow to parameterize the damage as a function of the flooding depth and flow velocity.

In the example considered, possible sources of damage are i) the contact between the flooding and the railway embankment, with earth erosion, ii) the direct flooding of the track level by the flow level rising, iii) the damage of retaining walls due to infiltration, iv) the flooding of the track level by overland flow, v) the pressurization of culverts and small bridges.

4 Preliminary Conclusions

The present paper proposes a methodology aimed at developing a Spatial Decision Support System (SDSS) that integrates GIS functionalities and predictive models to facilitate strategic decision-making for railway adaptation to hydrogeological hazards. The conceptual framework combines railway infrastructure management experiences with scientific knowledge to enhance railways resilience in the face of climate change and weather-related challenges.

In this work, the applicability of the methodology at the local scale and the feasibility of implementing the SDSS were tested through a case study involving a main railway track in Southern Italy that recently experienced damages and disruption due to an extreme storm event. By implementing a local-scale case study, we were able to (i) identify initial issues and challenges related to the application, (ii) assess the limitations of the employed approach, and (iii) explore potential opportunities. Some considerations on these aspects are reported in the following.

The data collection and homogenization phase proved to be laborious and complex. Moreover, the inhomogeneity of available topographic datasets introduced variability in the accuracy of 2D flooding simulations, leading to less reliable results of overland flow computations. The selection of the prediction model and the type of modelling to be carried out are crucial for the success of the analysis and must be carefully conducted, starting with the specific case study and then extending to a national scale. In fact, when flooding events result from combinations of an overflowing river channel and overland flows, rainfall data should be imposed directly as input in the 2D hydrodynamic model, for simulating the runoff generation and the subsequent inundation processes. In the specific case study, a distinction was made between flood events primarily related to river overflow and flood events directly linked to heavy rainfall, which generates hydraulic instability effects on slopes. Using the 2D HEC-RAS model with the *non-classical* direct rainfall modelling (DRM) approach allowed us to identify not only the portions of railway infrastructure intersecting with flooded areas but also potential damage sources caused by direct rainfall, which are currently not incorporated into the official hazard maps produced by the River Basin District Authorities (generally by means of the *classical* method for fluvial flooding that uses hydrographs as input boundary conditions).

The information presented here provides a fundamental understanding of the necessary data required to conduct such a comprehensive analysis, with the goal of obtaining accurate results describing the effects of extreme events on railway infrastructures. As for the planned future work, the roadmap for the SDSS development includes the following steps concerning the advancement of the methodology: (i) further two-dimensional hydrodynamic simulations will be conducted to identify best practices in numerical hydraulic modelling; (ii) a preliminary analysis of indirect effects of extreme events on the transportation system in a climate change context will be introduced. Another evolutionary line of work will focus on automating the calculation processes (hydraulic simulations and risk analysis) managed through the web interfaces of the SIMS system. This will allow authorized users to select the railway section for analysis, choose appropriate models, analysis types, and obtain corresponding results in the WebGIS application.

Acknowledgements. The work of Giada Varra is co-funded by the European Union program FSE-REACT-EU, PON Ricerca e Innovazione 2014–2020 DM1062/2021.

References

1. Ministero dell'Ambiente e della Tutela del Territorio e del Mare (MATTM): Piano Nazionale di Adattamento ai Cambiamenti Climatici (PNACC) (2018)
2. Armstrong, J., Preston, J., Hood, I.: Adapting railways to provide resilience and sustainability. Proc. Inst. Civil Eng. Eng. Sustain. **170**(4), 225–234 (2017)
3. Gattinoni, P., Scesi, L., Arieni, L., Canavesi, M., Zaffaroni, F.: A new rating system for hydrogeological risk management along railway infrastructures in Prealpine zone (northern Italy). Innov. Infrastruct. Solut. **6**(120) (2021)
4. Kellermann, P., Schöbel, A., Kundela, G., Thieken, A.H.: Estimating flood damage to railway infrastructure – the case study of the March River flood in 2006 at the Austrian Northern Railway. Nat. Hazards Earth Syst. Sci. **15**, 2485–2496 (2015)
5. Firmi, P., Iacobini, F., Rinaldi, A., Vecchi, A., Agostino, I., Mauro, A.: Methods for managing hydrogeological and seismic hazards on the Italian railway infrastructure. Struct. Infrastruct. Eng. **17**(12), 1651–1666 (2021)
6. IPCC. Summary for policymakers. In: Climate Change 2021: Masson-Delmotte, V., et al. (eds.) The Physical Science Basis. Contribution of Working Group I to the Sixth Assessment Report of the Intergovernmental Panel on Climate Change. Cambridge University Press, Cambridge (2021)
7. Oswald Beiler, M.R., Treat, C.: Integrating GIS and AHP to prioritize transportation infrastructure using sustainability metrics. J. Infrastruct. Syst. **21**(3) (2015)
8. Newman, J.P., et al.: Review of literature on decision support systems for natural hazard risk reduction: current status and future research directions. Environ Model Softw. **96**, 378–409 (2017)
9. Sugumaran, R., DeGroote, J.: Spatial Decision Support Systems - Principles and Practices, 1st edn. CRC Press, Taylor & Francis Group, Boca Raton (2010)
10. Mileu, N., Queirós, M.: Integrating risk assessment into spatial planning: RiskOTe decision support system. ISPRS Int. J. Geo-Inf. **7**(5), 184 (2018)
11. Palutikof, J.P., Street, R.B., Gardiner, E.P.: Decision support platforms for climate change adaptation: an overview and introduction. Clim. Change **153**, 459–476 (2019)
12. Sebillo, M., Vitiello, G., Grimaldi, M., Buono, D.D.: SAFE (safety for families in emergency). In: Misra, S., et al. (eds.) ICCSA 2019. LNCS, vol. 11620, pp. 424–437. Springer, Cham (2019). https://doi.org/10.1007/978-3-030-24296-1_34
13. Tartaglia, M., Fiduccia, A.: Geo-business intelligence and spatial data warehousing: a railway company case study. In: Borgogno-Mondino, E., Zamperlin, P. (eds.) ASITA 2022. CCIS, vol. 1651, pp. 141–155. Springer, Cham (2022). https://doi.org/10.1007/978-3-031-17439-1_10
14. Varra, G., et al.: Climate change on the Italian railway: adaptation options to weather extremes. In: Proceedings of the 3rd IAHR Young Professionals Congress (2022)

15. Santo, A., Santangelo, N., Forte, G., De Falco, M.: Post flash flood survey: the 14th and 15th October 2015 event in the Paupisi-Solopaca area (Southern Italy). J. Maps **13**(2), 19–25 (2017)
16. Guerriero, G., Focareta, M., Fusco, G., Rabuano, R., Guadagno, F.M., Revellino, P.: Flood hazard of major river segments, Benevento Province Southern Italy. J. Maps **14**(2), 597–606 (2018)
17. Revellino, P., et al.: Multiple effects of intense meteorological events in the Benevento Province Southern Italy. Water **11**, 1560 (2019)
18. Tarquini, S., et al.: TINITALY/01: a new triangular irregular network of Italy. Ann. Geophys. **50**, 407–425 (2007)
19. Costabile, P., Costanzo, C., Ferraro, D., Barca, P.: Is HEC-RAS 2D accurate enough for storm-event hazard assessment? Lessons learnt from a benchmarking study based on rain-on-grid modelling. J. Hydrol. **603** (2021)
20. David, A., Schmalz, B.: Flood hazard analysis in small catchments: comparison of hydrological and hydrodynamic approaches by the use of direct rainfall. J. Flood Risk Manag. **13**, e12639 (2020)
21. Szewrański, S., Chruściński, J., Kazak, J., Świąder, M., Tokarczyk-Dorociak, K., Żmuda, R.: Pluvial flood risk assessment tool (PFRA) for rainwater management and adaptation to climate change in newly urbanised areas. Water **10**(4), 386 (2018)
22. Schanze, J.: Pluvial flood risk management: an evolving and specific field. J. Flood Risk Manag. **11**, 227–229 (2018)
23. Marchi, L., Borga, M., Preciso, E., Gaume, E.: Characterisation of selected extreme flash floods in Europe and implications for flood risk management. J. Hydrol. **394**(1–2), 118–133 (2010)
24. Borga, M., Stoffel, M., Marchi, L., Marra, F., Jakob, M.: Hydrogeomorphic response to extreme rainfall in headwater systems: flash floods and debris flows. J. Hydrol. **518** Part B, 194–205 (2014)
25. Falconer, R.H., Cobby, D., Smyth, P., Astle, G., Dent, J., Golding, B.: Pluvial flooding: new approaches in flood warning, mapping and risk management. J. Flood Risk Manag. **2**(3), 198–208 (2009)
26. Soil Conservation Service (SCS). National Engineering Handbook; Section 4, Hydrology (NEH-4). U.S. Department of Agriculture: Washington, DC, USA (1985)
27. Legislative Decree no. 49/2010. Attuazione della direttiva 2007/60/CE relativa alla valutazione e alla gestione dei rischi di alluvioni. [Implementation of the Floods Directive 2007/60/EC concerning the assessment and management of flood risk]. Official Gazette of the Italian Republic n.77/2010 (2010)
28. Legislative Decree no. 180/1998. Misure urgenti per la prevenzione del rischio idrogeologico ed a favore delle zone colpite da disastri franosi nella regione Campania [Urgent measures for the prevention of hydrogeological risk and for areas affected by landslide disasters in the Campania region]. Official Gazette of the Italian Republic n.134/1998 (1998)
29. Legislative Decree no. 152/2006. Norme in materia ambientale [Environmental law]. Official Gazette of the Italian Republic n.88/2006 (2006)
30. Trigila, A., Iadanza, C., Lastoria, B., Bussettini, M., Barbano, A.: Dissesto idrogeologico in Italia: pericolosità e indicatori di rischio - Edizione 2021. ISPRA, Rapporti 356/2021 (2021)

Comparison Between the Vegetation Indices Obtained from Sentinel-2 and Planet: A Case Study over a Rice Farm in Northern Italy

Christian Massimiliano Baldin$^{(\boxtimes)}$ ⓘ and Vittorio Marco Casella ⓘ

DICAR, Università degli Studi di Pavia, Pavia, Italy
{christianmassimiliano.baldin,vittorio.casella}@unipv.it

Abstract. Precision Agriculture has shown how to improve the production chain by reducing fertilizers and consequently reducing pollution and costs, sometimes with improvements in yield. This research is carried out in Italy, in collaboration with the agronomic consultancy agency "Dr.Agr. P.A. Barbieri and Dr.Agr.G.L. Rognoni" (Casteggio - Pavia, Lombardia) over "Riserva San Massimo", a farm near "Gropello Cairoli", made up of rice crops and a forest (about 15 km^2 in total). Agronomists have been using Sentinel-2 images in rice crops for many years and have found the need to use images with higher spatial and temporal resolution: this is the research question. Sentinel-2 has a temporal resolution of 5 days and a spatial resolution of 10 m (at best): some results have been found using Planet images. Sentinel-2, free, is considered a reference in this field; Planet, for a fee, has a higher spatial resolution (3 m) and a longer revisit time (almost daily). The research was conducted through 3 main phases: availability and usability of the images, self-consistency of the Planet images acquired quite simultaneously and coherence between the Sentinel-2 images and those of Planet, captured on the same day. The NDVI and NDRE indices have been studied for their importance in fertilization. It has been shown that Sentinel-2 is not sufficient for all required applications and that Planet could represent an opportunity under some conditions. The planet-derived indices have good self-consistency and the comparison between the Sentinel-2 and Planet indices showed seasonal miscalibration: lower for NDVI, higher for NDRE.

Keywords: Precision Agriculture · Remote Sensing · Rice

1 Introduction

1.1 Rice Cultivation in Northern Italy

Rice cultivation in Italy is mostly located in the North: the need of water is substantial for water-seeded crops which are the majority. Lack of precipitation is the most important problem to deal with and especially during 2022 drought, water lacked in many territories [1].

Fertilizers impact the production chain due to their cost and pollution (if abused): the prices of nitrogen-based ones have undergone exponential increase never seen in

E. Borgogno Mondino and P. Zamperlin (Eds.): ASITA 2023, CCIS 2088, pp. 257–284, 2024.
https://doi.org/10.1007/978-3-031-59925-5_18

the past. The main culprit is the anomalous increase in the cost of energy: the political-military crisis has exacerbated the already difficult situation. Russia, a strong producer of urea, is currently out of the European trade and North Africa meets the needs of the Northern Italy [1].

Irrigation by submersion involves expensive land management works, in perfectly leveled environments delimited by embankments: the high winter rainfall and clayey soils do not allow the inclusion of rice cultivation in adequate crop rotations, due to the impossibility of implementing the autumn-spring cycle crops [1].

Numerous solutions have been studied: identification of the best rice genotypes, experimental varietal comparison tests, adaptability analysis of available rice varieties, organization of agronomic rotation in the absence of the submergence irrigation technique and, finally, precision agriculture [1].

1.2 Precision Agriculture as an Opportunity

Quantifying fertilizer needs is an opportunity to consider instead of providing crops with the same amount of product. VRA (Variable Rate Application) gives the possibility of dosing chemical products through prescription maps. These types of maps could be realized virtually tiling crops to decide how much fertilizer to put inside each of them. Prescription maps can be created through vigor maps obtainable thanks to Remote Sensing techniques and multispectral images [2] (acquired from tractors during field work or by aerial imaging via drones, airplanes, satellites).

Quantifying the use of fertilizer allows us to understand where its use is not necessary: this leads to a reduction in costs and pollution. From the Agronomist's experience it can be stated that sometimes an improvement in yield can be obtained compared to the use of a uniform quantity of product (especially where it is not possible, with field work, to understand that the crop is in a worse situation) [3].

1.3 Multispectral Images as Diagnostic Tool to Define Tailored Prescription Maps Through NDVI and NDRE Indices

Multispectral images are the key to the entire process because they contain data within specific wavelengths across the electromagnetic spectrum (generally detected through instruments sensitive to these). Every application needs specific bands: prescription maps for fertilization require mostly "Red", "NIR and "Red Edge" [3].

Each band is related to a specific range of wavelengths based on the sensor's capability and project: acquisitions need to be analyzed in relation to the instrument which took it. Even though instruments don't share the same ranges it is possible to compare them through statistical evaluations. Dealing with precision agriculture, and specifically with fertilization, means using some indexes that give the ability to numerically express some vegetation properties: NDVI (Normalized Difference Vegetation Index) and NDRE (Normalized Difference Red Edge Index) are considered the most important when people are dealing with precision agriculture [20].

$$\text{NDVI} = \frac{NIR - RED}{NIR + RED} \tag{1}$$

$$\text{NDRE} = \frac{NIR - Red\ Edge}{NIR + Red\ Edge} \tag{2}$$

These formulas are applied to each pixel: results have a range between -1 and 1 where values below zero mostly determine areas of no vegetation, construction, streets, and other infrastructures. Values ranging from 0 to 1 represent the status of vegetation: NDVI is usually ranging from 0.4 to 0.9 while NDRE is often ranging from 0.3 to 0.7. NIR, Red and Red Edge (in the formulas mentioned before) indicate the intensity obtained after processing the data recorded by the instrument for each pixel. NDVI (1) is the best known and the oldest index used in Agriculture because it gives the ability to create vigor maps by measuring quantities proportional to the amount of chlorophyll (with Red and NIR). NDRE (2) is best used (thanks to its sensitivity) in mid-to-late growing season when the plants are mature and ready to be harvested [3, 20, 27].

1.4 Rice Cultivation and Precision Agriculture: State-of-the-Art

Sentinel-2 is considered the gold standard for multispectral image acquisition used in precision agriculture: it is free and available on tractors that use these technologies.

By knowing the operational limits of the machine (each company has its own), it is possible to create prescription maps based on the owner's specific requests: crop tiling is an important example given that the tractor (GNSS guided) must follow a precise path to dose the right amount of fertilizer inside each tile. The dosage derives from the agronomic curve which relates the indices and the quantity of fertilizer.

The limits for correct tiling depend on the operating machines (and their ability to vary the speed). In the Agronomist's experience, the tiles generally measure 7 m × 24–28 m because 7 m is the minimum longitudinal distance in which the tractor can effectively vary the cadence: the transversal distances depend on the characteristics of the crop and the owner's preferences.

1.5 Sentinel-2 Issues: Planet Could Be the Solution?

This work was born from a specific request from the agronomist: they already use Sentinel-2 images as a support for precision agriculture in rice cultivation and would like to switch to images with greater spatial and temporal resolution.

The spatial resolution of Sentinel-2 is not sufficient if the crops are small and non-uniform due to the edge effect which leads to incorporating non-cultivated areas into the pixels of the crops: 10 m of spatial resolution is only effective when it comes to huge fields.

The Sentinel-2 revisit time is 5 days, not enough if the weather is cloudy, and agronomists need acquisitions to prepare prescription maps in a short time: this leads agronomists to plan drone acquisitions.

Planet could be the solution thanks to its almost daily visit time and its spatial resolution of 3 m. The need from which this work was born is to demonstrate that images of the Planet can be used in precision agriculture with the cultivation of rice. It is necessary to understand whether their numerous acquisitions are consistent over time and whether the indices obtained by Planet are comparable with those obtained by Sentinel-2. The scientific gap that this research seeks to overcome is to demonstrate whether the experience gained with the well-known Sentinel-2 can be used in some way with images of smaller and more irregular planets and crops.

1.6 Literature Review on Planet Images and Rice Cultivation

The literature review went through a long and in-depth process of studying articles and books to understand previous experiences and proven knowledge on various topics [3–35]: precision agriculture, indices used, rice cultivation and related use of images satellite. None of them directly correlates the use of images of the Planet to the cultivation of rice (and specifically to fertilization): the lack of information was balanced by the Agronomist's experience on the crops he usually deals with. This research, in fact, was carried out in collaboration with the agronomic consultancy company "Dr. Agr. P.A. Barbieri and Dr. Agr. G.L. Rognoni" (Casteggio - PV): its experience on optimizing rice yield comes from previous work, carried out in collaboration with the "Ente Nazionale Risi" [3].

The experiences of the Geomatics Laboratory in the GIS and Remote Sensing sectors was also fundamental.

2 Aims

The aim of this work was to demonstrate the usability of images of the Planet in precision agriculture for the cultivation of rice during the fertilization period: this objective can be achieved through 3 types of analysis.

2.1 Assessment of the Availability of Useful Images for Sentinel-2 and Planet

Two significant image-related issues were noted: availability and usability. The first problem is related to the path of the satellites that capture the images, the second problem is related to cloud cover because the earth can be obscured.

2.2 Planet Images Internal Congruence Analysis

Understanding the capabilities of the Planet sensor to acquire coherent multispectral images needed to be demonstrated: Planet revisit time (for any location, as declared by the manufacturer) is almost daily due to the many satellites available. The real question is that all these satellites could acquire multispectral images in the same way and specifically for the NDVI.

2.3 NDVI and NDRE Indices Congruence Between Sentinel-2 and Planet Constellation

Studying the comparison between the images of the planet and those of Sentinel-2 was essential since Sentinel-2 is a benchmark for precision agriculture, even if it has a lower spatial resolution and revisit time. Table 3 and Table 4 in the appendix show an overview of the two sensors, as declared by the manufacturer.

Spatial resolution is a key factor for working with these 2 sensors: Planet has all its bands with a resolution of 3 m, Sentinel-2 has non-homogeneous bands. The main objective of this article is the comparison between NDVI and NDRE: the first requires the NIR and Red bands (where the resolutions are 10 m for Sentinel-2 and 3 m for Planet), the second requires the NIR and Red Edge bands (where the resolutions are 10 and 20 m respectively for Sentinel-2 and 3 m for Planet).

3   Material and Methods

3.1   Sentinel-2 Images

The Copernicus Sentinel-2 [35–48] mission comprises a constellation of two polar-orbiting satellites placed in the same sun-synchronous orbit, phased at 180° to each other.

Sentinel-2 offers a 5-day revisit time (combining Sentinel-2A and Sentinel-2B for major areas of the world). The spatial resolution for the most important bands used in this research is 10 m for the Red and NIR (Near InfraRed) bands and 20 for the Red Edge band (it was necessary to homogenize them). The overview of the bands is shown in Table 3 in the Appendix.

Use of Sentinel-2 Images is under license: Copernicus Sentinel satellite – Open Access compliant, CC BY-SA 3.0 IGO.

3.2   Planet Images

Planet constellation [49–52] consists of more than 200 satellites: after August 2021 the satellites with the recent PSB.SD have replaced the old ones giving the possibility of an almost daily revisit time with 8 bands.

The Red, Red Edge and NIR bands with wavelengths of 665 nm, 705 nm, 865 nm respectively have a resolution of 3 m. Planet offers two types of geometries: those used in the article are orthorectified (radiometrically interoperable with Sentinel-2 images). The overview of the bands is shown in Table 4 in the Appendix.

Use of Planet Images is under license: ©Planet Labs PBC, CC BY-NC-SA 2.0.

3.3   Methodology Assessment of the Availability of Useful Images for Sentinel-2 and Planet

The verification of the availability and usability of the Planet and Sentinel-2 Images was carried out through statistics for 4 significant months for Precision Agriculture for 2022: from April to July. The analysis of the archive was carried out through the evaluation of 5 characteristics:

1. N° of expected images depends on the producer revisit time declaration
2. N° of available images depends on the archive availability for each producer
3. N° of unavailable images = N° of Expected images – N° of Available images

4. N° of good images depends on the Cloud Cover over the Test-Site ($<$10% is usable)

5. N° of Bad images = N° of Available images – N° of good images

Through this analysis it has been possible to evaluate the longer period without usable images for the two constellations.

3.4 Methodology for Planet Images Internal Congruence

Planet internal congruence has been studied to understand if indices obtained are reliable. Planet declares nearly daily revisit time but sometimes its satellites acquire the same area: a demonstration was made through multiple images acquired on the same day on the NDVI index. Each analysis was performed and automated on Matlab.

Methodology for NDVI analysis between each pair of Planet images (the results reported in Sect. 7 comprise the essential part of this work to evaluate the internal congruence):

1. Acquisition of available images from Planet archive.
2. Search for multiple images, acquired the same day by the same type of sensor without cloud cover.
3. Computation of NDVI index for any couple of images acquired the same day.
4. Computation of NDVI Maps and their histogram (Full Image Analysis).
5. Computation of Delta NDVI Map and its histogram (Full Image Analysis).
6. Scatter Plot of Planet NDVI #2 against NDVI #1 (Full Image Analysis) to understand if NDVI #2 is consistent with NDVI #1.
7. Scatter Plot of Delta NDVI (#2-#1) against #NDVI #1 (Full Image Analysis) to understand possible dependence of Delta NDVI respect to NDVI.
8. Outlier rejection of 1% of data for Full Image, considered as possible random errors.
9. Plot of histogram with outlier rejection and statistical analysis (with scatter plot including outliers) to understand how many there are and plot over the maps to understand where they are.
10. Region of interest is masked through crops' shapefile to evaluate data only inside the area of interest: a new scatter plot is done over only crops.
11. Scatter plot including of NDVI #2 against NDVI #1: Full Image data divided in Inliers of the Full Image, Outliers of the Full Image, Crops
12. Scatter plot of Delta NDVI (#2-#1) against #NDVI #1: Full Image data divided in Inliers of the Full Image, Outliers of the Full Image, Crops
13. Evaluation of RMSE on NDVI through the formula (3) for the Full Image, for the Inliers (99% of data), Crops (through the mask).
14. Evaluation of NDVI Mean on Crops.
15. Time Series plot to understand possible seasonality of crops: RMSE NDVI and NDVI Mean over time (extracting march-august time frame)

$$RMSE = \sqrt{\frac{1}{n} \sum_{i,j} (NDVI_2(i,j) - NDVI_1(i,j))^2} \qquad (3)$$

This methodology was also applied also to a single day with 5 Planet acquisitions to prove the internal consistency of all 5 images.

3.5 Methodology Used for Congruence Analysis Between Sentinel-2 and Planet Over NDVI and NDRE Indices

Planet and Sentinel-2 congruence across indices was assessed through acquisition on the same day: the archival search began for Sentinel-2 images without cloud cover and concluded by finding all contemporaneous Planet acquisitions without cloud cover itself. The demonstration was carried out using the NDVI and NDRE indices.

Sentinel-2 images required resampling via the NN method [53] to 3 m to be comparable to Planet Images without losing information.

Methodology for NDVI and NDRE analysis between each pair of Sentinel-2 and Planet images (the results reported in Sect. 7 include the essential part of this work to evaluate the congruence of the Planet, Sentinel-2):

1. Acquisition of available images from Sentinel-2 and Planet archive.
2. Search images acquired the same day by the two types of sensors without cloud cover.
3. Computation of NDVI and NDRE index for any couple of images acquired the same day.
4. Computation of NDVI and NDRE Maps and their histogram (Full Image Analysis).
5. Computation of Delta NDVI Map and Delta NDRE and its histogram (Full Image Analysis).
6. Scatter Plot of Planet NDVI #2 against NDVI #1 (Full Image Analysis) to understand if NDVI #2 is consistent with NDVI #1.
7. Scatter Plot of Planet NDRE #2 against NDRE #1 (Full Image Analysis) to understand if NDRE #2 is consistent with NDRE #1.
8. Scatter Plot of Delta NDVI (#2-#1) against #NDVI #1 (Full Image Analysis) to understand possible dependence of Delta NDVI respect to NDVI.
9. Scatter Plot of Delta NDRE (#2-#1) against #NDRE #1 (Full Image Analysis) to understand possible dependence of Delta NDRE respect to NDRE.
10. Outlier rejection of 1% of data for Full Image, considered as possible random errors.
11. Plot of histogram with outlier rejection and statistical analysis (with scatter plot including outliers) to understand how many there are and plot over the maps to understand where they are.
12. Region of interest is masked through crops' shapefile to evaluate data only inside the area of interest: a new scatter plot is done over only crops.
13. Scatter plot including of NDVI #2 against NDVI #1: Full Image data divided in Inliers of the Full Image, Outliers of the Full Image, Crops
14. Scatter plot including of NDRE #2 against NDRE #1: Full Image data divided in Inliers of the Full Image, Outliers of the Full Image, Crops
15. Scatter plot of Delta NDVI (#2-#1) against #NDVI #1: Full Image data divided in Inliers of the Full Image, Outliers of the Full Image, Crops
16. Scatter plot of Delta NDRE (#2-#1) against #NDRE #1: Full Image data divided in Inliers of the Full Image, Outliers of the Full Image, Crops
17. Evaluation of RMSE on NDVI through the formula (3) for the Full Image, for the Inliers (99% of data), Crops (through the mask).
18. Evaluation of RMSE on NDRE through the formula (4) for the Full Image, for the Inliers (99% of data), Crops (through the mask).

19. Evaluation of NDVI Mean on Crops.
20. Evaluation of NDRE Mean on Crops
21. Time Series plot to understand possible seasonality of crops: RMSE NDVI and NDVI Mean over time (extracting march-august time frame)
22. Time Series plot to understand possible seasonality of crops: RMSE NDRE and NDRE Mean over time (extracting march-august time frame)

$$RMSE = \sqrt{\frac{1}{n} \sum_{i,j} (NDRE_2(i,j) - NDRE_1(i,j))^2} \tag{4}$$

4　Area of Interest: Riserva San Massimo

The Farm, chosen in agreement with the agronomic consultant agency managed by Dr. Agr. P.A. Barbieri and Dr. Agr. G.L. Rognoni, is "Riserva San Massimo" (Fig. 1). It's located near Pavia, and it consists of a complex (about 15 Km^2) of crops inside a wildlife reserve: the main activity in this area is rice cultivation through biological farming.

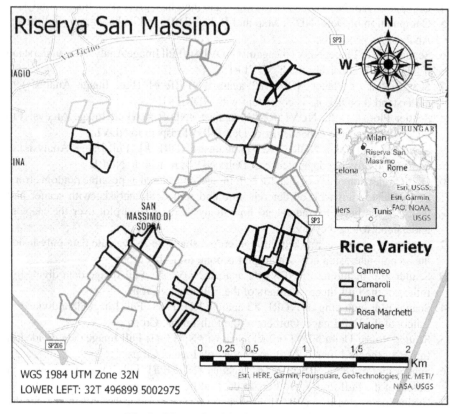

Fig. 1. Riserva San Massimo – Rice Variety

5   Available Data

Three types of data were used during this research:

- Riserva San Massimo ESRI shape file (provided by the agronomic consultant agency)
- Sentinel-2 Images, Level-2A Images [41]
- Planet Images, Superdove Sensor [48]

Sentinel-2 images had these characteristics: atmospherically corrected surface and reflectances in cartographic geometry [41]. Granules were ortho-images in UTM/WGS84 projection.

Planet images had these characteristics: acquired by the latest sensor (SuperDove – 8 bands), calibrated surface reflectance, rectified assets and radiometrically harmonized Sentinel-2. Even Planet uses UTM/WGS84 projection [48].

- Images found in Sentinel-2 archive: 73 for 2021 and 71 for 2022.
- Images found in Planet archive: 222 for 2021, 345 for 2022

6   Analysis

The availability and usability analysis gave the longest time span without available images for Planet and Sentinel-2: archive availability and cloud cover need to be considered when choosing the constellation, also for plan drone acquisitions when necessary. The analysis was carried out for a time span ranging from March to July for 2022: the availability of images of the Planet constellation grows over time and the SuperDove satellite acquires them from 2020 but at a slower pace. The March-July quarter is considered important in precision agriculture for fertilization. The results and methodology of this analysis are illustrated respectively in Sect. 7.1 and Sect. 3.3.

The analysis of multiple Planet images was also carried out during 2022 and for 07/10/2021 (only one day for which 5 images are available). Multiple Planet images, quite contemporary, were an opportunity to demonstrate the self-consistency of the sensor: the hypothesis is that the images acquired over a period between 10 min and an hour should have given similar results in relation to the calculation indices. The results and methodology of this analysis are illustrated respectively in Sect. 7.3 and Sect. 3.4.

Comparing Planet and Sentinel-2 images acquired on the same day gave the opportunity to understand the difference between the calculated indices. NDVI and NDRE were initially calculated for all 2022 pairs: the analysis was subsequently extended to 2021 due to lower cloud cover during the year. The results and methodology of this analysis are illustrated in Sect. 7.4 and Sect. 3.5 respectively.

7   Results

7.1   Assessment of the Availability of Useful Images for Sentinel-2 and Planet

The longest time span found without usable imagery was 9 days for Planet and 30 days for Sentinel-2. When agronomists need to perform field operations, 30 days of unusable crop images are limiting. If no other imagery is available, they must use other techniques, such as drone imagery, which can be acquired even with higher cloud cover (Table 1).

Table 1. Comparing Sentinel-2 and Planet Images: availability and usability

	Planet				Sentinel-2			
2022	April	May	June	July	April	May	June	July
Expected	30	31	30	31	6	7	6	6
Available	20	20	19	20	6	7	6	6
Unavailable	10	11	11	11	0	0	0	0
Good	8	13	10	19	2	4	2	2
Bad	12	7	9	1	4	3	4	4

7.2 Times Series Results

The numerical results of the entire process (described in the paragraph relating to the methodology) have been reported in full in the Appendix: within this paragraph only the essential part of the work that demonstrates the purpose of the article is reported.

Multiple values were reported for each time series:

- Full Image RMSE (without masking or outlier rejection)
- Inliers RMSE (Full Image with outlier rejection)
- Crops RMSE (with masking and outlier rejection)
- Index mean value over Crops.

The difference between each calculated RMSE, for each individual pair of images, suggests that the indices need to be evaluated with the specific crop type in mind. Within Sect. 7.3, a single case with low and high outliers is shown as an example because the focus of the paper is on rice crops for the region of interest.

7.3 Planet Images Internal Congruence

The internal congruence results of the planet are reported in full only in the Appendix for completeness (see Appendix, Table 5) and demonstrate a high coherence over time of multiple acquisitions of Planets. The analysis was conducted initially for the year 2022 and subsequently for a specific day in 2021 (10/07) in which 5 images were acquired within a period of one hour. Figure 2 represents a comparison between two images of the Planet acquired on the same day (13/07/2022) over a period of 10 min: each point represents a pair of pixels (NDVI Image #1, NDVI Image #2). The values of each pair of pixels were displayed only for the crops and, for most of them, they are on the diagonal: this shows that the NDVI values are similar for each pixel examined. Figure 3 plots the 2022 time series for RMSE on NDVI (crops) versus the average NDVI, both plotted over time at different scales. This graph demonstrates that during the fertilization period (July) the RMSE to NDVI is low, with an average RMSE of 0.02 and an average NDVI of 0.8978 for that time period. The maximum RMSE found is 0.0429 on 16/05: in this period the cultivation of rice does not completely cover the land and could lead to a higher value which however is low (and not useful for fertilization). The results demonstrate the self-consistency of Planet and that there is however a seasonal variation in coherence over time.

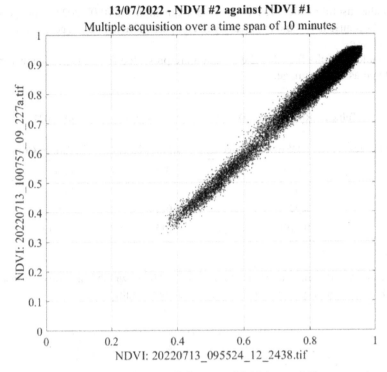

Fig. 2. 13/07/2022 - NDVI #2 against NDVI #1: crops. Multiple acquisition over a time span of 10 min

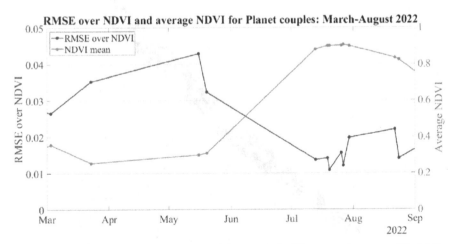

Fig. 3. Time series: RMSE over NDVI and NDVI mean for Planet couples: crops. Useful time frame for precision farming: March-August 2022

Another useful result is related to the 5 acquisitions of 10/07/2023 in the period of one hour because it was the opportunity to compare more than 2 images, as done in the previous case.

In Table 2 results for RMSE evaluation are presented for 4 images against the #1, considered as master image.

Table 2. RMSE over NDVI: 5 Planet images available on 10/07/2021

Planet Images	RMSE: Full Image	RMSE: Inliers	RMSE: Crops
#2-#1	0.0265	0.0253	0.0135
#3-#1	0.0346	0.0317	0.0186
#4-#1	0.0211	0.0174	0.0101
#5-#1	0.0191	0.0151	0.0113

The average RMSE over crops (Table 2) is of 0.0133 which is a good demonstration of the Planet capability to obtain the same value with multiple acquisitions.

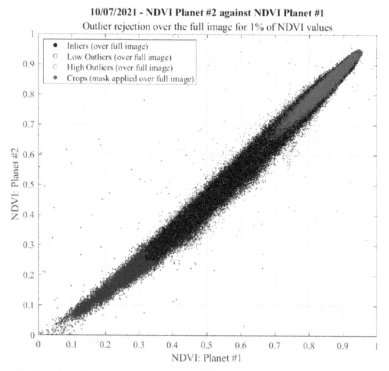

Fig. 4. 10/07/2021 – NDVI Planet #2 against NDVI Planet #1. Outlier rejection over the full image for 1% of NDVI values and crops highlighted

Figure 4 represents the comparison between the couple #1,#2 (as in Table 2): green dots are the pixels of the crops. Outlier rejection is presented only in this case to demonstrate that the 2 NDVIs are congruent (the points are displayed along the diagonal). Higher differences in NDVI are minimal along the NDVI value (Fig. 5): the Delta NDVI map (Fig. 6) shows where the higher values are located: buildings, roads, artefacts. The results demonstrate that Planet is consistent across all 5 five acquisitions.

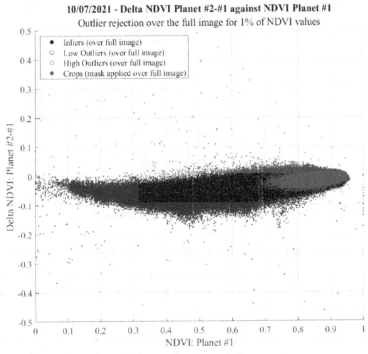

Fig. 5. 10/07/2021 – Delta NDVI Planet #2-#1 against NDVI Planet #1. Outlier rejection over the full image for 1% of NDVI values and crops highlighted

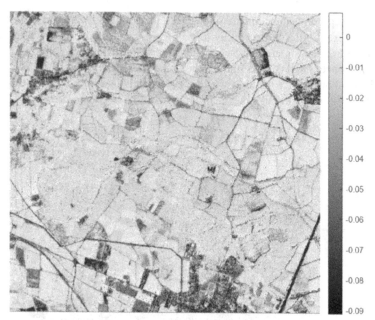

Fig. 6. Delta NDVI Map Planet #2-#1 filtered as shown in scatter in Fig. 5. Low Outliers (Blue), High Outliers (Red): for the most are outside the crops (Green) (Color figure online)

7.4 Congruence Analysis Between Sentinel-2 and Planet (NDVI and NDRE)

The results of the congruence analysis of Sentinel-2 and Planet are displayed for completeness in the Appendix: only the essential part of the work is displayed within the paragraph focused on the improvement made.

The analysis was initially carried out for 2022, where the availability of images was greater, and subsequently also extended to 2021 where the lower cloud cover during the year gave a greater quantity of images available to analyze even if only one is available date for comparison in July 2021.

Results summary (Full data and Plot):

- 15/07/2022 NDVI Scatter Plot: Planet against Sentinel-2, Plot: Fig. 7
- 2022 NDVI full data: Appendix A.1, Table 7, Plot: Fig. 8
- 15/07/2022 NDRE Scatter Plot: Planet against Sentinel-2, Plot: Fig. 9
- 2022 NDRE full data: Appendix A.2, Table 9, Plot: Fig. 10
- 2021 NDVI full data: Appendix A.1, Table 6, Plot: Fig. 11
- 2021 NDRE full data: Appendix A.2, Table 8, Plot: Fig. 12

The results are displayed in this paragraph only for crops as in the previous time series (Fig. 3).

Figure 7 represents a comparison for a pair of images (Sentinel-2, Planet) acquired the same day (15/07/2022) in a time span of 10 min: each point represents a pair of pixels (NDVI Sentinel-2, NDVI Planet). The values of each pair of pixels were displayed for crops only: a slight miscalibration is shown throughout the scatter plot because pixels have higher values for Planet NDVI than for Sentinel-2.

Figure 8 plots 2022 time series for RMSE over NDVI (crops) versus the average NDVI, both plotted over time at different scales. This graph demonstrates that during the fertilization period (July) the RMSE over NDVI is low, with an average RMSE of 0.0561 and an average NDVI of 0,864 for that time frame.

Figure 9 represents a comparison for a pair of images (Sentinel-2, Planet) acquired the same day (15/07/2022) in a time span of 10 min: each point represents a pair of pixels (NDRE Sentinel-2, NDRE Planet). Values of each pair of pixels were displayed for crops only: a miscalibration is shown throughout the scatter plot (higher than for the NDVI) because pixels have higher values for Planet NDRE than for Sentinel-2.

Figure 10 plots 2022 time series for RMSE over NDRE (crops) versus the average NDRE, both plotted over time at different scales. This graph demonstrates that during the fertilization period (July) the RMSE over NDVI is lower than other time intervals, but it is still considerable, with a mean RMSE of 0.0904 and an average NDRE of 0,6312 for that time interval.

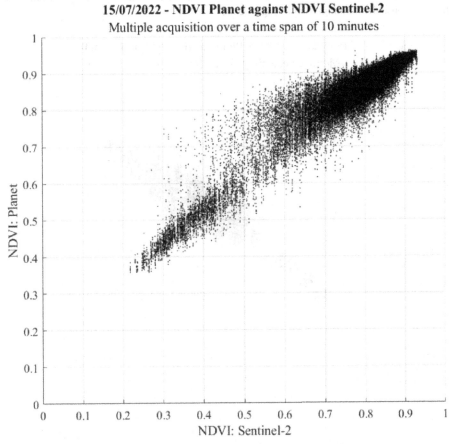

Fig. 7. 15/07/2022 – NDVI Planet against NDVI Sentinel-2: crops. Multiple acquisition over a time span of 10 min

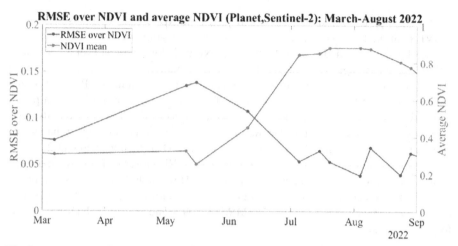

Fig. 8. Time Series: RMSE over NDVI and NDVI mean (Planet.Sentinel-2): crops. Useful time frame for precision farming: March-August 2022

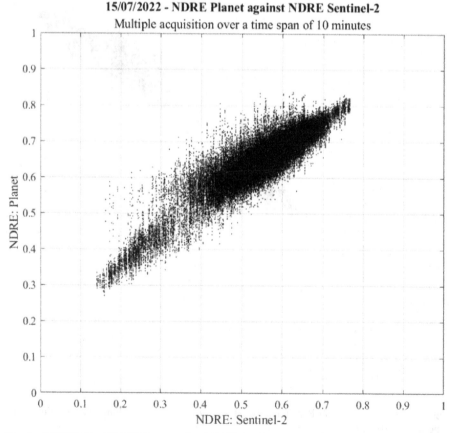

Fig. 9. 15/07/2022 – NDRE Planet against NDRE Sentinel-2: crops. Multiple acquisition over a time span of 10 min

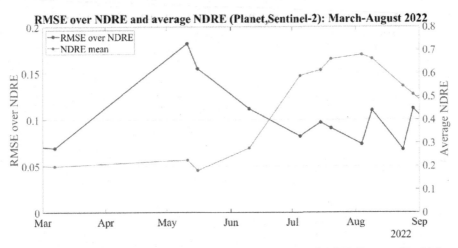

Fig. 10. Time Series: RMSE over NDRE and NDRE mean (Planet.Sentinel-2): crops. Useful time frame for precision farming: March-August 2022

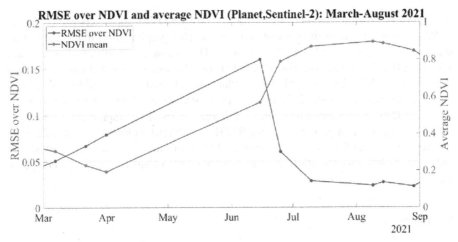

Fig. 11. Time Series: RMSE over NDVI and NDVI mean (Planet.Sentinel-2): crops. Useful time frame for fertilization: March-August 2021

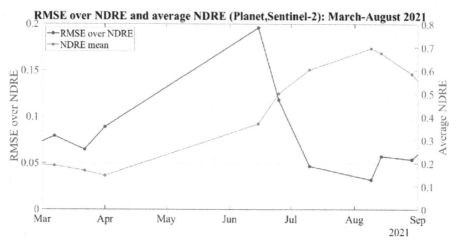

Fig. 12. Time Series: RMSE over NDRE and NDRE mean (Planet.Sentinel-2): crops. Useful time frame for fertilization: March-August 2021

Figure 11 plots 2021 time series for RMSE over NDVI (crops) versus the average NDVI, both plotted over time at different scales. This graph demonstrates that during the fertilization period (July) the RMSE over NDVI is low, as in 2022, with an average RMSE of 0.0320 and an average NDVI of 0,8698 for that period (but only a multiple image for 10/07/2021 is available with 5 Planet acquisitions compared to 1 Sentinel-2 acquisition). Figure 12 plots 2021 time series for RMSE over NDRE (crops) versus the average NDRE, both plotted over time at different scales. This graph demonstrates that during the fertilization period (July) the RMSE over NDRE is lower than in 2022, with an average RMSE of 0.0567 and an average NDRE of 0,6077 for that time period (but only a multiple image for 10/07/2021 is available with 5 Planet acquisitions compared to 1 Sentinel-2 acquisition).

8 Discussion

The availability and usability analysis (Sect. 7.1) has shown importance in the context of precision agriculture. Sentinel-2 is an excellent data source for agronomists and farmers (with more bands than Planet) but in case of cloud cover, with only one image every 5 days, there can also be long periods without usable images. Often, when planning fertilization interventions, it is necessary to carry out short-term planning and it is necessary to use drones to compensate for the lack of data. In the 4 most significant months of 2022 it was seen that there was a period of 30 days without Sentinel-2 images: Planet seems to be able to compensate for this problem, having an almost daily frequency, and reaching a maximum of 9 days without images available (mainly due to cloud cover). Planet, from this point of view, certainly represents a good alternative given the increase in the number of satellites in the constellation (today already over 200) compared to the good results already obtained in previous years as indicated in this paper [54].

The internal congruence of Planet images was good for crops throughout the analyzed period, with a significant reduction in RMSE in July, during the most important period for rice fertilization (Sect. 7.3). The opportunity to use images acquired almost simultaneously made it possible to validate the coherence of the sensor over time.

Sentinel-2–Planet congruence demonstrated a miscalibration: lower for NDVI and higher for NDRE. The main result is that during the fertilization period, in July, the alignment of the 2 sensors is greater: the miscalibration must however be considered (RMSE over NDVI $\approx$ 0.05; RMSE over NDRE $\approx$ 0.09). This analysis allows the use of Planet images, with experience acquired with Sentinel-2 in precision farming and the knowledge of the results highlighted in this paper. The Sentinel-2 literature and the experience of agronomists allow the use of NDVI and NDRE through agronomic curves that relate the indices to the quantity of fertilizer needed: studies have been conducted using handhelds crop sensors (as RapidScan [55]) compared to Sentinel-2 indices. The agronomic curves for rice cultivation have been studied empirically by "Ente Nazionale Risi", Paper [6] has demonstrated that there is a need to align the Rapidscan and Sentinel-2 data by analyzing rice crops for years with field instruments such as Green Seeker and Rapid Scan [18]. Adapting results to drone and satellite images with statistical and empirical calibration could be done through some of the analysis shown in this paper through data acquired for 2021 and 2022.

Although the focus of the paper is fertilization, it is interesting to highlight that the RMSE for crops has a peak in May (sometimes even in June) where it is higher than the RMSE calculated for the full image and inliers. This effect could be linked to the different spatial resolution of the 2 sensors and to the fact that rice grows from May until mid-June: the vegetation covers neither terrain nor the water (depending on the type of cultivation) [1]. Higher resolution images from the Planet constellation appear to acquire the phenomenon differently than Sentinel-2.

9   Conclusion

Planet offers a good solution for both spatial and temporal resolution: acquisitions are consistent over time (internal congruence) and given the almost daily revisit time, Planet images are more likely to overcome the cloud cover problem.

The analysis demonstrates that the difference between the indices calculated for a pair of Sentinel-2 and Planet images, acquired the same day, is seasonal and the alignment must be considered.

During the fertilization period, in the month of July, Planet images appear to be more consistent with those of Sentinel-2 although with calibration errors that are not always negligible: lower for NDVI and higher for NDRE (which may require an alignment). Planet images can be applied to rice cultivation under the above conditions.

Acknowledgments. Authors thank Dr. Agr. G. L. Rognoni and Ing. C. Bergonzi for their contributions in choosing test-site and in interpreting field data through their experience, gained through a long collaboration with "Ente Nazionale Risi".

Authors thank "Riserva San Massimo" owners and workers for their support in sharing their experience during field work.

Funding. The research described in this paper is part of a doctoral position funded by the PON DM 1061 call.

Appendix

(See Table 4).

Table 3. Overview of the Sentinel-2 Bands [35]

Sentinel-2

Band N°	Type	Central wavelength (nm)	Bandwidth (nm)	Spatial resolution (m)
1	Coastal Aerosol	442.7	20	60
2	Blue	492.7	65	10
3	Green	559.8	35	10
4	Red	664.6	30	10
5	Red Edge 1	704.1	14	20
6	Red Edge 2	740.5	14	20
7	Red Edge 3	782.8	19	20
8	NIR	832.8	105	10
8a	Plateau NIR	864.7	21	20
9	Water Vapor	945.1	19	60
10	SWIR	1373.5	29	60
11	SWIR	1613.7	90	20
12	SWIR	2202.4	174	20

Table 4. Overview of the Planet Bands [50]

Band N°	Type	Central Wavelength (nm)	Bandwith (nm)	Resolution (m)	Interoperability with S2 band (declared)
1	Coastal Blue	443	20	3	Sentinel-2 Band 1
2	Blue	490	50	3	Sentinel-2 Band 2
3	Green I	531	36	3	–
4	Green	565	36	3	Sentinel-2 Band 3
5	Yellow	610	20	3	–
6	Red	665	31	3	Sentinel-2 Band 4
7	RedEdge	705	15	3	Sentinel-2 Band 5
8	NIR	865	40	3	Sentinel-2 Band 8

Table 5. Time Series 2022: RMSE NDVI vs. NDVI Mean Crops. Results developed for Planet internal congruence

Date	RMSE Full Image	RMSE Inliers	RMSE Crops	Average NDVI Crops
25/02	0.0485	0.0465	0.0416	0.3410
26/02	0.0357	0.0339	0.0273	0.3344
03/03	0.0329	0.0311	0.0265	0.3556
23/03	0.0441	0.0414	0.0352	0.2548
16/05	0.0411	0.0394	0.0429	0.3000
20/05	0.0359	0.0325	0.0323	0.3097
13/07	0.0241	0.0226	0.0136	0.8803
19/07	0.0225	0.0202	0.0140	0.8992
20/07	0.0214	0.0177	0.0108	0.9000
26/07	0.0276	0.0258	0.0155	0.9015
27/07	0.0199	0.0175	0.0120	0.9065
30/07	0.0463	0.0350	0.0197	0.8996
22/08	0.0404	0.0333	0.0220	0.8340
24/08	0.0206	0.0188	0.0140	0.8237
10/09	0.0219	0.0206	0.0192	0.6836
11/09	0.0207	0.0165	0.0151	0.6789

A.1 Sentinel-2 vs. Planet: Time Series 2021–2022 RMSE vs. NDVI Mean Crops. Results Developed for Planet vs. Sentinel-2 Congruence Analysis

Table 6. Time Series 2021: RMSE NDVI vs. NDVI Mean Crops

Image N°	Sentinel-2 AVBL: 73	Planet AVBL: 222	RMSE Full Image	RMSE Inliers	RMSE Crops	Average NDVI Crops
1	11/01	11/01	0.0528	0.0488	0.0378	0.3466
2	16/01	16/01	0.0808	0.0777	0.0525	0.3359

(continued)

Table 6. (*continued*)

Image N°	Sentinel-2 AVBL: 73	Planet AVBL: 222	RMSE Full Image	RMSE Inliers	RMSE Crops	Average NDVI Crops
3	26/01	26/01 (1)	0.0827	0.0782	0.0550	0.3631
4	26/01	26/01 (2)	0.0895	0.0852	0.0613	0.3589
5	15/02	15/02	0.0541	0.0504	0.0343	0.3503
6	07/03	07/03 (1)	0.0698	0.0672	0.0623	0.3130
7	07/03	07/03 (2)	0.0563	0.0530	0.0508	0.3065
8	22/03	22/03	0.1058	0.1033	0.0668	0.2301
9	01/04	01/04	0.0670	0.0648	0.0788	0.1946
10	15/06	15/06	0.1326	0.1304	0.1600	0.5678
11	25/06	25/06	0.0849	0.0806	0.0603	0.7895
12	10/07	10/07 (1)	0.0567	0.0524	0.0301	0.8683
13	10/07	10/07 (2)	0.0649	0.0612	0.0339	0.8712
14	10/07	10/07 (3)	0.0672	0.0636	0.0322	0.8695
15	10/07	10/07 (4)	0.0707	0.0665	0.0353	0.8719
16	10/07	10/07 (5)	0.0563	0.0523	0.0286	0.8683
17	09/08	09/08 (1)	0.0482	0.0439	0.0190	0.8964
18	09/08	09/08 (2)	0.0475	0.0432	0.0199	0.8957
19	09/08	09/08 (3)	0.0632	0.0575	0.0236	0.8935
20	14/08	14/08 (1)	0.0663	0.0622	0.0237	0.8824
21	14/08	14/08 (2)	0.0707	0.0665	0.0271	0.8853
22	29/08	29/08	0.0568	0.0513	0.0226	0.8455
23	08/09	08/09	0.0651	0.0607	0.0346	0.7700
24	13/10	13/10	0.0746	0.0717	0.0772	0.4466
25	18/10	18/10 (1)	0.1080	0.1062	0.1120	0.4006
26	18/10	18/10 (2)	0.1071	0.1052	0.1080	0.3985

Table 7. Time Series 2022: RMSE NDVI vs. NDVI Mean Crops

Image N°	Sentinel-2 AVBL: 71	Planet AVBL: 345	RMSE Full Image	RMSE Inliers	RMSE Crops	Average NDVI Crops
1	07/03	07/03	0.0750	0.0733	0.0762	0.3037
2	11/05	11/05	0.1056	0.1034	0.1350	0.3230

(*continued*)

Table 7. (*continued*)

Image N°	Sentinel-2 AVBL: 71	Planet AVBL: 345	RMSE Full Image	RMSE Inliers	RMSE Crops	Average NDVI Crops
3	16/05	16/05 (1)	0.0835	0.0810	0.1023	0.2340
4	16/05	16/05 (2)	0.1123	0.1101	0.1385	0.2525
5	10/06	10/06	0.0877	0.0851	0.1077	0.4505
6	05/07	05/07	0.0824	0.0793	0.0537	0.8435
7	15/07	15/07	0.0895	0.0866	0.0651	0.8510
8	20/07	20/07 (1)	0.0927	0.0884	0.0524	0.8805
9	20/07	20/07 (2)	0.0914	0.0878	0.0533	0.8810
10	04/08	04/08	0.0762	0.0727	0.0387	0.8814
11	09/08	09/08	0.1015	0.0993	0.0687	0.8753
12	24/08	24/08	0.0661	0.0630	0.0395	0.8045
13	29/08	29/08	0.0815	0.0784	0.0628	0.7750
14	18/09	18/09	0.0605	0.0566	0.0482	0.5856
15	23/09	23/09	0.1196	0.1185	0.1066	0.4881
16	08/10	08/10	0.1288	0.1278	0.1444	0.3620
17	18/10	18/10	0.1733	0.1725	0.1802	0.3561

A.2 Sentinel-2 vs. Planet: RMSE 2021–2022 Time Series for NDRE vs. NDRE Mean. Results Developed for Planet vs. Sentinel-2 Congruence Analysis

Table 8. Time Series 2021: RMSE NDRE vs. NDRE Mean Crops

Image N°	Sentinel-2 AVBL: 73	Planet AVBL: 222	RMSE Full Image	RMSE Inliers	RMSE Crops	Average NDRE Crops
1	11/01	11/01	0.0727	0.0667	0.0573	0.2041
2	16/01	16/01	0.0700	0.0641	0.0530	0.1991
3	26/01	26/01 (1)	0.0712	0.0646	0.0516	0.2150
4	26/01	26/01 (2)	0.0719	0.0652	0.0520	0.2147
5	15/02	15/02	0.0669	0.0622	0.0588	0.1994

(*continued*)

Table 8. (*continued*)

Image N°	Sentinel-2 AVBL: 73	Planet AVBL: 222	RMSE Full Image	RMSE Inliers	RMSE Crops	Average NDRE Crops
6	07/03	07/03 (1)	0.0796	0.0770	0.0728	0.1866
7	07/03	07/03 (2)	0.0874	0.0847	0.0793	0.1895
8	22/03	22/03	0.0822	0.0803	0.0647	0.1668
9	01/04	01/04	0.0771	0.0750	0.0890	0.1456
10	15/06	15/06	0.1655	0.1633	0.1959	0.3596
11	25/06	25/06	0.1191	0.1150	0.1183	0.4997
12	10/07	10/07 (1)	0.0704	0.0662	0.0478	0.6018
13	10/07	10/07 (2)	0.0915	0.0880	0.0643	0.6120
14	10/07	10/07 (3)	0.0872	0.0837	0.0602	0.6094
15	10/07	10/07 (4)	0.0899	0.0864	0.0647	0.6124
16	10/07	10/07 (5)	0.0695	0.0659	0.0467	0.6029
17	09/08	09/08 (1)	0.0534	0.0495	0.0272	0.7056
18	09/08	09/08 (2)	0.0521	0.0479	0.0282	0.6991
19	09/08	09/08 (3)	0.0613	0.0564	0.0320	0.6948
20	14/08	14/08 (1)	0.0819	0.0781	0.0480	0.6688
21	14/08	14/08 (2)	0.0913	0.0877	0.0573	0.6742
22	29/08	29/08	0.0832	0.0784	0.0539	0.5842
23	08/09	08/09	0.0907	0.0861	0.0737	0.4871
24	13/10	13/10	0.1013	0.0976	0.0955	0.2732
25	18/10	18/10 (1)	0.1031	0.0999	0.1014	0.2466
26	18/10	18/10 (2)	0.0999	0.0966	0.0951	0.2434

Table 9. Time Series 2022: RMSE NDRE vs. NDRE Mean Crops

Image N°	Sentinel-2 AVBL: 71	Planet AVBL: 345	RMSE Full Image	RMSE Inliers	RMSE Crops	Average NDRE Crops
1	07/03	07/03	0.0758	0.0728	0.0692	0.1987
2	11/05	11/05	0.1541	0.1518	0.1821	0.2263
3	16/05	16/05 (1)	0.1132	0.1108	0.1234	0.1659

(*continued*)

Table 9. (*continued*)

Image N°	Sentinel-2 AVBL: 71	Planet AVBL: 345	RMSE Full Image	RMSE Inliers	RMSE Crops	Average NDRE Crops
4	16/05	16/05 (2)	0.1399	0.1374	0.1551	0.1819
5	10/06	10/06	0.0998	0.0971	0.1119	0.2771
6	05/07	05/07	0.1036	0.1010	0.0823	0.5888
7	15/07	15/07	0.1219	0.1193	0.0970	0.6136
8	20/07	20/07 (1)	0.1267	0.1233	0.0914	0.6614
9	20/07	20/07 (2)	0.1223	0.1193	0.0909	0.6613
10	04/08	04/08	0.1130	0.1100	0.0737	0.6801
11	09/08	09/08	0.1449	0.1427	0.1101	0.6630
12	24/08	24/08	0.0896	0.0864	0.0680	0.5444
13	29/08	29/08	0.1257	0.1225	0.1121	0.5086
14	18/09	18/09	0.0746	0.0695	0.0663	0.3660
15	23/09	23/09	0.1054	0.1036	0.0900	0.3309
16	08/10	08/10	0.1452	0.1436	0.1539	0.2403
17	18/10	18/10	0.1675	0.1661	0.1729	0.2376

References

1. Varetti, G.: L'almanacco del riso 2023. Le più importanti news 2022 di Risoitaliano.eu (2022). Independently Published. https://www.risoitaliano.eu/
2. Baldin, C.M., Rocca, M.T., Franzini, M., Casella, V.M.: L'uso di immagini Planet nell'agricoltura di precisione: una prima sperimentazione relativa al riso. Convegno Nazionale SIFET Arezzo (2023)
3. Cordero, E., et al.: Fertilisation strategy and ground sensor measurements to optimise rice yield. Eur. J. Agron. **99**, 177–185 (2018). https://doi.org/10.1016/j.eja.2018.07.010
4. Farbo, A., Sarvia, F., De Petris, S., Borgogno-Mondino, E.: Preliminary concerns about agronomic interpretation of NDVI Time Series from Sentinel-2 data: phenology and thermal efficiency of winter wheat in Piemonte (NW Italy). Int. Arch. Photogramm. Remote Sens. Spatial Inf. Sci. ISPRS-Archives XLIII-B3-2022 (2022). https://doi.org/10.5194/isprs-archives-XLIII-B3-2022-863-2022
5. Borgogno-Mondino, E., Farbo, A., Novello, V., De Palma, L.: A fast regression-based approach to map water status of pomegranate orchards with sentinel-2. MDPI Horticulturae 8(9), 759 (2022). https://doi.org/10.3390/horticulturae8090759
6. Farbo, A., Meloni, R., Blandino, M., Sarvia, F., Reyneri, A., Borgogno-Mondino, E.: Spectral measures from sentinel-2 imagery vs ground-based data from Rapidscan© sensor: performances on winter wheat. In: Borgogno-Mondino, E., Zamperlin, P. (eds.) ASITA 2022. CCIS, vol. 1651, pp. 211–221. Springer, Cham (2022). https://doi.org/10.1007/978-3-031-17439-1_15
7. Ghilardi, F., De Petris, S., Farbo, A., Sarvia, F., Borgogno-Mondino, E.: Exploring stability of crops in agricultural landscape through GIS tools and open data. In: Gervasi, O., Murgante, B.,

Misra, S., Rocha, A.M.A.C., Garau, C. (eds.) ICCSA 2022. LNCS, vol. 13379, pp. 327–339. Springer, Cham (2022). https://doi.org/10.1007/978-3-031-10545-6_23

8. Sarvia, F., De Petris, S., Orusa, T., Borgogno-Mondino, E.: MAIA S2 versus sentinel 2: spectral issues and their effects in the precision farming context. In: Gervasi, O., et al. (eds.) ICCSA 2021. LNCS, vol. 12955, pp. 63–77. Springer, Cham (2021). https://doi.org/10.1007/978-3-030-87007-2_5

9. Sona, G., et al.: UAV multispectral survey to map soil and crop for precision farming applications. Int. Arch. Photogramm. Remote Sens. Spatial Inf. Sci. **XLI-B1**, 1023–1029 (2016). https://doi.org/10.5194/isprs-archives-XLI-B1-1023-2016

10. Benedetti, R., Rossini, P.: On the use of NDVI profiles as a tool for agricultural statistics: The case study of wheat yield estimate and forecast in Emilia Romagna. Remote Sens. Environ. **45**, 311–326 (1993). https://doi.org/10.1016/0034-4257(93)90113-C

11. Sruthi, S., Mohammed Aslam, M.A.: Agricultural drought analysis using the NDVI and land surface temperature; a case study of Raichur District. Aquatic Procedia **4**, 1258–1264 (2015). https://doi.org/10.1016/j.aqpro.2015.02.164

12. Lenney, M.P., Woodcock, C.E., Collins, J.B., Hamdi, H.: The status of agricultural lands in Egypt: the use of multitemporal NDVI features derived from landsat TM. Remote Sens. Environ. **56**(1), 8–20 (1996). https://doi.org/10.1016/0034-4257(95)00152-2

13. Kovalev, I.V., Testoyedov, N.A.: Modern unmanned aerial technologies for the development of agribusiness and precision farming. In: IOP Conference Series: Earth and Environmental Science, vol. 548, p. 052080 (2020). https://doi.org/10.1088/1755-1315/548/5/052080

14. Boiarskii, B., Hasegawa, H.: Comparison of NDVI and NDRE indices to detect differences in vegetation and chlorophyll content. J. Mech. Continua Math. Sci. (4) (2019). https://doi.org/10.26782/jmcms.spl.4/2019.11.00003

15. Milas, S.A., Romanko, M., Reil, P., Abeysinghe, T., Anuruddha, M.: The importance of leaf area index in mapping chlorophyll content of corn under different agricultural treatments using UAV images. Int. J. Remote Sens. **39**(15–16), 5415–5431 (2018). https://doi.org/10.1080/01431161.2018.1455244

16. Bellón, B., Bégué, A., Lo, S.D., De Almeida, C.A., Simões, M.: A remote sensing approach for regional-scale mapping of agricultural land-use systems based on NDVI time series. Remote Sens. **9**(6), 600 (2017). https://doi.org/10.3390/rs9060600

17. Conferenza ESRI Italia 2019 – Concimazione Azotata di Precisione in Risaia. https://www.esriitalia.it/media/sync/Gian_Luca_Rognoni_esri_2019.docx.pdf. Accessed 24 July 2023

18. Miniotti, E., et al.: Riso, sensori ottici e droni per ottimizzare la concimazione, Terra è Vita (Aprile 2015, Edizioni Agricole). https://terraevita.edagricole.it/wp-content/uploads/sites/11/2015/04/Riso-Pagine-da-TV15-2015-3.pdf

19. Huang, S., et al.: Potential of RapidEye and WorldView-2 satellite data for improving rice nitrogen status monitoring at different growth stages. Remote Sens. MDPI (2017). https://doi.org/10.3390/rs9030227

20. Rehman, T.H., Lundy, M.E., Linquist, B.A.: Comparative sensitivity of vegetation indices measured via proximal and aerial sensors for assessing N status and predicting grain yield in rice cropping systems. Remote Sens. MDPI (2022). https://doi.org/10.3390/rs14122770

21. Brinkhoff, J., Dunn, B.W., Robson, A.J.: Rice nitrogen status detection using commercial-scale Imagery. Int. J. Appl. Earth Obs. Geoinf. (2021). https://doi.org/10.1016/j.jag.2021.102627

22. Nutini, F., et al.: An operational workflow to assess rice nutritional status based on satellite imagery and smartphone apps. Comput. Electron. Agric. (2018), https://doi.org/10.1016/j.compag.2018.08.008

23. Späti, K., Huber, R., Finger, R.: Benefits of increasing information accuracy in variable rate technologies. Ecol. Econ. (2021). https://doi.org/10.1016/j.ecolecon.2021.107047

24. Gebbers, R., Adamchuk, V.: Precision agriculture and food security. Science (2010). https://doi.org/10.1126/science.1183899
25. Meier, J., Mauser, W., Hank, T., Bach, H.: Assessments on the impact of high-resolution-sensor pixel sizes for common agricultural policy and smart farming services in European regions. Comput. Electron. Agric. (2020). https://doi.org/10.1016/j.compag.2019.105205
26. Roy, D.P., Huang, H., Houborg, R., Martins, V.S.: A global analysis of the temporal availability of PlanetScope high spatial resolution multi-spectral imagery. Remote Sens. Environ. **264** (2021). https://doi.org/10.1016/j.rse.2021.112586
27. De Lima, P.I., Gerardo, J.R., De Lima, P.J.L.M.: Remote sensing monitoring of rice fields: towards assessing water saving irrigation management practices. Frontiers (2021). https://doi.org/10.3389/frsen.2021.762093
28. Annovazzi-Lodi, L., Casella, V., Baldin, C.M., Bernini, A., Adeniyi, O.D., Maerker, M.: Per un uso del suolo dinamico: classificazione di serie storiche di immagini Sentinel-2. #AsitaAcademy2021, 1-2-9-16-23 luglio 2021. http://atti.asita.it/ASITA2021/Pdf/037.pdf
29. Burt, J.E., Barber, G.M., Rigby, D.L.: Elementary Statistics for Geographers, 3rd edn. The Guilford Press (2009). ISBN 978-1-57230-484-0
30. Lavender, S., Lavender, A.: Practical Handbook of Remote Sensing, 2nd edn. CRC Press (2023). ISBN 978-1-03221-433-7
31. Tassinari, G., Ugulini, D., AA. VV.: Manuale dell'Agronomo, il nuovo "TASSINARI". Reda Edizioni per l'agricoltura. 6th edn. (2018). ISBN 8883613562
32. AA. VV.: Manuale dell'esame abilitante alla professione di agrotecnico e di agrotecnico laureato, nonché per l'Agronomo, il Forestale ed il Perito Agrario. Società Editoriale Nepenthes, 5th edn. (2021). ISBN 8890767170
33. Ribaudo, F.: Prontuario di agricoltura. Hoepli, 2nd edn. (2021). ISBN 978-88-203-7662-8
34. NDRE – Eos data analytics. https://eos.com/industries/agriculture/ndre/. Accessed 24 July 2023
35. Sentinel-2 User Handbook. https://sentinel.esa.int/documents/247904/685211/Sentinel-2_User_Handbook. Accessed 24 July 2023
36. Copernicus. https://www.esa.int/Applications/Observing_the_Earth/Copernicus. Accessed 24 July 2023
37. About Copernicus. https://www.copernicus.eu/en/about-copernicus. Accessed 24 July 2023
38. Sentinel-2 Satellite Description. https://sentinel.esa.int/web/sentinel/missions/sentinel-2/satellite-description. Accessed 24 July 2023
39. Sentinel-2 Mission Guide. https://sentinel.esa.int/web/sentinel/missions/sentinel-2. Accessed 24 July 2023
40. Sentinel-2 Revisit and Coverage. https://sentinel.esa.int/web/sentinel/user-guides/sentinel-2-msi/revisit-coverage. Accessed 24 July 2023
41. Sentinel-2 Product Types. https://sentinel.esa.int/web/sentinel/user-guides/sentinel-2-msi/product-types. Accessed 24 July 2023
42. Sentinel-2 Spatial Resolution. https://sentinel.esa.int/web/sentinel/user-guides/sentinel-2-msi/resolutions/spatial. Accessed 24 July 2023
43. Sentinel-2 Radiometric Resolutions. https://sentinel.esa.int/web/sentinel/user-guides/sentinel-2-msi/resolutions/radiometric. Accessed 24 July 2023
44. Sentinel-2 MSI User Guide. https://sentinel.esa.int/web/sentinel/user-guides/sentinel-2-msi. Accessed 24 July 2023
45. Sentinel-2 MSI Technical Guide. https://sentinel.esa.int/web/sentinel/technical-guides/sentinel-2-msi. Accessed 24 July 2023
46. Sentinel-2 MSI Instrument. https://sentinels.copernicus.eu/web/sentinel/technical-guides/sentinel-2-msi/msi-instrument. Accessed 24 July 2023
47. Sentinel-2 License. https://open.esa.int/copernicus-sentinel-satellite-imagery-under-open-licence/. Accessed 12 Oct 2023

48. Sentinel-2A (10 m) Satellite Sensor – Satellite Imaging Corporation. https://www.satimagin gcorp.com/satellite-sensors/other-satellite-sensors/sentinel-2a/. Accessed 24 July 2023

49. Planet Imagery Product Specifications. https://assets.planet.com/docs/Planet_Combined_Ima gery_Product_Specs_letter_screen.pdf. Accessed 24 July 2023

50. Understanding PlanetScope Instruments. https://developers.planet.com/docs/apis/data/sen sors/. Accessed 24 July 2023

51. Planet – PSScene. https://developers.planet.com/docs/data/psscene/. Accessed 24 July 2023

52. Planet – Scene Level Normalization and Harmonization of Planet Dove Imagery. https://assets. planet.com/docs/scene_level_normalization_of_planet_dove_imagery.pdf. Accessed 24 July 2023

53. Matlab – Change Image Size. https://it.mathworks.com/help/visionhdl/ug/image-downsize. html. Accessed 17 Oct 2023

54. Roy, P.D., Huang, H., Houborg, R., Martins, V.S.: A global analysis of the temporal avail-ability of PlanetScope high spatial resolution multi-spectral imagery. Remote Sens. Environ. 264, 112586 (2021). https://doi.org/10.1016/j.rse.2021.112586. https://www.sciencedirect. com/science/article/pii/S0034425721003060. ISSN 0034-4257

55. RapidSCAN CS-45, Handheld Crop Sensor. https://www.ecosearch.info/sites/default/files/ prodotti_documentazione/CS45_DataSheet_v3.pdf. Accessed 19 Oct 2023

Classification of Water in an Urban Environment by Applying OBIA and Fuzzy Logic to Very High-Resolution Satellite Imagery

Dario Perregrini[✉] and Vittorio Casella

Department of Civil Engineering and Architecture, University of Pavia, 27100 Pavia, Italy
{dario.perregrini,vittorio.casella}@unipv.it

Abstract. When it comes to soil classification, especially if performed in an urban area, the distinction between water and shadows cast by buildings is a well-known problem. Recently the geomatics laboratory of the University of Pavia purchased an image of the WorldView3 satellite of the entire municipal area of Pavia. The work area was a portion of Pavia called "Città giardino", in which there is a canal in a context characterised by residential buildings with heights ranging from 6 to 20 m, therefore it was necessary to identify a classification strategy capable of distinguishing effectively between the shadows of the buildings and the water of the canal. The classification was performed on the multispectral image with a Ground Sampling Distance (GSD) of 30 cm, obtained by fusing with the Gram-Schmidt pan-sharpening technique, the panchromatic and the 8-band multispectral image (respectively 30 and 120 GSD) of the study area. A good result was obtained by accurately describing the *water class* with different membership functions applied to the most relevant band statistics (mainly the mean and standard deviation of the pixels in each object), in fact an overall accuracy of 96.13% was achieved, by comparing it with the ground truth obtained by manually classifying most of the elements present in the scene in the "water" "vegetation" and "impermeable soil" classes.

Keywords: OBIA · WorldView3 · Satellite imagery · Land use classification · Fuzzy logic · Water classification

1 Introduction

Part of my research for the preparation of the PhD thesis, consists in the classification of the soil at the urban level of very high-resolution satellite images for the creation of soil permeability maps. This type of maps can be a source of great information, for example for sustainable development and planning in cities, in the hydraulic field by quickly providing information over a very large area on the type of soil and how it interacts with

E. Borgogno Mondino and P. Zamperlin (Eds.): ASITA 2023, CCIS 2088, pp. 285–301, 2024.
https://doi.org/10.1007/978-3-031-59925-5_19

rainfall events, nowadays more and more intense and frequent. Moreover, the heavily cemented areas typically tend to have a direct link with higher temperatures and with higher air pollution values, in short, a very versatile tool. For the creation of these maps, a fundamental step is the classification that can be performed and its accuracy, in which, especially in an urban environment a recurring problem is distinguishing between water and shadows, as already known in the literature [1, 2], because they tend to have a very similar spectral response. In our case study to correctly classify the image we had to distinguish the water in the canal from the shadows cast by the buildings, a problem that typically only occurs when working with high resolution images, at lower resolutions the shadows of the buildings don't interfere as much or are not even visible except for very tall buildings. While rural areas, typically used for agricultural purposes, the NDWI index is sufficient to effectively extract watercourses, unfortunately the same cannot be said for urban areas where there are many disturbing elements. To avoid this problem, we have applied to a small area of the city of Pavia a detailed description of the water class, made up of different membership functions logically combined with each other, to try through fuzzy logic to replicate the process that drives a person to distinguish between the two elements. For us it is easy to distinguish the shaded areas because within them it is possible to distinguish several objects on background, while in the case of watercourses, especially if they have a good depth, only a homogeneous color will be seen. Taking advantage of this fact, the description of the water class, in addition to identifying objects with high NDWI values, will take into consideration the standard deviation of the red, coastal blue, and blue bands. Shadows cast by buildings tend to have higher values of standard deviation in these three bands, due to the presence of a variety of different elements visible within them, cars, roads, perhaps the roofs of lower buildings and so on. By knowing that, using only fuzzy logic it was possible to distinguish between the two classes, accurately classifying only the watercourse within the city and a small lake present in the scene at the top right. The study area is a small portion of an image taken by the WorldView3 satellite on the entire area of the city of Pavia, a panchromatic with a GSD of 30 cm and an 8-band multispectral with a GSD of 120 cm, subsequently joined using the Gram-Schmidt pansharpening technique. This area is particularly interesting due to the presence of the canal and its proximity to the buildings and consequently with their shadows, furthermore in the city there are no other small waterways, therefore develop the classification technique on this area makes us think that it will probably be adequate for the classification of the whole city. In addition to this, it is important to mention that for this area a very detailed ground truth was carried out in recent years by a member of the university's geomatics laboratory before the start of my PhD, allowing an exceptionally rigorous validation of the classification obtained. The classification was carried out using a method "object-based" with the software Trimble eCognition™, by applying different segmentations and refining a first classification obtained, finally, the validation of the results was also done within the eCogntion™ software, exploiting the very rich ground truth in our possession. From this comparison, summarized with a confusion matrix, it is shown how the technique of describing the classes through the combination of different membership functions is an effective method for distinguishing between water and shadows in an urban environment. In the case study it is important to specify that the classification of the elements that make up the urban fabric of the city was not studied in detail, leaving both the streets and the buildings under the same class, for various reasons, both these elements are impermeable, and therefore have the same permeability value, because it is not a simple distinction to make with spectral information alone and does not particularly affect the classification of objects water and finally the ground truth is not present for most roads, but only for buildings.

2   Material Used

The geomatics laboratory of the University of Pavia purchased an image of the World-View3 satellite of the entire municipal area of Pavia taken on March 2021, for which we have a multispectral image with 8 bands and a higher resolution panchromatic image, respectively 120 cm and 30 cm (Table 1).

Table 1. Multispectral bands acquired by the WorldView3 satellite.

WorldView3 multispectral bands	Wavelengths	GSD at nadir	GSD 20° off-nadir
Panchromatic	450 – 800 nm	31 cm	34 cm
Coastal Blue	400 – 450 nm	124 cm	138 cm
Blue	450 – 510 nm	124 cm	138 cm
Green	510 – 580 nm	124 cm	138 cm
Yellow	585 – 625 nm	124 cm	138 cm
Red	630 – 690 nm	124 cm	138 cm
Red edge	705– 745 nm	124 cm	138 cm
Near infrared 1 (Nir 1)	770 – 895 nm	124 cm	138 cm
Near infrared 2 (Nir 2)	860 – 1040 nm	124 cm	138 cm

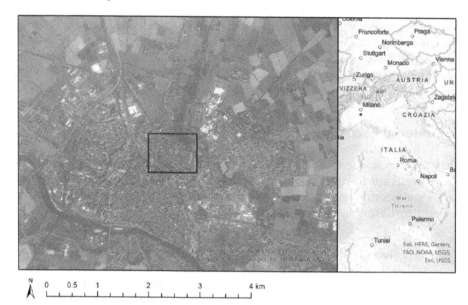

Fig. 1. A portion of the municipal area of Pavia, acquired by the WorldView3 satellite on March 22, 2021, with the area under study highlighted in red (Color figure online).

    Panchromatic band and multispectral bands were combined using the pansharpening method based on Gram-Schmidt orthogonalization [3], implemented in ESRI's software ArcGIS pro ™, which allowed us to carry out the classification of a small portion of the city of Pavia by exploiting the high resolution of 30 cm and the information of the 8 multispectral bands. To further improve the quality of the image obtained, different algorithms could have been evaluated and compared, in order to reduce the spectral error as much as possible [4], also improving the quality of the image classification, even if this was not done the degree of detail achieved is remarkable and represents a key factor in distinguishing between the different elements that make up the urban area of a city. In the center of the image, we see the city of Pavia, just below the Ticino river and around it a vast area for agricultural use. In order to be able to classify the whole image into different elements, it is essential to identify different test areas to reduce computer calculation times. For the development of the description of the classes that make up the urban area, water, vegetation, and impermeable soil, which includes both streets and buildings, the *"città giardino"* area was chosen. Which in addition to being a fairly balanced test site in terms of classifiable elements is an area for which we have abundant ground truth acquired in previous years by our laboratory. So, for us it is a portion of the city to test the membership functions that define the three classes, especially water class, which has to be classified without the influence of interfering shadows near buildings. Which in this case, being all more or less between 6 and 20 m in height, generate shadows of similar dimensions and with a spectral response similar to those classifiable as water (Figs. 1 and 2).

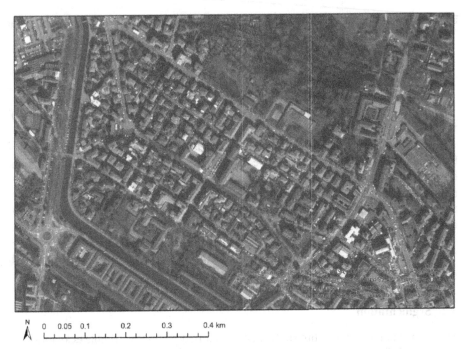

N
A

0   0.05   0.1   0.2   0.3   0.4 km

Fig. 2. Sub-area of the city of Pavia that has been classified and studied.

3   Methodology

The work performed can be divided into three main steps, calculation of the indices, segmentation and classification, each step will be explained in more detail in the respective subchapters. The first three phases are directly connected to each other, in the sense that a variation of the parameters that characterize each phase have a direct impact on the classification of the entire scene, we adjusted all the parameters necessary for the classification looking for a visually satisfactory result which was then confirmed by the validation. This last process was carried out by converting the polygons present in a shapefile, created in the past years by the members of our laboratory, into objects within eCognition™ and then comparing the pixels belonging to these objects with the classification obtained by the developed method.

3.1   Index Calculation

In addition to the bands present in the image (Table 1), we used two well-known indexes in the literature for the classification of water and vegetation objects in the study area. For water classification, the use of the NDWI (**N**ormalized **D**ifference **W**ater **I**ndex) greatly simplifies the process, but in such a detailed image it is not sufficient by itself to rigorously distinguish the water from the shadows of the buildings [5]. Instead, the NDVI (**N**ormalized **D**ifference **V**egetation **I**ndex) was more than enough for our purposes, widely used for many years now for the classification of different types of vegetation and their condition of stress/health [6], in our case we limited ourselves to using it to identify the vegetation zones present in the urban area of the city of Pavia studied.

$$NDWI = \frac{(Band\_Nir\_2 - Band\_Red)}{(Band\_Nir\_2 + Band\_Red)} \tag{1}$$

$$NDVI = \frac{(Band\_Green - Band\_Nir\_2)}{(Band\_Green + Band\_Nir\_2)} \tag{2}$$

These indices have been used not only in the classification process with fuzzy logic by defining membership functions based on them, but also in the image segmentation process, allowing to obtain objects that are very representative of the elements present in the scene. For the calculation the nir2 band was used instead of the nir1 because I typically have higher pixel values, it highlights vegetation and water more than the rest of the scene. And subsequently the limits of the membership functions were calibrated on these values. This choice is totally subjective, the same result can be obtained using the nir1 band if the limits of the membership functions involving the indices are modified in coherently with the values of the recalculated index.

3.2 Segmentation

The segmentation of the entire study area was carried out in the Trimble eCognition™ software environment, there are several algorithms already prepared to segment an image, for which the user only needs to define parameters that can influence the shape, size, and weights to be attributed to the spectral component rather than the geometry of the resulting object. In our specific case among all possible algorithms, we have used the *Multiresolution segmentation* algorithm [7], this algorithm proceeds to merge the pixels present in the image into objects, evaluating the spectral heterogeneity of the objects based on the specified *scale factor*. A low scale factor will give less heterogeneous and therefore smaller objects, on the contrary high values will allow to have larger objects with more pixels and therefore more heterogeneous. It is also possible to modify the weight that is attributed to the spectral component and by increasing the *shape factor*, higher values cause the influence of the spectral characteristics of individual pixels to matter less during segmentation. In addition to this, the user can also manipulate resulting shape through the *compactness factor*, the higher this value is, the more the objects will tend to be compact. For the test site chosen by us, after several attempts, the following values 50, 0.3 and 0.5 were identified as optimal values for the *scale factor*, the *shape factor,* and the *compactness factor* respectively, the segmentation was performed only on the red band, green band, yellow band, blue band and on the two indices calculated in the previous step. During the segmentation all the bands were given the same weight, while the indices were weighted more, weight equal to 1 for the bands, while a weight equal to 3 was used for the indices. In this case the information contained in the visible bands was sufficient to classify the entire area, the coastal blue, red edge and nir1 bands were not used, while the nir2 band was indirectly used including in the segmenting the two indices calculated in the previous step. Since the image does not always have an urban area as its subject, before this segmentation a specific segmentation is made to classify the uncultivated fields, on this image in particular it has no effect, but otherwise the fields would be classified and only on the remaining objects would the subsequent segmentation be performed to proceed with the classification of water, vegetation, and impermeable soil. No checks have been made on the quality of the segmentation achieved, because the dimensions of the area examined are quite small and it is therefore possible to visually have immediate feedback on the quality of the result achieved. In addition to this, different segmentations are made according to the classes to be identified, the uncultivated fields are classified following a segmentation with larger objects and with different weights, while for the remaining classes it is possible to use the same segmentation. However, in

Fig. 3. Comparison between the image of a portion of the area studied before, top, and after segmentation, bottom.

areas with greater extension the parameters used in the multi resolution segmentation algorithm could be optimized to increase the goodness of the final result [8, 9], (Fig. 3).

The images show a comparison of an area of the study area before and after the segmentations, it can be seen how the dimensions of the objects recognized within the artificial canal are very similar to the shadows near the buildings both in terms of colour and size. While the shadows that are cast on the green areas, there are no particular problems because they are classified as vegetation in any case, if the shadows are cast on a road, the NDWI values alone are very similar to the segmented objects in the canal i.e. water.

3.3 Classification

The classification of the objects obtained from the segmentation was done by combining, through logical operators, the values of belonging to a class or not obtained from the individual membership functions, in this way it was possible to combine different characterizing aspects, from the shape to the spectral response and the spectral homogeneity of pixels within an object. The membership functions used are shown below and in the following subchapters for each identified class the limits of each membership function are reported, they are very simple functions, our attempt was to combine them with each other trying to replicate the mental process of a person in recognizing different objects. In this work we have focused particularly on the water class to precisely address the problem of the misclassification of shadows in the water class, while for a person the difference is evident and he is perfectly capable of recognizing them, for a machine it is not the same (Fig. 4).

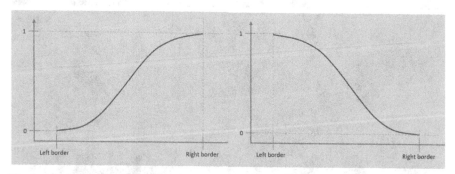

Fig. 4. Membership function directly proportional on the left (function A) and indirectly proportional on the right (function B).

These functions are defined in the range fixed for a certain feature, 1 indicating complete membership while 0 no membership in that class. So, depending on the function adopted on a feature, whether function A or function B, we can have belonging values equal to 1, 0, or a value in between. For each class, various key features have been identified for the classification, from the combination of the membership values resulting in each feature chosen through logical combinators, a value is obtained which, if greater than 0.1, a set threshold below which the object remains unclassified, is assigned to the class with the highest overall membership value. The classes in which it will be possible to classify the scene are four, impermeable, uncultivated fields, vegetation and water, there is also the uncultivated fields, because in a broader perspective we aim at a classification of the entire image of Pavia. In this specific case, there are no objects in the scene that can belong to the class uncultivated fields and therefore we will not describe it, while this is not the case in the other study areas we are working on, where the elements present are part of a rural context. After the description of the classes into which the image will be divided, an explanatory example is reported in order to better understand how the class is attributed to the objects obtained from the segmentation.

Water Class

For the water class it was necessary to develop a combination of different membership functions for the various features taken into consideration, from parameters to consider the extension of the object to others capable of evaluating the spectral characteristics of water bodies. Our attempt was to transmit to the machine through the fuzzy logic the cognitive process that allows a person looking at the image to distinguish between the shadows of the buildings and the real watercourse. Observing the shadows, it is always possible to distinguish some detail of the image inside them, whether it is a vehicle or simply the road in the background, while for watercourses generally if they are sufficiently deep a more homogeneous colour is observed. Consequently, it is logical to think that in the objects segmented by the software, for the visible bands, red, green, and blue, the standard deviation values are higher in the shadows than in the canal (Fig. 5).

Looking at the distribution of standard deviations in the various segmented objects, we noticed that the red and blue bands are more significant in distinguishing between water and shadows than the green band. In its place we have introduced a membership function which is evaluated on the standard deviation of the coastal blue band, which, having the left edge and right edge values very close, is set to be practically a threshold value. As shown in the diagram, initially the average values of the indices on each object are evaluated, the NDVI index to immediately reject any object with a minimal trace of vegetation even if in the shade, and the NDWI index to highlight possible objects classifiable as in the class water. Of the membership values of these two functions, we keep the lowest, which we will call A, then multiply it with the membership value deriving from the size of the object, which we will call B, by doing so we can already greatly reduce the number of possible candidate objects as water class. Finally, the C value obtained from the multiplication of A and B is multiplied by the D value, the minimum value deriving from the membership functions applied to the standard deviation of the red, coastal blue and blue band. From the value of this last multiplication, we obtain the "water class value" which if greater than 0.1, a threshold below which no class is attributed to the object, the examined object will be classified in the water class. Adding component D, to the result obtained previously by multiplying the information deriving from the indices and the extension of the objects, allows you to further filter the objects that could be classified incorrectly, introducing a natural aspect for us in the distinction of the various elements present in an image.

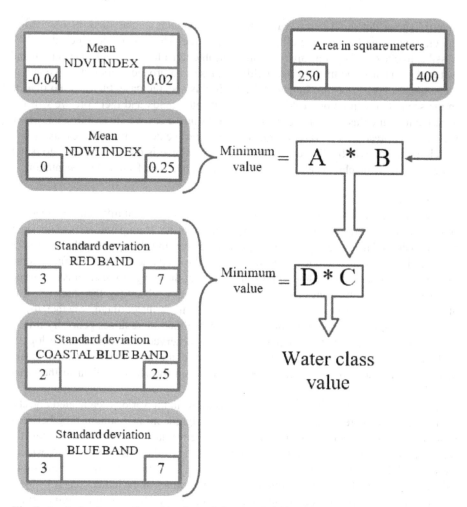

Fig. 5. Logical scheme of combination of the membership functions applied to the features involved in the description of the water class, the features to which the membership function A has been applied are highlighted in red, while those to which the function B has been applied are highlighted in blue, in the two lower corners the values of the left border and right border between which the functions are defined with values between 0 and 1 (Color figure online).

Vegetation Class

For the classification of the vegetation within the image, only the membership function A applied to the mean value of the NDVI index within the objects was used, with the left border and right border values of 0.1 and 0.2, respectively. It must also be considered that the image was acquired by the satellite in March 2021 and many trees do not yet have a very developed crown and therefore the NDVI values are lower than they could be, however in the analysed context this parameter was more than sufficient to efficiently distinguish the green areas present in the studied area.

Impermeable Class

It was decided in this work not to further investigate the classification of the different elements that make up the urban area, the distinction for example between buildings, roads and other elements that may be of interest can be made in many ways depending on the type of data available and from what you need to identify. Since the classification of the various elements that make up the urban fabric at this point can be done by working exclusively on the objects classified as impermeable soil, we will not go into this aspect in this article.

3.4 Refinement Process

Initially only the water and vegetation classes are classified, from the result of this first classification we have seen how carrying out a refining step of the water class improves the results considerably. Instead of trying to immediately classify all the objects that correspond to the water class, only the most significant ones are classified and subsequently made to grow by expanding them in the neighbouring pixels that respect certain parameters. The software used makes many algorithms available and to perform the refinement of the raw classification we used the algorithm called Pixel-Based Object Resizing, which does exactly what was described above. So, we first eliminated the objects classified under the water class which are completely isolated, i.e. with the edges in contact only with objects without any class yet attributed, this because with the segmentation parameters adopted it is very rare that in such a detailed image a course of water or a lake are composed of a single object, as shown in the figure below (Fig. 6).

Once these "solitary" elements have been eliminated, often shadows or ambiguous objects in the urban area, we proceed to make the remaining objects classified with the water class grow in the pixels adjacent to them, applying a single restriction that they must have an NDWI index value greater than 0.3, exploiting the continuity of water courses in nature. This step of growth of the objects is repeated indefinitely, until no more changes occur in the image, i.e. when there are no more pixels in contact with the objects classified as water that complies with the imposed condition. In this way instead of having to immediately classify all the elements that should belong to the water class, which would inevitably lead to the incorrect classification of some shadow objects, only those with the most suitable parameters are classified as water, reducing the risk of error during the classification. From the comparison with the two images of the same area, before and after this process, it is clearly seen how in terms of precision, a higher step is reached. The artificial canal is almost perfectly outlined, and by constraining the growth only in the pixels with values of the NDWI index greater than 0.3, values that typically do not belong to objects in the shade, it is possible to avoid interference with objects that have nothing to do with water. In areas where there are uncultivated fields, the same procedure is carried out before starting with the segmentation for the identification of the other three classes, obviously changing the constraints applied to the growth algorithm, obtaining well-defined fields. Approaches of this type allow to obtain good results if calibrated correctly, unfortunately they depend a lot on the image and cannot be adopted unconditionally without taking into consideration the distribution of the elements to be classified.

Fig. 6. Comparison between the image of a portion of the area studied before, above, and after refining the classification of the water class, below.

4 Validation

The validation of the results obtained was done by comparing the classification made with a shapefile of the entire area analyzed, where the elements present in the image were divided into blue *water class*, green *vegetation class*, and red *impermeable soil class*. This area of the city of Pavia over the years has been the subject of several studies by our laboratory, so gradually a very dense ground truth of the entire area has been created, which is why it has been chosen over other urban areas of the city (Fig. 7).

Fig. 7. Shape file used for validating the classification, after being transformed into objects within eCognition™, the same colors used during classification are kept, blue - Water, green-Vegetation, red - Impermeable soil (Color figure online).

The shape file has been imported into the eCognition™ software, the various polygons that make up the shape have been transformed into objects and all the pixels inside them have been given the class indicated as an attribute in the shapefile. Subsequently, for all the pixels contained within the objects obtained from the ground truth, the class deriving from the ground truth is compared to that obtained from the image classification, the accuracy assessment is done directly within the software and the result is a confusion matrix with an overall accuracy value of 96.13%, (Fig. 8).

The classified image shows a clear distinction between the water contained in the artificial canal and the shadows projected by the buildings, and also from the confusion matrix, reported in the next chapter, we see how out of a total of 141774 pixels of ground truth belonging to the water class, only 3302 are classified incorrectly as *impermeable soil* along the edges. As previously mentioned, there are no objects belonging to the uncultivated fields class, neither in the classified image nor in the ground truth, because in the examined scene we do not have any, but the algorithm used is designed to classify the entire image of the municipality of Pavia. The purpose of this test area was to develop a fairly detailed description of the water class, applying fuzzy logic to the features of the segmented objects, to overcome the problem of misclassification of shadows in urban areas.

Fig. 8. Result of the classification of the entire area under study *"città giardino"*.

5 Discussion

Although the classification strategy developed in this work allows for good results, it has some limitations, mainly the need to manually investigate the ideal values to be attributed to the limits of the membership functions, similarly it may be necessary to carry out some segmentation tests before obtaining suitable parameters. While the logical scheme with which it can be reused independently of the image, the spectral parameters on which the membership functions are applied must be calibrated on each image in order to obtain the same results, an operation that requires the user to make several attempts before reaching the ideal combination. The best strategy therefore consists in identifying small areas representative of the most typical situations that one intends to classify on which to carry out tests, and subsequently extending the classification to the entire image. Which nowadays, given the acquisition capabilities of high-resolution satellites is a good compromise between the time needed to fine-tune the parameters and the quality of the result obtained. Compared to methods based on deep learning that are very popular in recent years and with which it is possible to obtain excellent results [10], as said we clearly need to spend some time adjusting the various parameters in the initial phase. There is the advantage of being able to use all the ground truth for validation and not having to sacrifice any of it for the algorithm training phase, information that in some way must either already be in possession in the best-case scenario or must be created in a good quantity, an operation that requires time and computing power. The other key point of the work is the distinction between shadows and water, a well-known problem for those who classify images of urban areas, various approaches are found in the literature, one of the most used strategies is to exploit the brightness of an object to determine its nature, in particular a low brightness indicates an object that can be classified as a shadow. The choice to adopt a method based on the homogeneity of the objects investigated serves to free us from the fact that within an urban area there may be parts of the canal covered by shadows. Parts that could therefore be classified incorrectly if the brightness was evaluated, or it would be necessary to carry out other checks and filtering to remove the misclassified elements. A condition that does not occur specifically in the area studied, but could occur in a densely built urban context, it could also be influenced by the season in which the photo is acquired, for example in the case of canals flanked by rows of trees. Exploit the presence of elements in the background in my opinion is a more "human" approach to classification, for which observing an image regardless of the degree of brightness would be able without problems to distinguish between a shade and an area with water.

Table 2. Confusion Matrix

User Class\ Sample	Water	Vegetation	Uncultivated Fields	Impermeable	Sum
Water	135832	1280	0	0	137112
Vegetation	2640	1035386	0	31605	1069631
Uncultivated Fields	0	0	0	0	0
Impermeable	3302	80291	0	1788885	1872478
Sum	141774	1116957	0	1820490	

Accuracy	Water	Vegetation	Uncultivated Fields	Impermeable
Producer	0.9581	0.927	-nan(ind	0.9826
User	0.9907	0.968	-nan(ind	0.9556
Hellden	0.9741	0.947	-nan(ind	0.9688
Short	0.9495	0.8994	-nan(ind	0.9395
Kappa Per Class	0.9561	0.8881	-nan(ind	0.9557

Totals	
Overall Accuracy	0.9613
Kappa	0.9245

6 Conclusions

In conclusion, the work carried out has allowed us to improve the description of the water class, to allow its classification also in urban environments without being too much influenced by shadow objects. The algorithm applied is designed to classify larger areas, for this reason it also includes the class of uncultivated fields and even if they are not present in the study area, a segmentation with different parameters is carried out for their identification. Subsequently, once the uncultivated fields have been classified, on the remaining objects we proceed as explained in detail in this article with the classification process of the water and vegetation classes, and finally attributing the impermeable soil class to all the unclassified objects. It is important to underline that it was not our intention to distinguish between buildings and roads, this aspect may be the subject of future investigations by carrying out a detailed study only on the part of the image classified as impermeable soil, which in our case would also require a more detailed ground truth. In the confusion matrix shown below, we can see how an accurate description of a class through the application of fuzzy logic allows not only to effectively distinguish between shadows and water, but to achieve an overall accuracy of 96.13% over the whole scene (Table 2).

7 Future Development

Future implementations could consist in an optimization of the parameters applied for the segmentation, which on the scene was evaluated only visually and for the definition of the left border and right border in the various membership functions, the application of a statistical approach evaluating on a large number of objects the histogram corresponding to the various features to identify the most suitable membership function to describe the objects. Obviously in a broader perspective, where some smaller portions of the bigger image are used for the construction of the membership functions which will then be applied to the whole image or other test sites, in fact a limit is precisely linked to the image that is used and to the sensor who took it. The description of the various features that make up a class, in particular the values that are adopted as left and right border, could change from sensor to sensor and for this reason, even if maintaining the same basic logic, it would be necessary to set again the values applied in the description of the single classes, optimizing them on the image being studied. Apart from the previous considerations, we are satisfied with the result obtained, although it is possible to optimize the results further, with more accurate descriptions of the classes and further detailing the urban area, the introduction of the standard deviations of different bands and their logical combination with other elements, has led to a clear distinction between two elements that typically in an urban context is easy to misclassify.

References

1. Zhang, X.: Object-based distinction between building shadow and water in high-resolution imagery using fuzzy-rule classification and artificial bee colony optimization. J. Sens. **2016** (2016).https://doi.org/10.1155/2016/2385039

2. Shahtahmassebi, A., Yang, N., Wang, K., Moore, N., Shen, Z.: Review of shadow detection and de-shadowing methods in remote sensing. Chin. Geogra. Sci. **23**, 403–420 (2013). https://doi.org/10.1007/s11769-013-0613-x

3. Maurer, T.: How to pan-sharpen images using the Gram-Schmidt pan-sharpen method - a recipe. In: ISPRS - International Archives of the Photogrammetry, Remote Sensing and Spatial Information Sciences. XL-1/W1, pp. 239–244 (2013). https://doi.org/10.5194/isprsarchives-XL-1-W1-239-2013

4. Yilmaz, V., Serifoglu Yilmaz, C., Güngör, O., Shan, J.: A genetic algorithm solution to the gram-schmidt image fusion. Int. J. Remote Sens. **41**, 1–28 (2019).https://doi.org/10.1080/01431161.2019.1667553

5. McFEETERS, S.K.: The use of the normalized difference water index (NDWI) in the delineation of open water features. Int. J. Remote Sens. **17**(7), 1425–1432 (1996). https://doi.org/10.1080/01431169608948714

6. Huang, S., et al.: A commentary review on the use of normalized difference vegetation index (NDVI) in the era of popular remote sensing. J. For. Res. **32**, 1–6 (2021). https://doi.org/10.1007/s11676-020-01155-1

7. Baatz, M., Schape, A.: Multiresolution segmentation-an optimization approach for high quality multiscale image segmentation. In: Strobl, J., Blaschke, T. (eds.) Angewandte Geographische Informationsverarbeitung XII. Beitrage zum AGIT-Symposium Salzburg 2000, Karhlsruhe, Herbert Wichmann Verlag, pp.12–23 (2000)

8. Chen, Y., Chen, Q., Jing, C.: Multi-resolution segmentation parameters optimization and evaluation for VHR remote sensing image based on meanNSQI and discrepancy measure. J. Spat. Sci. **66**(2), 253–278 (2021). https://doi.org/10.1080/14498596.2019.1615011

9. Zhao, M., Meng, Q., Zhang, L., Hu, D., Zhang, Y., Allam, M.: A fast and effective method for unsupervised segmentation evaluation of remote sensing images. Remote Sens. **12**, 3005 (2020). https://doi.org/10.3390/rs12183005

10. Zhang, P., Ke, Y., Zhang, Z., Wang, M., Li, P., Zhang, S.: Urban land use and land cover classification using novel deep learning models based on high spatial resolution satellite imagery. Sensors **18**, 3717 (2018). https://doi.org/10.3390/s18113717

Author Index

E. Borgogno Mondino and P. Zamperlin (Eds.): ASITA 2023, CCIS 2088, pp. 303–304, 2024.
https://doi.org/10.1007/978-3-031-59925-5

Printed in the United States
by Baker & Taylor Publisher Services